CROSS-EXAMINING SOCRATES

This book is a re-reading of Plato's early dialogues from the point of view of the characters with whom Socrates engages in debate. Socrates' interlocutors are generally acknowledged to play important dialectical and dramatic roles, but no previous book has focused mainly on them. Unlike existing studies, which are thoroughly dismissive of the interlocutors and reduce them to the status of mere mouthpieces for views which are hopelessly confused or demonstrably false, this book takes them seriously and treats them as genuine intellectual opponents whose views are often more defensible than commentators have standardly thought. The author's purpose is not to summarize their positions or the arguments of the dialogues in which they appear, much less to produce a series of biographical sketches, but to investigate the phenomenology of philosophical disputation as it manifests itself in the early dialogues.

JOHN BEVERSLUIS is Professor of Philosophy at Butler University, Indianapolis.

CROSS-EXAMINING
SOCRATES

A Defense of the Interlocutors in Plato's Early Dialogues

JOHN BEVERSLUIS

Butler University, Indianapolis

CAMBRIDGE
UNIVERSITY PRESS

PUBLISHED BY THE PRESS SYNDICATE OF THE UNIVERSITY OF CAMBRIDGE
The Pitt Building, Trumpington Street, Cambridge, United Kingdom

CAMBRIDGE UNIVERSITY PRESS
The Edinburgh Building, Cambridge CB2 2RU, UK   http://www.cup.cam.ac.uk
40 West 20th Street, New York NY 10011–4211, USA   http://www.cup.org
10 Stamford Road, Oakleigh, Melbourne 3166, Australia

First published 2000

Printed in the United Kingdom at the University Press, Cambridge

Typeset in Baskerville and Greek New Hellenic [A O]

A catalogue record for this book is available from the British Library

Library of Congress cataloguing in publication data

Beversluis, John, 1934–
Cross-examining Socrates: a defense of the interlocutors in
Plato's early dialogues/John Beversluis.
p.   cm.
Includes bibliographical references and indexes.
ISBN 0 521 55058 0 (hardback)
1. Plato. Dialogues.   2. Socrates.   3. Sophists (Greek philosophy)   I. Title.
B395.B445   1999
184–dc21   99–11232 CIP

ISBN 0 521 55058 0 hardback

To the Memory of
Gregory Vlastos
(1907–1991)

In your present situation what are your philosophers doing, except incessantly demonstrating to you, that almost upon every subject you think wrong, that you are almost continually acting wrong, that in your constitution, police, and way of living, almost every thing ought to be otherwise, than it is? – This is to convince a sick man of his illness. To recover him again, is the chief point! – But I will lay a wager, that they are as little serious in re-establishing your health, as you are in desiring it. I could give you a good reason for my opinion; but people must not tell every thing they know.

Christopher Martin Wieland,
Socrates out of his Senses: or Dialogues of Diogenes of Sinope

Contents

viii Contents

Preface

Many books have been written about Plato's early dialogues, but they all focus mainly on Socrates. Everyone acknowledges that Socrates' interlocutors play important dialectical and dramatic roles, but no one has ever written a book which focuses mainly on them. That is what I propose to do. Unlike existing studies, which are thoroughly dismissive of the interlocutors and reduce them to the status of mere mouthpieces for views which are hopelessly confused or demonstrably false, this book takes them seriously and treats them as genuine intellectual opponents whose views are often more defensible than commentators have standardly thought. It is a re-reading of the early dialogues from the interlocutors' point of view. My purpose is not to summarize their positions or the arguments of the dialogues in which they appear, much less to produce a series of biographical sketches, but to investigate the phenomenology of philosophical disputation as it manifests itself in the early dialogues.

The idea for such a book first occurred to me during the summer of 1983 while I was a participant in Gregory Vlastos's NEH Seminar "The Philosophy of Socrates" at the University of California at Berkeley. I had applied in hopes of reviving a waning interest in philosophy which had derailed me professionally and even prompted thoughts of a career change. What the encouragement of family and friends had not accomplished in more than half a decade, this seminar accomplished in a few weeks. It was a turning point in my life.

Every session was absorbing and illuminating – a claim one can seldom honestly make and a tribute to Gregory's inspired leadership. Of course, everyone who knew him also knows that he would have scolded me for saying this. For one thing, he disliked the term "inspired" – a "glib" term which "says nothing" and "bestows empty praise." He also hated to be accused of leadership and always insisted that he was not our teacher but our colleague and fellow student. But it was inspired leadership all the same.

His preparation and industry were prodigious, and he expected the same from us. When it was not forthcoming, he could be very blunt and did not pull his punches. No one ever disappointed him twice. In addition to meting out unsparing (and occasionally scathing) criticism, he invited ours. The invitation was matter-of-factly extended, without a trace of condescension or the slightest nuance to convey the unspoken message that we were always to bear in mind that the speaker of these words was Gregory Vlastos. His openness to criticism was indelibly imprinted on my mind by a remark he made during one of our early sessions: "I am one of those scholars who can never get anything completely right by himself." This should not be dismissed as mock modesty or fake self-deprecation. Although it was his writings and seminars which had almost singlehandedly triggered the recent explosion of interest in Anglo-American Socratic studies, he refused to take credit for it and saw himself as part of an international community of scholars whose work he studied and whose "reasoned censure" he solicited. There are few authors whose published writings are so generously sprinkled with acknowledgments of indebtedness to others.

But, of course, he *was* Gregory Vlastos – a man who had meticulously worked out and tirelessly refined a systematic, original, and often highly controversial interpretation of Socratic philosophy which represented the intellectual fruits of a lifetime. His remarkable willingness to countenance criticism coexisted with an equally remarkable unwillingness to budge an inch unless absolutely compelled by textual evidence or analytical rigor. He clung to his views tenaciously. Trying to extract a concession from him was like trying to extract a stick from the jaws of a bulldog. But it could occasionally be done. Having made the concession, he dropped the adversarial stance in the spirit of the Socrates of the *Gorgias* who is happy to refute others but no less happy to be refuted himself because then it is he who benefits.

Although in later years I saw him rarely and corresponded with him infrequently, I was deeply affected by the news of his death. It was hard to believe that there would be no more bulky airmail envelopes stuffed with curious sheets of paper of various sizes and colors – some typed, some hand-written in his characteristic scrawl – covered with criticism buttressed with all-but-indecipherable citations from the Greek text but always ending with some word of encouragement and the warmest personal regards. My acute awareness that he would have found the overall thesis of this book shockingly wrongheaded is partially alleviated by the fact that although he welcomed agreement wherever he found it, he did not suppress disagreement and never asked for disciples. It is for these reasons that I have been bold enough to dedicate it to his memory.

Although I had been toying with this project since 1983, it was not until my sabbatical in 1988–89 – spent in Cambridge, England – that I began working on it in earnest. I am grateful to the Sabbatical Leaves Committee and the administration of Butler University for approving my sabbatical; and to the Academic Grants Committee for funding subsequent research during the summers of 1990, 1993 and 1994. I am also grateful to the Classics Faculty of Cambridge University for allowing me to use its libraries, for permitting me to attend lectures, and for welcoming me into its weekly Ancient Philosophy Colloquium. For criticism and discussion, I am indebted to Professors G. E. R. Lloyd, Malcolm Schofield, David Sedley, and, above all, Myles Burnyeat who generously read large chunks of my early drafts and graciously invited me to read a paper based on this material to the Cambridge B Club – an honor I accepted with fear and trembling. For further criticism and discussion, I am indebted to Robert Arrington, Linda Bell, Nathaniel Beversluis, Joanne Edmonds, Thomas Fox, George Hoffmann, and, particularly, C. Grant Luckhardt whose willingness to talk about Plato's early dialogues over the years went far beyond the normal limits of human tolerance and whose enthusiasm for this project never flagged. More recently, I simultaneously benefited and suffered at the hands of two readers for Cambridge University Press – initially anonymous but later revealed to be Myles Burnyeat and David Sedley – whose searching criticism required me to re-write the whole book and whose exhilarating encouragement provided me with the incentive to do it. My debt to them is incalculable. I cannot delude myself into believing that I have adequately responded to all their objections. I can only hope that they will find the final version open to fewer. More recently still, I benefited from the detailed and incisive criticism of Debra Nails. My warmest thanks also to Pauline Hire,

Classics Editor, for her initial interest, helpful advice, and re-markable patience; and to Linda Woodward, my copy-editor, whose keen eye and scrupulous attention to detail caught many errors, ambiguities, and obscurities, and improved this book in many ways.

Finally, I am grateful to my wife, Susan, whose acts of super-erogation over the years have been so numerous and untrumpeted that they have almost ceased to be surprising. Not only did she urge me to spend my sabbatical in England in the face of my periodic worries about uprooting our children; she also commuted to work between Cambridge and London five days a week for the whole year without ever once complaining and still found the time and energy to plan weekend family excursions throughout the length and breadth of the United Kingdom – "dragging us off to yet another castle," as our son unwisely observed early one foggy Saturday morning. As for our "uprooted" and castle-satiated children, Nathaniel and Ellen, now young adults, I cannot find words to re-capture my memories of them during that golden year. So I will simply thank them for the aplomb with which they adapted to life in England, affecting an astonishingly authentic British accent almost overnight, and for being so much fun.

Introduction

Socrates[1] believed that the unexamined life is not worth living (*Ap.* 38a5–6). He also believed that his interlocutors were living unexamined lives. Generations of commentators have endorsed his assessment. For centuries, they have been berating the interlocutors and exulting in the effortless brilliance and utter finality with which they are refuted in one early dialogue after another. The result is a time-honored reading which may be summed up as follows: Searching for moral truth and disavowing moral knowledge, Socrates relentlessly examines his interlocutors, only to discover that they are ignorant about moral matters – often the very matters about which they profess expertise. Unable to define the terms they so carelessly employ or to defend the assertions they so confidently advance, they are helpless in the face of Socratic interrogation, reduced to *aporia*,[2] and exposed as theoretically and morally bankrupt. Worse still, they are not committed inquirers, as is evidenced by their stubborn refusal to acknowledge the cogency of Socrates' criticism and by their perverse tendency to return to the workaday world unchanged and ready to go

---

[1] By "Socrates" I mean the Socrates of Plato's early dialogues among which I include the *Apology* (*Ap.*), *Charmides* (*Ch.*), *Crito* (*Cr.*), *Euthyphro* (*Eu.*), *Gorgias* (*G.*), *Hippias Minor* (*HMi.*), *Ion* (*I.*), *Laches* (*La.*), *Protagoras* (*Pr.*), and *Republic* I (*R.*). Passages cited are from J. Burnet, *Platonis Opera*. Unless otherwise indicated, all English translations are from *Plato: Complete Works*, ed. John M. Cooper.

[2] Although *aporia* is usually translated as theoretical "perplexity," it has wider practical implications which may be seen by noticing its connection to other terms of the same family. A *poros* is a means of passage – a way out or through. Hence to be *aporos* is to be without passage. Uncharted seas induce *aporia* in sea-farers who lack the *technē* of navigation which enables them to find their way through unfamiliar territory. Socrates tries to induce the same state in his interlocutors by making the familiar unfamiliar. The victim is not just in intellectual difficulty ("un embarras de la pensée," Manon, 1986: 24); he is also at a loss as to how to act. See also Kofman, 1983: 51–53.

about their business as if these confrontations had never taken place.

This account is so widely accepted that it may safely be dubbed "the standard view." I use the term "view" advisedly, for what is really at work is not so much an explicit theory as an implicit picture. Those who have fashioned it paint with a wide brush, favoring bold outlines and stark contrasts. On the one hand is Socrates, the paradigmatically rational man, resolutely "following the argument wherever it leads" and tirelessly exhorting his interlocutors to do the same in hopes of convincing them that they do not know what they think they know, and motivating them to join him in searching for the knowledge which is virtue and leads to that true happiness which all men desire and of which no one is voluntarily ignorant. On the other hand are the interlocutors, paradigmatically irrational men, resisting the argument at every turn and the most unlikely assortment of blunderers it was ever a sage's misfortune to endure. Unlike Socrates, whose examined life is lived in accordance with Reason and whose genuine wisdom – or kind of wisdom (σοφίαν τινά, *Ap.* 20d7) – consists in acknowledging that he is not wise (23a5–b4), the interlocutors are impervious to Reason and content with a semblance of wisdom. Secure in their false conceit of knowledge, they neglect the care of their souls. In thus turning aside from what is of supreme importance and pursuing trivialities such as power, reputation, and wealth, they serve as permanent witnesses to the folly of the unexamined life – instructive case-histories of men desperately in need of a gadfly to sting them into moral awareness. It is a very seductive picture. And as an account of what is going on in the early dialogues, it has never been seriously challenged.

In this book I challenge it. The standard picture is not based on a comprehensive and rigorously empirical study of the early dialogues; it is a highly selective and unabashedly pro-Socratic account based almost entirely on the *Apology*. The textual evidence that can be adduced in support of it is actually quite meager, and its apparent plausibility depends on assigning undue weight to a handful of superficially impressive but thoroughly unrepresentative passages scattered throughout the early dialogues in which Socrates' dialectical behavior embodies his announced seriousness and concern for the souls of his fellows, as expressed in the *Apology*, and on withholding due weight from a host of other, much more representative passages in which these lofty ideals are not much in evidence.

Before defending himself against the formal indictment brought by Meletus, which accuses him of not believing in the gods of the city, of introducing new gods, and of corrupting the youth (24b8–c1), Socrates tries to discredit a cluster of earlier charges which accuse him of being a wise man, a wrongdoer, and a busybody who speculates about cosmology, makes the weaker argument stronger, and teaches these things to others (18b4–c1, 19b4–c1). His defense is prompted by his recognition that these charges have not arisen in a vacuum and by his belief that his conduct has been misconstrued by his accusers. In an attempt to prove that where there is smoke there need not be fire, he sets out to convince the jury that he is not wise and to explain why he is mistakenly thought to be. In the course of defending himself he offers his only public (and more or less "official") explanation of what he has been up to for all those years.

He begins by flatly denying that he speculates about cosmology and teaches it to others. Indeed, he teaches *nothing* to others for the very good reason that he knows nothing and, therefore, has nothing to teach.

How, then, is his present notoriety and reputation for wisdom to be explained? The question is a fair one, and Socrates replies by recounting a remarkable incident which had taken place many years ago but which, as is clear from the incredulous outburst from the jurors, had not gained wide currency. It seems that his lifelong but recently deceased friend Chaerephon had once asked the Delphic oracle whether anyone is wiser than Socrates and had been told that there is not.[3] Puzzled by this oracular pronouncement and unaware of possessing any wisdom, great or small, Soc-

---

[3] The historicity of this incident – never alluded to again in the Platonic corpus – has often been impugned on the ground that it is a transparent attempt to absolve Socrates of the charge of impiety by a spurious appeal to divine approval (see Robin, 1910: 30, n. 1; Joël, 1921: 769; Dupréel, 1922: 46, 412, 418, 419, n. 1; Hackforth, 1933: 101–4; Gigon, 1947: 95; Chroust, 1957: 32–33; and Montuori, 1981: 57–143, and 1988: 17, 50–62). However, most commentators think it unlikely that Plato would have invented the story (see J. Adam, 1894: 57–58; Gomperz 1905, II: 105; Burnet, 1924: 170–71; A. E. Taylor, 1932: 76–77; Ferguson, 1964: 70–73; Guthrie, 1971b: 85–86; Fontenrose, 1978: 34; Brickhouse and Smith, 1989: 4–9, 88–90; Reeve, 1989: 21; and Stokes, 1992: 52–54).

rates had initially tried to refute the oracle (ἐλέγξων τὸ μαντεῖον, 21c1)[4] by interrogating numerous people with a reputation for wisdom – including politicians, poets, and craftsmen – in hopes of finding someone wiser. But he had failed. This disappointing venture had convinced him that the god was right: no one *is* wiser than Socrates – albeit only in the modest sense that, unlike these others, he does not claim to know what he does not know. Since anyone can become wise in this sense, he concluded that the god had merely used him as an example (παράδειγμα, 23b1): anyone is wise who, like Socrates, realizes that he has no wisdom. He also concluded that he had been commanded to live the life of a philosopher, examining himself and others, and demonstrating that they are in the same deplorable epistemic condition as he (28e4–6).

Proponents of the standard picture accept all this at face value. But it is highly problematic. First, Socrates' account is too general: he claims to have interrogated *many* people with a reputation for wisdom, but he does not identify specific individuals. Second, his assessment is unsubstantiated: he *claims* to have demonstrated that none of these people knew what they thought they knew, but he offers no evidence in support of this claim. We are, in effect, asked to take Socrates' word for the fact – if it is a fact – that, when subjected to interrogation, all these unidentified interlocutors had been exposed as fraudulent claimants to wisdom.

Why not take his word for it? Has Plato not immortalized Socrates doing exactly what he claims to have done? Why not say that the *Apology* contains the claim and the early dialogues contain the evidence?

This reply on Socrates' behalf is as question-begging as his own account. There is a serious discrepancy between what Socrates

---

[4] Ἐλέγχω need not mean "refute," as it is rendered by Burnet 1924: 172, according to whom Socrates tried "to prove the god a liar" (so too Ryle, 1966: 177; West, 1979: 106–7, 125; Nehemas, 1986: 305–6; Teloh, 1986: 111; Dorion, 1990: 332; and Brisson, 1997: 138, n. 75); it can also mean "examine" or "test." Hence eager to rid Socrates of even the slightest hint of impiety, many commentators claim that he was not trying to refute the oracle, but simply trying to unravel the true meaning of this riddling utterance; his strategy was "interpretative only" (Reeve, 1989: 23; so too Allen, 1970: 48; Navia, 1985: 185–86; Woodruff, 1988: 83–84; Brickhouse and Smith, 1989: 96–97; Nagy, 1989: 79; Stokes, 1992: 34–35; and McPherran, 1996: 224). Since ἐλέγχω has multiple meanings, the dispute cannot be settled on linguistic grounds. Although I think the overall context favors "refute," I will not wage a polemical campaign on this already crowded textual battlefield.

claims to have achieved, as reported by Plato in the *Apology*, and what his interlocutors think he has achieved, as depicted by Plato in the early dialogues. Although these encounters convinced Socrates that his interlocutors were devoid of wisdom, they did not have the same effect on the interlocutors. They are not as uniformly annihilated as Socrates would have us believe. Unlike Xenophon's Socrates, who is so persuasive that, "whenever he argued, he gained a greater measure of assent ... than any man I have ever known" (*Mem.* 4.6.15), Plato's Socrates is singularly unpersuasive.

This is not a novel claim. Gregory Vlastos said the same thing almost thirty years ago when he declared that Plato's Socrates "is not persuasive at all. He wins every argument, but never manages to win over an opponent."[5] Like other proponents of the standard picture, Vlastos is fully aware of the discrepancy, and he accounts for it in the same way. If we accept his diagnosis, the discrepancy is easily explained: we simply blame the interlocutors – "those misguided, confused, wrongheaded people whose souls [Socrates] seeks to improve."[6] The implication is that Socrates' arguments are always (or almost always)[7] cogent and that his interlocutors' resistance is always (or almost always) indefensible and traceable to their impenetrable obstinacy. Proponents of the standard picture say, in effect, "True, the interlocutors are 'seldom, if ever', persuaded by Socrates' arguments; but they should have been."

I offer a different assessment. Instead of focusing on the interlocutors' resistance to Socrates' arguments and accounting for it in psychological terms, I will focus on the quality of the arguments resisted. On my reading, many of them are fallacious or unsound,

---

[5] 1971: 2. In 1991: 292, n. 161, "never" is replaced by "seldom, if ever."

[6] 1983a: 56. Cf. Blundell, 1992: 133–34: "Socrates' interlocutors suffer from a whole spectrum of human weaknesses and failings, whether moral, intellectual, or both, which interfere with their ability to philosophize ... [They] rarely seem to progress from elenctic bewilderment to increased philosophical insight." Commentators who offer similar assessments are legion. Here as elsewhere, I cite only representative opinion; detailed documentation would fill volumes.

[7] Almost everyone acknowledges that Plato is occasionally guilty of minor logical slips and that he sometimes employs elliptical arguments in need of supplementation (see, e.g., C. C. W. Taylor, 1976: 178–81; Santas, 1979: 233–40, 272–80; and Vlastos, 1991: 140–48). Irwin, 1977: 4, goes further: "Much of what Plato says is false, and much more is confused, vague, inconclusive, and badly defended" – a remark which draws stinging criticism from Allen, 1996: 166.

and the interlocutors' resistance is defensible. Socrates' arguments are not only *criticized* by his interlocutors; they often *warrant* criticism and are criticized for exactly the right reasons.

The black and white contrast between Socrates and his interlocutors is evident not only in the standard picture's account of the early dialogues but also in its approach to them. Its proponents revere Socrates and treat his every utterance with meticulous care, reconstructing the man and his thought with complete fidelity down to the minutest detail. But they do not lavish comparable attention on his interlocutors, skeptically scrutinizing them with the clinical detachment of the laboratory technician and methodically consigning them to neatly labelled categories – Naive Youth, Complacent Businessman, Religious Fanatic, Slippery Sophist, Arrogant Rhapsode, Cynical Nihilist – in which, like bottled specimens, they are placed on permanent exhibit as intellectually inconsequential and morally dubious figures unworthy of even the perfunctory attention they usually receive. Like the account, the approach is unrelentingly one-sided, humorless, and unfriendly: the interlocutors are never right, seldom likeable, rarely even tolerable; wrong and wrongheaded, they elicit only criticism and contempt.

I want to substitute a different picture based on a different approach. Instead of accepting Socrates' uniformly negative assessment of his interlocutors at face value, I will examine them one by one, assessing them independently on the basis of their own merits and individual showings. I will not approach the early dialogues with the presumption that Socrates is always right and that the interlocutors are always wrong and that it is only their logical incompetence and psychological obstinacy which prevent them from being "won over." In short, mine will be a much less tidy picture. The contrasts between Socrates and his interlocutors will not be etched in such sharp relief, the battle between Reason and Unreason will not be so edifyingly obvious, and the outcome will not be so unanimously pro-Socratic.

Proponents of the standard picture peruse the texts in search of arguments, and they are astonishingly good at extracting them. Having done so, however, they often examine them *in vacuo* – in isolation from the persons who marshal them, the situations which generate them, and other contextual considerations which inform them and shape their direction. In the process, dialectical interaction tends to become superfluous, and dramatic detail and psychological nuance tend to be dismissed as mere fluff.[8]

In saying this, I am not smuggling in any esoteric hermeneutical assumptions about "the dialogue form" and why Plato employed it. Nor am I minimizing the importance of the arguments. A study of the early dialogues must attend closely to their argumentative content: the definitions and theses advanced by the interlocutors, the arguments Socrates deploys against them, their responses to his arguments, the ensuing complications, and the final resolution or lack of resolution. But the early dialogues do not proceed by argumentation alone, and a study of them should not emphasize the reason*ing* at the expense of the reason*ers*. We must also attend closely to the psychological dynamics between Socrates and his interlocutors: the character of the interlocutors, the manner in which they advance their definitions and theses, the manner in which Socrates argues against them, the strategies they employ in response to his arguments, his counterstrategies, the reasons why some remain active participants while others try to extricate themselves, and, insofar as it is discernible, the degree of their respective commitments to pursue the argument seriously and in a spirit of moral earnestness.

We must immerse ourselves in a world of subtleties in which no one *simply* wins or loses, and in which logic, although powerfully present, seldom fully penetrates and is not the only operative instrument of persuasion. The single-minded approach, which attends only to the arguments, resembles the boxing fan who watches only in anticipation of the knockout punch, oblivious to the incessant infighting which gradually undoes an opponent and renders him vulnerable to the knockout punch when it finally arrives. The more prolonged and gruelling exchanges between Socrates and interlocutors like Protagoras and Callicles are strik-

---

[8] An instructive example is provided by J. Adam, 1893: x. Commenting on the psychologically climactic moment in the *Protagoras* when Socrates finally locks horns with the great sophist, he declares: "At this point the true business of the dialogue begins" – as if all that had gone before had been "nothing but a sort of cranking-up, or a big spoonful of jam to cover up the pill that is now to be administered" (Kitto, 1966: 235) and hence not part of the "business" (or, at least, not the "true" business) of the dialogue. Of course, not all commentators neglect dramatic context. Notable exceptions include Deschoux, 1980; Stokes, 1986, and 1992: 26–92; Cornford, 1987: 221–38; Coventry, 1990: 174–96; Arieti, 1991: 2–11; Klagge, 1992: 1–12; Frede, 1992: 201–19; Thayer, 1993: 47–59; and Nails, 1995: 36–50, 228–31.

ingly similar to such brawls. In witnessing them, we must lay aside our contemporary academic preconceptions, forgo the unspeakable niceties of stylized peer debate before impeccably behaved colleagues, and elbow our way into the crowded Athenian marketplace where the philosopher is a street fighter and philosophy a spectator sport.[9]

Instead of treating Socrates' interlocutors as disposable dramatic packaging, we must engage in the joint exercises of imaginative identification and psychological reconstruction, making every effort to grasp their perceptions of these encounters and taking empathetic note of their wide-ranging emotions – their moments of high enthusiasm and buoyant confidence, their flagging interest and mounting despair, their rising gorges and outraged protests, and their desperate attempts to salvage their views – not to mention their egos – in spite of heavy damages sustained. Plato often depicts their responses in considerable detail; in fact, he often seems as interested in exploring the roots of the interlocutors' resistance as he is in providing Socrates with the arguments whose ostensibly rigorous entailment relations they are so determined to resist. Taken seriously, these details invest the early dialogues with a deeper and much less manageable dimension.[10]

Socrates' interlocutors are not faceless dramatic devices – mere stylistic pegs on which to hang an argument. Nor are they flat, one-dimensional characters who are of interest only for the grist they provide for the Socratic mill. They are living presences – vivid and credible dramatic stand-ins for real people whose strengths and weaknesses, formidableness and absurdity, complexity and simplicity have been brilliantly captured by Plato's dramatic genius.

---

[9] The popular picture of Socrates accosting people in the marketplace is rejected by Ryle, 1966: 175–77: first, because bedlam is not conducive to philosophical discussion; and, second, because most of the conversations depicted in the early dialogues are not impromptu "kerb-side pesterings," but semi-formal and (sometimes) previously arranged debates which take place in secluded palaestrae or private homes. Cf. Burnet, 1924: 87. However, this low-profile Socrates is hard to reconcile with the Socrates of the *Apology* who reminds his jurors of his ubiquitous presence: not only in the marketplace, but also at the bankers' tables and many other public places (17c7–d1) where, gadfly-like, he had lighted on each of them, everywhere, and all day long (30e5–31a1; cf. 19d1–7, 23b4–7, 31c4–7, 33a6–b3, and 36b5–d1).

[10] We must be cautious in ascribing inner psychologies to Socrates' interlocutors. Unlike actually existing people, fictional characters may legitimately be said to have inner experiences only when they are manifested in their behavior or attested to by a narrator. Plato's masterly depiction of character in the dramatic dialogues and his subtle employment of *oratio obliqua* in the narrated ones insure that these conditions are satisfied.

These are recognizable human types – men from different walks of life, with different levels of understanding, and with different reasons for entering into disputation with Socrates. But however they differ, in the final analysis they are remarkably similar: they are seldom, if ever, persuaded by Socrates' arguments. Their individual and collective resistance poignantly underscores the difference between refuting a thesis and persuading a person. It also reveals that the human stakes are high and that genuine persuasion requires more than crushing dialectical skill and periodic assurances of one's salutary intentions.

The early dialogues do not just depict theoretical debates about matters of perennial philosophical importance, they also depict the intensely personal nature of these debates. They confront us again and again with a phenomenon which is common in philosophy (and in intellectual debate generally) but seldom squarely faced: it is possible to silence the opposition without persuading it. These dialogues seldom end on the note of triumph sounded by proponents of the standard picture. It is true that by the time the argument has run its course Socrates' interlocutors have typically been numbed by his stingray-like attack (*M.* 79e7–80b2)[11] and can no longer say a word, but they are just as typically unpersuaded of the falsity (or inadequacy) of their views. However paralyzing momentarily, Socrates' arguments have no lasting effect.[12] Nor are the interlocutors noticeably grateful for the indefatigably optimistic, destructive-for-constructive-purposes-let's-start-all-over-again manner by which he reduces them to confused silence. On the contrary, they often manifest deep resistance towards his apparently devastating but strangely unconvincing arguments and comparably deep resentment towards him. Proponents of the standard picture pass lightly over these awkward facts too, seldom pausing to ask what it is about Socrates' arguments that his interlocutors find so unconvincing and, on occasion, infuriating.

[11] The image of Socrates as a stingray appears for the first time in the *Meno*, but it is an apt description of his effect on his interlocutors in many of the early dialogues. Although Socrates' preferred image of himself is that of a gadfly which awakens and arouses (*Ap.* 30e1–31a1), he accepts Meno's characterization with the proviso that his philosophical discussions leave him even more numbed than his interlocutors (*M.* 80c6–d1).

[12] As is clear from Alcibiades' would-be testimonial to Socrates' extraordinary effect on him: having confessed that Socrates is the only man alive who can make him feel ashamed, he adds that the minute he is out of Socrates' sight, he behaves exactly as he pleases (*Sym.* 216a8–b5).

Socrates' interlocutors have had a very bad press. To be sure, there are a few who resist his arguments for silly or transparently self-serving reasons. Their all-but-complete lack of engagement with the issues; their unwillingness to follow the most elementary argument; their refusal to draw the required inference or to acknowledge it when it is drawn for them; their jejune quibbling, frequent red herrings, and predictable face-saving exits – all this limpidly reveals the lengths to which uncommitted inquirers will go to circumvent criticism.

But the interlocutors are not all like that. There are many others whose encounters with Socrates begin quite promisingly and whose gradually eroding responsiveness, palpably increasing impatience, and eventual recalcitrance cannot be adequately explained by cataloging their shortcomings. Although Socrates periodically assures them that he is simply "following the argument wherever it leads," this universally acclaimed profession of philosophical malleability should not be taken in any naively literal sense. Socrates does not passively follow the argument wherever *it* leads. *Arguments* do not "lead" anywhere. Contrary to what Socrates sometimes implies,[13] the "direction" taken by an argument is not vouchsafed to the elenctic practitioner by a presiding Cosmic Logos in relation to which he is merely the logically attuned and morally neutral medium. It is dependent on the systematically operative, usually unargued, and often even unstated methodological assumptions and substantive views of the practitioner: his views about the nature and role of definition, his implicit ontology and epistemology, his first-order moral judgments, and his analogies between morality and the *technai*. These are the factors that determine the "direction" in which the argument "leads." Socrates' more astute interlocutors resist his arguments not because they are pig-headed and perversely unwilling to follow them to where *he* says they lead, but because they do not think they lead there. These interlocutors are not the intellectual pushovers we have read so much about. Even when reduced to silence, they usually behave as if it is the argument itself (or the way in which Socrates has conducted it) which is at fault; and the blame for their logical

---

[13] See Louis, 1945: 43–44: "Le raisonnement auquel se livre le dialecticien, autrement dit le Logos, est fréquemment présenté comme un être vivant." See also Robinson, 1953: 8; Diès, 1972: 111–25; and Dixsaut, 1994: 27–39.

difficulties is unhesitatingly laid at his doorstep. And when he proceeds to announce that it is not he but the *logos* that is refuting them, they find the situation intolerable. Although their objections are usually rejected out of hand by Socrates and proponents of the standard picture, I think they are often exactly on target.

Socrates' interlocutors not only criticize his arguments; they also complain bitterly about his dialectical tactics. A recurring case in point is his rule against long speeches (*I.* 530d9–531a1, *Eu.* 6c8–9, *G.* 461d6–7). Socrates cannot tolerate people who go on at length, like gongs that continue to resonate long after being struck (*Pr.* 328e5–329b1); his "poor memory" makes it impossible for him to follow them (*Pr.* 334c8–d5, *HMi.* 364b5–c2). He wants (and often demands) short answers: a simple "Yes" or "No" will suffice. Many interlocutors resent this restriction. The (at least partial) validity of their protest is never acknowledged. No one advocates unbridled verbosity, but laconic brevity bordering on monosyllabic utterance is not the only alternative. Although Socrates' brevity requirement is routinely endorsed as a necessary safeguard against rhetorical excess and as a precondition of rigor, its less salutary consequences usually go unnoticed. It not only prevents his interlocutors from being long-winded; it also prevents them from explaining what they mean and do not mean, from qualifying their assertions, and from making important distinctions to ensure that their views will get a fair hearing. The requirement is also selectively enforced. Socrates himself is inordinately prone to speech-making – many of them much longer than anyone else's.[14] Although proponents of the standard picture find endless excuses for him,[15] Socrates himself is mildly sensitive to this charge and occasionally "apologizes" for breaking his own rule. But he con-

[14] Stone's description, 1988: 146, of Socrates as "the most talkative man in Athens" had precedents in classical antiquity. In Plautus' *Pseudolus* (464) Simo warns Callipho that Pseudolus "will talk your head off till you feel as if you're arguing with Socrates." (I owe this source to C. Grant Luckhardt.) Socrates' propensity for incessant talk prompted Aristophanes to coin the verb "to Socratize" (σωκρατεῖν) and to describe those who fell under its spell as having been "Socratified" (ἐσωκράτουν, *Birds* 1281–82).

[15] Socrates "adapts rhetorical techniques to a moral end" and "offers his long speeches for questioning and investigation, rather than expecting them to be swallowed whole" (Rutherford, 1995: 146–47); Socrates employs the "Phaedrus principle," according to which "different conditions of *psychai* educationally require different types of *logoi*," and sometimes making a speech is the only way that he can "educate" his interlocutor (Teloh, 1986: 1); Socratic rhetoric is "philosophical" rhetoric which tries to inculcate "excellence of soul" (Allen, 1984: 108).

tinues to break it, thereby tacitly sanctioning the double standard
which allows him to exploit to the hilt the persuasive possibilities
of rhetoric while forbidding his interlocutors to do the same.

Socrates' interlocutors accuse him of many other things: of deliberately misconstruing their assertions and of deducing absurd
and obviously unintended inferences from them, of employing
faulty analogies, of leading them into carefully prepared traps, of
employing shame tactics, and of arguing for victory. Above all,
they accuse him of tendentiously reformulating their theses in the
weakest possible form and refuting straw men.[16] Although these
objections are usually dismissed as the disingenuous subterfuges of
soreheads, I think they are also often exactly on target.

Having said this, I want to add two disclaimers.

First, in endorsing the interlocutors' objections, I am not treating them as actually existing people who operate independently of
Plato's authorial control and have spotted weaknesses in Socrates'
arguments. The early dialogues are not stenographic transcripts
that preserve the *ipsissima verba* of actual conversations to which
Plato was privy. As Vlastos rightly points out, "It is Xenophon
who professes to be recalling Socratic conversations he had witnessed personally. Plato does no such thing."[17] My claims about
the interlocutors are put forth in the full realization that they are
dramatic characters whose scripts were written by Plato. Although
most of them correspond to actual historical figures, their portrayal, like that of Socrates himself, is fictionalized. Accordingly,

---

[16] I cannot accept Shorey's contention, 1937, 1: xi, that "[i]t is Plato's method always to
restate a satirized and controverted doctrine in its most plausible form before proceeding
to a definitive refutation."

[17] 1991: 49. Cf. Horneffer, 1904: 22: "Die Platonische Dialoge sind völlig frei Dramen.
Diese Art freier Behandlung entspricht der allgemeinen Anschauungsweise des Alter-
tums, die in derartigen Schriftwerken keinerlei historische Treue verlangt." See also
Munk, 1857: 49–53; Schleiermacher, 1858: 34–35; Bruns, 1896: 211–12; Bury, 1909: 243–
44; Ryle, 1966: 161–62; and Kidd, 1992: 83–84. Classical antiquity had no concept of
biography in the post-eighteenth-century sense which burdens the modern biographer
with the requirement of scrupulous fidelity to fact. For an illuminating discussion of the
relation between biography and fiction in the early dialogues (and in the *Sōkratikoi logoi*
generally), see Momigliano, 1971: 23–64. Of course, the fact that Plato nowhere *professes*
to be recalling actual conversations does not license us to infer that the early dialogues
contain *no* reliable information about Socrates or Socratic philosophy and that they simply perpetuate a Platonically-contrived "Socratic legend," as has been argued, *inter alia*,
by Maier, 1913; Joël, 1921; Dupréel, 1922; Robin, 1910; Gigon, 1947; Magalhães-Vilhena,
1952a, and 1952b; Chroust, 1957; Humbert, 1967; and Montuori, 1981, and 1988.

the focal point of this study is not the historical figures themselves, but as portrayed by Plato.[18]

Second, in defending the interlocutors against Socrates, I am not rejecting the standard picture as a misreading of the early dialogues. The standard picture derives ultimately from Plato, and its proponents read the early dialogues exactly as he intended them to be read. Nor am I just criticizing Socrates. As Myles Burnyeat has said, "The programme [of the early dialogues] is one there is every reason to accept as no less a genuine mark of the historical Socrates than the recurrent irony which enlivens its execution. The arguments themselves, however, are ... the creation of Plato."[19] If Burnyeat is right – and surely he is – then to criticize Plato's Socrates is ultimately to criticize Plato. Like proponents of the standard picture, Plato greatly overestimates the arguments he puts into the mouth of Socrates, and he greatly underestimates the objections he puts into the mouths of the interlocutors.

Since this is not a book about Socrates but a book about his interlocutors, many issues which would otherwise cry out for sustained attention are treated cursorily in the text, consigned to the notes, and sometimes bypassed altogether. For example, in discussing the Socratic elenchus, I am much more interested in discovering how Socrates actually argues in specific contexts than I am in providing yet another general elucidation of the elenchus itself. I am also much more interested in determining how his interlocutors are actually affected by his arguments than I am in making theory-laden pronouncements about how they ought to be affected by them. Similarly, in discussing the "What-is-*F*?" question, I am much more interested in what the interlocutors make (or do not make) of this question than I am in the question itself, how its formulation may vary from one dialogue to another, whether these variations signal a "development" in Plato's thought, how

---

[18] The always interesting but often unreliable Diogenes Laertius reports that, upon hearing Plato read the *Lysis*, Socrates remarked, "By Heracles, what a number of lies this young man tells about me" (3.5). Although probably apocryphal, the remark bears witness to an ever-present possibility. Had the historical counterparts of Socrates' interlocutors read the dialogues in which they appear, they might have registered similar complaints. Indeed, if the ancient *testimonia* are trustworthy, some of them did. See Athenaeus (*The Deipnosophists* 505e4–8). For full documentation, see Riginos, 1976: 96–100.

[19] 1971: 214.

Socratic *eidē* differ from Platonic forms, and in what sense, if any,
Socrates has a theory of forms. In short, I discuss problems internal to Socratic philosophy only when they shed light on the theses
advanced by particular interlocutors or on the arguments Socrates
employs against them. Any other procedure would have led me
down interesting but (for my purposes) distracting byways and
resulted in a much longer book – indeed, in two books at cross-
purposes with each other and coexisting uneasily between a single
cover.

   In place of the usual dialogue by dialogue format, I have sub-
stituted an interlocutor by interlocutor approach, devoting a sepa-
rate and self-contained chapter to each, except for Charmides/
Critias and Laches/Nicias whose dialectical interaction with Socrates (and with each other) is so intimately connected as to preclude individual treatment. As for the chapter sequence, it is based
on philosophical and thematic considerations, not on chronological
ones.[20] Hence from the fact that I discuss Laches and Charmides
before Euthyphro or Protagoras before Gorgias, no inferences
should be drawn about my views – to the extent that I have views
– about the chronology of the dialogues in which these interlocutors appear.

   Of course, a book about Socrates' interlocutors cannot completely avoid Socrates. Eschewing Erasmus' "St. Socrates, pray
for us," I will take a hard look at him too, making no attempt to
prettify the results. The Socrates of the early dialogues is not
the thoroughly whitewashed Socrates of the standard picture. In
their determination to defend his often faulty arguments and to
vindicate his often unscrupulous dialectical tactics at almost any
cost, its proponents have neglected the insatiably polemical and
all-too-human Socrates who operates in full view in Plato's pages
and replaced him with a more admirable but largely imaginary
substitute – a hitherto unchallenged way of reading Plato against

[20] Many commentators think chronology is the key to understanding Plato and for distinguishing Platonic from Socratic thought (see, e.g., Hermann, 1839; Guthrie, 1975: 39–
56; Vlastos, 1991: 45–80; and Irwin, 1977: 291–93, n. 33). According to this "devel-
opmentalist" methodology, the views espoused by the Socrates of the early dialogues
are (as nearly as can be determined) those of the historical Socrates whereas the views
espoused by his (in many respects very different) counterpart of the middle dialogues are
those of Plato. For critiques of this hermeneutical approach, see Kahn 1981, 1988b, 1988c,
1991, and 1992; Cooper 1997, xii–xviii; and, more massively, Nails 1993, and 1995: 53–135.

which this book is a long-overdue protest. In it, I will identify and render explicit a disturbing layer of Socratic philosophizing which, although not completely unnoticed by previous commentators, has been relegated to comparative obscurity. Until it has been convincingly delineated, Plato's Socrates will continue to enjoy a reputation which is out of proportion to his achievement and he will continue to evade responsibility for a lack of achievement which is not yet part of his reputation.

There is a dark and even ominous side to this alleged moral gadfly who claims to care for the souls of his fellows but does everything in his power (often by whatever means) to deprive them of whatever shred of insight they possess, offering them nothing in return and (more often than not) leaving them in a state of complete confusion without so much as a hint about what to do next. It was precisely this deliberate inculcation of a moral void against which P. T. Geach protested when he judged Socratic dialectic morally harmful.[21] Although few have gone that far, the fact remains that, however true or untrue to the historical Socrates, Plato's Socrates is a complex and enigmatic figure.

In saying this, I am not just repeating the complaints of other philosophers. One recalls the impatience of Wittgenstein:

Reading the Socratic dialogues one has the feeling: what a frightful waste of time. What's the point of these arguments that prove nothing and clarify nothing?[22]

And Ryle's characteristically trenchant quip:

Socrates has, like a gadfly, to sting Athens into wakefulness, with almost nothing to show what she is to be awakened to, save to the existence of the gadfly.[23]

My complaint is different.

I dare say that at one time or another almost everyone has laid aside a Socratic dialogue with the nagging suspicion that something is amiss. But what? No diagnosis can carry full conviction

---

[21] 1966: 372. Presumably not even Geach would go as far as the anonymous author of a 1768 Godwyn Pamphlet, entitled *Socrates Diabolicus: or, The Old Man Exploded. A Declamation Against Socrates*, according to whom Socrates' "captious subtleties" were designed "to poison the affections of men, and to seduce them from the road of duty and morality" (4–5, 13).

[22] 1989: 14e.

[23] 1966: 177.

unless it answers to one's settled intellectual and emotional experience in reading the dialogues. This is hard to achieve – partly because the texts are often difficult to interpret and partly because of other more subtle factors which install themselves between reader and text: sympathy with the Socratic philosophical enterprise, antipathy towards particular interlocutors, worries about one's ignorance of the staggering (and constantly growing) secondary literature, and so on. But perhaps the most powerfully influential factor of all is the standard picture itself – that venerable interpretive tradition painstakingly constructed by the best minds in the history of classical scholarship, past and present, whose scholarly erudition, linguistic competence, and analytical rigor one can never hope to equal. Hence instead of reporting one's findings and airing one's misgivings, one minimizes them or explains them away. In any event, that is what I did. For years, I suppressed my misgivings in respectful – albeit begrudged – deference to the standard picture. Under its spell, I often reported what I did not think and often failed to report what I did think. As a result of this considerably less-than-honest response to what, in my heart of hearts, I thought was going on in the early dialogues, I found myself accumulating more and more skeletons in my Socratic closet. To what extent my experience is shared by others, I have no way of knowing; I speak only for myself. In this book, I open that long-locked door and allow my shadowy closet dwellers to emerge into the light of day.

We have never lacked monumental studies of Plato's works, and the past several decades have produced a new wave of contemporary scholarship in the form of books, articles, commentaries, and published colloquia proceedings whose rigor, clarity, and attentiveness to detail have revolutionized our understanding of Socratic philosophy and set new standards for studying it. But our understanding of Socrates' interlocutors has lagged far behind. Since embarking on this study, I have spent so much time in their company that by now they seem like old friends. In this book, I undertake to rescue them: not only from Socrates, but also from the mythology which has accumulated around them as the result of generations of unabashedly pro-Socratic scholarship. I do not claim that this study will require a reassessment of all these dialectical underdogs, but I do claim that it will require a reassessment of many of them. At the very least, by resisting the urge to berate and by presenting them in a way which makes their resistance to Socrates intelligible, it may make us less inclined to stand naively aghast at their imperviousness to Socratic argumentation and disabuse us of the too-easy criticism with which we have abused them.

CHAPTER I

The Socratic interlocutor

The term "interlocutor" is standardly used in referring to the people with whom Socrates converses in the early dialogues.[1] According to the *O.E.D.*, an interlocutor is "one who takes part in a dialogue, conversation, or discussion" – an etymological definition which slices the term into its Latin derivatives: *inter* (between) and *loquor* (to speak). Interlocutors are people between whom there is speech; less cumbersomely, they are people who talk to each other.

This does not take us very far. There are all kinds of conversations and all kinds of interlocutors, though in ordinary language the term is seldom used. Few would refer to the person with whom they chatted on the morning train as their interlocutor. It is a stiff and uncolloquial term, a term that elicits raised eyebrows, suggesting affectation and alerting those within earshot that they are in the presence of a stuffed shirt. In short, it is a term to be avoided – unless, of course, one is writing about Plato, in which case one can hardly get along without it.

Even some students of Plato reject the term "interlocutor" in favor of less pedantic alternatives like "partner," "respondent," or "answerer." But these remedial substitutes are equally problematic. "Partner" fosters the illusion of intellectual equality between participants who are, in most cases, spectacularly unequal and, on occasion, mismatched. "Respondent" errs in the opposite direction by reducing one participant to a completely passive role. "Answerer" is unsatisfactory too; Socrates' interlocutors do much more than answer questions. What is needed is not a new term or even a better definition of an old term, but an elucidation of the concept of the Socratic interlocutor which clarifies his dialectical

---

[1] The Greek equivalent is προσδιαλεγόμενος – a term Plato uses sparingly (see *Pr.* 342e4; *Th.* 161b3, 167e8; *S.* 217d1–2, 218a1, 268b4; and *Laws* 887e1).

and philosophical functions. Accordingly, I will retain the term "interlocutor." In spite of its terminological awkwardness, it best captures the announced philosophical goals and methodological principles which underlie the Socratic elenchus[2] and are allegedly operative throughout the early dialogues.

Although Socrates never systematically formulates these goals and principles, they can be extracted from what he periodically does say by way of contextual explanations, rebukes, expressions of puzzlement, directives, and asides. They will emerge even more clearly if we approach the early dialogues indirectly and briefly highlight some important differences between Socratic interlocutors and the very dissimilar non-Socratic interlocutors who appear in dialogues written by philosophers other than Plato. There are not many of them. Most philosophers have opted for the prose treatise as the preferred vehicle for the dissemination of philosophical ideas. Comparatively few have written dialogues; of these, fewer still have done so effectively.[3]

Since philosophers who write dialogues presumably do so for a reason, some commentators think it is impossible to understand the Platonic dialogues until we have discovered that reason. Hence the notorious question: Why did Plato write dialogues? This question, which has given rise to a kind of sub-field in Platonic studies, implies that Plato's decision to write dialogues cries out for explanation. Numerous answers have been given – many of them based on the controversial (and usually unargued) assumption that "the dialogue form" is *sui generis* and that "dialogical" content cannot be communicated "non-dialogically" owing to the fact that Plato never speaks *in propria persona*.[4]

Everyone agrees that there are important differences between a piece of reasoning advanced by an author in a prose treatise and a piece of reasoning advanced by a character in a dialogue. However, before trying to coax esoteric doctrine from this, two points should

---

[2] Although Socrates says next to nothing about his philosophical method – the term "method" (μέθοδος) does not appear until *Ph.* 79e3 (see Robinson, 1953: 67; and Vlastos, 1983a: 28, n. 5) – and although he employs ἐλέγχω more or less interchangeably with a variety of other verbs (e.g., σκοπέω, ἐρευνάω, ἐρωτάω, ἐξετάζω, σκέπτομαι, and ζητέω) and their various compounds to describe his dialectical role *vis-à-vis* his interlocutors, the term "elenchus" has become permanently entrenched in Anglo-American scholarly parlance.

[3] Burnyeat, 1987: 24, thinks the only philosopher who even approaches Plato is Hume.

[4] See, e.g., Griswold, 1988: 1; Bowen, 1988: 58–63; and Sayre, 1988: 94–95.

be noted. First, the distinction between the prose treatise and the dialogue is not exhaustive. Philosophers have set forth their views in a
wide variety of literary *genres*: poetry (Parmenides and Xenophanes),
confessions (Augustine and Rousseau), the question-and-answer
format (Aquinas), meditations (Marcus Aurelius and Descartes),
geometrical proofs (Spinoza), diaries and pseudo-autobiographical
narratives (Kierkegaard), novels and plays (Camus and Sartre),
aphorisms (Nietzsche), "remarks" and "*Zettel*" (Wittgenstein), and
so on. Second, the distinction between the prose treatise and the
dialogue is not sharp. Philosophers who do not write dialogues
often employ interlocutor-like figures as pedagogical devices: to
anticipate objections, to bring ambiguities to light, to forestall misunderstandings, and to show how easy it is to get things wrong.
Even philosophers who do write dialogues often insert long speeches
during which the interlocutor is mute and all-but-forgotten. Plato
himself is a case in point. The middle and late dialogues make
copious use of the method of continuous exposition in the form of
elaborate (and virtually uncontested) chains of reasoning, myths,
historical narratives, quasi-scientific discourses, and legal promul-
gations. Although dialogues in name, they read more like extended
monologues with occasional audience participation. Even the early
dialogues contain long speeches during which dialectical interaction is temporarily suspended. I conclude that, in spite of weighty
pronouncements about "the dialogue form" with which some commentators afflict us, an empirical approach to the Platonic corpus
reveals that the Platonic dialogue is not a unitary, *sui generis*, and
consistently employed alternative to the prose treatise, but a *carte
blanche* stylistic format which assigns high priority to sustained dialectical interaction but is not restricted to it. In this book, I will
proceed on the assumption that Plato did not write dialogues for
mysterious reasons, but rather because, given his Socratically influenced conception of philosophy as a collaborative enterprise,
the dialogue form was the ideal vehicle for celebrating his mentor
and conducting his own philosophical investigations.

Since philosophers who write dialogues do so in very different
ways and for very different reasons, the concept of the interlocutor
cannot be elucidated *in general*. We must examine each interlocutor
– Socratic and otherwise – on his own terms and in relation to the
philosophical goals and methodological principles of the philosopher in whose dialogue he appears. Since limitations of space

prohibit a full-scale comparative study, I offer the following remarks as illustrative.

I begin with Augustine's *De Libero Arbitrio*. In the course of refuting the errors of his interlocutor, Evodius, Augustine does not employ any single method of argumentation. However, his dialectical procedure often bears a striking resemblance to that peculiarly Socratic method of argumentation which Aristotle calls "peirastic" in which the interlocutor is refuted "from [his] own beliefs" (ἐκ τῶν δοκούντων τῷ ἀποκρινομένῳ, *S.E.* 165b3–4; *T.* 100a29–30). For example, asked why he judges adultery wrong, Evodius replies that it is because he would not tolerate adultery on the part of his own wife; and whoever does to another what he does not wish done to himself does what is evil (1.3.6). Augustine responds with the counterexample of the aspiring adulterer whose desire is so overpowering that he offers his wife to the husband of his prospective partner in sin – an action which Evodius also judges wrong. Alas, retorts Augustine, not according to the principle he has just espoused; for in the counterexample the aspiring adulterer is willing to do the very thing Evodius abhors.

Scattered examples of "peirastic" argumentation aside, *De Libero Arbitrio* consists mostly of extended monologues in which Augustine is neither refuting Evodius nor (apparently) even conversing with him.[5] In these passages, the dialogue form is purely external and the interlocutor's role becomes increasingly perfunctory and, in the end, non-existent. Highly visible and actively involved in the discussion throughout Book 1, Evodius gradually recedes from view. The eclipse of Evodius continues in the succeeding books, where his participation is minimal, and he vanishes altogether during the last nineteen pages of the "dialogue." Augustine's propensity for monologue and conspicuous neglect of Evodius suggest that, in his hands, the dialogue form is little more than a pedagogical device which enables him to expound positive doctrine.

Anselm also wrote dialogues for primarily pedagogical purposes. That this is so is clear from the preface to *Cur Deus Homo*:

[I]ssues which are examined by the method of question-and-answer are clearer, and so more acceptable, to many minds – especially to minds

---

[5] A tendency about which he is a trifle self-conscious and for which another interlocutor, Adeodatus, profusely thanks him: "I am specially grateful that latterly you have spoken without the interruption of questions and answers, because you have taken up and resolved all the difficulties I was prepared to urge against you" (*De Magistro* 14.46).

that are slower ... Therefore ... I shall take as my fellow disputant the
one who has been urging me to this end more insistently than the others,
so that Boso may ask and Anselm answer. (3: 49–50)

Although Anselm often replies to Boso's questions with questions
of his own, his purpose is not to draw him into philosophical debate, but to pave the way for his own forthcoming solution of the
difficulty at hand by eliciting Boso's assent to other propositions
on which the solution depends. For example, asked whether men
would have died had they not sinned, Boso replies, "As we believe,
[they] would not, but I want to hear from you the rationale of this
belief" (3 : 61). He adds that he fears he would be sinning were he
to say anything else (3 : 68). In prefacing his reply with the locution, "As we believe" – a locution which occurs frequently
throughout *Cur Deus Homo* – Boso is not appealing to prevailing
orthodox opinion. Although his "we" denotes the collective body
of believers, it is not the empirical fact that these propositions are
believed that recommends them to Boso. They are not theological
endoxa – religious beliefs common to all the faithful – but unassail-
able truths appropriated by faith independently of and prior to
philosophical investigation. If they were merely theological *endoxa*,
Boso's dissent would only be atypical and not, as he fears, sinful.

As an interlocutor, Boso is a generic stand-in for the religiously
committed but intellectually perplexed believer. What he wants
from Anselm is not truth – he already has that – but understanding: "We believe it, but I would like to have a reason for it"
(3 : 74). Yet although Boso is already in possession of truth, it is
truth imperfectly grasped. Understanding is not the condition of
belief, but it is a coveted *desideratum*; and the intellectually consci-
entious believer makes every effort to augment his understanding
(1 : 1; 2 : 50). That God became man is beyond dispute; Boso merely
wants to know why. Anselm's explanation follows, set forth dialectically by means of question-and-answer, so as to render the Doctrine of the Incarnation intelligible "to minds that are slower."

The philosophical function of the Anselmian interlocutor, like
that of his Augustinian counterpart, is largely pedagogical: he asks
questions which Anselm answers, he expresses confusions which
Anselm dispels, he poses objections which Anselm demolishes. His
humble contributions are dialectically uneventful and rarely influence the direction of the discussion. His responses are unfailingly

docile and characterized by a studied passivity: "It is up to you to explain and up to me to pay attention," "You have satisfactorily answered my objection," "I am ashamed for having asked that question." And so it continues for hundreds of pages. In *De Veritate* the interlocutor is so anonymous that he lacks even a name. Identified simply as "Pupil," he earnestly implores "Teacher" to impart truth and promises to be a good listener (2:77). Discussion with such interlocutors is almost wholly devoid of philosophical excitement. There is little sense of intellectual struggle, even less dialectical give-and-take, and never the slightest possibility that the interlocutor might remain unpersuaded. We know from the very first page whose view will prevail. Tame and tractable throughout, Evodius, Boso, and "Pupil" comport themselves like well-behaved catechumens in the presence of a revered authority, gratefully embracing the truths vouchsafed to them and devoutly resolving never again to be overtaken by doubt or error.

If the dialogues of Augustine and Anselm are little more than thinly-disguised monologues and if their interlocutors are rather too accommodating, Hume's *Dialogues Concerning Natural Religion* are genuinely confrontational and Cleanthes, Demea, and Philo are not interlocutors at all. They are rather philosophical protagonists – flesh and blood proponents of divergent points of view which they defend with considerable acumen. Hume is very sensitive about this point. Speaking through Pamphilus, he says:

[T]hough the ancient philosophers conveyed most of their instruction in the form of dialogue, this method of composition has been little practiced in later ages, and has seldom succeeded in the hands of those who have attempted it ... To deliver a *System* in conversation scarcely appears natural; and while the dialogue-writer desires, by departing from the direct style of composition, to give a freer air to his performance, and avoid the appearance of *author* and *reader*, he is apt to run into a worse inconvenience, and convey the image of *pedagogue* and *pupil*.[6] (1983: 1)

In Hume, the participants are intellectual equals – "[r]easonable men [who] may be allowed to differ where no one can reasonably be positive" (1–2).

---

[6] On the differences between the "pedagogical" dialogue (as employed, e.g., by Cicero, Augustine, Anselm, Galileo, Malebranche, Schopenhauer, and Shelley), which presupposes the inherent inequality of the participants, and the "dialogue of relative equality" (as employed, e.g., by Descartes, Berkeley, and Hume), see Levi, 1976: 1–20. See also Koyré. 1962: 17–19, esp. 18, n. 4.

The traditional dialectical roles disappear: there is neither a designated questioner nor a designated answerer – no specific participant whose views are singled out for sustained scrutiny and who must bear full dialectical responsibility for them. Sustained scrutiny there is, but of arguments antecedently formulated and delivered for the occasion, not of theses contextually elicited and jointly explored. The method of criticism is also significantly different from that of Augustine and Anselm. A representative example occurs in Part III where Philo sets out to discredit Cleanthes' formulation of the Argument from Design. His critique does not take the form of a joint exploration in which Cleanthes is required to assent to each step; instead, he proceeds cumulatively with a series of objections which continues uninterrupted for several pages. But he pays a high price for this strategy. Having gone on at considerable length and, as he thinks, brought into play his heaviest artillery, he is more than a little disconcerted when Cleanthes disputes an earlier premise on which the entire chain of reasoning depends but to which he never assented. Having undercut Philo's argument, Cleanthes disparages it on the ground that it proceeds "from too luxuriant a fertility which suppresses [his] natural good sense by a profusion of unnecessary scruples and objections" (26). The rejection of this single premise enables Cleanthes to circumvent the massive critique launched by Philo who is left "a little embarrassed and confounded" (26).

By contrast, Berkeley's dialogues are genuine dialectical exchanges, and Hylas is an authentic interlocutor and the designated answerer to Philonous' questions. Unlike his Augustinian and Anselmian counterparts, the Berkeleyian interlocutor is not a rapt disciple eager to imbibe wisdom from a revered sage. The champion of common sense, Hylas enters the discussion with strongly held opinions, which he defends with considerable acumen, and with clearly formulated objections, which he advances with clarity and force. As for Philonous, he is remarkably attuned to these objections and takes them very seriously. Unwilling merely to silence Hylas or to settle for his grudging acquiescence, he strives for genuine persuasion, considering his objections one by one, ignoring his trivial inadvertences, refusing to put words into his mouth, and allowing him time for stocktaking during which he may review the arguments which have been deployed against him and examine them for possible logical flaws. Realizing that the hold of custom is strong, that people often remain wedded to beliefs after acknowledging them to be indefensible, and that what is needed is not just a refutation of false beliefs, but an explanation of their apparent plausibility, Philonous leaves no stone unturned and will not rest until he has dispelled Hylas' doubts.

Unlike Hume, Berkeley makes extensive use of "peirastic" argumentation. Philonous continually requires Hylas to assent to each step of the argument and continually reminds him of his previous admissions (see, e.g., 227, 231, 234, 239, 240–41, 243, 246–47, 261), so that he will be "convinced out of [his] own mouth" (270). However, Berkeley's purpose is not purely negative. Like Augustine and Anselm, he is not just bent on refuting error; he also wants to expound positive doctrine – in particular, the "immaterialism" he had set forth in his previously published but largely ignored *Treatise Concerning the Principles of Human Knowledge*. Disappointed by its lukewarm reception, he resolved to try again by presenting his views in more accessible form. The result was the *Three Dialogues between Hylas and Philonous* which "introduces [his] notions ... into the mind in the most easy and familiar manner" (220) in hopes of inducing the reader, presumably sympathetic to Hylas, to abandon his own materialism as he witnesses its champion going down to defeat. In that sense, Berkeley's dialogues are as pedagogically motivated as Augustine's and Anselm's.

For these philosophers, the dialogue form is not a methodological necessity, but a stylistic option – a pedagogical device which enables them to set forth their views in a comparatively untechnical and undemanding way. Since, for them, philosophical truth can be presented either dialectically (in dialogues) or non-dialectically (in prose treatises), there is only a contingent connection between the end of expounding positive doctrine and the means by which it is expounded. The choice of means is, in fact, secondary – an afterthought, a purely strategic matter to be determined by the intellectual capacities of one's audience.

It is time to sum up this brief survey of non-Socratic interlocutors. First, however different in other respects, the Augustinian, Anselmian, and Berkeleyian interlocutors are alike in that they are all, to varying degrees, spokesmen for, and dramatic embodiments of, error; and error must be refuted. Second, in spite of the considerable amount of space allotted to refutation, it is only a preliminary. Simply to have refuted the interlocutor is not enough; his false beliefs must be replaced with true ones. Finally, since refutation leads the interlocutor into perplexity and uncertainty – states of mind which Augustine, Anselm, and Berkeley regard as regrettable and potentially dangerous – if the interlocutor cannot find his way out of his difficulties, they stand ready to come to his aid.

In turning to Plato's early dialogues, one enters a different world. Here, too, are interlocutors aplenty and refutation by "peirastic" argumentation. But Socratic interlocutors bear little resemblance to their non-Socratic counterparts.

For one thing, the philosopher with whom they have to do operates with radically different motives. Unlike Augustine, Anselm, and Berkeley, Socrates is not interested in expounding positive doctrine – not because he is indifferent to truth, but because he has none to impart. However, although devoid of wisdom, he claims to be a lover of it – a searcher in search not only of truth, but also of other searchers. The early dialogues reflect the Socratic conception of philosophy as a collaborative enterprise – a joint search for truth. By a "joint" search, Socrates does not just mean a discussion between two (or more) participants. The dialogues of Augustine, Anselm, and Berkeley satisfy *that* criterion; but they are not joint searches in Socrates' sense. In these dialogues only one participant is searching for truth; the other participant already has it. The interlocutor plays no vital role in the discovery; he merely provides the occasion for the author of the dialogue to communicate the truth he has already discovered – "[t]o deliver a *System*," in Humean phrase. Socrates has no system. Anyone who claims to have one disqualifies himself as a philosopher.

Second, unlike Augustine, Anselm, and Berkeley, Socrates does not refute his interlocutors in hopes of replacing their false beliefs with true ones, but in hopes of convicting them of ignorance and replacing their false beliefs with a *desire* for true ones. The proximate end of philosophizing is not the discovery of truth, but the realization that one does not have it. The etymological definition of "philosophy" as the love of wisdom has become so hackneyed through repetition that it is easy to forget that it originally meant something important. As a lover of wisdom, the philosopher dissociates himself from all who claim to *be* wise. But although philosophy is, in that sense, a means to an end – an activity which (one hopes) will culminate in the discovery of truth – it is also, for Socrates, an end in itself – an activity which enables one to live an examined life. It is in living that life, rather than in enjoying the epistemic benefits which result from living it, that the highest human happiness is to be found:

[T]he greatest good for a man [is] to discuss virtue every day and those other things about which you hear me conversing and testing myself and others, for the unexamined life is not worth living for men. (*Ap.* 38a1–6)

In short, the activity of philosophizing is not a *means* to happiness, understood as an end distinct from philosophizing and contingently connected to it as a causal consequence; it *is* happiness.[7]

Finally, unlike Augustine, Anselm and Berkeley, who deplore perplexity and uncertainty as regrettable and potentially dangerous states of mind and do everything in their power to uproot them, Socrates prizes perplexity and uncertainty as desirable and potentially salutary states of mind and does everything in his power to inculcate them. If the interlocutor cannot find his way out of his difficulties, Socrates will not bail him out; he is on his own.

Unlike Evodius and Boso, the Socratic interlocutor is not a rapt disciple who has come to sit at the feet of a revered sage.[8] Indeed, insofar as Socrates denied having ever taught anyone anything (*Ap.* 33a5–6, 33b5–8), he had no disciples (μαθητής).[9] He did, however, have intimates,[10] many of whom were present at his exe-

---

[7] In this life and possibly the next. It is precisely the opportunity of talking endlessly about virtue which makes the prospect of immortality so attractive to Socrates (*Ap.* 41c2–4).

[8] The interlocutors encountered by Xenophon's Socrates are very different. Excruciatingly aware of their intellectual inadequacies and embarrassingly susceptible to his instant "wisdom," they have much in common with the Augustinian and Anselmian interlocutors and would have found them kindred spirits.

[9] In referring to Socrates' interlocutors, neither Plato nor Xenophon uses the term "disciple" (μαθητής). Socrates calls Chaerephon his companion (ἑταῖρος, *Ap.* 21a1), and Xanthippe alludes to his friends (οἱ ἐπιτήδειοι, *Ph.* 60a6). Xenophon typically employs τοὺς συνόντας (*Mem.* 1.2.64, 1.1.4, 1.2.8, 1.2.17, 1.6.3, 4.3.1, 4.4.25), although he occasionally substitutes τοὺς συνδιατρίβοντας (1.2.3, 1.3.15, 1.4.1), τοὺς ἐπιτηδείους (1.1.6), τοὺς ἀποδεξαμένους (1.2.8), and τοὺς συγγιγνομένους (1.2.61).

[10] In view of their allegedly close proximity to Socrates, one would expect Xenophon and Plato to be authoritative sources about the members of the Socratic inner circle. But their lists are strikingly different. Interestingly, neither includes the other. Xenophon's writings contain only one oblique allusion to Plato (*Mem.* 3.6.1), and Plato never mentions Xenophon. Diogenes Laertius attributes this mutual chilliness to the intense rivalry between them (2.57, 3.34). Athenaeus also reports that Plato and Xenophon were envious of each other (*The Deipnosophists* 504e4–f6). He adds that Plato was inimical (δυσμενής, 506a6) and filled with malice (κακοηθείας, 507a8–10) towards everyone: "[T]he day would fail me if I should wish to proceed with all who were abused by the philosopher" (507a1–3).

cution.[11] Unlike Xenophon's *Memorabilia*, which depicts endless conversations between Socrates and these people, Plato's early dialogues depict only one – the celebrated exchange with Crito.[12]

But if the Socratic interlocutor is not a rapt disciple like Evodius and Boso, neither is he an independent thinker like Hylas. The typical Socratic interlocutor is no intellectual and, in spite of Critias' application of the term φιλόσοφος to the young Charmides (*Ch.* 154e8–155a1), none is a philosopher. Unlike the "Socrates" of the *Phaedo*, who surrounds himself with philosophers, and the "Socrates" of the *Republic*, for whom philosophy is a specialized discipline reserved for the select few and then only after years of intensive preliminary immersion in mathematics, geometry, astronomy, and harmonics, the Socrates of the early dialogues thinks it is open to anyone and everyone to philosophize and is willing to debate all comers – young or old, foreigner or fellow citizen (*Ap.* 30a2–4). The prerequisites are minimal: one need only speak Greek and possess a modicum of intelligence, though it is arguable that some of his interlocutors lack even that.

Socrates' interlocutors fall into three fairly distinct categories: they are either young men (Charmides is a mere boy), established professionals (Nicias and Laches are generals, Polus is a rhetorician, Euthyphro is a theologian, Ion is a rhapsode, and Gorgias,

---

[11] See *Ph.* 59b6–c6. Diogenes Laertius (3.35–36) reports that many of the Socratics were ill-disposed towards Plato and that some were openly hostile. Antisthenes attacked him in a dialogue entitled *Sathon*; Aristippus criticized him for not being present at Socrates' execution, "though he was no farther off than Aegina"; and Aeschines claimed that the arguments advanced in the *Crito* in favor of Socrates' escaping from prison were actually his own and that Plato put them into the mouth of Crito because he despised Aeschines for being poor – a remark which Burnet, 1924: 173, dismisses as "a piece of spiteful Epicurean tittle-tattle." If even a fraction of the gossip, rumor, and innuendo reported by Diogenes Laertius is true, the Socratics were a petty and quarrelsome lot who not only disagreed monumentally among themselves about Socrates' philosophical views but also intensely disliked one another.

[12] The others are occasionally alluded to – albeit usually unflatteringly. This unlikely group included Aristodemus, who worshiped Socrates and went about barefoot in imitation of him (*Sym.* 173b1–2); Apollodorus, who lamented his pre-Socratic years as wasted and wretched (*Sym.* 172c2–173a3); and Chaerephon, who behaved like a wild man (μανικός, *Ch.* 153b2) whenever he was in the presence of Socrates and who considered himself so adept at his method that he would cross-examine people on demand (*G.* 447c9–448c3). Although Xenophon never tires of recounting how Socrates improved his companions by teaching them to master their passions, Plato's portrayal suggests that he improved few and that his own inner strength and stability of character were conspicuously lacking in his intimates: Chaerephon was impulsive (*Ap.* 21a3), unpunctual (*G.* 447a7–8), and overly-susceptible to physical beauty (*Ch.* 154c8–d5); Aristodemus could not hold his liquor (*Sym.* 176c1–3); and Apollodorus lacked self-control (*Ph.* 59a7–b4, 117d3–6).

Protagoras, and Hippias are sophists), or prosperous employers of manual laborers (Cephalus and Polemarchus owned what was probably the largest shield factory in the Piraeus, and Crito is an urban dweller who owns several farms).[13]

Socrates' interlocutors are comprised of a comparatively narrow sociological group. For one thing, they are all men. Women appear infrequently and fleetingly in Plato's dialogues. At *Sym.* 176e4–10 Socrates unceremoniously enjoins a female flutist to vacate the premises so the men can talk philosophy in peace.[14] Except for (the probably mythical) Diotima, whose remarks are narrated by Socrates (*Sym.* 201d1–212a8), and Aspasia, whose speech he repeats for the benefit of Menexenus (*Men.* 236d4–249c9), the only woman in the whole Platonic corpus who actually says anything is Xanthippe; and she is allotted only one sentence which is narrated by Phaedo: "Socrates, this is the last time your friends will talk to you and you to them" (*Ph.* 60a5–6). Although Phaedo pillories her remark as "the sort of thing that women usually say" (60a4–5), I find it quite touching and, in view of her reputation, decidedly unshrewlike.[15] But it falls on deaf ears. Absorbed in philosophical reflection about the mixed sensations of pleasure and pain in his chained legs, Socrates has no time for irrelevancies. He responds to his wife with a stony silence and instructs Crito to have her escorted from the cell forthwith – which he does, with Xanthippe wailing and beating her breast. Moments before his execution she makes another appearance accompanied by their three sons and "the

---

[13] For an illuminating survey of the walks of life from which Socrates' interlocutors are drawn, see Vidal-Naquet, 1984: 273–93.

[14] Actually, it is hard to tell whether she is banished because she is a female or because she is a flutist. Plato had an inordinate dislike for the instrument because of its wide harmonic range (*R.* 561c6–d2), and he excluded flutes, flutists, and even flute-makers from his ideal society (*R.* 399c7–d6).

[15] Xanthippe's reputation as a shrew derives largely from Diogenes Laertius who reports that she regularly scolded Socrates and once tore his coat from his back in the marketplace and then proceeded to drench him with water (2.36–37). (One suspects that many interlocutors would have liked to do the same thing.) In response to Alcibiades' criticism of his wife as an intolerable nag, Socrates sagely confides that he puts up with her for the same reason that riders put up with spirited horses: just as, having mastered these, they can more easily cope with docile creatures, so he, owing to the society of Xanthippe, can more easily cope with humanity at large. Diogenes solemnly adds that it was to such words that the Pythian priestess bore witness when she declared that no one is wiser than Socrates (2.36–37). The only commentator known to me who interprets Xanthippe's remark in the *Phaedo* as that of a shrew is Brun, 1960: 25: "Dès que Xanthippe nous eut aperçus, ce furent des malédictions et des discours tout à fait dans le genre habituel aux femmes."

women of his household" (αἱ οἰκεῖαι γυναῖκες, *Ph.* 116b2), but is again quickly dispatched. Not only are there no female interlocutors in the early dialogues, Plato never portrays Socrates conversing with a woman.[16] Although willing to enter into philosophical debate with anyone and everyone – "young and old, foreigner and fellow citizen," he does not add "man or woman."[17]

Socrates' interlocutors are comprised of a comparatively narrow sociological group in a second way. Although the early dialogues abound with allusions to skilled craftsmen whose expertise, grounded in an understanding of the rational principles underlying their *technai*, serves as a model for the moral expertise for which Socrates is searching, and although Socrates numbers the craftsmen among those he interrogated during his search for someone wiser than himself, Plato never portrays him conversing with a craftsman.[18] However his interlocutors may differ in age, background, and education, they all move in the higher echelons of society – Athenian and otherwise.

Unlike their non-Socratic counterparts, who participate eagerly in philosophical discussion and often initiate it, Socrates' interlocutors typically become embroiled unwittingly and against their better judgment. A casual remark, instantly rued, about being on the way to court (or something equally humdrum) suddenly acquires momentous importance, and they quickly find themselves being drawn into a discussion for which they have little relish and less competence. Socrates' method of argumentation is coercive. He tries to force his interlocutors to a particular conclusion – "to get [them] to believe something, whether [they] want to believe it

[16] Xenophon, on the other hand, portrays him conversing with the beautiful and scantily clad hetaera Theodete (*Mem.* 3.11.1–18) and reports another conversation with Aspasia (2.6.36).
[17] However, he does add that in the hereafter, if there is one, it would be a source of "extraordinary happiness" to examine the men *and women* there (*Ap.* 41c2) – a remark which prompts Vlastos, 1991: 110, n. 15, to conclude that women were not excluded, in principle, from philosophical debate and that their absence from the early dialogues is traceable to the fact that they were "not in the public places where Socrates could reach them" – a sociological barrier which is removed in the next life. Vidal-Naquet, 1984: 282, is less apologetic: "Les femmes sont citoyennes de la *République*, elles ne sont pas reçues dans la société platonicienne des dialogues."
[18] Neither does Xenophon. However, he does depict a conversation between Socrates and Euthydemus that takes place in a cobbler's shop where Socrates and his companions often gathered (*Mem.* 4.2.1).

or not.''[19] But although his method of argumentation is coercive, his manner of engaging his interlocutors in discussion is not: participation is voluntary (*Ch.* 158e3, *La.* 188a6–c3, and 189a1–3). At the same time, it is all-but-impossible to avoid. Socrates' unfailing urbanity, combined with his willingness to discuss any subject, however trivial, and his uncanny ability to judge character, enable him to lure people into discussion in spite of their misgivings.

But if Socrates' interlocutors enter into philosophical discussion voluntarily, they also enter into it blindly, advised neither of the constraints which govern the Socratic elenchus nor that its purpose is refutation. Lysimachus is one of the few who is forewarned about this – albeit not by Socrates but by Nicias:

> You don't appear ... to know that whoever comes into close contact with Socrates and associates with him in conversation must necessarily, even if he begins by conversing about something quite different ... keep on being led about by the man's arguments until he submits to answering questions about himself concerning both his present manner of life and the life he has lived hitherto. And when he does submit to this questioning, you don't realize that Socrates will not let him go before he has well and truly tested every last detail. (*La.* 187e6–188a3)[20]

The typical Socratic interlocutor is unaware of all this and is told only that he must refrain from making long speeches and say what he really believes. Some are not even told that.

Although seemingly spontaneous and even desultory, the Socratic elenchus is, in fact, highly rigorous. Having been lured into discussion – often on false pretenses (Euthyphro is flattered into believing he can be of genuine assistance) – the Socratic interlocutor has no idea of what he is in for. Entering into disputation with Socrates is like inadvertently strolling into a minefield. By the time he realizes what is happening, it is too late. The refutation is as swift as it is unexpected. His astonishment is compounded by the fact that the refutation is apparently self-inflicted. At each step of the argument, he is pointedly asked whether he assents to the propositions proposed for his assent. Dissent is not only possible, it is invited. But he does not dissent. The propositions seem perfectly

---

[19] Nozick, 1981: 4. For a different view, see Irwin, 1986: 49–74.
[20] At *Ap.* 29e3–30a2 Socrates describes his treatment of his interlocutors in almost identical terms.

innocuous – even truisms. Yet once his assent is given, it assumes a life of its own and quickly becomes the instrument of his undoing. Although freely offered, his every utterance binds and fetters him; his every assertion negates something else he has said or wants to say. It is an unpleasant and unnerving experience – the experience of the interlocutor as dialectical target and of refutation not only as annihilation but, apparently, as *self*-annihilation.

Embellishing the *O.E.D.*'s definition, a Socratic interlocutor is "one who takes part in a dialogue, conversation, or discussion" which is conducted for the surreptitious but allegedly salutary purpose of refuting him "from his own beliefs," thereby exposing his false conceit of knowledge and infusing him with self-knowledge. From Socrates' point of view, an interlocutor is someone who mistakenly (and often arrogantly) supposes that he knows something which he does not know. Such persons are deluded and in need of having their delusions exposed. In thus engaging his interlocutors, he claims to be caring for their souls and discharging his divine mission.

A further insight into the concept of the Socratic interlocutor may be gained by reviewing how Socrates came to believe he had this mission. As we have seen, when confronted with the astonishing – and, to his mind, dubious – Delphic pronouncement that no one is wiser than he, Socrates had initially tried to refute it by interrogating various people with a reputation for wisdom in hopes of finding someone wiser. Having found such a person, he had intended to appear before the Pythia and confront her with living proof of her error: "This man is wiser than I, but you said I was [the wisest]" (*Ap.* 21c2).[21] In short, he had treated the Delphic pronouncement like any other dubious claim. Although not an interlocutor in the strict sense, since he cannot be directly inter-

---

[21] Contrary to what Socrates implies, the oracle did not say that he is the wis*est* of men, but that no one is wis*er* – a claim which is compatible with others being as wise insofar as they, too, acknowledge that they have no wisdom and which seems to entail that these other hypothetical wise men would have the same divine mission. I say "seems to entail" because Socrates goes out of his way to explain that his belief in his divine mission was not based solely on the oracle's pronouncement, but also on dreams, commands, and every other way in which the gods make their wishes known to human beings (*Ap.* 33c4–7). In any event, he does not object to others behaving as if they had the same mission. Without a trace of disapproval and even with a trace of amusement, he approvingly alludes to certain young men who, with him as their model, go about examining people who think they know something when, in fact, they know little or nothing (*Ap.* 23c2–7).

rogated, the god is nevertheless treated as a kind of interlocutor – an interlocutor *in absentia* – and his claim is targeted for refutation. The search for someone wiser than Socrates is on.

Unlike Socrates' typical allusions to wise men, these remarks should not be taken ironically. The search was undertaken in complete seriousness and in hopes of refuting the oracle, that is, in hopes of demonstrating that, on any straightforward interpretation, the proposition "No one is wiser than Socrates" is false. This proposition can be false only if there *is* someone wiser than (or as wise as) Socrates. And it can be *known* to be false only if Socrates can find him. Hence his disappointment upon discovering that the very people thought to be the wisest were, in fact, the most deficient in wisdom (*Ap.* 22a1–4). This was not a mere corroboration of what he had expected all along; it was a genuine empirical discovery. The search for a counterexample with which to refute the oracle had failed.

Since the class of persons wiser than Socrates is now known to be a null class, it would be the height of folly to continue searching for its members. And Socrates did not. Unable to demonstrate that the oracle's claim was false, he concluded that it was true, reinterpreted its meaning, and concluded that he had been commanded to live the life of a philosopher (φιλοσοφοῦντά ... δεῖν ζῆν, *Ap.* 28e5), examining himself and others, thereby *helping* the god's cause (*Ap.* 23b4–c1). The hitherto dubious claim that no one is wiser than Socrates has been pronounced irrefutable (ἀνέλεγκτος, *Ap.* 22a7–8),[22] and the purpose of the divine mission is to vindicate it. The serious search for someone wiser than himself has been replaced by tongue-in-cheek irony about pretenders. The Socrates of the early dialogues has been born.

There is another "kind of interlocutor" in the early dialogues – an omnipresent, sinister, and undifferentiated entity which darkens Plato's pages and hovers over them like a menacing cloud. This entity is "public opinion" and it is embodied in the views of "the Many." Like the god at Delphi, it cannot be directly interrogated; but it is sometimes indirectly interrogated with some unfortunate

---

[22] Those who translate ἐλέγχω as "examine" or "test" (rather than as "refute") are committed to translating ἀνέλεγκτος as "unexaminable" or "untestable" – thereby foisting on Socrates the decidedly odd (if not self-contradictory) claim that his purpose in testing the oracle was to demonstrate that it is untestable.

interlocutor serving as its representative. I say "unfortunate" because it is axiomatic in the early dialogues that the opinions of
"the Many" are, at best, muddled and, at worst, false. Any interlocutor foolish enough to answer on their behalf has dug his own
dialectical grave.

I said earlier that I would retain the term "interlocutor" because, in spite of its terminological awkwardness, it best captures
the announced philosophical goals and methodological principles
which underlie the Socratic elenchus and are allegedly operative
throughout the early dialogues. One final principle needs to be
mentioned.

Socrates sometimes suggests that there is an important and peculiarly Socratic kind of reciprocity between himself and his interlocutors. This reciprocity is easily overlooked if we attend only to
their respective roles as questioner and answerer. Superficially
considered, the questioner seems to enjoy all the dialectical advantages. Everyone knows it is easier to pick apart someone else's
position than to set forth a coherent position of one's own. According to Socrates, however, there is a deeper dimension to the
Socratic elenchus which reveals that this initial impression is false.
What it is may be seen by recalling that his announced goal is to
care for the souls of his fellows by convicting them of their ignorance and motivating them to take up the philosophical quest.
Hence arises the view of the interlocutor as a person whose life is
on the line – the patient, the defendant, the accused, who is (in
Jaeger's phrase) intellectually "stripped."[23] According to official
Socratic elenctic theory, one cannot pursue philosophy with maxi-
mum profit by oneself in isolation from others. One needs a questioner, an examiner, a critic – someone to save one from oneself,
from one's ignorance, complacency, and sloth by calling into
question one's deepest certainties and revealing that one does not
know what one thinks one knows.

However, if the early dialogues show anything, they show Socrates' monumental failure. The recalcitrant and unpersuaded interlocutor is not a phenomenon peculiar to some of the dialogues,
but a phenomenon common to most of them – to all of them if
Vlastos is right in claiming that Socrates *never* manages to "win
over" an opponent. Hence if Socrates' announced goal is his only

[23] 1943–45, I: 34. Socrates uses the same metaphor at *Ch.* 154e5–7.

reason for living the life of a philosopher, why, in view of his universal (or all-but-universal) failure, does he continue to believe it is a worthwhile activity – not to mention the highest form of human happiness? Why does he not abandon his divine mission as a singularly hopeless and thankless task? What are we to make of his apparently inexplicable willingness to invest such inordinate amounts of time and energy in the company of these unresponsive and seemingly impenetrable interlocutors?

A possible explanation is that he persists because he understands that the examined life is difficult and is not unduly discouraged by failure. A second possibility is that he persists because, although he never completely "wins over" an opponent, he occasionally makes marginal progress. Yet another possibility is that he persists out of obedience to the god of Delphi.

Although each of these explanations has a certain plausibility, Socrates gives a different one. It is this explanation which reveals the allegedly deeper dimension of the Socratic elenchus. According to Socrates, he persists in the face of universal (or all-but-universal) failure because caring for the souls of his fellows is *not* his only reason for living the life of a philosopher; it is not even his most important one. Although Socrates' divinely appointed task is to examine his interlocutors and deprive them of their false conceit of knowledge, the Socratic elenchus is neither wholly adversarial nor wholly altruistic. Socrates seeks out interlocutors: not just for their sakes, but also for his own sake. If his interlocutors need him, as he manifestly believes, he needs them, too. Elenctic examination is always *self*-examination (*Ap.* 38a4–5).

Rebuked by Critias on the ground that he is just trying to refute him, Socrates replies:

[H]ow could you possibly think that even if I were to refute everything you say, I would be doing it for any other reasons than the one I would give for a thorough investigation of my own statements – the fear of unconsciously thinking I know something when I do not. And this is what I claim to be doing now, examining the argument for my own sake primarily, but perhaps also for the sake of my friends. (*Ch.* 166c7–d4)

Similarly, before refuting Gorgias, Socrates expresses the hope that his interlocutor is the same kind of man as he:

And what kind of man am I? One of those who would be pleased to be refuted if I say anything untrue, and who would be pleased to refute anyone who says anything untrue; one who, however, wouldn't be any less pleased to be refuted than to refute. For I count being refuted a greater good, insofar as it is a greater good for oneself to be delivered from the worst thing there is than to deliver someone else from it. (*G.* 458a2–7)

In short, the deeper dimension of the Socratic elenchus consists in the fact that, in examining his interlocutors – and, presumably, improving their souls – Socrates is simultaneously examining himself – and, presumably, improving his soul. To philosophize by oneself in isolation from others is to deny the necessity and to decline the risk of scrutiny by others. These passages shed further light on the concept of the Socratic interlocutor and the indispensable dialectical and philosophical functions he allegedly performs. It is, in fact, no exaggeration to say that the whole Socratic philosophical enterprise is unalterably grounded in the necessity of having interlocutors. Without them, the enterprise collapses, and the possibility of philosophizing in the deepest and potentially most beneficial sense is lost. Without a questioner, fraudulent claimants to wisdom are deprived of what they need most – a critic. But without an answerer, the questioner is deprived of what he needs most – an interlocutor against whom his own views can be tested. If the answerer has access to the *logos* only when subjected to interrogation, the questioner has access to it only when provided with an answerer. In the process, the views of both are tested: the answerer's by the questioner and the questioner's by the *logos*.

This, then, is the concept of the interlocutor which underlies the Socratic elenchus. At least, it is the "official" view. Socrates is hard on his interlocutors, but for excellent reasons – he is improving their souls – and he is equally hard on himself. This announced goal is at once noble and puzzling: noble, because it bespeaks a deep moral seriousness; puzzling, because it is (for the most part) a misdescription of his actual goal – which is not to improve anyone, but simply to win arguments. In the following chapters, we will see that, and how often, this is the case.

CHAPTER 2

Elenchus and sincere assent

Before turning to the interlocutors and defending my thesis that Socrates' frequent use of faulty arguments and unscrupulous dialectical tactics calls into question his announced seriousness and concern for the souls of his fellows, I must address an objection which will have occurred to many readers and which, if sound, would undercut my thesis and render this study superfluous. The objection is that I am ignoring "the 'say what you believe' constraint,"[1] that is, the Socratic methodological principle that his interlocutors may neither advance theses which they do not believe nor concur with theses propounded by Socrates unless they sincerely assent to them.[2] Socrates' allegedly unwavering commitment to this principle is one of the orthodoxies of contemporary Anglo-American Socratic scholarship. I say "allegedly" because although Socrates occasionally invokes this sincere assent requirement, its importance has been greatly exaggerated by many recent

---

[1] The terminology is Vlastos's, 1983a: 35. In 1994: 7, "constraint" is replaced by "requirement."

[2] The requirement is variously interpreted. Some commentators think that it applies not only to the interlocutors but also to Socrates, and that it forbids him to employ premises which he does not believe (see Crombie, 1962, i: 26; C. C. W. Taylor, 1976: 155–61; Irwin, 1977: 39; Méron, 1979: 211; Vlastos, 1981b: 223, n. 5; 1991: 132–35, esp. 134, n. 17. Others think that it applies only to the interlocutors on the ground that Socrates always argues *ad hominem*, i.e., from his interlocutors' beliefs; hence it is not necessary that *he* believe the premises he employs, it is sufficient that *they* believe them (see Stokes, 1986: 1–35; Teloh, 1986: 1–2, 16–18; Kahn, 1983: 113, n. 62; Frede, 1992: 212; Brickhouse and Smith, 1994: 14–16. Even Vlastos admits that Socrates occasionally employs premises he does not believe; but he exonerates him on the ground that in these passages he is not engaged in "standard" elenchus, which demonstrates that his interlocutors' beliefs are false and requires him to employ only premises he thinks are true, but in "indirect" elenchus, which demonstrates that their beliefs are inconsistent and does not require this (1983a: 38–39, esp. nn. 29 and 32). Brickhouse and Smith find other excuses, denying that Socrates is "directly deceitful" in employing premises he does not believe and asserting – for reasons unknown to me and undisclosed by them – that he must divulge his actual views only "[w]hen asked directly" (1994: 16, n. 30).

37

commentators.[3] In this chapter, I will try to show that it is not nearly so ubiquitously present and systematically operative as they think.

Passages in which the requirement is invoked include *Cr.* 49c11–d1:

Crito, see that you do not agree to this, contrary to your belief (παρὰ δόξαν);

R. 349a4–6:

[W]e mustn't shrink from pursuing the argument and looking into this, just as long as I take you to be saying what you really think (ἅπερ διανοῇ);

Pr. 331c4–d1:

Don't do that to me! It's not this "if you want" or "if you agree" business I want to test. It's you and me I want to put on the line, and I think the argument will be tested best if we take the "if" out;

and *G.* 500b5–7:

[B]y Zeus, the god of friendship, Callicles, please don't think that you should jest with me ... or answer anything that comes to mind, contrary to what you really think (παρὰ τὰ δοκοῦντα).

Indeed, at *G.* 495a8–9 Socrates tells Callicles that he cannot be a suitable dialectical partner if he speaks contrary to what he really believes.

No one has attached greater weight to these (and other similar) passages than Vlastos, according to whom Socrates "will not debate unasserted premises – only those asserted categorically by his interlocutor, who is not allowed to answer 'contrary to his real opinion'."[4] Insofar as the sincere assent requirement disallows "iffy" – that is, tentative and non-committal assertions – it invests the Socratic elenchus with an "existential dimension"[5] which en-

---

[3] Among them, Robinson, 1953: 15–16; Gulley, 1968: 33–34, 41; Burnyeat, 1971: 214; Irwin, 1977: 39; 1995: 20, 29–30, 48–49, 121; Stokes, 1986: 29–33; Teloh, 1986: 11; Saunders, 1987: 31, 278, n. 3; Benson, 1989: 591–99; Frede, 1992: 211–12; Penner, 1992b: 144–45; Brickhouse and Smith, 1994: 13–14; and Rutherford, 1995: 79. The requirement is so deeply entrenched in and taken for granted by Anglo-American Socratic scholarship that one recent commentator merely alludes to it in passing as "a familiar feature" of the Socratic elenchus (McPherran, 1996: 54, n. 70).
[4] 1983a: 29. See also 1956: liv, n. 13; 1971: 20; 1991: 14, 111–13, 123, n. 69; 1994: 7–10, 135–36.
[5] The terminology is Vlastos's, 1983a: 37.

ables Socrates to examine his interlocutors' lives as well as their theses[6] and radically distinguishes Socratic dialectic, which is concerned with truth, from sophistic eristic,[7] which is only concerned with victory.[8]

Although this edifying dichotomy is deeply entrenched in Anglo-American Socratic studies, it should be taken with a grain of salt. In particular cases it is very hard to distinguish Socratic dialectic from sophistic eristic;[9] in fact, they are often indistinguishable.[10] The Socrates of the early dialogues is not all of a piece; on the contrary, he is a complex and elusive figure whose overall dialectical performance cannot be adequately accounted for by either category. Although he habitually affirms that he is searching for truth and habitually denies that he is arguing for victory, he seems inordinately intent on winning arguments – often by whatever means. In a word, his actual elenctic practice often bears little resemblance to his official elenctic theory. This duality of purpose is expressive of a corresponding duality of character which accounts

---

[6] There is no scholarly consensus about how – or even whether – the testing of theses and lives are connected. Vlastos, 1983a: 36, denies that there are two kinds of elenchus – one philosophical, the other therapeutic – and claims that there is only one which must do both jobs at once – a claim contested (albeit for very different reasons) by Woodruff, 1986: 26, and Penner, 1992b: 144–45.

[7] Eristic (from ἔρις – strife, quarrel, contention) was a competitive or "agonistic" form of argumentation in which one participant tried to defeat the other by any means – fair or foul.

[8] For standard discussions of the differences – real or alleged – between dialectic and eristic, see Moraux, 1968: 277–311; Guthrie, 1971b: 27–54; Kerferd, 1981: 59–67; Rankin, 1983: 13–29; Irwin, 1986: 61–63, 1992b: 63–69; Benson, 1989: 591–99; Poulakos, 1995; and Wardy, 1996. Robinson's magisterial study (1953) is notable for its familiarity with the texts and its non-apologetic tone. With disarming forthrightness, Robinson points out that although Plato always praises dialectic and always denounces eristic, he never adequately explains the difference. At each stage of his life, he applied the term "dialectic" to "whatever seemed to him at the moment the most hopeful procedure" and he applied the terms "eristic" and "sophistry" to "whatever seemed to him at the time the danger most to be avoided" (70).

[9] As Robinson, 1953: 85; Kidd, 1967: 481; and Irwin, 1992b: 65, candidly acknowledge.

[10] Ryle, 1966: 119, thinks the early dialogues *are* specimens of eristic and, with characteristic irreverence, characterizes them as "elenctic question-answer tussles." Although this view has found little favor among recent and contemporary commentators, the fact is that Socrates' dialectical tactics often render him liable to the charge of eristic. His demand for brief answers is a case in point. Requiring short answers was a common sophistic tactic: at *Euthyd.* 295b6 Dionysodorus prohibits Socrates from requesting clarification and requires him to answer questions even if he does not fully understand what he is being asked, at 296a1–2 he faults him for answering more than he was asked, and at 296a8–c2 he tells him to stop qualifying his answers. Socrates often employs the same tactics.

both for the "best, wisest, and most just" Socrates celebrated at
Ph. 118a16–17 – and for the "not too scrupulous" Socrates mildly
rebuked by Guthrie[11] and severely taken to task by many interlocutors. His dialectical aberrations include numerous violations –
some of them quite blatant – of the sincere assent requirement.

Socrates' unscrupulous dialectical tactics have not gone unnoticed. Although few endorse Grote's contention that "[a] person
more thoroughly Eristic than Sokrates never lived,"[12] many accuse
him of deliberate sophistry – of feeding his interlocutors premises
he thinks false, of drawing inferences he thinks fallacious, and of
"every [other] trick of logic and rhetoric."[13] Having done so, however, they vindicate him on the ground that although his tactics
are often dubious, his motives are always exemplary: he is exposing ignorance and caring for souls. As we shall have many occasions to observe during the course of this study, many commentators – Vlastos is not one of them – think that the crucial difference
between dialectic and eristic is a difference *in motivation*: the former
is serious and aims at moral improvement whereas the latter is
frivolous and merely aims at victory. Apparently, the philosophical
end justifies the dialectical means.[14]

I reject this approach. Throughout this book, I will proceed on

---

[11] 1975: 439.

[12] 1867, III: 479 – a criticism rejected by Vlastos, 1983a: 31, n. 14, on the ground that Grote
employs the term "eristic" with "culpable looseness" to mean "contentiousness" which,
although admittedly one of Socrates' failings as a philosopher, is not the same thing as
sophistry.

[13] See, e.g., Woodbridge, 1929: 269–70; Robinson, 1942: 101–2; Jaeger, 1943–45, II: 64;
Dodds, 1959: 249; Sprague, 1962; Friedländer, 1964, II: 19, 181, 254; Sinaiko, 1965: 14–15;
Ryle, 1966: 119; Gulley, 1968: 24, 45; Diès, 1972: 296; Guthrie, 1975: 439; Kahn, 1983: 93,
1992: 252–53, and 1996: 110–11, 112, n. 13, 114–16, 189, n. 11, 237; Kidd, 1967: 481;
McTighe, 1984: 226; Stokes, 1986: 34; Teloh, 1986: 1–2, 16–18; Chrétien, 1987: 3–6; and
Graham, 1992; 152–54. Angélopoulos, 1933: 29, thinks that Socrates *was* a sophist
between 430 and 420. According to his analysis, the sophist depicted by Aristophanes in
the *Clouds* is an accurate description of the Socrates *he* knew while the moral philosopher
depicted by Plato and Xenophon is an equally accurate description of the very different
Socrates *they* knew many years later. So, too, Mazel, 1987: 27–29.

[14] The lengths to which some commentators are prepared to go in vindicating Socrates' dialectical tactics are vividly illustrated by Nickolas Pappas's assessment of the arguments
against Thrasymachus in *Republic* I. Having faulted Socrates, *inter alia*, for changing the
subject, for failing to define crucial terms, for using faulty analogies, for generalizing
from particular cases, and for employing sloppy arguments which depend on ambiguity,
wordplay, and legerdemain, Pappas defends him on the ground that these "flawed" arguments are merely "first sketches [whose] obvious faults ... betray the overcompression
of deep truths" (1995: 45–50 *passim*).

the assumption that allegations of faulty reasoning are a serious matter. Unlike Teloh,[15] who thinks that Socratic dialectic should not be judged primarily by "the excellence of its logic," I think that is the sole criterion by which it should be judged. In response to McKim's puzzling contention[16] that "the very features of Socrates' argument[s] that are logically objectionable are precisely those that render [them] psychologically telling," it is sufficient to point out that a "logically objectionable" argument is a worthless argument; and it remains worthless in spite of the fact that some unwary interlocutor is taken in by it or finds it "telling."

Vlastos acknowledges that Socrates sometimes employs unscrupulous dialectical tactics. In chapter five of *Socrates, Ironist and Moral Philosopher* – entitled "Does Socrates Cheat?" – he cites several passages (mostly from the *Protagoras*) in which he is portrayed as "complicated, devious, cunning, and not averse to playing pranks on his interlocutors upon occasion."[17] However, he categorically denies that Socrates ever cheats and vigorously defends him against all charges of eristic and deliberate sophistry. Although he is sometimes guilty of dialectical trickery, he always remains "free of resort to deceit ... *when arguing seriously*."[18] This, of course, presupposes a criterion by which to tell when Socrates is "arguing seriously" and when he is not. According to Vlastos, the early dialogues provide one: "*when Socrates is searching for the right way to live, in circumstances in which it is reasonable for him to think of the search as obedience to divine command*, his argument cannot involve wilful untruth."[19] Whenever this criterion is satisfied, Socrates is "arguing seriously" and is never guilty of dialectical trickery or deviousness; however, whenever it is not satisfied, he is not "arguing seriously" and is often guilty of these things. In producing this criterion, Vlastos is trying to tie down "a loose thread" in an earlier paper[20] in which he had denied that "for good purposes (pedagogical or polemical) ... [Socrates] would ever (knowingly, and in a serious vein) assert

[15] 1986: 1.

[16] 1988: 37.

[17] 1991: 133. Criticism of Socrates is not novel in Vlastos's writings (see 1956: xxiv–xxv, xxxviii: 1971: 15–17; 1983a: 31, n. 14; and 1988: 92).

[18] *Ibid.*: 133–34.

[19] *Ibid.*: 134. Specific passages from which Vlastos extracts his criterion include *Ap.* 28d6–a1, 29d2–30a7; *Ch.* 166c7–d2; and *G.* 500c1–4.

[20] 1981b: 223, n. 5.

categorically a false premise or endorse a fallacious argument." What was missing there – a sufficiently precise criterion of Socratic "seriousness" – is ostensibly supplied here.

But there is still something missing. Given Vlastos's account of the Socratic elenchus, "arguing seriously" is not a sufficient condition for Socrates' never knowingly endorsing a false premise or drawing a fallacious inference; it is only a necessary condition. Another condition must be added, namely, when he is engaged in "standard" elenchus, which does not countenance these maneuvers, rather than in "indirect" elenchus, which does.[21] Only when both these individually necessary conditions are satisfied does the required sufficiency obtain. So whenever Socrates knowingly asserts a false premise or endorses a fallacious argument, Vlastos's analysis provides him with two outs: (i) "I was not 'arguing seriously'," and (ii) "I was 'arguing seriously', but I was not engaged in 'standard' elenchus."

Vlastos's criterion of Socratic "seriousness" signals a valiant attempt to explain something which those who accuse Socrates of deliberate sophistry never even attempt to explain, namely, how a philosopher who knowingly employs fallacious and unsound arguments can be reconciled with a morally earnest truth seeker.[22] The difficulty is a real one, but Vlastos has not solved it. His criterion is open to several objections.

First, it restricts the range of applicability of "elenctic argument" to those passages in which Socrates is "searching for the

---

[21] See n. 2.

[22] Whether Plato portrays Socrates knowingly employing fallacious or unsound arguments is a controversial question. According to Robinson, 1942: 97–103, Plato had no word for "fallacy" and his "consciousness" of "fallacy-as-such" was "very small"; however, he clearly recognized some fallacies – in particular, those involving ambiguity and illicit conversion – and often portrayed Socrates employing them to "deceive" his interlocutors. The same thesis is advanced by Sprague, 1962; McKim, 1988: 36–37, 46–48; Vickers, 1988: 84–119; and Rutherford, 1995: 91. It is, of course, emphatically rejected by Vlastos. I myself am as wary of Robinson's (largely unverifiable) speculation about Plato's "consciousness" of fallacy as I am of Vlastos's (sometimes excessively apologetic) justifications of Socrates' often faulty arguments and unscrupulous dialectical tactics. Both are insufficiently attentive to Ryle's salutary reminder, 1966: 206–7, that logic was in its infancy in Plato's day – a fact which makes it unlikely that a clear distinction between a valid and an invalid argument predated the early dialogues and, therefore, ill-advised anachronistically to assume that Plato "just knew from the start" the differences between good and bad arguments. See also Lloyd, 1979: 60–61, 100–102, 123, n. 331). Whether Plato "realized" that some of the arguments he puts into Socrates' mouth are fallacious, I do not pretend to know. Since my purpose is not historical but philosophical, I avoid all authorial inferences and assess Socrates' arguments *as arguments*.

right way to live" in obedience to the god at Delphi and, there-fore, "arguing seriously." This overly strict criterion entails that all non-argumentative or argumentative but "non-serious" pas-sages fall outside the purview of the Socratic elenchus and must be described in some other way, for example, as dialectical pre-liminaries, interludes, or postludes, during which Socrates is not searching for the right way to live and may, therefore, presumably behave however he pleases. This way of carving up the dialogues into "serious" and "non-serious" portions smacks of overinter-pretation the sole purpose of which is to excuse Socrates' dia-lectical lapses and to protect his reputation as "the honest arguer we know him to be."[23]

Second, I suspect that a rigorous application of Vlastos's crite-rion to the early dialogues would yield an alarming number of pas-sages in which it would be impossible to determine on the basis of any non-arbitrary criterion of "seriousness" (as opposed to play-fulness, playful seriousness, serious playfulness, tongue-in-cheek irony, mockery with serious intent, lighthearted bubble-pricking, etc.) when, and to what extent, Socrates is "arguing seriously" and hence when, and to what extent, the criterion has been satisfied. Part of what makes him so endlessly fascinating – not to mention infuriating – is that his "serious" moments cannot be divorced from his "non-serious" ones without doing violence to both. His behavior cannot be consigned to one of two luminously clear and transparently obvious categories in a way that enables us to say, "Now he is being serious, but now he is not." Indeed, if by "seri-ous" one means humorless, unrelieved gravity, and the complete absence of the sense that he is thoroughly enjoying his interlocu-tor's befuddlement, Socrates is seldom, if ever, completely serious; on the other hand, if by "not serious" one means flippant, cavalier, and wholly unconcerned about the right way to live, he is seldom, if ever, not serious.

Third, it is not only impossible to apply Vlastos's criterion in a way that enables us non-arbitrarily to distinguish passages in which Socrates is "arguing seriously" from those in which he is not; it is not even clear how the criterion itself is to be understood. Ac-

---

[23] 1991: 279. Klosko, 1983: 363, rightly points out that Vlastos is often "sorely taxed" to rid Socrates' arguments of the appearance of sophistry. He adds that "by unearthing suit-able tacit premises, a determined scholar would be able to absolve *any* argument of this charge, no matter how sophistical in appearance."

cording to Vlastos, Socrates is "arguing seriously" whenever he is "searching for the right way to live," that is, whenever he is philosophizing, examining himself and others, in obedience to the god at Delphi. But how are we to determine when he is doing *that*? Here Vlastos provides no help. His criterion purports to tell us what counts as "seriousness," but it does not tell us what counts as *philosophizing*. Although apparently perspicacious and unproblematically applicable, it is, in fact, vacuous: Socrates is never knowingly guilty of dialectical trickery or deviousness when he is "arguing seriously"; therefore, whenever he *is* knowingly guilty of these things, he is *not* "arguing seriously." In short, instead of elucidating the criterion of "seriousness" independently of dialectical trickery and deviousness in a way that enables us to approach the early dialogues empirically, criterion in hand, and ask whether Socrates is, in fact, ever guilty of these things, Vlastos defines "arguing seriously" in a way that precludes the possibility. So, of course, he never is. That is not exegesis; it is apologetics. Vlastos's refusal to allow anything to count against his assertion that Socrates never cheats renders it textually unfalsifiable. Either we need a more satisfactory criterion of Socratic "seriousness"[24] or we need to abandon the distinction between "serious" and "non-serious" argumentation. I opt for the latter.[25]

If we do abandon it, we are left with an enigmatic figure whose astonishingly mixed bag of tricks and constantly fluctuating attitudinal stance towards his interlocutors invest his overall dialectical performance with an ambiguity that resists all neat classifications. If those critics who accuse him of being an accomplished sophist are guilty of exaggeration, it is an exaggeration of a truth worth retrieving.

What that truth is may be seen by looking more closely at the sincere assent requirement and its alleged role in (what Vlastos calls) "standard elenchus" – that peculiarly Socratic form of

---

[24] Méron, 1979: 41–42, offers one: Socrates is being serious whenever he reveals his true thoughts ("sa vraie pensée"). But this criterion is as difficult to apply as Vlastos's. Indeed, if Michael Stokes (about whom more later) is right, Socrates never (or rarely) reveals his "true thoughts."

[25] For further criticisms of Vlastos, see Beversluis, 1993. For a different assessment, see Irwin, 1992a: 242–43, who is "entirely convinced" by Vlastos's "devastating case" against the charge that Socrates cheats.

"peirastic" argumentation by which Socrates refutes his interlocutors "from their own beliefs" and which Vlastos has schematized as follows:

(i)   The interlocutor asserts a thesis, *p*, which Socrates considers false and targets for refutation.
(ii) Socrates secures agreement to further premises, say *q* and *r* (each of which may stand for a conjunct of propositions). The agreement is *ad hoc*: Socrates argues from {*q, r*}, not to them.
(iii) Socrates then argues, and the interlocutor agrees, that *q* and *r* entail *not-p*.
(iv) Socrates then claims that he has shown that *not-p* is true, *p* false.[26]

This is a lucid schematization of the formal structure of (some of) Socrates' arguments. But it purchases its lucidity at the intolerably high price of neglecting the informal complexity of the Socratic elenchus and the contexts in which it is conducted.

Socrates' interlocutors resist his arguments for many reasons. Sometimes they disagree with one (or more) of the premises. Sometimes they dispute the analogy by which he deduces a damaging inference from their previous admissions. Sometimes they dispute the inference itself. But the most interesting form of resistance occurs when an interlocutor, intimidated by the deftness with which Socrates can deduce unwelcome consequences from whatever he says, is reluctant to say anything at all. In such cases, Socrates' task is to elicit his initial assent.

But the phenomenon of giving (or withholding) one's assent is not as straightforward as it seems. Assent is not an either/or affair. There are *degrees* of assent, ranging from the unqualified "Certainly" (πάνυ γε) and "Yes, by Zeus" (ναὶ μὰ Δία), to the more circumspect "It seems so" (φαίνεται or ἔοικε), to the still less accommodating "I suppose" (οἶμαι), to the downright grudging "If you say so" and "So be it" (ἔστω). Except for "Certainly" and its semantic equivalents, all these locutions signal *qualified* assent; and qualified assent is not assent *simpliciter*. Accordingly, in recording the logical commitments that Socrates manages to extract from his interlocutors, it is not sufficient to report that they have *assented* to

---

[26] 1994: 11. For an earlier (and marginally different) formulation, see 1983a: 39.

the propositions proposed for their assent – not even if one adds, as some do,[27] that they never renege on their assent once they have given it. Reneging is not an either/or affair either. We also need to know *the manner in which* and *the degree to which* they have assented. Socrates' interlocutors do not typically "assert categorically" the premises proposed for their assent; their responses are usually more qualified and guarded.

Nor should we overlook the equally important and rather more surprising fact that Socrates seldom acknowledges his interlocutors' reluctance to give their unqualified assent. Indeed, he habitually minimizes (or ignores) their misgivings and presses for their assent: by asking leading questions, by resorting to mock flattery, by employing shame tactics, by soliciting the aid of other auditors, and even by threatening to leave (*Pr.* 335c2–6). These psychologically manipulative tactics suggest that, although officially insisting on sincere assent, he is often willing to settle for qualified, and sometimes heavily qualified, assent.

In view of the momentous importance that many commentators have ascribed to the sincere assent requirement, it is surprising that they have paid almost no attention to the question of what counts as sincere assent. Accordingly, before proceeding further, I will try to elucidate this murky – and almost wholly unanalyzed – concept.

The first thing to notice is that it is not the case that you are authorized to ascribe a belief that p to me only if I assert p or assent to it when it is proposed as a belief candidate. Beliefs are not (or are not merely) occurrent mental states which are only contingently connected to behavior; they are also partly dispositional. Bain[28] may have gone too far in saying that belief has *no* meaning except in reference to actions, but he was surely right in saying that nothing can count as a belief "that does not directly or indirectly implicate our voluntary exertions." The same point is made more clearly by Price,[29] according to whom "A believes that p" is a dispositional statement which is equivalent to a series of conditional statements describing how A would behave in certain circumstances. Similarly, Braithwaite[30] distinguishes "entertaining

---

[27] See Kraut, 1983: 65–66; and Vlastos, 1983b: 72–73.   [28] 1880: 112.
[29] 1969: 275–76.   [30] 1932–33: 132–33.

p" – the "subjective or phenomenological" component of belief –
from "being disposed to act as if *p* were true" – the "objective or
behaviouristic" component – and argues that the latter is the *differentia* which distinguishes actually believing *p* from merely entertaining it in thought. By the "*differentia*" of belief, he does not
mean a set of specific actions, but rather a set of dispositions to
act which are "actualized in suitable circumstances."[31] Beliefs are
often ascribed to (or withheld from) people on the basis of their
behavior: not just their overt actions, but also their emotions (or
lack of them), their responses (or failures to respond), their facial
expressions and tone of voice (or lack of them), and other things
they say (or do not say) and do (or do not do). It is not the case
that it is only in asserting (or assenting to) *p* that I incur epistemic
responsibility for believing *p* together with whatever logical or behavioral commitments believing (or assenting to) it may entail. In
short, asserting (or assenting to) *p* is not a necessary condition for
ascribing a belief that *p* to me.

But neither is it a sufficient condition. Just as I can believe (or
assent to) *p* without asserting it, so I can assert (or assent to) *p*
without believing it. The mere fact that I assert (or assent to) some
proposition *p* is not an adequate criterion for ascribing a belief
that *p* to me – not even if I preface my assertion with hearty assurances that I "mean what I say" and other displays of sincerity.
Sincerity is not (or is not merely) an occurrent inner state either. If
it were, there would be no public criteria of sincerity and hence
no way of telling who is (and who is not) sincere. But although
sincerity is not wholly behavioral and dispositional, the criteria for
ascriptions of it are. Like belief ascriptions, sincerity ascriptions
are criteriologically connected to behavior. Far from being an
inner state which must be inferred, often problematically, *from*
behavior, sincerity (or insincerity) is often manifested *in* behavior.
People radiate sincerity (or insincerity). It is written all over them.

It is, of course, reasonable for you to assume that if I believe
that *p*, I will assert *p* in apposite circumstances and assent to *p*
when it is proposed for my assent. But the converse is not true.

---

[31] *Ibid.*: 137. So, too, Cohen, 1992: 115: "[T]o accept that *p* is to adopt the policy of taking
the proposition that *p* as a premiss in appropriate circumstances," i.e., to include *p*
"among one's premises for deciding what to do or think in a particular context."

Taken by itself – detached from specific contexts and disconnected from my past, present, and future behavior – no utterance (assertorial or otherwise) is a sufficient condition for a belief ascription. Like ascriptions of inner states generally, belief ascriptions have public criteria. If you are reasonably to ascribe a belief that p to me, there must be some discernible connection between my belief that p and my past, present, and future behavior. If I claim to believe that p but never (or seldom) behave in appropriate ways or behave in ways which are incompatible with believing it, you may reasonably doubt that I believe it, however vigorously I assure you that your doubts are groundless.

This behavior includes linguistic behavior. Not only must my beliefs be compatible with my past, present, and future *actions*; they must also be compatible with my past, present, and future *beliefs and broader set of linguistic practices*. Beliefs are seldom analyzable individually in isolation from a person's belief-set. Belief-candidates do not typically present themselves individually in a way that enables a person to acquire them one at a time. Nor are they typically abandoned one at a time. To acquire or to abandon a belief is not typically to change one's mind about the truth-value of a single proposition; it is typically to acquire or to abandon a cluster of propositions whose truth-values are systematically interconnected and which stand or fall together. Hence if I assert (or assent to) some proposition p which is not manifested in, or is incompatible with, my past, present, and future behavior – linguistic or otherwise – and which stands in no discernible connection to, or is incompatible with, my overall belief-set, you may reasonably doubt that I really believe what I say I believe. Such utterances do not count as sincerely held beliefs.

The importance of all this for determining whether the propositions to which Socrates' interlocutors assent are expressive of their sincerely held beliefs can hardly be exaggerated. Any even remotely plausible account must take careful note both of the compatibility (or lack of it) between what they say and how they behave and of the continuity (or lack of it) between the propositions to which they assent *during* their dialectical encounters with Socrates and the propositions they brought with them into the discussion and to which they would have assented (or would have been disposed to assent) *before* these encounters.

In saying this, I am not succumbing to the temptation of turning the early dialogues "face-about" in hopes of "finding more on the back."[32] To ask: What would Socrates' interlocutors have said (or have been inclined to say) before their encounters with him? is not like asking: What subjects did Hamlet study in Wittenberg? or: How many children had Lady Macbeth? Unlike the latter, which are pseudo-questions about quasi-factual details to which the text provides no answers, the former are questions about character, belief, and motivation. The fact that Socrates' interlocutors are fictional characters does not entail that they did, thought, and believed nothing "before" their encounters with him. As in literary works generally, the chronology of a Platonic dialogue is not confined to the events that take place between its covers. Although fictional characters have no empirical reality (and hence no empirical pasts and futures), they have imaginative reality (and hence imaginative pasts and futures). Imaginatively considered, they are "real" enough – as "real" as Tess of the D'Urbervilles or Hamlet.[33]

Critics who write books with titles like *What Happens in Hamlet?* do not confine themselves to events that take place during the play. They also talk about events that took place before it begins. In doing so, they are not guilty of conceptual confusion. Lots of things happened before *Hamlet* begins: Claudius killed Hamlet's father, Gertrude hastily (albeit unwittingly) married her husband's murderer, Hamlet was overtaken by melancholy and became disenchanted with Ophelia and with women generally, and so on. In addition to performing many actions before the play begins, Hamlet held many beliefs – some of them true (e.g., Ghosts exist), others false (e.g., My father died of natural causes). He was also a very different person. We know this because the other characters are constantly pointing out that he is not his old self and marveling at the change that has come over him.

If it is intelligible to talk about what Shakespeare's characters did and believed before the play begins, it is equally intelligible to talk about what Socrates' interlocutors did and believed before the dialogues begin. To cite but a single example, before the *Euthyphro* begins, Euthyphro's father had been guilty of criminal negligence which resulted in the death of one of his slaves – an act which had

---

[32] The terminology is Kitto's, 1966: 15–16.
[33] As Stanley Cavell, 1987: 102–3, rightly observes, to say that the existence of the characters encountered in literature is "fictional" is not an answer to a question; it is the name of a philosophical problem.

morally outraged Euthyphro and impelled him to prosecute his
father for murder. To deny that these events took place and that
propositions about them and about the beliefs of the persons who
performed or witnessed them have truth-values – i.e., are true
or false within the world of the work – is to misunderstand the
"logic" of fictional statements and the "reality" of the characters
who utter them. It is also to trivialize the early dialogues by
depriving them of their dramatic power and their psychological
impact.

Since it is intelligible to say that Socrates' interlocutors held
beliefs before their dialectical encounters with him, it is important
to determine whether the beliefs they bring with them into the
discussion are the same as the propositions they assert (or to which
they assent) during it. If there are good reasons for thinking that
they are not, then there are also good reasons for denying that
Socrates elicits their sincere assent.

What do Socrates' interlocutors believe? The obvious answer is
that they believe what they say they believe, that is, they believe
the propositions which they assert and to which they assent. If
Michael Stokes[34] is right, Socrates never (or rarely) advances assertions himself; he merely asks questions to ascertain what his
interlocutors believe, and the subsequent course of the discussion
depends entirely on the answers he receives. For example, when
he asks Charmides whether temperance is noble, whether temperate men are good, and whether only that which is good can be
productive of good (*Ch.* 160e6–13), we should not assume that he
himself believes these propositions. And similarly throughout the
early dialogues. In a word, Socrates' questions are *questions*, not
disguised assertions to which he himself is committed.[35] The interlocutor is free to answer these questions in any way he wishes. He
need not answer them affirmatively; but if he does, the answers
are his and, therefore, the theses examined are also his.

In support of these contentions, Stokes produces two pieces of
textual evidence: first, when Socrates' interlocutors realize that
their previous admissions entail the negation of their original
theses, they often try to avoid logical shipwreck by saying that

---

[34] 1986: 6–7.
[35] *Ibid.*: 4–9. The same analysis is given by Teloh, 1986: 1–2; Kidd, 1992: 82–92; and Frede,
    1992: 205–6.

their original theses are indefensible *if what Socrates has said is true.*
Second, Socrates never countenances this move. He always insists
that he himself has advanced no assertions whatever and that the
inconsistent propositions are traceable to his interlocutor. For example, when Protagoras tries to saddle Socrates with the thesis
that the "parts" of virtue are related in such a way that none resembles any other, Socrates replies: "I didn't say that. Protagoras
here said that in answer to my question" (*Pr.* 330e7–331a1).[36]
Stokes is right on both counts. But the logical situation is more
complicated than he seems to think.

It is true that Socrates is the questioner. And questioners ask
questions. However, Stokes overlooks the fact that grammatical
interrogatives are not always logical interrogatives and, therefore,
not always (or not merely) straightforward requests for information. Every question has its own logic which is a function of the intention and purpose of the questioner in asking it. Differences in
intention or purpose on the part of the questioner invest the questions asked with different illocutionary forces (and illocutionary-
force potential) which enable the questioner to perform a wide variety of speech-acts under cover of "just asking questions."

Of course, some questions are straightforward requests for information, asked either in ignorance or with incomplete understanding which the questioner is trying to remedy, for example,
"Is there a faculty meeting this afternoon?" But others are not so
innocent, e.g., "There is a faculty meeting this afternoon, isn't
there?" Although this could be a straightforward request for information, it need not be. Indeed, it need not (logically) be a *question* at all. Such locutions – which J. L. Austin calls "utterances in

---

[36] The *Alcibiades I* contains what is perhaps the clearest example of this common Socratic
rejoinder. When Alcibiades tries to saddle Socrates with an equally unwelcome conclusion, Socrates asks: "Who do you think is saying these things – me, the questioner, or
you, the answerer?" (113a1–2). When Alcibiades admits that it is his views which are
under examination, Socrates emphatically asserts that, in that case, he himself cannot be
held responsible (ἐμὲ ... αἰτιᾷ μάτην, 113c4) either for the theses advanced or for the
conclusions arrived at; his interlocutor must bear full responsibility for both (112d7–
113c4). (Even if the *Alcibiades* was not written by Plato, as many believe, few would disagree with Shorey's claim, 1933: 415, that it contains nothing which is "necessarily un-
Platonic.") Méron is one of the few commentators who questions the claim that it is
always the interlocutor's thesis that is examined. She adds that, in interpreting the early
dialogues, we need to be more subtle and examine the overall context to determine
which interlocutors respond spontaneously and which respond in ways influenced by
Socrates (1979: 13–14).

a speech situation"[37] – often have a hidden agenda which enables the speaker to "do things with words": to seek reassurance, to bemoan his poor memory, to issue a reminder to his hearer, or even to deplore his habitual lack of attendance. Such "questioners" advance an assertion – "There is a faculty meeting this afternoon" – and then ask their interlocutor to endorse it – "Isn't there?"

What if he does endorse it? Whose assertion is it? According to Stokes, it is the interlocutor's. Is Stokes right?

If, in response to my "question," "There is a faculty meeting this afternoon, isn't there?", my hearer says, "Yes," it is his answer in the sense that it was he who produced the affirmative response. However, he *was* responding; and the proposition to which he was responding was mine. Had I not asked the "question," the matter would probably not have occurred to him. Furthermore, in answering my "question" affirmatively, he did not perform the speech-act of *asserting* a proposition but the very different speech-act of *confirming* a proposition; and the proposition confirmed was not his, but mine. Some questions are more loaded still and clearly calculated to secure the desired response, e.g., "You did promise that I could borrow your car for the weekend, didn't you?" or "Jimmy is sorry, aren't you Jimmy?" Similarly, when queried in the presence of his suspicious wife about whether he approves of adultery, the habitual adulterer can be relied on to issue vehement denials.

Although many commentators attach great weight to the sincere assent requirement and gravely observe that if the answerer fails to abide by it, the discussion will suffer in serious ways, they seldom add that the questioner has analogous responsibilities and that if he fails to discharge them, the discussion will suffer in equally serious ways. Socrates often fails. His questions often have a hidden agenda and are calculated to secure the desired responses. Although these responses are (usually) effortlessly elicited and (often) monotonously predictable – "Yes," "Necessarily," "To be sure," "Apparently," and so on – they should not be taken at face value and as necessarily expressive of the interlocutors' sincerely held beliefs. They often signal nothing more than the philosophically uninteresting fact that the interlocutor sees no good reason for not assenting. But it does not follow that he believes the

---

[37] 1962: 138.

propositions to which he has assented, i.e., that they are expressive of antecedently formulated and sincerely held beliefs which he brought with him into the discussion and would have affirmed (or been disposed to affirm) before it. To cite but a single example, would anyone seriously suggest that, in "assenting" to the Socratically proposed thesis that there is a single *eidos* or *idea* common to all pious actions "by which" they are pious and which constitutes the standard for distinguishing pious actions from impious ones, Euthyphro is giving expression to a belief he held prior to being asked? The suggestion taxes credulity.

Although Socrates implies that nothing could be easier, saying what one really believes is often very difficult. People hesitate: not because they are unreflective or dishonest or hedging, but because they are not sure. Beliefs are not "cognitive" states of mind carried about "in one's head" like groceries in a bag, so that, upon being asked whether one believes a particular proposition, one need only look within to see whether the belief is there, as one inspects one's grocery bag to see whether one remembered to buy shampoo. Then, too, we are often asked for our opinions on subjects about which we have not made up our minds ("For whom do you intend to vote?") or on subjects about which we have no opinions and probably never will ("Have you ever heard anyone modulate so effortlessly into such a distant key?"). Nor, *pace* Vlastos, does the absence of sincere assent necessarily render the interlocutors' assent "iffy" – tentative, non-committal – and, therefore, insincere. Here, as elsewhere, radical dichotomies and exclusive disjunctions will only lead us astray. Socrates' interlocutors often assent to propositions routinely, perfunctorily, and uncomprehendingly. They do so for a variety of reasons: to seem more astute than they really are, to give the impression of having followed the argument more closely than they really have, or simply because Socrates expects them to. Judging from the hopeless predicaments in which they often become embroiled, it seems that the answer they should have given – the only truly sincere one – is neither "Yes" nor "No," but rather "I have no opinion one way or the other. The proposition has never entered my head."

Vlastos has a ready reply. The fact that a proposition has never entered an interlocutor's head is perfectly compatible with saying that he believes it "in that marginal sense of the word in which we may all be said to 'believe' innumerable things that have never entered our heads, but are nonetheless entailed by what we believe in the common or garden use of the word."[38] Such beliefs are not "overt," but "covert." Hence – the example is Vlastos's – if I overtly believe that Mary is John's sister and that John is Bill's grandfather, then I covertly believe that Mary is Bill's great-aunt – "even if I have never thought of that fact – indeed, even if I do not have a word for 'great-aunt' in my vocabulary." Formulated in full generality, anyone who overtly believes p and who also overtly believes q and r, which entail $not\text{-}p$, covertly believes $not\text{-}p$. Socrates apparently holds the same view. Why else would he breezily assure Polus that he does not "really" believe that it is worse to suffer injustice than to commit it and that he "really" believes the converse, since he believes other propositions which entail it ($G.$ 474b2–5)?

Something is wrong here. If I overtly believe p and also overtly believe q and r, which entail $not\text{-}p$, then I am, of course, logically committed to believing $not\text{-}p$. Hence upon learning the meaning of "great-aunt," I will instantly concur that "Mary is John's sister" and "John is Bill's grandfather" jointly entail "Mary is Bill's great-aunt." But it does not follow that I covertly believed this all along.[39] A proposition which I do not overtly believe (and, in fact, claim to disbelieve) but which is entailed by other propositions which I do overtly believe is not thereby proved to be a proposition which I covertly believe. Polus no more entered the discussion covertly believing that it is worse to commit injustice than to suffer it than Crito entered Socrates' prison cell covertly believing that he should remain in prison and drink the hemlock.

This theory of covert belief is also incompatible with Socrates' claim that his divine mission consists in demonstrating that his interlocutors are ignorant. On the view before us, Polus is not ignorant; he is just muddled. He *thinks* he believes that it is worse to suffer injustice than to commit it, but he "really" believes the converse. In that case, however, the required conclusion is not that Polus does not know what he thinks he knows, but rather that he is not aware of what he does know or, at least, truly – albeit covertly – believes – a remarkable claim which entails either that

---

[38] 1983a: 51; see also 1994: 23.
[39] On the unintelligibility of the notion of covert belief, see Dummett, 1975: 285–86, and Méron, 1979: 14.

Polus differs from every other interlocutor in the early dialogues or that all the other interlocutors are in the same epistemic condition and Socrates' description of his divine mission in the *Apology* is inaccurate.

It is equally misleading for Vlastos to claim that whenever an interlocutor advances a thesis which Socrates considers false, he is confident that he will always find others in his interlocutor's belief-set which entail the Socratic thesis.[40] Since Socrates' "questions" are often calculated to secure the desired response, it is not a matter of complete indifference to him how his interlocutor replies, provided that his reply is expressive of what he really believes. It is not as if, owing to incredible good luck, Socrates always just happens to elicit the very answers he needs to refute his interlocutor; on the contrary, he knows exactly what answers he needs and his questions are tailored to secure them. He does not ransack his interlocutor's belief-set to *find* the propositions needed to refute him; he supplies them himself. And if his initial questions do not secure the desired response, he continues asking questions until they do.

This policy is often defended on the ground that Socrates cannot accept just *any* answers his interlocutor happens to give; he must elicit the *right* answers. And one elicits the right answers by asking the right questions. Although Socrates has traditionally been celebrated for his ability to do precisely this, the celebration is premature. A questioner can no more claim that he asks the right questions than a clothing retailer can claim that he sells the right sizes. Questions are not right or wrong in themselves, and their rightness or wrongness cannot be assessed in a vacuum. The "right" question is the one that accomplishes the questioner's purpose(s); the "wrong" question is the one that does not. Accordingly, a question can be "right" in one context but "wrong" in another. Furthermore, insofar as Socrates ignores what his interlocutor really believes and elicits his assent to premises which he himself supplies, he operates with a surreptitious criterion of what counts as a satisfactory answer which is very different from his announced criterion: a satisfactory answer is no longer one which is expressive of what his interlocutor really believes, but rather one which enables Socrates to refute him, even if, as is often the case, it is not expressive of what he really believes.

---

[40] 1983a: 52–53. See also 1985: 18, n. 44; and 1994: 56, n. 43.

However, the most crucial question of all is not whether Socrates' interlocutors sincerely assent to the propositions proposed for their assent, but the degree of Socrates' own commitment to the sincere assent requirement. And this, I submit, is open to question on several counts. The first, inconclusive in itself but worth mentioning, is that the requirement is absent from most of the early dialogues. It is, in fact, only invoked in four: the *Crito*, the *Protagoras*, the *Gorgias*, and *Republic* 1.[41] Second, even when it is invoked, it is often nothing more than an effective psychological technique for luring the interlocutor into discussion. (Euthyphro is assured that Socrates envies his uncommon theological grasp and wishes to become his disciple.) Third, and more problematic, having invoked the requirement at the outset of a discussion, Socrates does not always enforce it and sometimes waives it altogether. Indeed, in the *Gorgias* and *Republic* 1, he waives it the minute the exchange becomes heated, and in the *Protagoras* he waives it almost immediately.[42] Finally, and most problematic of all, even when he does enforce it, he does not always take pains to insure that the thesis he refutes is the one his interlocutor originally affirmed rather than some tendentious reformulation of it. Thrasymachus is a case in point. In response to his definition of justice as the advantage of the stronger, Socrates asks whether he means that the person who eats the most beef, and hence is strongest, is the most just. Thrasymachus' outraged reply is exactly on target:

You disgust me, Socrates. Your trick is to take hold of the argument at the point where you can do it the most harm. (*R.* 338d3–4)

In this passage Socrates is caught in the act of deliberately misrepresenting his interlocutor's thesis. His ostensibly humorous but patently lame reply – "I was just trying to get you to express yourself more clearly" (338d5–6) – is idle. Other interlocutors register similar complaints. Yet even in the face of their protests, Socrates continues to claim that he is refuting them "from their

---

[41] Vlastos, 1991: 111, n. 21, accounts for its absence by claiming that although the requirement is "generally taken for granted" and "mentioned only when there is special need to bring it to the interlocutor's notice," it is a "standing rule" of elenctic debate.

[42] According to Vlastos, 1983a, Socrates waives the requirement "only as a *pis aller* and under protest, so that the argument may go on" (38); at *R.* 340c1–2 his "apparent willingness" to waive it is "ironical" (34, n. 24), and at *Pr.* 333b8–c9 he suspends it only to allow Protagoras to "save face" (38). As we will see, Socrates waives the requirement much more often than Vlastos thinks and for very different reasons.

own beliefs." All the more important, then, that he attend to what they actually say instead of tendentiously reformulating their assertions and then refuting his own reformulations.

To sum up, Socrates explicitly invokes the sincere assent requirement with only four interlocutors (Crito, Protagoras, Thrasymachus, and Callicles); he enforces it with only one (Crito); and he does not so much as mention it with twelve (Euthyphro, Hippias, Charmides, Critias, Gorgias, Polus, Ion, Laches, Nicias, Cephalus, Hippocrates, and Polemarchus).[43] This meager textual base is too precarious a foundation on which to erect so momentous a methodological principle. The requirement is too infrequently invoked, too arbitrarily enforced, and too often suspended to justify elevating it to the status of a "standing rule" which, although "generally taken for granted" and "mentioned only when there is a special need to bring it to the interlocutor's notice," is nevertheless presupposed throughout the early dialogues.[44]

Given Socrates' frequent violations of the sincere assent requirement, we need to distinguish the arguments to which Vlastos's schematization of "peirastic" argumentation is applicable (in which Socrates abides by the requirement and refutes the thesis affirmed by his interlocutor) from those to which it is not (in which he disregards the requirement and refutes a tendentiously reformulated thesis). We also need to amend Vlastos's schematization of "standard" elenchus as follows:

(i)   The interlocutor asserts some thesis, say, p, which Socrates construes, i.e., *mis*construes, as p^*.

---

[43] I anticipate the following objection. If A lays down a procedural stipulation in the presence of B, C, and D, it applies equally to them all. He need not repeat it to each successively. Once suffices for a group. Although this objection seems eminently reasonable, it overlooks the crucial question of time. If A lays down the stipulation during the initial discussion with B, it is reasonable to claim that it applies *subsequently* to C and D. However, if he does not lay it down until the subsequent discussion with D, it is unreasonable to claim that it applies *retroactively* to B and C. That is precisely what happens in the *Gorgias* and *Republic* I where the sincere assent requirement is not invoked until the discussion with the third interlocutor – Callicles in the former and Thrasymachus in the latter.

[44] To my knowledge, the only commentators to have noticed this are Kahn, 1992: 255–56, according to whom sincerity is more a "desideratum" than a rule or, at best, a rule "more honored (or at least more often mentioned) in the breach than in the observance" (see also 1996: 118), and Nails, 1993: 286–88; 1995: 92–95, according to whom Socrates "gave only lip service" to the sincere assent requirement and "merely pretends" that his interlocutors must answer in accordance with their actual beliefs.

(ii)   Socrates secures his interlocutor's qualified (sometimes *heavily* qualified) agreement to further premises, say, q and r.

(iii) Socrates then argues, and the interlocutor agrees, that q and r entail *not-p**.

(iv)   Thereupon Socrates claims that *not-p** has been proved true, p^* false.

Vlastos's schematization is inapplicable to all the Socratic arguments that fall into the second category.

Armed with this distinction, we can provide a less abusive explanation of the interlocutor who, having affirmed p and *to some degree* assented to q and r (which entail *not-p**), does not abandon p and affirm *not-p**. We need not berate him as stubbornly perverse and unwilling to follow the argument wherever it leads. There is a simpler and kinder explanation. The reason he does not affirm *not-p** is that he never affirmed p^*; he affirmed p.

Even if the thesis refuted is the one originally affirmed by the interlocutor, he often still has good reasons for refusing to abandon it. Every valid deductive argument is either a proof of its conclusion or a disproof of the truth of at least one of its premises. Clearly, the degree of the interlocutor's confidence in *not-p*, the conclusion of Socrates' argument, can be no stronger than the degree of his confidence in q and r, the premises from which it is deduced. Hence having affirmed p, having given only qualified assent to q and r, and having perceived that they entail *not-p*, he may reasonably begin to suspect that his assent to q and r had been hasty and that he had been ill-advised to yield to the pressure brought to bear on him by Socrates. In such a situation, his reluctance to abandon his original thesis would not only be intelligible; it would be justified.

Refutation by tendentiously reformulated thesis is not the only unscrupulous dialectical tactic employed by Socrates. But it is one of the more common ones – a fact which reveals that the sincere assent requirement is neither as important nor as systematically operative as we have been given to believe.

CHAPTER 3

Crito

Throughout this study we need to proceed carefully with our eyes on the texts. The reputations of Socrates' interlocutors go before them, and of no one is this more true than Crito. Universally dismissed as one of the most superficial and non-morally[1] motivated interlocutors in the early dialogues, he is usually described as a wealthy and well-connected businessman who is unduly worried about how his reputation will suffer if people mistakenly thought that he had been unwilling to provide the funds necessary to save Socrates' life and whose fear of public opinion has prompted him to spring Socrates from prison and thereby effect an eleventh-hour miracle. R. E. Allen's opinion is representative:

Crito's plea begins, ends, and is mainly based on "how things will look." The pivot of his reasoning, to the degree that it has a pivot, turns on the connected concepts of shame and success ... The good man succeeds and helps his friends ... The bad man fails, and in his failure he becomes disgraced ... Crito stands as an advocate, pleading a cause to his friend in behalf of his friend, using, as a pleader will, such terms as he can muster to persuade. The randomness of his persuasion answers to an underlying incoherence in his plea.[2]

Although this seems to be the received opinion among students of Plato,[3] it is a misdescription of Crito and a misdiagnosis of his motivation.

Crito is not the well-meaning but misguided simpleton he has

---

[1] Some commentators grudgingly concede that Crito's remarks bear witness to a morality of sorts, but they disparage it as "average Athenian morality" (see J. Adam, 1888: xvi; and A. E. Taylor, 1929: 170).

[2] 1984: 108–9.

[3] See, e.g., J. Adam, 1888: xv–xvi; A. E. Taylor, 1924: 258; Burnet, 1924: 178; Shorey, 1933: 84; Friedländer, 1964, II: 75; Santas, 1979: 11–12; Tejara, 1984: 17; Teloh, 1986: 118–19; Kraut, 1984: 25; and Brisson, 1997: 180.

been made out to be. He has not been belatedly spurred into action by the prospect of social disgrace; he has been involved with Socrates' escalating – and, to his mind, largely self-inflicted – problems with Athens from the very beginning. His caustic capsule summary of recent events betrays his mounting displeasure at the way things have been handled: the whole trial could have been avoided, Socrates' conduct was shameful, and his friends have emerged looking like cowards. Socrates' imminent death is the crowning absurdity (*Cr.* 45c5–46a8).[4] In short, Crito has had enough. He appears in Socrates' prison cell as a loyal but exasperated critic of his eccentric friend whose imprudent conduct has gotten so out of hand that it threatens death for him, grief for his friends, and abandonment and educational disaster for his sons. His impassioned case – multi-faceted but unified by an underlying moral principle – has been largely ignored by commentators. It is also largely ignored by the vaguely attentive Socrates who focuses on one aspect of the case and ignores the rest. It is about time that someone took Crito seriously.

The historical Crito was a lifelong friend and benefactor of Socrates. According to Diogenes Laertius, it was he who liberated Socrates from manual labor, "being struck by his beauty of soul" (2.20–21), educating him and providing for his needs. Diogenes also reports that Crito was the author of seventeen philosophical dialogues on a variety of topics ranging from *What is knowledge?* and *That men are not made good by instruction* to *What is expedient?* and *On tidiness* (2.121). This is more than a little surprising. As portrayed by Plato, Crito is not the sort of man who writes philosophical dialogues. His dramatic counterpart appears in three dialogues: the *Crito*, the *Euthydemus*, and the *Phaedo*. He is also mentioned among those present at Socrates' trial (*Ap.* 33d9, 38b6).

The Crito of the *Euthydemus* is a prosperous urban dweller and the owner of several farms. Unlike Cephalus, who is also wealthy but not overly fond of money (*R.* 330b8–c2), Crito is determined to accumulate as much wealth as possible so his sons will be handsomely provided for (*Euthyd.* 304c3–5, 306d2–e3). Although Socrates periodically alludes to Crito's obsession with wealth and jok-

---

[4] Grote, 1867, I: 298, n. b calls this a "remarkable passage" which reveals that, in the opinion of Socrates' closest friends, his trial and death could have been avoided "without anything which they conceived to be dishonourable to his character."

ingly urges him to study with Euthydemus and Dionysodorus, whose art is not a hindrance to money-making, he neither rebukes him for his obsession with money nor warns him about its potentially harmful effects on the soul of its possessor. Throughout the *Euthydemus* he seems to accept Crito pretty much for what he is.

That is not the case in the *Crito*. Whereas Socrates is comparatively gentle with and even slightly amused by the money obsessed and (apparently) morally neutral Crito of the *Euthydemus*, he is quite critical of and even somewhat disappointed by the altogether sober and morally earnest Crito of the *Crito*.

Although roughly the same age and from the same deme (*Ap.* 33d9–e1), Socrates and Crito are strikingly different: the former is poor,[5] shabbily clothed, and devoted to philosophy; the latter is rich, elegantly clothed, and devoted to augmenting his net profits. Unlike some members of the Socratic inner circle, who hang on Socrates' every word and even imitate his manner of dress, Crito is a no-nonsense businessman, and he acts and dresses the part. No going about bare-footed for him. Nor does he completely approve of some of Socrates' other activities: he rebukes him for associating with Euthydemus and Dionysodorus and scolds him for taking lyre lessons at his advanced age in a class made up of young boys who afflict him with such constant ridicule that he finally recruited several other senior citizens to enroll in the class in hopes of diffusing the abuse (*Euthyd.* 272c3–d1).

Crito enjoys eavesdropping on philosophical discussions in his spare time (*Euthyd.* 271a1–3) and praises philosophy as "a charming thing" (*Euthyd.* 304e6–7), but it has not taken hold of him. Unlike the other-worldly and metaphysically susceptible Simmias and Cebes, who are deeply affected by Socrates' discourse about the immortality of the soul and filled with longing for the bliss awaiting those whose lives have been holy and just, the utterly this-worldly and metaphysically impervious Crito abruptly breaks the spell by urging Socrates to refrain from talking so much on

---

[5] Like many commentators, Burnet, 1924: 98, explains that Socrates was not always poor and attributes his later (and largely self-induced) poverty to his divine mission. For a less awestruck explanation, see Wills, 1993: 37: "Those who draw a romantic picture of poor Socrates living free of material encumbrance resolutely overlook the fact that a person who could afford to study with the Sophist Prodicus, who lived as an intellectual inquirer without the need to work, and who qualified as a property-holding hoplite free to train and campaign in the wars, obviously had an estate of some sort ..."

the ground that over-excitement can counteract the effect of the poison he is soon to ingest (*Ph.* 63d5–e2). Not normally one to publicize his failures, Socrates candidly admits that he has failed to persuade Crito that the soul is immortal and that, in burying him, he will only be burying his body (*Ph.* 115c5–d6).

Crito lets the remark pass. He is a practical man who prides himself on living in "the real world." Right now he has more important things to worry about, and there is no time for philosophy; for busy people like Crito, there seldom is. Only when he is in the company of Socrates does it seem like madness (μανίαν) to have neglected the education of his sons – especially Critobulus, who is growing up and in need of guidance (*Euthyd.* 306d6–e3). Like Alcibiades, who is overcome by shame when he is in the presence of Socrates but backslides the minute he is out of his sight (*Sym.* 216a8–b5), Crito needs Socrates' sobering presence to keep his parental responsibilities in the forefront of his consciousness. *Of course* it is madness to worry more about his sons' financial security than about their education, and he wonders why it is so hard to remember this.

But if Socrates' presence is a powerful reminder of the importance of philosophy and education, his counsel falls on deaf ears:

[P]ay no attention to the practitioners of philosophy, whether good or bad. Rather give serious consideration to the thing itself: if it seems to you negligible, then turn everyone from it, not just your sons. But if it seems to you to be what I think it is, then take heart, pursue it, practice it, both you and your sons. (*Euthyd.* 307b6–c4)

Good advice, perhaps; but it is largely wasted on Crito who, in spite of his periodic twinges of guilt and mild attacks of self-knowledge, is an unlikely candidate for philosophy.

In turning to the *Crito*, we encounter a recognizable but, in many respects, very different person. A dramatic rather than a narrated dialogue, the *Crito* depicts a conversation that takes place before dawn in Socrates' prison cell. Asked why he is up and about so early, Crito divulges that he is the bearer of bad news. The ship from Delos, whose sacred voyage had delayed Socrates' execution, has been sighted at Sunium and will soon reach Athens – which means that Socrates will be executed the next day. Socrates begs to differ. He has just awakened from a dream in which a beautiful woman in white informed him that he would not die for three more days. Crito is unimpressed. Like sensible men everywhere, he gives little credence to nocturnal revelations; besides, this is no time to be quibbling about the empirical accuracy of prophetic utterances. The situation is desperate. There are decisions to be made and things to be done. In the interim between Socrates' trial and execution, Crito has not been idle; he and several other friends of Socrates have arranged for his escape. In the conversation that follows, Crito tries to persuade him to avail himself of this golden opportunity.

He begins by pouring out his heart. Socrates' death will be a double calamity: not only will he lose an irreplaceable friend; his reputation will also be dealt a shattering blow. People will not believe that he had tried to help and that Socrates had repeatedly resisted his overtures – a remark which suggests that Crito's present plea had been preceded by others.[6] And what, he rhetorically asks, could be more shameful (αἰσχίων) than to be thought of as a man who cares more about his money than about his friends (44c2–3)?[7]

Socrates' response is surprising. We expect him to tell Crito to ignore the unstable and fluctuating opinions of "the Many." But although he says this a few Stephanus pages later, he does not say it here. Instead, he tries to soften the blow that Crito thinks his reputation will suffer by offering him a piece of consolation: the most reasonable people (οἱ ... ἐπιεικέστατοι), whose opinion alone is worthy of consideration, will understand what has happened and not think less of him (44c6–9). The distinction Socrates makes is not between worrying about what people will think and not worrying about it, but between worrying about what *reasonable*, as opposed to *un*reasonable, people will think. In saying this, he seems (temporarily at least) to be operating on Crito's own ground – not urging him to renounce *all* concern for his reputation, but directing it to a more worthy object.

Crito disagrees. One must worry about public opinion, as is

---

[6] The same thing is implied at *Cr.* 48e1–3. Socrates tells Crito to stop trying to persuade him with the same arguments.

[7] Woozley, 1979: 15–16, thinks Crito's worries are unfounded on the ground that Socrates was not a popular hero and it was highly unlikely that his friends would have been accused of stinginess or cowardice for failing to rescue him.

abundantly clear from Socrates' present legal predicament. Get a bad name with "the Many" and their capacity for inflicting the greatest evils has no limit (44d1–5). Socrates thinks otherwise: would that "the Many" could inflict the greatest evils; for then they would also be capable of the greatest good.[8] In fact, they can do neither. Unable to make a man either wise or foolish, they do what they do haphazardly (ποιοῦσι δὲ τοῦτο ὅτι ἂν τύχωσι, 44d9–10).[9]

Crito does not dispute the point, but neither does he pursue it. Instead, he returns to his previous train of thought and confesses that his impending sense of loss is particularly hard to bear because it is a preventable loss. Socrates need not die. Further attempts at persuasion follow. Crito hopes that Socrates' reluctance to escape is not prompted by worries about his friends' safety; if so, his worries are groundless. The required amount is comparatively small, everyone is willing to contribute and to incur whatever risks are necessary, and potential informers can be bought off.[10] Finally, Socrates would be welcome in many other cities – especially in Thessaly where Crito has powerful friends who will give him asylum.

In addition to these personal and prudential reasons, Crito offers several *moral* reasons – none of which is based on worries about his reputation. What Socrates is about to do is not right (οὐδὲ δίκαιόν, 45c5). In opting for death, he is knowingly embarking on a course of action which is harmful to himself and injurious to his friends. He is also derelict in his parental duties, abandoning his

---

[8] Woozley, 1979: 14, thinks this is a *non sequitur*: from the fact that "the Many" can inflict the greatest evils, it does not follow that they are also capable of the greatest good. But Woozley has misread the passage. Socrates is not deducing an inference. His remark should be understood in light of his belief that no one errs voluntarily. Men do evil because of ignorance which, if replaced by knowledge, would enable them to do good; hence the greater their present capacity for evil, the greater their future capacity for good.

[9] The Greek cannot mean "'The Many' do whatever occurs to them" (as many translations have it). See J. Adam, 1888: 32; and Burnet, 1924: 260.

[10] Crito is not implying that there are informers lying in wait to testify specifically against Socrates. The allusion is to a group of professional informers (συκοφάντας, 45a8) – public busy-bodies who made their living by threatening to bring charges (often false ones) against the rich who were usually willing to pay them off, thereby settling cheaply out of court. Xenophon reports that Crito himself was constantly besieged by these predators, and that Socrates had advised him to employ a counterinformer who could induce them to drop their charges by discovering skeletons in their own closets and threatening them with countersuits (*Mem.* 1.2.9).

sons and voluntarily consigning them to the status of orphans.[11] Instead of acting like a good and courageous (ἀγαθὸς καὶ ἀνδρεῖος) man, Socrates is taking the easy way out and is guilty of a kind of cowardice (ἀνανδρίᾳ τινι, 45d4–8) – disreputable conduct on the part of someone who professes to care about virtue.

I have summarized Crito's case at some length – partly to convey its urgency and partly to call attention to the variety of arguments it contains. Unlike most commentators,[12] who think Crito's single (or overriding) reason for urging Socrates to escape is his preoccupation with his reputation, Woozley recognizes that he advances numerous reasons. He also recognizes that, insofar as Crito explicitly invokes the principle that one should never knowingly do what is harmful to others – much less to one's own children[13] – several of his reasons are moral ones based on considerations about justice.[14]

---

[11] Socrates' apparent lack of concern for his sons also surfaces at the end of the *Apology*. At 41e1–42a2 he makes a request in their behalf, but it is a very unusual one. Instead of imploring the jurors to look after them and to educate them in his stead, he implores them to avenge him by troubling his sons, as he has troubled Athens, if they care about anything more than virtue or if they think they are something when they are nothing. This request, utterly devoid of weak-kneed sentimentality about children and childhood, strikes many modern readers as decidedly cool, if not downright callous. (Woozley, 1979: 121, speaks of Socrates' "distasteful detachment" from his children.) It struck Crito the same way. Socrates' views about parental responsibility are highly contra-endoxic – not only by modern standards, but also by ancient ones. Although the early dialogues provide no reason for thinking that Socrates was unconcerned about his sons, they provide every reason for thinking that he was fundamentally concerned about them not *qua* sons, but *qua* potential fraudulent claimants to wisdom. That is, his most fundamental concern was a concern rooted in his divine mission.

[12] Grote, 1867, 1: 287–98; Teloh, 1986: 119–21; and Arieti, 1991: 137–38, are notable exceptions. Teloh acknowledges Socrates' "cavalier dismissal" of most of Crito's reasons, but adds that he does respond to some of them and that the rest have "clear Socratic answers" (119).

[13] Crito's reasoning is based on the general principle that one should either not have children at all or one should take their upbringing and education seriously (45d4–5). Socrates does not deny the principle, but he does deny that escaping from prison and avoiding death is the best way of discharging his parental obligations, thereby relocating Crito's principle within a Socratic hierarchy of value in which one's supreme obligation is not to be a good father, as conventionally understood, but to be a just man (48c2–d5, 54a1–d1).

[14] According to Woozley, 1979: 12–13, those who deny that Crito's reasons are moral because they spring solely from worries about his reputation have overlooked an important principle of moral reasoning, namely, "If it is a good moral reason why A should not act in a certain way that B will suffer if he does, then it is a good reason, whoever utters it ... If that Crito and others will suffer an undeserved reputation in the event of Socrates' death was a good moral reason in favor of Socrates' agreeing to the escape plan, then it was no less a good reason because it was Crito himself who advanced it."

Although Woozley penetrates further than most, his analysis is incomplete. That this is so is borne out by his overly harsh assessment of (what he takes to be) Crito's first reason, namely, that Socrates' death will deprive him of an irreplaceable friend. According to Woozley, Socrates "does not bother" to reply to this reason – a reason which Plato included simply to reveal Crito's "muddleheadedness in argument."[15] This criticism is unfounded. However deep Crito's personal attachment to Socrates, he does not offer this heartfelt sentiment as a *reason* for escaping from prison. He is not appealing to Socrates' pity ("Your death will make me very sad, therefore you should escape"); he is stating a fact. This is not "muddleheadedness in argument," it is friendship. The reason Socrates "does not bother" to reply is that there is nothing to reply to.

It is only after giving vent to these personal apprehensions that Crito offers his first reason – a reason which must be assessed in light of the declaration of friendship that preceded it. He fears that people who do not know them well will think he refused to save Socrates' life because he cares more about his money than about his friends. This troubles Crito: not because he is a slave to public opinion, but because the allegation is false. He *has* tried to save Socrates' life – repeatedly: not simply because Socrates is his friend, but also because he thinks that it is right (δίκαιοί), i.e., just, for him to escape and, therefore, that it is also right, i.e., just, for his friends to help him to escape (44e6–45a5). Crito does not want to be morally censured for being unwilling to do the very thing he has been trying to do. He is right. In view of his persistent efforts, it *would* be shameful if people upbraided him with these false allegations. It is idle to deny that Crito is worried about his reputation, but his worries are those of a principled moral agent shrinking from unjust criticism, not those of a spineless sociopath in quest of peer approval.

Again Socrates' reply is puzzling. Although Woozley goes too far in saying that Socrates treats this reason "with contempt,"[16] he does not take it seriously. He again faults Crito for being unduly concerned about what people will think and again assures him that "the Many" cannot inflict the greatest evils.

---

[15] *Ibid.*: 17.   [16] *Ibid.*: 13.

Has Socrates contradicted Crito's claim? It certainly looks like it. A few Stephanus pages ago, Crito asserted that "the Many" *can* inflict the greatest evils, and Socrates now asserts that they can*not*. In fact, however, there is no contradiction here. *P* and *not-p* are genuine (as opposed to apparent) contradictories, which signal genuine (as opposed to apparent) disagreement, if and only if both speakers mean the same thing. Crito and Socrates do not. In saying that "the Many" can inflict the greatest evils, Crito means that they can inflict irreversible harm on others, for example, they can put innocent people to death. Socrates is not denying *that*. The disagreement between them is not about whether "the Many" are capable of doing such things, but about whether, in doing them, they are inflicting the greatest evils. Crito thinks they are; Socrates thinks they are not. In saying this, he is not so much denying Crito's claim but redefining – and presumably deepening – the meaning of "the greatest evils." As he sees it, the greatest evils are not evils inflicted on the body, but on the soul – "that part of us, whatever it is (ἐκεῖνο, ὅτι ποτ' ἐστὶ τῶν ἡμετέρων), which is concerned with justice and injustice" (47e8–48a1). It is true that "the Many" can put innocent people to death, but death is not the greatest evil. The greatest evil is not to be killed, but to be made unjust. Hence, appearances to the contrary, Socrates has not contradicted Crito's claim.

But he has done something else. In redefining "the greatest evils," he has introduced a new – and single – criterion for determining whether it would be just for him to escape. Unlike Crito's multiple criteria, which focus exclusively on bodily harms inflicted on other people – in particular, one's friends and children – Socrates' single criterion treats these as secondary considerations and focuses on harms inflicted on oneself – in particular, on one's soul. It is true that "the Many" cannot inflict this kind of evil on a person, but a person can inflict it on himself by acting unjustly; for, in so doing, he makes himself unjust. According to this criterion, the ultimate reason for calling an action just or unjust is its effect on the soul of the agent who performs it.[17] It follows that insofar as Crito

---

[17] As J. Adam rightly observes, this principle, "far from being altruistic, was dictated by conscious egoism." Socrates "refrained from doing wrong, not out of regard for others, but because of its effect upon his own soul" (1888: xviii). See also Santas's discussion of the "prudential paradox" and Socrates' "egoistic theory of motivation" according to which it is always to one's advantage to be just (1979: 185–93).

confines his arguments to bodily harms and ignores the effects of wrongdoing on the soul of the wrongdoer, he is wasting his time.

Socrates is not completely unappreciative of Crito's efforts; he acknowledges that his zeal is estimable – provided that it is rightly directed (μετά τινος ὀρθότητος, 46b1–2). But if it is not, then the greater his zeal, the harder it will be to bear. Accordingly, they must examine his proposal:

> I am the kind of man who listens only to the argument that on reflection seems best to me. I cannot, now that this fate has come upon me, discard the arguments I used; they seem to me much the same. I value and respect the same principles as before, and if we have no better arguments to bring up at this moment, be sure that I will not agree with you. (46b4–c3)

In short, unless Crito can produce better reasons for escaping from prison, Socrates will not budge. Although unfailingly courteous towards his old friend, he treats him as one who "speaks an infinite deal of nothing ... [H]is reasons are as two grains of wheat hid in two bushels of chaff; you shall seek all day ere you find them, and when you have them they are not worth the search."[18]

Before presenting his reasons for remaining in prison and going to his death, Socrates alludes to several previous discussions between Crito and himself during which they had agreed about a number of important matters; and he wonders whether Crito still holds the same opinions. Crito thereupon dutifully agrees with a series of statements. More accurately, he dutifully gives affirmative answers to a series of questions, thereby committing himself to their assertorial reformulations: (i) that we should attend only to the useful opinions (τὰς ... χρηστάς) of the wise (τῶν φρονίμων) that is, those who know (τῷ ἐπιστάτῃ) and understand (ἐπαΐοντι) and ignore the useless (τὰς ... πονηράς) opinions of the foolish (τῶν ἀφρόνων); (ii) that we should pay heed to the praise and blame of the wise but ignore the praise and blame of the foolish; (iii) that, in yielding to the opinions of "the Many," we harm that within us which is benefited by justice and harmed by injustice and which makes life worth living; and (iv) that we should attend to the opinions of him "who understands justice and injustice" (ὅτι ἐπαΐων περὶ τῶν δικαίων καὶ ἀδίκων) – "the one, that is, and the

---

[18] Shakespeare, *The Merchant of Venice* I.I.114–18.

truth itself" (ὁ εἷς καὶ αὐτὴ ἡ ἀλήθεια) "before whom we should feel fear and shame more than before all the others" – "if there is one who has knowledge of these things" (47a2–48b2).[19]

Having elicited Crito's assent to these theses, Socrates gently but firmly rebukes him:

So ... you were wrong to believe that we should care for the opinion of the many about what is just, beautiful, good, and their opposites [even though] the many are able to put us to death ... [T]he most important thing is not life, but the good life. (48a7–b6)

Here a protest is in order. Crito said nothing of the kind. What he said was that he had decided *on moral grounds and independently of* the opinions of "the Many" that it is just for Socrates to escape. However, given Socrates' refusal to escape, Crito finds himself worrying about what "the Many" will think. Although this may show that he looks to "the Many" for moral approval – or, at least, shrinks from their disapproval – it does not show that he looks to them for moral guidance.

Not only has Socrates failed to rebut Crito's case; he has also misrepresented it. The heart of his case is that, insofar as Socrates voluntarily inflicts avoidable harm on his friends, his family, and himself, he is behaving unjustly. Ignoring the moral dimension of Crito's case and focusing exclusively on his worries about his reputation – worries which Socrates misunderstands – he accuses him of basing his moral beliefs on the opinions of "the Many." This is both inaccurate and unfair. Even if Crito is completely wrong about Socrates' duties to his friends, his family, and himself, as Socrates (and most commentators) firmly believe, the claim for which Socrates faults him is a claim he never made.

Uncorrected by Crito, Socrates next undertakes to demonstrate that it would not be just for him to escape. Before doing so, he again emphasizes that he wishes to conduct a joint investigation and again announces that he will withdraw his claim if Crito can refute it. Another series of questions follows, all of which are again answered affirmatively by Crito who thereby again commits himself to their assertorial reformulations: (i) that we should never

[19] The *Crito* is the only early dialogue in which the existence of a moral expert is treated as a serious possibility. At *Pr.* 319a10–320b5 Socrates explicitly denies that any such person exists on the ground that virtue cannot be imparted from one person to another. Cf. *M.* 89e1–96c10.

do wrong voluntarily (ἑκόντας); (ii) that wrongdoing is always shameful to the wrongdoer; and, above all, (iii) that we should never requite evil with evil – no matter how unjustly we ourselves have been treated (49a4–e3). Before allowing Crito to answer these questions, Socrates gravely observes that there are not many people who hold these views, and that those who do and those who do not have nothing in common and even despise one another. Accordingly, before affirming these theses and allowing them to serve as the starting point (τῆς ἀρχῆς, 49d9) of the ensuing discussion, Crito should consider these matters very carefully and not answer contrary to what he really believes (πάρα δόξαν, 49d1).

This prominent invocation of the sincere assent requirement is one of the star texts cited by commentators intent on installing it as a "standing rule" of elenctic debate – the guarantor of truthfulness in argumentation and the provider of the "existential dimension" which enables Socrates to examine his interlocutors' lives as well as their theses.[20] However, Socrates himself seems to attach much less importance to the requirement and is not as intent on securing Crito's sincere assent as these commentators suppose. If he were, he would simply ask his questions, invoke the requirement, and await Crito's honest answers. But he does not. Behaving as if he half-suspects that Crito might have changed his mind about these previously agreed-on theses, he surreptitiously introduces a new ingredient into the discussion which insures that Crito will reaffirm them. The invocation of the sincere assent requirement is preceded by a powerful psychological appeal to Crito's sense of shame. Socrates sagely observes that he certainly hopes Crito still holds these opinions because they would be no better than children if they were to change their minds about something so fundamental as the injustice of requiting evil with evil (49a4–b1). The strategy works: Crito assures Socrates that he still holds these opinions.

There is no reason to doubt him. I am not claiming that the admission Socrates wrings from Crito is dishonest; I am simply pointing out that he *does* wring it from him. This is the answer Socrates wants, and it is the answer he makes sure he gets. However, the decisive instrument of persuasion is not the sincere assent

---

[20] Like many Anglo-American commentators, Brisson attaches great weight to the requirement and describes it as a "[r]ègle essentielle à la discussion" (1997: 234, n. 59).

requirement but the appeal to Crito's sense of shame with its subtle, irresistible, *and patently false* suggestion that it is childish to change one's mind about an important issue in one's old age.

Having elicited Crito's "sincere" assent, Socrates declares that the next thing he will say – or, rather, ask (μᾶλλον δ' ἐρωτῶ, 49e5) – is whether we should always keep our agreements, provided that they are right (τῷ δίκαια ὄντα, 49e6), or whether we are free to break them. Predictably, Crito opts for the former. Very well then. In escaping from prison, would Socrates not be breaking his agreement with Athens and thereby trying to destroy the city by disobeying its laws? And would it be a sufficient justification to say that, having been wronged by the city, Socrates may wrong it in return, thereby requiting evil with evil? It looks like the Socratic elenchus is on its way, like a rollercoaster irretrievably set in motion, and that the by-now helpless Crito is just along for the ride.

In view of his recent "reaffirmation" of and "sincere assent" to the principle that it is always and unconditionally wrong to requite evil with evil, we expect Crito to say that the fact that Athens has wronged Socrates is *not* a sufficient justification for him to wrong it in return by escaping from prison. But he surprises us by saying – emphatically and with an oath – that it *is* a sufficient justification; indeed, that is exactly what we *should* say (50c3) – an astounding reply which reveals that even at this comparatively late stage of the discussion Crito is still in fundamental disagreement with Socrates: not only about whether he should escape from prison, but also (and more fundamentally) about whether it is always and unconditionally wrong to requite evil with evil.

Perceiving that Crito is still unpersuaded, Socrates renews his efforts. But with a difference. Again abandoning logic in favor of psychology, he opts for yet another strategy – neither a "joint" investigation in which Crito is required to say what he "really" believes nor another appeal to his sense of shame, but rather a long and largely uninterrupted piece of rhetoric – the famous speech which he puts into the mouth of the personified Laws of Athens (50a6–54d1). This speech – a Socratic *epideixis* if there ever was one – is designed to persuade Crito that were Socrates to escape from prison, he would be breaking his contract with Athens – a contract which provided him (and his family) with all the benefits of citizenship in exchange for unconditional obedience to its laws – and thereby acting unjustly, disobeying the laws, destroying the city, and harming his own soul.[21] Again, the psychological strategy works.[22]

Having concluded his speech, Socrates again addresses Crito in his own person and informs him that although the words of the Laws resonate so loudly within him that he can hear nothing else, he is still free to dissent. However, unlike his previous invitation, which was prefaced by assurances that he would take Crito's objections seriously and yield if he found them convincing (48d8–e1), this one is prefaced by assurances that further objections would be futile (μάτην, 54d6). Crito sensibly replies that he has nothing more to say. His studied resignation, preceded by his renewed insistence that Socrates should escape from prison, reveal that in his heart of hearts he is still unpersuaded. The end of the *Crito* presents us with an interlocutor who has heard Socrates out and "assented to" each of the premises put to him but who continues to disagree with him and finally lapses into silence because he realizes that further protests would indeed be futile. Although Socrates achieves a victory of sorts in this dialogue, it is not a *dialectical* victory. Crito remains loyal: not because he agrees with Socrates, but because he is his friend.[23]

Henceforth he abandons the role of critic, remaining with Socrates until the very end and attending to the many mundane and often gruesome details. He had been present at the trial where he had offered to pay a fine as an alternative to the death penalty. Failing in this, he had tried to prevent Socrates' imprisonment by posting bail. During his imprisonment, he had visited him frequently – perhaps daily. In any event, the jailer had grown accustomed to him and had given him special privileges. On the day of execution, he acts as manager of Socrates' estate and personal affairs. Unlike Socrates' other friends, Crito is not self-indulgent,

---

[21] See Brisson, 1997: 194: "Il ... s'agit du seul dialogue où un argument moral sérieux est mis dans la bouche non de l'un des interlocuteurs, mais dans celle d'une abstraction personnifiée, les Lois d'Athènes."

[22] Grote, 1867, I: 307–8, notes that in spite of Socrates' strictures on long speeches, he often makes them himself "with ability and effect." J. Adam, 1888: xx–xxi, goes further: Socrates' long speeches reveal "[t]he limitation of [his] genius" and the "half-complete" nature of his rationalism; had it been complete, "he would not have shrunk from submitting to the test of his dialectic the whole question of the validity and authority of law, as a condition of the stability of social life."

[23] This is argued with great eloquence by Méron, 1979: 212–13. The same point is made in passing by Mazel who observes that Crito remains loyal to Socrates "[p]ar amitié plus par conviction" (1987: 207–8).

and his grief has not rendered him useless. At Socrates' request, he directs someone to escort Xanthippe from the cell. He later delivers a message from the executioner and solicits final instructions from Socrates about the children and his burial. He assists him with his bath, is present during his last moments with his family, and finally signals the executioner to administer the hemlock. Temporarily overcome by emotion, he slips from the cell; but soon he is back. In deference to Socrates' last wish, he promises to sacrifice a cock to Asclepius[24] and, moments later, closes the eyes and mouth of the corpse. It would be hard to find a more devoted and steadfast friend.

All this seems to go unnoticed by Socrates. Even as Crito efficiently and unobtrusively discharges his thankless task, Socrates seems to remain completely oblivious of him. The Socrates of the *Phaedo* is a man who seems to have no need of other people and is willing to tolerate them only if they will talk philosophy and conduct themselves in a way that measures up to his impossibly high standards. He makes little allowance for normal human weakness or even for normal human response.[25] When Xanthippe breaks down at the prospect of losing her husband, she is removed from his presence. When his friends are overcome by similar emotions, they are reprimanded and placed on notice that, unless they can control themselves, the same fate awaits them.

If his friends are all-too-human, Socrates hardly seems human at all. He seems more like a disembodied intellect, a rational soul temporarily housed in a body and awaiting release – if not eagerly, at least without discernible regret. His serenity in the face of death is undeniably impressive, but it is a remote and chilly serenity. As time slips away, his conversation and general demeanor suggest that he would be perfectly content to spend his final hours in solitude, pondering the mixed sensations of pleasure and pain in his legs and setting the verses of Aesop to music. While the banished Xanthippe grieves elsewhere and his emotion racked friends do their best to avoid "womanly" behavior, Crito takes control of

---

[24] As Chambry astutely notes, "Socrate mourant a les mêmes inquiétudes que Céphale" (1989: 9, n. 2).

[25] J. Adam is one of the few commentators who is sensitive to this. According to him, Plato put "the fatal argument" which requires Socrates to place his obligation to the city above his obligation to his family and friends into the mouth of the personified Laws of Athens "to save Socrates from the charge of selfishness and lack of feeling" (1888: 61).

the situation and tries to make Socrates' final hours as comfortable and as conducive to rational discussion as the oppressive circumstances permit. Although Socrates seems completely oblivious of him, Plato most certainly was not.

In saying this, I am not denying that Plato's ultimate sympathies lay with Socrates. He apparently agreed that he should remain in prison and that the objections he had put into Crito's mouth were feeble and beside the point. At the same time, his portrayal suggests that the bond between them is not an intellectual one which stands or falls with their theoretical agreement or disagreement. Crito entered Socrates' cell hoping to persuade him to escape. The reasons he advanced seemed cogent to himself and would have persuaded most people. Socrates knows that too, and in his emotionally detached way he "appreciates" Crito's genuine – albeit, in his opinion, misguided – concern. Although he ignores a good deal of what Crito says and misrepresents much of what he does not ignore, Crito seems not to notice; if he does, he does not protest. But even if Socrates had examined Crito's case for escaping more carefully, it is unlikely that he would have persuaded him that it would be unjust to escape. The gap between them cannot be bridged by argumentation. Fortunately for Socrates, Crito found another way to bridge it.

Crito's loyalty, selflessness, and remarkable capacity for unconditional friendship do not bespeak shallowness and superficiality. Such a man does not deserve to have his portrait permanently housed in the Gallery of Inept Interlocutors of which proponents of the standard picture are the self-appointed curators. It is not only false but cruel to suggest that his presence in Socrates' cell is traceable to his worries about "how things will look" and "what people will think." Nor will it do to assert without qualification that he is living an unexamined life. In spite of his lack of philosophical acumen, Crito is a man of considerable stature. His less than imposing mind is more than compensated for by his royal heart.

CHAPTER 4

Ion

"There is an ancient quarrel between poetry and philosophy," declares the "Socrates" of *Republic* x, and "if you admit the pleasure-giving Muse ... pleasure and pain will be kings in your city instead of law or the thing that everyone has always believed to be best, namely, reason" (*R.* 607a5–8). It is often said that the quarrel was started by the poets who claimed to be men of great wisdom. But that is to account for it from the point of view of the philosophers. It might equally be said that the quarrel was started by the philosophers who denied that the poets were men of great wisdom, thereby accounting for it from the point of view of the poets. And if we are speaking chronologically, that is exactly what we should say. The poets pre-dated the philosophers by centuries. In any event, there *was* a quarrel; and it was intensified by the fact that the poets were taken much more seriously than the philosophers by the general public. Their works had shaped the beliefs and sensibilities of Greece for generations, and they were looked upon as the definitive embodiments and final arbiters of human virtue. What was believed to be true of the poets generally was believed to be preeminently true of Homer – "the encyclopaedist" whose poetry "as an epic archetype of the orally preserved word was composed as a compendium of matters to be memorized, of a tradition to be maintained, of a *paideia* to be transmitted."[1]

All these claims are vigorously contested by the "Socrates" of the *Republic* according to whom the writings of the poets – understanding the term broadly enough to include comic, lyric, and tragic authors – must be closely scrutinized and methodically purged of their morally objectionable content which, owing to the craft and cunning with which it is presented, inculcates falsehood

---

[1] Havelock, 1963: 49.

by misrepresenting the nature of the gods and heroes (*R.* 377b5–392c5) and, what is worse, penetrates the soul of the reader/auditor, causing him to assimilate these images unawares and to become like the objects depicted (*R.* 395b8–d3). In view of these immanent dangers, it is not enough to instruct the young about what is good (ἀγαθόν) and beautiful (καλόν); they must be habituated in goodness and beauty from earliest infancy so that, like carefully selected and pretreated wool, their souls are permanently imbued with the indelible dye of virtue which pleasure, fear, and passion can never rinse out (*R.* 429d4–430b2). Thus forearmed against the seductive but morally corrupting offerings of the banished poets, and immersed in the didactic but morally edifying efforts of their approved counterparts, who write according to the prescribed patterns (τοῖς τύποις, *R.* 398b3), they will grow into properly formed adults in whom the love of the Good has taken root.

These recurring denunciations of poets and poetry, so characteristic of middle and later Plato, are wholly absent from the early dialogues. Unlike his (in many respects) very dissimilar counterpart in the *Republic*, the Socrates of the early dialogues promulgates no theories of education, banishes no poets, and compiles no approved lists of appropriately excised poetry. Misgivings he has, but they are infrequently expressed and, by the standards of the *Republic*, comparatively mild. Confronted with Euthyphro's claim that, in prosecuting his father, he is following in the footsteps of Zeus, the best and most just of the gods, who punished his father for his crimes (*Eu.* 5e2–6a5), Socrates does not deplore Euthyphro's moral corruption at the hands of the poets and advocate curricular reform; he merely marvels at Euthyphro's credulity and confesses that he himself finds it hard to believe these Homeric tales (*Eu.* 6a6–b4). Similarly, when Protagoras recounts how, in distributing the skills necessary for survival, Epimetheus had provided so lavishly for the animal kingdom that he exhausted his supply before he had made provision for human beings – a blunder which prompted Prometheus to steal fire and technical expertise from Athena and Hephaestus, thereby infuriating them and incurring the wrath of Zeus (*Pr.* 320d3–322a2) – Socrates does not rail against theological anthropomorphism and lobby for a morally purged poetic canon; he merely changes the subject. The Homeric tales which elicit severe moral censure from the "Socrates" of the

Republic, evoke little more than skeptical eyebrow-raising from the Socrates of the early dialogues whose periodic allusions to poetry and poets are made in a mildly amused, tongue-in-cheek manner which suggests that he does not take them seriously enough to warrant sustained criticism.

But although the early dialogues do not bear witness to any overt quarrel between poetry and philosophy, this ostensibly unruffled surface is deceptive. As Grube[2] rightly observes, there is no quarrel so long as the poets make no claim to knowledge. But, of course, they do; and so there is.[3]

However, it focuses on different issues. Whereas the Platonic protest is basically a moral one which focuses on objectionable poetic content and its potentially harmful effects, the Socratic protest – if "protest" is not too strong a term – is basically epistemological. Socrates' complaint is not that the poets are potential menaces to the moral well-being of society, but that they cannot provide a rational justification for what they say or a rational explanation of their ability to say it (*Ap.* 22b8–c3). In short, the utterances of the poets do not count as knowledge (ἐπιστήμη). And neither, by implication, do those of the rhapsodes – who are the interpreters of the poets.

Rhapsodes – from ῥάπτω (to stitch together) and ᾠδή (song) – were professional reciters of poetry and a familiar phenomenon throughout Greece and Asia Minor. Poetic recitation was not confined to intellectual literary guilds and select coffee-houses. Poetry was part and parcel of Greek popular culture, and it was available to the masses from the globe-trotting rhapsodes whose performances at religious festivals and annual games were heavily advertised and well-attended forms of entertainment which attracted crowds of 20,000 and upwards (*I.* 535d4–5). Prominently positioned and clothed in elaborate costumes, they delivered their spell-binding speeches, competing for victory and (usually) large purses – the Hellenic version of show-biz.

But the rhapsodes' importance far transcended their entertainment value. Insofar as their recitations were one of the principal

---

[2] 1980: 182.
[3] See Flashar, 1958: 1: "Dadurch wird der 'alte Streit zwischen Philosophie und Dichtung', von dem Platon spricht, zu einem unmittelbar philosophischen Anliegen, das sich durch fast alle Dialoge Platons verfolgen lässt und das im Ion zum erstenmal Gestalt gewinnt." See also Jowett, 1871, 1: 496; and Murdoch, 1977: 8.

means by which the Homeric tradition was handed down from one generation to the next, they also performed an indispensable educational and cultural function.[4] Although books (in the form of papyrus rolls) existed, they were neither readily available nor much in demand.[5] Except for the educated few, the Greeks were not readers, but listeners. As a result, their relation to the Homeric texts was analogous to that of most music lovers to music in every era. Either lacking scores or unable to read them, their only access to music is through public performances. Hence the importance of competent performers. The same was true of public access to poetry in classical antiquity. Hence the importance of competent reciters. Only by being transmitted anew to each succeeding generation could this poetic tradition continue to survive as a coherent, standardized, and shared set of normative beliefs, attitudes, and practices, and thus continue to articulate the criteria that provided content for the term *aretē* and defined what it meant to be human. As the transmitters of this rich but precarious tradition, the rhapsodes answered to an immense and – except for atypical dissenters like Socrates and Plato – universally perceived cultural need.[6]

Like the sophists, who answered to a different and – except for the same dissenters – equally perceived need,[7] the rhapsodes are often assessed in isolation from the historical context that produced them. Usually maligned as opportunistic charlatans whose superficially impressive but substantively empty recitations pandered to public taste and provided them with handsome incomes, they are routinely numbered among the contributors to the decline of Athenian morality. No doubt there were some who answered to this description. But the abuse of a function does not undercut its

---

[4] According to the *Hipparchus* – a dialogue traditionally believed to be authentic but now almost universally regarded as spurious – it was Hipparchus, the oldest son of Peisistratus, who brought the Homeric poems to Greece and compelled the rhapsodes to recite them in hopes of educating the citizenry (228b4–c6). Diogenes Laertius claims that the credit belongs to Solon (1.57).

[5] For a discussion of Athenian literacy, books, and the minor educational role they played in classical antiquity, see Roberts, 1984: 103–5.

[6] In Xenophon's *Symposium* (3.6) Niceratus reports that he listens to the rhapsodes almost every day.

[7] On the unavailability of an education that went beyond the fundamentals, see Kerferd, 1981: 37–38; Roberts, 1984: 94–103; and de Romilly, 1992: 30–56.

need – a point clearly grasped by the "Socrates" of the *Republic* who, although convinced that existing poetry cannot provide adequate moral habituation for the young, never doubted the need for poetry that can. Convinced that neither the sophists nor the rhapsodes were adequate to the educational task, Plato's attitude towards both fluctuated between covert distrust and overt hostility. Although he recognized that they were merely symptoms of the lamentable state of Athenian society and not its cause (*R.* 490e2–496a9), he seldom had anything good to say about them. For that reason, it is as unwise to rely solely on the Platonic corpus for information about the sophists and rhapsodes as it is to rely solely on the New Testament for information about the Pharisees and the Sadducees. Plato's estimate of the rhapsodes emerges most clearly in his portrayal of the celebrated Ion of Ephesus in the dialogue which bears his name.

The *Ion* depicts a discussion between Ion and Socrates. Although its dramatic date cannot be precisely determined, Ion's passing remark that his native city is presently under Athenian rule (541c3–4) indicates that it must be before 416[8] when the alliance between Athens and Ephesus was dissolved. The preliminary chit-chat suggests that this is not the first meeting between the pair, but Ion's pitiful helplessness in the face of Socratic interrogation suggests that it is their first philosophical encounter.

In answer to the question: who is Ion? one can only say that Ion is Ion, and there is none like him. Unknown apart from this dialogue, he is arguably the most intellectually marginal character in the early dialogues and a strong contender for the title of Socrates' Silliest Interlocutor. If Xenophon is right, he was typical of his profession:

[T]he rhapsodes are consummate as reciters, but they themselves are utter fools. (*Mem.* 4.2.10)

It is hard to imagine a more damning criticism, coming as it does from a writer whose heartfelt but (after a few pages) repetitious and uninteresting "recollections" of Socrates leave one with the distinct impression that his hero was little more than an inexhaustible conduit of numbingly predictable and eminently forgettable

---

[8] Unless otherwise indicated, all dates are BCE.

platitudes. If the intellectually inconsequential Xenophon judges
you foolish, you must be foolish indeed.[9]

But if Ion is one of Socrates' most intellectually marginal and
dialectically inept interlocutors, he is also one of the most likeable.
Although he labors under an inordinately high opinion of himself
– he thinks he is worthy of being awarded a gold crown by the
Homeridae[10] – his vanity is not the off-putting vanity of intellectual
arrogance, but the endearing vanity of intellectual naivete – the
vanity of the precocious, but untested adolescent.[11] Here is a linguistic virtuoso whose auditors are putty in his hands whom he can
alternately convulse with laughter and move to tears but who, upon
being administered a mild dose of Socratic cross-examination, can
explain neither the Homeric wisdom he imparts nor how he is able
to impart it.

Having just returned from Epidaurus where he had won first
prize at the festival of Asclepius, the jubilant Ion is anticipating
similar successes and triumphs in Athens – if the god wills (530b4).
Never one to discourage a braggart, Socrates feigns admiration
for Ion's erudition which enables him not only to recite the poet's
words, but also to elucidate his thought – the exegetical task which
Ion thinks is the most difficult part of his job and on which Socrates focuses most of his critical attention. Oblivious to the irony,
Ion immodestly confides that, in addition to elucidating the poet's
ideas, he embellishes them with such fine ideas of his own that
his epideictic displays excel those of any other rhapsode the
world has ever seen. Having good-naturedly endured all this self-
congratulatory fanfare, Socrates uncharacteristically requests a
demonstration of Ion's rhetorical ability – the very thing he usu-

---

[9] Strictly, the source of this extremely negative assessment is not Xenophon but Euthydemus. Interestingly, the Xenophontic Socrates does not fully endorse it. Although he
agrees that no one is "more stupid" (ἠλιθιώτερον) than the rhapsodes, he does not attribute their stupidity to lack of intelligence, but to the fact they do not know the "inner
meaning" (τὰς ὑπονοίας) of the poems they recite (*Symposium* 3.6–7). That the rhapsodes
were far from being fools is implied by Grote, 1867, 1: 455, and argued with great eloquence by Flashar, 1958: 21–24.

[10] The Homeridae (or Sons of Homer) was a guild of professional rhapsodes located in
Chios who claimed to be direct descendants of Homer.

[11] A few commentators agree. Stock thinks Ion's vanity is "harmless" (1909: vii). So, too,
Méron, 1979: 162: "Il est infatué de lui-même ... non sans cause apparemment." But
most do not. Woodruff judges Ion "proud" and "a fit target" for Socratic criticism
(1983: 6). Bloom describes him as "self-satisfied" and "as far from the radical self-doubt
of philosophy as a man can be" (1987: 371).

ally goes out of his way to avoid – only to beg off the minute Ion agrees. On second thought, he would rather ask a few questions.

Having declined the role of audience in favor of that of questioner, Socrates is surprised to learn that Ion's skill as a rhapsode is confined to Homer. Other poets bore him; when their names come up, his attention wanes. He frankly dozes (532b8–c4). This remarkable self-evaluation should not slip by unnoticed. Unlike every other interlocutor in the early dialogues, Ion acknowledges his intellectual and professional limitations at the very outset: when it comes to reciting Homer, he is unsurpassed; but when it comes to reciting other poets, he is useless.

Socrates' response is surprising. Instead of rejoicing that he has finally found an interlocutor who is aware of his limitations and willing to acknowledge them, he feigns puzzlement and sets out to show that Ion's skill as a rhapsode cannot be confined to Homer. Unlike most Socratic interlocutors, who need to realize that they are *less* competent than they think they are, Ion apparently needs to realize that he is *more* competent than he thinks he is. To drive this point home, Socrates advances two arguments. The first – 531a5–d2 – is as follows:

(i)   There are many subjects about which Homer and the other poets say the same things (ταὐτὰ λέγετον), and in those cases Ion can elucidate them all equally well.

(ii) But there are many other subjects about which Homer and the other poets do not say the same things (μὴ ταὐτὰ λέγουσιν), e.g., divination; and in such cases a diviner could adjudicate their disagreements better than Ion.

(iii) However, if Ion were a diviner himself, he could adjudicate these disagreements equally well.

(iv) Therefore since Homer and the other poets speak about many of the same things, e.g., war, dealings between gods and men, and since Ion has agreed that insofar as the poets say the same things, he can expound and elucidate them equally well, his skill as a rhapsode cannot be confined to Homer.

Before proceeding to Socrates' second argument, it is worth noticing that the first is fallacious. In saying – in (i) and (ii) – that Homer and the other poets sometimes do and sometimes do not "say the same things," Socrates means that they *agree* about some things, but *disagree* about others. However in (iv) he means something else. Here "saying the same things" does not mean agreeing (as opposed to disagreeing) about the subjects on which they write; it means *writing about the same subjects* (as opposed to *writing about different ones*). Not noticing this shift of meaning, Ion concurs: "That's true, Socrates" (531d3). What he should have said is: "That's true, Socrates, but it is irrelevant. We were not discussing whether Homer and the other poets write about the same subjects but whether, in writing about them, they agree or disagree. You are equivocating on 'say the same things'."[12]

Instead of lodging this objection, Ion shifts ground and introduces a new consideration: he admits that Homer and the other poets write about many of the same subjects, but he thinks that Homeric poetry is better (ἄμεινον, 531d10). Although it is often risky to speculate about what is going on in the mind of a fictional character, that is not the case here. In saying that Homeric poetry is "better" than non-Homeric, Ion clearly means that it is better *qua* poetry, i.e., that it is better written and hence superior when judged by aesthetic criteria.[13] My use of the term "aesthetic" is, of course, anachronistic. As Guthrie[14] rightly points out, aesthetic criteria are never mentioned in the *Ion*. However, they are clearly implied. In saying that Homeric poetry is better than non-Homeric, Ion is making an implicit aesthetic judgment and hence making an implicit distinction between what the poets say and how they say it, that is, an implicit distinction between content and style. As we will see, Socrates does the same thing a few Stephanus pages later.

We expect Socrates to challenge Ion by asking on what ground he claims that Homeric poetry is better than non-Homeric and by demanding a definition of beauty which may serve as a standard (παράδειγμα) for individual and comparative ascriptions of it. But he does not. Ignoring Ion's implicit appeal to aesthetic criteria

---

[12] Woodruff, 1983: 9–10, acknowledges that at least one of Socrates' arguments trades on an equivocation; however, instead of faulting him for fallacious reasoning, he defends him on the ground that the argument "plays on words in an illuminating way." Guthrie, 1975: 202, n. 1 is less apologetic: "It is hardly worth pointing out all the fallacies committed by S. in this little work."

[13] For a different interpretation, see Méron, 1979: 164–65, according to whom Ion is not offering an aesthetic evaluation of Homeric poetry, but merely expressing his personal taste: he just *likes* Homeric poetry better than non-Homeric.

[14] 1975: 205.

and his implicit distinction between content and style,[15] he tries to demolish Ion's claim that his skill as a rhapsode is confined to Homer with a second argument (531d12–532b7):

(i) When several people talk about the same subject, e.g., mathematics or wholesome food, and one speaks better (ἄριστα) than the rest, the person who is most competent to judge the good speaker (τὸν εὖ λέγοντα) is also most competent to judge the bad (τοὺς κακῶς λέγοντας), i.e., these comparative judgments are necessarily made by the same person, namely, the one who possesses the *technai* of mathematics or nutrition.[16]

(ii) Formulated in full generality, in any *technē*, whoever is most competent to judge who speaks better is also (and for that reason) most competent to judge who speaks worse.

(iii) Therefore if Ion is competent to judge that Homer speaks better than the other poets, he must be equally competent to judge that they speak worse. So, again, his skill as a rhapsode cannot be confined to Homer.

Exulting in Socrates' apparent victory, Guthrie[17] exclaims: "Who ever heard of an art critic who could assess Polygnotus but no other painter?" Guthrie is right. It would be patently absurd to say such a thing. But Ion never said it.

The apparent cogency of Socrates' second argument depends on his tendentious interpretation of what Ion did say. The argument tries to demonstrate that it is inconsistent for Ion simultaneously to assert:

(i) that he is competent to judge which poets speak well and which speak badly,

and:

(ii) that his skill as a rhapsode is confined to Homer.

---

[15] See Schaper, 1968: 25: Socrates "ruthlessly" overrides Ion's "rather sensible suggestion."

[16] The term *technē* has no exact English equivalent and applies to any activity that involves expertise. The Greeks made no distinction between what we broadly call "crafts" (cobbling, carpentry, pottery, etc.) and the so-called "fine" arts (poetry, music, painting, etc.). Although often translated as "art," Dodds, 1959: 190, prefers the more neutral "skill." See, too, Murray, 1996: 108.

[17] 1975: 202.

But these propositions are not inconsistent. All Socrates has shown is that to be a competent judge of the superiority of Homeric poetry over non-Homeric, one must be acquainted with both – hardly an insight to be shouted from the housetops. Furthermore, Ion *is* acquainted with both. He did not say that he has no *knowledge* of non-Homeric poetry;[18] he said only that he has no *interest* in it. His claim was that his skill as a rhapsode is confined to Homer, not that his acquaintance with Greek poetry is confined to him. And from the fact that he is acquainted with non-Homeric poetry and judges it inferior to Homeric it does not follow that he must be equally skilled at reciting both.

In addition to ignoring Ion's implicit appeal to aesthetic criteria and his implicit distinction between content and style, Socrates redefines "speaks better." Instead of agreeing that anyone who is competent to judge who speaks well and badly about mathematics (or any other *technē*) must be a practitioner of that *technē*, Ion should have pointed out that this is only true if, by "speaks better," one means "speaks correctly" (ὀρθῶς). He should then have explained that this is not what he meant. By "speaks better" (εὖ), he did not mean "speaks correctly," but "speaks with more stylistic elegance, beauty, and charm." Socrates' argument has force only if "speaks better" means "says what is true" in the sense of correctly assessing the factual accuracy of what the poets say about the subject matter that falls under the *technē* in question – in this case, mathematics. Ion never made such a claim. He claimed only that he could assess the stylistic effectiveness with which the poets speak about the subject matter that falls under the *technē*.

An author less favorably disposed towards Socrates (and more favorably disposed towards rhapsodes) might have provided Ion with the following rejoinder: "Although I am neither a diviner nor a mathematician nor a doctor, and, therefore, lack the technical expertise necessary to adjudicate substantive disagreements about divination, mathematics, and medicine, I am a competent judge of who speaks better about these subjects from a non-substantive and purely stylistic point of view. You have overlooked the fact that although one must be a surgeon in order to assess the medical content of a lecture on a complicated surgical procedure, one need not be a surgeon in order to judge which of two lecturers is the

---

[18] *Pace* Friedländer, 1964, I: 129–30.

better speaker. Hence you have not shown that I am an incompetent judge of the aesthetic qualities by virtue of which Homeric poetry is better than non-Homeric." It follows that Socrates' second attempt to refute Ion's claim that his skill as a rhapsode is confined to Homer is as unsuccessful as the first.

None of this is detected by Ion. Thunderstruck by this apparently devastating argument and unaccustomed to trafficking in such profundities, Ion is reduced to *aporia*:

Then how in the world do you explain what *I* do, Socrates? When someone discusses another poet I pay no attention, and I have no power to contribute anything worthwhile ... But let someone mention Homer and right away I'm ... paying attention and I have plenty to say. (532b8–c4)

Puzzled (apparently for the first time) by his inability to recite non-Homeric poetry, he implores Socrates to unravel this mystery by explaining him to himself. The result is the Socratic theory of poetic inspiration.

It is not "by art and knowledge" (τέχνη καὶ ἐπιστήμη) that Ion recites Homeric poetry well (532c6); if it were, then he could recite non-Homeric poetry equally well, just as someone who understands the *technai* of painting, sculpture, and music is not confined to discoursing about particular painters, sculptors, and musicians, but can discourse equally well about them all. Those who have knowledge of something have knowledge of the whole and not merely knowledge of some of its parts – much less, of only one part. Since Ion's skill as a rhapsode is confined to Homer, it must be explained in some other way. According to Socrates, he does so by divine inspiration (θείᾳ μοίρᾳ, 534c1). Before proceeding further, it should be noted that Socrates' acknowledgment in this passage that Ion's skill as a rhapsode is confined to Homer contradicts the conclusion of the two foregoing arguments according to which his skill is *not* – indeed, *cannot be* – confined to Homer. Clearly, Ion's skill as a rhapsode either is or is not confined to Homer. If it is not, then the Socratic theory of divine inspiration which follows is superfluous; we need no esoteric explanation of how Ion recites Homer. On the other hand, if it is, then, insofar as the conclusion of the two foregoing arguments is incompatible with this theory, it follows that in this dialogue Socrates simultaneously argues for both *p* and *not-p*.

Having explained that Ion does what he does by divine inspiration, Socrates goes on to claim that the same is true of the poets:

> For a poet is an airy thing, winged and holy, and he is not able to make poetry until he becomes inspired (ἔνθεος) and goes out of his mind and his intellect is no longer in him ... [I]t's not by mastery that they make poems or say lovely things (καλά) about their subjects ... [but] by a divine gift ... That's why the god takes their intellect away from them when he uses them as his servants ... so that we who hear should know that *they* are not the ones who speak ... [but] the god himself. (534b3–d4)[19]

As empirical evidence for these claims, Socrates adduces the sad case of Tynnichus of Chalcis – an inconsequential and obscure poet who during his whole literary career produced only one poem worth mentioning (ἀξιώσειεν μνησθῆναι) – the hymn of praise which everyone is singing (534d6–8). The existence of this poem – one of the most beautiful (κάλλιστον, 534d8) ever written – demonstrates that even the most unaccomplished poet in all Greece[20] can become the chosen mouthpiece of the gods.

Socrates' use of κάλλιστον should not go unnoticed. In employing this term – an unmistakably evaluative one – he, too, is making an implicit aesthetic judgment and hence making an implicit distinction between what the poets say and how they say it, thereby evaluating Tynnichus' poem *qua* poem.[21] According to the Socratic theory of the creative process, insofar as a poet is uninspired and composes voluntarily, he is aesthetically impotent. Such

---

[19] It is sometimes said that Plato did not hold this theory of poetic inspiration and merely interjected it as an ironical polemic with no serious philosophical content – a "polemische Ironic ohne sachlichen Gehalt" (Pohlenz, 1913: 186). See also A. E. Taylor, 1929: 40; Tigerstedt, 1969: 28; Tejera, 1984: 320; Levi, 1985: 356; and, more cautiously, Woodruff, 1983: 5, 8–9). This is vigorously contested by Grote, 1867, I: 459–60; Friedländer, 1964, I: 132–33; Schaper, 1968: 29–34; and, above all, Flashar, 1958: 20–21, according to whom Ion's earlier remark that he will be victorious in Athens "if the god wills" (ἐὰν θεὸς ἐθέλῃ, 530b4) is not mere pious clap-trap, but a phrase which has "einen tieferen Sinn" for Plato and reveals that the theory of poetic inspiration which follows is indeed his. The phrase is not uncommon in Plato (see, e.g., *Ph.* 69d6, 80d7–8, *HMa.* 286c3, *Laws* 632e7, 688e2, 739e5, and 752a8).

[20] Woodruff, 1983: 38, points out that, in spite of Socrates' low opinion of Tynnicus, he was admired by Aeschylus.

[21] Cf. *Sym.* 198b1–199b5 where "Socrates" is astounded (ἐξεπλάγη) by the beauty of Agathon's speech about love in spite of the fact that he judges its content false. Both passages count against Allen's contention, 1996: 6, that "[n]owhere in the *Ion* is it supposed that poetry possesses an autonomous value" and Grote's similar contention, 1867, I: 456–57, that Plato "takes no account" of the poet "who touches the chords of strong and diversified emotion."

poets can write poems, but none "worth mentioning." It follows that Tynnichus' single aesthetically estimable poem is an involuntary achievement – and hence not an *achievement* at all – for which he is as little deserving of praise as he is deserving of blame for his previous and subsequent failures. All credit belongs to the Muse.[22]

Socrates' theory of poetic inspiration differs radically from the prevailing view.[23] Traditionally, the poet invokes the aid of the Muse; but inspiration does not preclude conscious craftsmanship. According to the Socratic theory, on the other hand, it does; the inspired poet is not a skilled craftsman who composes voluntarily in accordance with the rational principles of his *technē*. Indeed, the inspired poet has no *technē* – and hence no skill or craftsmanship at all.[24] Insofar as he produces anything of aesthetic merit, he is the passive vehicle of the gods. Out of his mind and devoid of understanding, he literally does not know what he is talking about. Accordingly, to call a poet "inspired" is not a compliment[25] but a kind of insult. Little wonder that the poets resented Socrates' claim that they did not compose "by art or knowledge," but by divine inspiration (*Ap.* 22b8–c2), and that they engaged Meletus to prosecute him on their behalf (23e3–5).

In the *Ion*, then, the term "poet" has two distinct senses – one, descriptive; the other, normative. Descriptively, a poet is someone who writes verse voluntarily and unaided by divine inspiration. Normatively, a poet is someone who writes verse involuntarily and under the influence of divine inspiration. Although there are many poets in the descriptive sense, the class of poets who are never inspired is a null class; no one is a poet in this sense during his whole literary career – not even Tynnichus who, in spite of his otherwise dreary efforts, was on one happy occasion the inspired mouthpiece of the gods. In short, there are three classes which serve as referents of the term "poet": first, the null class of universally unin-

---

[22] Woodruff, 1983: 5, describes the Ion as "one of Plato's riddles" – a dialogue in which Socrates tries to convince his interlocutor of the importance of poetry, which is the result of divine inspiration, and of the unimportance of the poet, who is merely the passive medium through which the gods speak.

[23] Woodruff, 1983: 8, describes it as "quite startlingly new." See also Grote, 1867, I: 459–60; Stock, 1909: viii–ix; Tigerstedt, 1969; Guthrie, 1975: 206–8; Saunders, 1987: 42–43; Canto, 1989: 10–13, 47–50; and Murray, 1996: 7–9, 114.

[24] As Woodruff, 1982: 145, rightly observes, Socrates "will not allow the poets a *technē*, even of pure style. All the beauty of a poem comes from the inspiring gods." See also Murray, 1996: 10, 102.

[25] This is noticed by Stock, 1909: viii–ix; and Allen, 1996: 7.

spired poets; second, the "mixed" class of poets who are inspired on some occasions, but not on others; and third, the class of poets who are universally inspired – which is also a null class if even Homer, "the best and most divine" of the poets, occasionally had his uninspired moments – a subject on which Socrates does not express an opinion.

What is true of the poets, who interpret (ἑρμηνεύετε) the utterances of the gods, is equally true of the rhapsodes, who interpret the utterances of the poets and are, therefore, interpreters of interpreters (ἑρμηνέων ἑρμηνῆς, 535a9). So Ion's inability to recite non-Homeric poetry has a simple explanation: the necessary inspiration is lacking. Accordingly, it is not a contingent fact about inspired poets and rhapsodes that they do not know what they are talking about; given the Socratic theory of the creative process, inspiration necessarily precludes understanding. It follows that "Tynnichus is inspired" and "Tynnichus understands the poem he just composed" are logically incompatible propositions. So are "Ion is inspired" and "Ion understands the poem he just recited."

Enchanted by this image of poets and rhapsodes as inspired mouthpieces of the gods, Ion endearingly confesses that Socrates' words have touched his very soul and becomes an instant convert to the Socratic theory of poetic inspiration. But apostasy threatens when Socrates proceeds to deduce an unexpected and unwelcome implication: just as the inspired poet is out of his mind and, therefore, mad, so is the inspired rhapsode. That is, so is Ion.

Ion balks at this conclusion. Although willing to acknowledge that he is inspired when he recites, he is unwilling to concede that he is mad. Monique Canto[26] judges him rather harshly for this, describing him as "un des personnages les plus antidialectiques des dialogues platoniens" – a person who accepts Socrates' conclusions when they are flattering to himself but rejects them when they are not. But surely Ion's reluctance to concede that he is mad admits of a less negative assessment. To concede *that* would be to concede that the alleged skill for which he is so highly sought after (and so handsomely paid) is not a *skill* at all and hence not an ability resident in himself and an appropriate object of praise, but a state to which he is involuntarily reduced and for which he de-

---

[26] 1989: 21.

serves no credit. The rest of the dialogue is devoted to convincing him that this is, in fact, the case.

Asked about which things in Homer he speaks well (εὖ), Ion confidently retorts that he speaks well about everything. Asked whether "everything" includes things he knows nothing about, he squirms a bit and warily asks which things Socrates has in mind. Socrates thereupon cites a passage from the *Iliad* which contains instructions about driving a chariot and asks whether a charioteer would not be a better judge of its correctness than a doctor. Ion agrees. But this admission is a mere preliminary to a more general and far more damaging one, namely, that if a charioteer knows more about driving chariots than a doctor, then it would seem that he also knows more about it than a rhapsode. That is, he knows more about it than Ion.

Before Socrates can elicit this admission, however, he needs a further argument. It is this. Since many *technai* exist and since each has a unique function (ἔργον, 537c6) which is defined by its object – it follows that the practitioner of a particular *technē*, e.g., carpentry, cannot, by that *technē*, know the subject matter which falls under another *technē*, e.g., medicine, and, therefore, cannot make authoritative judgments about it. Ion concurs, thereby rendering himself a sitting duck for the sequel. Just as charioteers know more than Ion about driving chariots, so also doctors and fishermen know more about medicine and fishing than he. Since Ion possesses none of these *technai* or any others, it follows, by his own admission (κατὰ τὸν σὸν λόγον, 540a5–6), that he is not a competent judge of who "speaks well" about any of them. Now comes the final blow. Since Ion is not a poet either, it follows that he cannot make authoritative judgments about poetry and hence is not competent to judge that Homeric poetry is better than non-Homeric – unless, of course, he makes this judgment under the influence of divine inspiration, devoid of understanding and in a state of madness.

If Ion insists that it *is* "by art and knowledge" that he makes these judgments, he must prove it. Since so far he has not, he is either refusing to prove it (and is, therefore, behaving unjustly towards Socrates) or he cannot prove it (and is, therefore, inspired and mad when he recites). So which is it? Is Ion unjust or divine (ἄδικος ... ἢ θεῖος)? Not surprisingly, Ion opts for the latter on the ground that divinity is nobler than madness (542a7). Thus the

answer to the question: Why is Ion's skill as a rhapsode confined to
Homer? is no longer a mystery. It is only when he recites Homeric
poetry that he is inspired. Ion concedes the point.

But his concession is premature. Although he has been silenced,
he has not been refuted. Socrates' argument depends on three demonstrably false assumptions: (i) that poetry is reducible without
remainder to its factual content about the various *technai*; (ii) that
the factual accuracy of this information is the only criterion by
which poetry can be assessed; and (iii) that only the practitioners
of the relevant *technai* are competent to assess it.[27]

However, before pursuing these objections, a disclaimer is in
order. It is both anachronistic and unfair to criticize an ancient
thinker's views about a given subject by appeal to more recent
views about that subject. As Guthrie[28] rightly observes, although a
modern reader may marvel at Socrates' "total incomprehension"
of the nature of poetry, which reduces it to a handbook of technical instructions, in Plato's day poetry was in fact viewed as "primarily didactic." Guthrie's point is well taken. However, it is significant that, in making it, he finds it necessary to use the term
"primarily." Although Plato (and the Greeks generally) viewed
poetry as primarily didactic, its aesthetic dimension did not entirely escape them. If it had, the qualification "primarily" would
have been superfluous. Ion and Socrates do indeed look to poetry
for technical instructions about the various *technai*, but they also
look to it for entertainment and delight. That this is so is borne
out by the fact that Socrates heaps high praise on Tynnichus' solitary poetic achievement and describes it as one of our most beautiful (κάλλιστον) poems and one which everyone is singing. People
do not usually sing technical instructions.

Although Ion fails to avail himself of it, his earlier implicit distinction between speaking correctly (ὀρθῶς) and speaking well (εὖ),
provides him with a reply to this argument and the (even by ancient standards) excessively narrow view of poetry on which it is
based. Confronted with Socrates' dilemma – either you are unjust
or you are divine – Ion is not logically compelled to opt for the
latter and to embrace the Socratic theory of poetic inspiration.
The dilemma is a false one. Several replies are open to him.

First, he could have invoked his earlier implicit distinction

---

[27] See Murray, 1996: 106.   [28] 1975: 205.

between content and style, and pointed out that although he is
neither a diviner nor a mathematician nor a doctor, and hence
incapable of making comparative *substantive* judgments about divination, mathematics, and medicine, that does not prevent him
from making comparative *aesthetic* judgments about passages in
which Homer talks about these *technai*. To be a competent judge
of Homeric poetry, which contains technical instructions about
the various *technai*, does not require that one be a practitioner of
those *technai*. Ion's claim that his skill as a rhapsode is confined to
Homer is problematic only if it is interpreted in light of Socratic
doctrine. There is nothing suspect about the ability to discourse
authoritatively about a single author. A specialist in Shakespeare
at a modern university would not be denied tenure on the ground
that his expertise does not extend to other dramatists (Elizabethan
and otherwise) who "talk about the same things." Contrary to
what Socrates implies, there is no Art-of-Poetry-in-the-Abstract,
mastery of which qualifies one as an expert about all poets and
ignorance of which disqualifies one as an expert about any.[29]
Second, Ion could have pointed out that Socrates' contention that
only practitioners of a *technē* are equipped to make authoritative
judgments about it is simply false. Possessing a *technē* is not a necessary condition for speaking authoritatively about it. Dramatic
and musical expertise are cases in point. Many teachers and critics
are uncannily adept at detecting faults in (and improving) the performances of actors and instrumentalists far more gifted than
themselves. Nor is it a sufficient condition. Many able performers
are reduced to incoherent stammering when called upon to explain how they do what they do. Finally, Ion could have pointed
out that although he has no idea how he sends his audiences into
raptures when (but only when) he recites Homeric poetry, from
the mere fact that he cannot explain how he does it (or why he
cannot do it when he recites non-Homeric poetry), it does not
follow that his ability to do so can only be explained by tracing it
to some causal agent other than himself – namely, the Muse. And
it certainly does not follow that he must be mad.

Ion denies that he is mad: not because he is intellectually arro-

---

[29] Kahn, 1996: 109–10, is also skeptical about Socrates' "one-to-one mapping principle,"
according to which anyone who knows the art of poetry can discourse authoritatively
about all poets because "the whole thing is poetry."

gant and impervious to argumentation, but because he knows perfectly well that he has a *technē* – that he possesses a specifiable and
highly developed set of rhetorical and dramatic skills which enable
him to affect his audiences deeply and *by design*. Socrates' contention that his ability to produce these effects is not traceable to an
ability resident within himself is at odds with his experience as a
rhapsode.[30] That this is so is borne out by his tell-tale remark that
he is carried away by his own recitations and overcome by the
same emotions that course through his hearers – albeit not so
overcome that he forgets that the more they weep over his tales of
woe, the more he laughs over his soaring profits (535c4–e6). Ion
knows exactly what he is doing and how he does it.

The fact that he does not affect his audiences in the same way
and to the same degree when he recites non-Homeric poetry is
easily explained. Like most people called upon to do things in
which they have no interest, Ion's heart is not in it and his performance is perfunctory and ineffectual. Far from being an impenetrable mystery, this is one of the commonplaces of human experience. Only a person determined to quibble and to find fault – only
a Socrates – could fail to understand it and, having failed, relegate
rhapsodes to the status of opportunistic charlatans devoid of all
understanding and account for their genuine successes in such a
preposterous way. The contention that rhapsodes and poets are
devoid of all intelligence and skill and merely passive vehicles of
the gods awaiting the necessary "inspiration" bespeaks an extraordinarily mechanical understanding of a skill and an adolescent,
moonstruck view of the creative process. A *Divine Comedy* or a
"Hammerklavier" Sonata does not trickle effortlessly from the
pen as the involuntary response to an externally applied divine
stimulus. As is obvious from the notebooks of countless poets,
composers, and artists, what we loosely call "art" is hard work
which involves meticulous planning, agonizing trial-and-error,
and incessant rethinking. And so does its interpretation.

It is often said[31] that Plato portrays Ion as a simpleton so that
Socrates can make sport of him. But this is not borne out by the
philosophical content of the dialogue. Socrates does not take Ion
seriously *qua* Ion, but he takes him very seriously *qua* rhapsode,

---

[30] As has been pointed out by Méron, 1979: 163, n. 20; and Canto, 1989: 142, n. 29.
[31] See, e.g., Elias, 1984: 5.

that is, *qua* mouthpiece of the gods. Plato portrays Ion as a simpleton: not to provide Socrates with entertainment, but to enhance the plausibility of the Socratic theory of poetic inspiration. A more intelligent rhapsode would have rendered it less plausible. What is needed is someone exactly like Ion – a rhapsode indisputably capable of stirring his audiences to the depths, but utterly incapable of explaining how he does it. Socrates never doubts Ion's competence as a rhapsode; he is concerned solely with its nature and source. By accentuating Ion's intellectual ineptness before presenting the theory of poetic inspiration, Plato prepares the reader for it.

It is easy to poke fun at Ion, and few commentators have resisted the temptation.[32] However, I want to conclude this chapter on a different note. Instead of pointlessly (and cruelly) maligning an admittedly incompetent interlocutor, I will pose a series of questions. Has Socrates cared for Ion's soul? Has he really tried to benefit and to improve him? Has he argued carefully, cogently, and on a level that Ion might reasonably be expected to understand? Is Ion really persuaded by Socrates' arguments? Does he really believe that he recites Homeric poetry under the influence of divine inspiration? Does he opt for being divine out of conviction or merely out of embarrassment and the desire to save face? Does he sincerely assent to the premises by which Socrates generates (or seems to generate) these conclusions? Does Socrates care whether he sincerely assents? Or whether his critique of poets and rhapsodes has registered? Does Ion depart a better man? Or a more modest rhapsode?

Since Ion is not an actually existing person, these are questions without answers. But insofar as fictional characters may be credited with imaginative futures, such questions have a restricted legitimacy and enable us to form a correspondingly imaginative estimate of the efficacy of the Socratic elenchus. In the *Ion* it has none.

---

[32] Most recently Murray, 1996: 98: "Ion ... is so stupid that he is not worth attacking"; and Kahn, 1996: 113: Socrates has "clearly won the argument, but his victory cannot be logically consummated because of the stubborn obtuseness of Ion."

CHAPTER 5

Hippias

With the dubious exception of Alcibiades,[1] Hippias is the only Socratic interlocutor with two dialogues named after him: the *Hippias Major* and the *Hippias Minor*. Since the former is rejected as inauthentic by some[2] and accepted but classified as transitional (rather than early) by others,[3] except for a few biographical details, this chapter will be confined to the latter.

Hippias is a sophist.[4] That, of course, is not sufficient to render him morally suspect and the enemy of virtue. Although traditional commentators tended to view the sophists as an undifferentiated entity and to portray them as intellectually inconsequential and even as morally corrupt, this unduly negative assessment is gradually being abandoned in favor of a more just estimate.[5] The possessors of a wide range of knowledge and an impressive array of skills, they answered to a perceived educational and cultural need and commanded high fees[6] – a policy much deplored by Plato's

---

[1] The *Alcibiades I* and *II* have had a strange history. Included in the third tetralogy of the Thrasyllean canon and regarded as authentic until the late nineteenth century, they were pronounced spurious by Schleiermacher, 1836: 328–36. Subsequent Platonic scholarship has largely endorsed his verdict.

[2] E.g., Thesleff, 1976: 105–17; Leggewie, 1978: 71–72; Kahn, 1985, and 1996: 37, n. 3; and Figal, 1995: 19–20.

[3] E.g., Irwin, 1977: 291, n. 33, and (more cautiously) 1995: 12; Vlastos, 1983a: 27, n. 2, 1991: 46–47, and 1994: 71, n. 14; and McPherran, 1996: 18, n. 46.

[4] The four so-called "older" sophists were all non-Greek: Hippias came from Elis, Protagoras from Abdera, Prodicus from Ceos, and Gorgias from Leontini. Before acquiring its pejorative connotations – a trend encouraged (and perhaps initiated) by Plato – the term "sophist" (σοφιστής) simply meant "wise man."

[5] For more sympathetic and appreciative assessments of the sophists, see the pioneering discussions of Sidgwick, 1872: 288–307, and 1874: 66–80; and Grote, 1888, VII: 346–99, according to whom Plato's "wholesale" condemnation of the sophists "betrays itself as the offspring ... of systematic peculiarity of vision, the prejudice of a great and able mind" (394–95). For more recent studies, see Havelock, 1957; Kerferd, 1981; Rankin, 1983; Vickers, 1988; and de Romilly, 1992.

[6] Protagoras' annual income allegedly surpassed that of Phidias and any other ten sculptors combined (*M.* 91d2–5), and Gorgias and Prodicus reportedly made more money than the practitioners of any other *technai* (*HMa.* 282b4–d5).

Socrates. Lovers of wisdom should not be lovers of gain.[7] But while Socrates never tires of faulting them for this,[8] he does not condemn the sophists *en bloc*; on the contrary, his attitude towards and treatment of them varies considerably. Unfailingly deferential towards Prodicus, uncharacteristically gentle with Gorgias, and alternately playful and rough with Protagoras, he is very hard on Hippias.[9]

In addition to being a sophist, Hippias is Elis' most distinguished foreign ambassador; and his earnings on these diplomatic missions exceed those of any other two sophists Socrates may care to name (*HMa.* 282d6–e8). Although much younger than his colleagues, he surpassed them in both range and depth. His knowledge, bordering on the encyclopaedic, included mathematics, mnemonics, music, rhetoric, grammar, astronomy, genealogy, mythology, and the history of antiquity. Possessed of a phenomenal memory, he can repeat a list of fifty words upon hearing it once, and boasts that he can answer any question he is asked. As if that were not enough, he composes tragedies and epics, and even makes his own clothes.[10]

If Plato's portrayal is accurate, Hippias was not notable for his modesty. He is constantly flaunting his knowledge and boasting about his achievements. Hippias is not only a braggart, he is also something of an exhibitionist – the sort of person who is forever praising his own abilities and, what is worse, forever threatening to display them. Unlike the less versatile and more modest Ion, who acknowledges that his skill as a rhapsode is confined to Homer, Hippias goes out of his way to let everyone know that he can recite *any* poet (*HMi.* 363c7–d4). His greatest claim to fame is his linguistic virtuosity which enables him to stage magnificent

[7] The Xenophontic Socrates has additional objections to charging fees: wisdom should be freely shared, especially among friends; to impart it only upon being solicited by a prospective client with ready cash is a kind of intellectual prostitution (*Mem.* 1.2.6–8, 1.5.6, 1.6.5, 1.6.13). Xenophon also reports that Antiphon traced Socrates' self-induced poverty, shabby wardrobe, and unappetizing cuisine to his inexplicable refusal to charge a fee (1.6.2–3).
[8] Harrison, 1964: 191, n. 44, has collected thirty-one passages from the Platonic corpus.
[9] Especially in the *Hippias Major* where Woodruff describes his treatment of Hippias as "remarkably savage" (1982: 127).
[10] The historical Hippias (*circa* 470–395) was far from being an empty showman. In addition to his intellectual achievements, he was a doxographer and the author of several treatises. Kerferd, 1981: 47–49; and de Romilly, 1992: 114–15, 181–82, describe him as a thinker of some consequence; and Guthrie, 1971a: 284, asserts that he "has better claims [than most sophists] to be accepted as a serious ethical thinker." It is hard to believe that Plato would have agreed.

epideictic displays – not only in Athens, where he is an annual sellout, but throughout the Greek world. Like many self-impressed people, he is monumentally imperceptive, regally accepting Socrates' mock flattery and ostentatiously confiding that he has yet to meet his superior at anything.

Hippias' self-congratulatory tendencies have repelled many readers. A. E. Taylor[11] describes him as "childishly conceited," Grote[12] thinks his "silliness and presumption" both invite and excuse the "derisory sting" of Socrates' comments, Woodruff[13] deplores the "empty core under [his] multifaceted veneer," Saunders[14] judges him "stupid and vain," and Allen[15] disparages him as "a professor who in his omniscience is unable to follow a Socratic argument." These somewhat churlish complaints are balanced by Guthrie's[16] characteristically humane remark that, although Hippias is "bombastic, humourless and thick-skinned," he is also a man of "unsuspecting innocence" and someone "with whom it would be difficult to be angry."

A dramatic dialogue and, by common consensus, one of Plato's earliest works,[17] the _Hippias Minor_ begins _in medias res_. Hippias has just completed an epideictic display and Eudicus, the promoter of the event, is eager to know what Socrates thinks of it. Characteristically, Socrates offers no assessment; he would, however, like to ask a few questions. Recalling Eudicus' father's remark that just as the _Iliad_ is a finer poem than the _Odyssey_, so also Achilles is a finer man than Odysseus, Socrates would like to know what Hippias thinks: which of the two is better (ἀμείνω)? and in what respect (κατὰ τί, 364b4–5)?

Hippias confidently replies that, of the heroes who sailed to Troy, Achilles is the best (ἄριστον), Nestor is the wisest (σοφώτατον), and Odysseus is the wiliest (πολυτροπώτατον, 364c3–7).[18]

---

[11] 1929: 29.
[12] 1867, I: 387.
[13] 1982: xii. He is more sympathetic later (see 127–29).
[14] 1987: 215.
[15] 1996: 25.
[16] 1971a: 281–82.
[17] Friedländer, 1964, II: 146, thinks that its composition predates the death of Socrates on the ground that Plato would not have portrayed his mentor so unflatteringly after his death. So, too, Ritter, 1933: 39, n. 1.
[18] The superlative of πολύτροπος – a term with multiple meanings ranging from the comparatively neutral "versatile," "resourceful," and "complex," to the more pejorative "cunning" and "wily."

When Socrates suggests that it is not Odysseus but Achilles who is the most wily, Hippias demurs on the ground that Achilles is the most simple (ἀπλούστατος), that is, the most straightforward and honest of men. In support of this contention, he cites a passage from the *Iliad* in which Achilles expresses strong disapproval of people who think one thing but say another, thereby denouncing liars; in short, Achilles is simple and true whereas Odysseus is wily and false (365b3–5).

Socrates finds this claim puzzling because it implies that the true man (ὁ ἀληθής) is different from the false (ὁ ψευδής), and he wonders whether that was really Homer's view. Hippias curtly assures him that it was; he adds that it is his view too. But Socrates is still unconvinced: *Is* the true man different from the false? Since it is impossible to interrogate Homer, he wonders whether Hippias would be willing to answer on his behalf? Hippias agrees.[19]

Before proceeding further, it is worth savoring the details of this carefully prepared tableau. Having been prevailed upon by Eudicus, after hours and free of charge, to answer Socrates' questions, the intellectually gifted but dialectically inept Hippias has inadvertently allowed himself to be drawn into a discussion for which his past experience has not prepared him. More accustomed to being "effective" than to being precise and more adept at discoursing at length and without interruption than at answering a series of specific questions which require him to explain exactly what he means, he is about to make his inauspicious debut as a Socratic interlocutor. Socrates palpably relishes the prospect. Unlike most moralists, for whom arrogance and overconfidence are intellectual vices to be rebuked and uprooted, Socrates welcomes them because they provide him with a polemical advantage which can be further exploited by the lethal combination of mock flattery and ironic self-deprecation. Like a wave that crests before breaking on the shore, arrogance and overconfidence provide the psychological momentum that propels the interlocutor into the discussion. Accordingly, they should not be rebuked but encouraged. The interlocutor must believe that he can provide Socrates with desperately needed instruction and thereby serve as his intellectual benefactor. The minute he begins to see through the ironic

---

[19] The shift from the opinion of a poet to that of an interlocutor who is in agreement with him is a common Socratic move. See *Pr.* 347e1–348a7 and *R.* 331d4–5.

facade, Socrates' task becomes harder; for he must then constantly
find new ways to prevent his interlocutor from trying to extricate
himself from the discussion. The psychologically irresistible strategy of encouraging him to spread his wisdom abroad is part of
Socrates' habitual concealment of purpose; he rarely divulges in
advance that his purpose is not to learn from his interlocutor, but
to refute him. The shock-value of the elenchus is an essential
ingredient.

Few Socratic interlocutors are as shocked as Hippias. Having
confidently asserted that the simple and true Achilles is better than
the wily and false Odysseus and that the true man is different from
the false, the walking encyclopaedia who can answer any question
he is asked suddenly finds himself burdened with two scandalously
paradoxical theses: (i) the true man is not different from the false,
they are one and the same (369b3–7); and (ii) the voluntary wrongdoer is better than the involuntary one (372d3–7).

Socrates deduces the first thesis as follows. Asked whether the
false, like the sick, are powerless to act or whether they have
power (δύναμις) to do things, Hippias replies that they have power
to do many things – in particular, to lie and to deceive others
(365d7–8). Furthermore, they deceive, not by foolishness, but by a
kind of intelligence (φρονήσεώς τινος). In short, the false know
(ἐπίστανται) what they are doing and are, therefore, wise in the
things about which they are false, that is they are wise at deception (365e6–10). Socrates thereupon defines "the false man" as
"the man who is intelligent and capable of speaking falsely"
(366b4–5). Hippias accepts the definition. He also agrees that
anyone who is ignorant and lacks this capacity cannot be false,
and that anyone who is intelligent and has it can do whatever he
wishes whenever he wishes. For example, being an able mathematician, Hippias is best qualified to speak truly about mathematics.
But for that very reason he is also best qualified to speak falsely
about it. A less able person might wish to speak falsely, but inadvertently speak truly. But if that is true, as Hippias agrees, then
the true man is not better than the false; they are one and the
same (367c7–d2).

This scandalously paradoxical thesis is then formulated in full
generality: the true and false man are one and the same – not only
in mathematics, but also in geometry, astronomy, and every other
science. Socrates thereupon challenges Hippias to find a single ex-

ception to this thesis and, with a rare burst of conviction, assures him in advance that he never will: "[I]f what I say is true" (εἰ δ' ἐγὼ ἀληθῆ λέγω, 369a4–5),[20] there are no exceptions. But if the true and false man are one and the same, then Achilles is not better than Odysseus: if Odysseus is false, he is also true; and if Achilles is true, he is also false (369b3–7).

Hippias can hardly believe his ears and vehemently protests:

Oh, Socrates! You're always weaving arguments of this kind. You pick out whatever is the most difficult part of the argument, and fasten on to it in minute detail, and don't dispute about the whole subject under discussion. (369b8–c2)[21]

His complaint is well founded. This argument has often been judged fallacious and even prompted charges of deliberate sophistry.[22]

But we need not become embroiled in polemical dispute. Even if the argument is not fallacious, it is unsound. "False man" does

---

[20] *Pace* Stokes, 1986: 5–7, Socrates here unambiguously advances an assertion himself.

[21] Woodruff, 1982: 85, and Rankin, 1983: 54–55, think that, in registering this protest, Hippias is merely expressing his preference for epideictic discourse which does not fasten upon some triviality (σμικρόν) but grapples with issues as a whole (ὅλῳ ... τῷ πράγματι, 369c1–2). However, a parallel passage in the *Hippias Major* suggests that his objection cuts deeper: "But Socrates, *you* don't look at the entirety of things, nor do the people you're used to talking with. You people knock away at the fine and the other beings by taking each separately and cutting it up with words. Because of that you don't realize how great they are – naturally continuous bodies of being. And now you're so far from realizing it that you think there's some attribute or being (τι ἢ πάθος ἢ οὐσίαν) that is true of these both but not of each, or of each but not of both. That's how unreasonably and unobservantly and foolishly and uncomprehendingly you operate" (*HMa.* 301b2–c3). See also *Pr.* 337c7–d1 where Hippias exhorts everyone to stop their petty bickering and to remember that they are all akin (συγγενεῖς) by nature, not by law, and that like resembles like by nature (τὸ ὅμοιον ... τῷ ὁμοίῳ φύσει συγγενές ἐστιν). Insofar as this passage suggests that all beings are naturally continuous and interconnected, it bespeaks an explicit and seriously held ontology. However, Socrates refuses to take Hippias' position seriously; on the contrary, he parodies it and construes it as a denial of the fact that Hippias and he are distinct individuals (*HMa.* 301d5–e8).

[22] According to Mulhern, 1968: 283–88, πολύτροπος is a *dunamis*-term which denotes a person's capacity to behave in a certain way, whereas ψευδής is a *tropos*-term which denotes a person's character (τρόπος) and typical behavior; in saying that Odysseus is false, Hippias does not mean that he is capable of lying, but that he is a liar. Mulhern argues that Socrates starts out with the *tropos*-sense of ψευδής and defines "the false" as "those who *speak* falsely" but later shifts to a *dunamis*-sense and redefines "the false" as "anyone who is capable of speaking falsely," thereby fallaciously deriving the paradoxical conclusion that the true and false man are the same by equivocation. See also Shorey, 1933: 86–87, 89–90; Hoerber, 1962: 121–31; Sprague, 1962: 67–70; and Kahn, 1996: 114. For a sustained critique of Mulhern's analysis, see Weiss, 1981: 289–90, according to whom Socrates argues solely from the *dunamis*-sense of ψευδής.

not mean "someone *capable* of speaking falsely." If it did, then the mere capacity to lie would be a sufficient condition for being a false man, and even the most scrupulously honest person, insofar as he has this capacity, would be a false man – which is absurd. To call someone a false man is not to say that he is *capable* of lying; it is to say that he *is* a liar.[23] The liar does not just *say* what is false; he *intends* to say what is false and does so *knowing* it to be false. Not only does he fail to speak the truth; he is untruth*ful*. Unlike the capacity to lie, which is a logically necessary condition that must be satisfied by any prospective liar, being a liar is a contingently true description of those who have the capacity and elect to exercise it. The class of those who are false is not coextensive with the class of those who are capable of being false.

It is, of course, true that knowledge is a necessary condition for lying confidently and successfully. But knowledge of what? According to Socrates, the confident and successful liar must have knowledge of that about which he speaks falsely; otherwise, he might inadvertently speak truly. In short, if one is confidently and successfully to say what is false, one must know what is true. But although this is so in some cases, there are many others in which it is not. The fact that I do not know Jill's telephone number does not prevent me from lying confidently and successfully if asked for it. I need only give out my own number or that of a friend. To lie about Jill's number, I need not know *it*; I need only know that the number I give out is *not* it. Provided that I know someone's telephone number, and my questioner does not know whose it is, I can lie about Jill's number as confidently and successfully as someone who does know it. So long as these conditions are satisfied, I need not worry about inadvertently disclosing her number and thereby inadvertently speaking truly. The examples could be multiplied indefinitely.

Even if, intending to lie, I panic and make up a number on the spot which by an incredible stroke of bad luck turns out to be Jill's, thereby inadvertently saying what is true, I am not thereby transformed into a "true man." Just as the false man does not just *say* what is false but *intends* to say what is false and does so *knowing*

---

[23] Or at least that he "is not what he pretends to be – that he is some kind of fake" (Vlastos, 1991: 277). The mistake was first detected by Aristotle who, criticizing this very argument, observes that "being false" does not consist in the capacity (ἐν τῇ δυνάμει), but in the choice (ἐν τῇ προαιρέσει), to speak falsely (*E.N.* 1127b12–13; and *Meta.* 1025a5–13).

it to be false, so also the true man does not just *say* what is true but *intends* to say what is true and speaks *believing* that what he says is true. Although one can inadvertently *say* what is true, one cannot inadvertently be truth*ful*. Unlike the former, which is an involuntary act performed in the mistaken belief that one is lying, the latter is a voluntary speech-act performed with the intention of being truthful.

Socrates is also mistaken in thinking that having the capacity to speak falsely entails that one is skilled (ἔμπειρος) at doing so. Like all forms of deception, lying is a social activity. It requires a deceiver (someone whose intention it is to deceive) and a deceivee (someone who is deceived). The true, i.e., truthful, man has no such intention. Nor would he be a good liar if he did.[24] It is not as if the true and false man are equally skilled at speaking falsely – and hence "the same" in that respect – and differ only in that the former elects not to do so. Unless "being skilled at speaking falsely" is defined in terms of a purely cognitive capacity – knowing the truth – in complete isolation from the situations in which, the persons to which, the intentions with which, and the characters of the persons by which those propositions are uttered, the true and false man cannot be said to have a common skill.

Unable to diagnose what is wrong with Socrates' argument but rightly rejecting its paradoxical conclusion, Hippias reaffirms his original thesis that Achilles is better than Odysseus and defends it by producing textual evidence from the *Iliad* in which Homer portrays the former as truthful and free of falsehood and the latter as wily and deceptive. Socrates feigns admiration for Hippias' exegetical prowess and momentarily debates him on his own turf by producing several counterexamples based on other passages from the *Iliad* in which it is not Odysseus but Achilles who is portrayed as wily and false. Hippias is unimpressed and accuses Socrates of being a careless reader of texts. What these passages actually show is something very different: unlike Odysseus, who speaks falsely voluntarily and by design (ἑκών τε καὶ ἐξ ἐπιβουλῆς), Achilles does so involuntarily (οὐκ ἐξ ἐπιβουλῆς ... ἀλλ᾽ ἄκων, 370e5–9) and because he is compelled by circumstances.

---

[24] As Vlastos, 1991: 277, n. 134, rightly points out, it is "surely false that, in general, truthful people are *skilled* at speaking falsely ... Considerable talent and much practice would be required to become a skillful liar."

Socrates has a ready reply: in that case, Odysseus *is* the better man; for, as the foregoing argument has shown, the voluntary liar is better than the involuntary one. At this point, Hippias is reduced to wondering out loud: How can that be true? Do not the laws (and people generally) make allowances for involuntary wrongdoing?

Of all the claims advanced by the interlocutors in the early dialogues, we expect Socrates to endorse this one. For he appeals to the same principle himself at *Ap.* 26a1–7 where he assures Meletus that any wrongdoing of which he may have been guilty was involuntary and thereupon reminds him that, according to both law and popular opinion, involuntary wrongdoers should not be punished, but admonished and instructed. However, he does not endorse it. Unlike Hippias and people generally, who believe that the involuntary wrongdoer is better than the voluntary one, Socrates claims to hold the opposite opinion (372d3–7). This unusually flagrant violation of the sincere assent requirement[25] is all the more culpable because in this passage Socrates not only fails to say what he believes, but says what he does *not* believe. Having done so, he adds that sometimes the popular view seems more plausible; in fact, he is constantly vacillating between the two and likens his present confusion to a fit brought on by the foregoing argument. Would Hippias be kind enough to cure his soul of ignorance by answering a few more questions?

Suspecting that Hippias' enthusiasm is waning, Socrates urges Eudicus to remind him of his earlier promise to answer any question he was asked. Disinclined to continue but perceiving that his reputation is on the line, Hippias reluctantly agrees.

To persuade Hippias that the voluntary wrongdoer is better than the involuntary one, Socrates advances the following argument (373c9–375c3):

(i)   There are good and bad runners.
(ii) Since rapidity is good and slowness evil, he who runs rapidly runs well and he who runs slowly runs badly.
(iii) He who runs slowly voluntarily is better (ἀμείνων) *qua* runner than he who runs slowly involuntarily.
(iv) Since running is a kind of doing and since doing is a kind of performing, he who runs badly performs badly and shamefully.

---

[25] The violation is noticed by Kahn, 1996: 118.

(v)   He who runs badly runs slowly.

(vi)   It follows that the good runner performs these bad actions voluntarily and the bad one involuntarily.

(vii) It also follows that he who runs badly voluntarily is better than he who does so unintentionally, and the same is true of every other activity.

(viii) Therefore in every activity he who errs voluntarily is better than he who does so involuntarily.

Hippias assents to each premise, but balks at the conclusion: it is monstrous (δεινόν) to say that voluntary wrongdoing is the mark of the good man and involuntary wrongdoing the mark of the bad (375d3–4). Socrates is unmoved: if a conclusion follows from an agreed-upon set of premises, it cannot be rejected simply because it is unwelcome. And the conclusion just arrived at certainly seems to follow from what had been said (ἐκ τῶν εἰρημένων, 375d5).

Since Hippias is still unpersuaded, Socrates must try again. His final argument – 375d8–376b6 – is as follows:

(i)   Justice is either a kind of capacity (δύναμίς τις) or knowledge (ἐπιστήμη) or both.

(ii)   If it is the former, then the more capable soul is more just; and if it is the latter, then the wiser soul is more just and the ignorant soul is more unjust.

(iii)   If justice is both a kind of capacity and knowledge, then the soul which has both is more just and the soul which has only one is more unjust.

(iv)   The more capable and wiser soul is the better soul and has greater capacity to do what is good or shameful.

(v)   When a soul does what is shameful, it does so voluntarily (ἑκοῦσα) by capacity or art (διὰ δύναμιν καὶ τέχνην) – or both – which are attributes of justice.

(vi)   Since to do injustice is to do evil and since to refrain from injustice is to do good, insofar as the more capable and better soul does what is just, it does so voluntarily; and insofar as the less capable and worse soul does what is just, it does so involuntarily.

(vii) Since the good man has a good soul and the bad man has a bad one, insofar as the good man does what is unjust, he does so voluntarily whereas the bad man does so involuntarily.

(viii) Hence he who errs voluntarily and does what is shameful and unjust – if there is such a man – is the good man.

Hippias again assents to each premise, but balks at the conclusion. He cannot agree with Socrates that the voluntary wrongdoer is the good man – a monstrous (δεινόν) idea, in his opinion. Nor can Socrates agree with himself (376b8).[26] Yet that seems to be the necessary (ἀναγκαῖον) conclusion.

What shall we say about this elusive little dialogue? Leaving aside the outraged Apelt, who called it "a kind of apology for sin,"[27] many commentators[28] think the interpretive key lies in the qualification "if there is such a man" (376b5–6). According to them, Socrates does not really believe that the voluntary wrong-doer is the good – much less the better – man; the argument is a *reductio ad absurdum* of the assumption that virtue is a *technē*. The more cautious Irwin and Kahn think the argument is intended to show either that virtue is not a *technē* or that it is a *technē* "unlike every other"[29] or "of quite an unusual sort"[30] in that its practi-tioners never voluntarily misuse it.[31] Since the end it promotes – happiness – is one which everyone necessarily wants, the misuse of the *technē* of virtue is psychologically impossible.[32] In short Soc-rates' psychological eudaemonism – the doctrine that everyone necessarily desires happiness – insures that voluntary wrongdoing will never occur. In short, Socrates' argument is a *reductio ad ab-surdum* intended to show that a denial of the so-called "Socratic paradox"[33] leads to the scandalous conclusion that the voluntary

---

[26] Interestingly, Xenophon's Socrates espouses the same view without batting an eyelash, and his interlocutor (Euthydemus) instantly concurs (*Mem.* 4.2.19–20).

[27] "[E]ine Art Apologie der Sünde" (1912: 226–27).

[28] Among them, Gomperz, 1905, II: 293–96; Pohlenz, 1913: 65; A. E. Taylor, 1929: 37–38; Shorey, 1933: 86–87; Gould, 1955: 41–43; Hoerber, 1962: 128; Sprague, 1962: 76; Fried-länder, 1964, II: 144; O'Brien, 1967: 104–7; Irwin, 1995: 69–70; and Allen, 1996: 25.

[29] Irwin, 1995: 69.

[30] Kahn, 1996: 118. See also Saunders, 1987: 268–69.

[31] See Aristotle (*Meta.* 1048a7–11), according to whom virtue is not a *technē*, since every *technē* is a "capacity for contraries" and, therefore, admits of misuse – something which is not true of virtue.

[32] Friedländer, 1964, II: 144, thinks Socrates' argument shows that the proposition "Volun-tary wrongdoers are better than involuntary ones" is self-contradictory and, therefore, that the voluntary misuse of the *technē* of virtue is logically impossible.

[33] By the "Socratic paradox," I mean (what Santas, 1979: 190, calls) "the moral paradox," i.e., the Socratic doctrine that "if a man has knowledge of what is virtuous and *also* knowledge that it is always better for one to do what is virtuous, then he will always (so long as he has this knowledge and virtuous behavior is in his power) behave virtuously" –

wrongdoer is better than the involuntary one – a conclusion which is avoided by denying that there is such a man.[34]

Although this interpretation is quite plausible in some respects, it is quite implausible in others. Its proponents too readily assume that the thesis that no one errs voluntarily – and that all wrong-doing is, therefore, involuntary – are already authentic, fully for-mulated, and self-consciously held Socratic doctrines in the *Hippias Minor* – one of Plato's earliest works. The assumption can (and should) be challenged. For one thing, the so-called "prudential paradox," that is, the thesis that everyone necessarily desires hap-piness, on which the so-called "moral paradox" depends, is never mentioned in the *Hippias Minor*. In fact, it is not until the *Euthydemus* – a dialogue variously classified as "transitional,"[35] "late-early,"[36] and "pre-middle"[37] – that Socrates unambiguously asserts that everyone wishes to prosper (εὖ πράττειν, 278e3–279a1), that is, to be happy. And it is not until the *Meno* that he unambiguously asserts that no one desires evil recognized as such, but only because he has mistakenly judged it to be good (77b6–78b2).

To be sure, at *Ap.* 37a5–6 Socrates emphatically declares that *he* never voluntarily wronged anyone. But the meaning of this asser-tion should not be divorced from its context. Socrates is on trial for his life. In saying this, he is proclaiming his own innocence, not advancing a philosophical thesis about human conduct univer-sally. Indeed, if we attend closely to what he says when his philo-sophical guard is down, we discover that he has grave doubts about other people. At *Ap.* 41d7–e1 he asserts that his accusers are morally blameworthy (ἄξιον μέμφεσθαι) for trying to harm him – apparently a blatant case of voluntary wrongdoing, for otherwise

---

a paradox which is distinct from and presupposes (what Santas calls) "the prudential paradox," i.e., the Socratic doctrine that men desire only good things, the corollary of which is that no one does what is evil knowing it to be evil, i.e., that all wrongdoing is involuntary. Unlike most commentators, who think that, for Socrates, knowledge of what is virtuous is both necessary and sufficient for virtuous conduct, Santas thinks that it is only a necessary condition; what is sufficient for virtuous conduct is not simply knowl-edge of what is virtuous, but knowledge of what is virtuous *in conjunction with* the univer-sal desire for happiness.

[34] Horneffer, 1904: 6–7, thinks that the argument of the *Hippias Minor* is a (Platonic) refuta-tion of the (Socratic) doctrine that virtue is knowledge. He finds a similar refutation of Socratic intellectualism in the *Laches*.

[35] Vlastos, 1983a: 27, n. 2, 1991: 46–47, and 1994: 71, n. 14.

[36] Guthrie, 1975: 266.

[37] Kahn, 1992: 38.

they would not be blameworthy. And at *G.* 480e5–481b1 he implicitly allows for the possibility of voluntary wrongdoing by presenting Polus with the hypothetical example of a person whose duty it is to harm someone for having wronged someone else and suggests that the most effective way of doing so would be by preventing the wrongdoer from coming to trial and being punished, thereby preventing him from being purged of wrongdoing and improved. He adds that should this prove to be impossible, the next best thing would be to arrange for the wrongdoer's escape so that, unpunished and unpurged of his evil, he will live a long and miserable life. One would be hard pressed to think of a more paradigmatic example of voluntary wrongdoing. Interestingly, at *Cr.* 49a4–5 Socrates asks Crito *whether* we should ever do wrong voluntarily – a pointless question if voluntary wrongdoing is psychologically (not to mention logically) impossible – and he proceeds to argue that we should not – thereby again implying that voluntary wrongdoing is possible. Why prohibit the psychologically (or the logically) impossible and fortify the prohibition with an argument? All this (by no means exhaustive) textual evidence suggests that the thesis that no one errs voluntarily – and that all wrongdoing is, therefore, involuntary – are not already authentic, fully formulated, and self-consciously held Socratic doctrines in the *Hippias Minor*, but rather doctrines at which Plato arrived later, gradually, and in conjunction with a more sophisticated moral psychology as a hard-earned solution to the problem posed in that dialogue.

Grote was one of the first to sponsor this view. Speaking of Hippias' unwillingness to draw the (apparently) required inference, he says:

If there be any argument, the process of which seems indisputable, while its conclusion contradicts, or seems to contradict, what is known upon other evidence – the full and patient analysis of that argument is indispensable, before you can become master of the truth and able to defend it. Until you have gone through such analysis, your mind must remain in that state of confusion which is indicated by Sokrates at the end of the Lesser Hippias.[38]

Grote thereupon faults Hippias: not only for affirming the premises of Socrates' argument and denying its conclusion, but also (and

---

[38] 1867, I: 397.

more fundamentally) for not being perplexed by Socrates' arguments and for not being dissatisfied with the outcome of the whole discussion. Instead of allowing himself to experience the full impact of *aporia* by taking the argument seriously, Hippias merely disagrees with its conclusion, thereby betraying that he is unwilling to acknowledge his own confusion – one of the "enemies [with which] the Searcher for truth must contend [and] the stimulus provocative of farther intellectual effort."[39] Grote does not deny that Socrates' arguments are problematic; on the contrary, he bluntly asserts that had Socrates' reasoning been put into the mouth of Hippias, most readers would dismiss the dialogue as "a tissue of sophistry."[40] However, since everything which in the mouth of Hippias would have been blatant sophistry is advanced by Socrates, with Hippias resisting every step of the way, a different assessment is in order. And Grote provides it: the *Hippias Minor* does not refute error; it documents confusion and records Socrates' inability to dispel it. In this dialogue, it is Socrates who is confused, and his confusion and resultant vacillation are not feigned, but real.[41]

It would be pointless to belabor the truism that an unwelcome conclusion which seems to follow necessarily from premises to which one has assented but which contradicts (or seems to contradict) what is known upon other evidence cannot be judged erroneous by proclamation. But does the unwelcome Socratic conclusion really follow?

It does not. The argument by which Socrates derives the paradoxical conclusion that the voluntary wrongdoer is better than the involuntary one is vitiated by two logical flaws. The first is a sys-

[39] *Ibid.*: 397–98.
[40] *Ibid.*: 394–98. So, too, Friedländer, 1964, II: 146, who thinks that Socrates' sophistry is so blatant in the *Hippias Minor* that, were it not for the testimony of Aristotle, few would endorse it as genuinely Platonic. See also Guthrie, 1975: 195–96, who complains about the "manifest absurdities" of this dialogue in which Socrates comes "perilously near" the "logical clowning" of the two sophists parodied in the *Euthydemus*.
[41] *Ibid.* The same interpretation is offered by Ovink, 1931: 176–77; and Vlastos, 1991: 275–79, according to whom the *Hippias Minor* documents "honest perplexity" and portrays Socrates "in a muddle" and victimized by a conceptual confusion shared by Plato whose moral insight at the time extended no further. This view is rejected by Dupréel, 1948: 197, and Annas, 1992: 50–51, according to whom Socrates is merely toying with Hippias. See also Kahn, 1992: 253: "Since there are serious moral issues here, for Vlastos the fallacies must be honest errors and the perplexity sincere. Why is Vlastos so blind ... to the malicious humor and flagrant bluffing of the *Hippias Minor*?"

tematic equivocation on the term "good" (ἀγαθός) and its comparative "better" (ἀμείνων).[42] According to Socrates, since the man best qualified to speak truly about mathematics (or any other subject) is also, and for that very reason, best qualified to speak falsely about it, it follows that the man who is good at these things (ὁ ἀγαθὸς περὶ τούτων, 367c4) is the good man (ὁ ἀγαθός, 367c5–6). But the inference is fallacious. "A is *good at* X-ing" does not entail "A is *good*." The proposition "A is *good at* X-ing" does not evaluate character. It does not even primarily evaluate performance. It evaluates capacity. It is, in short, a dispositional statement. The only conclusion that can validly be derived from Socrates' argument is a non-moral one, and it is not paradoxical at all. There is a sense in which skilled and voluntary wrongdoers *are* better than their less skilled and involuntary counterparts. No one would deny that a runner who voluntarily loses a race by running slowly is better *qua* runner than a runner who would have lost the race no matter how fast he had tried to run. The same applies to wrestlers who voluntarily lose matches, vocalists who voluntarily sing flat, and archers who voluntarily miss targets. All are better *qua* runners, wrestlers, vocalists, or archers. All could have avoided the blunder in question by exercising their respective skills. The fact that they elect not to exercise them does not cast doubt on their expertise or their capacity, but it does cast doubt on their character. The runner who voluntarily loses a race is better *qua* runner, but not *qua* participant in the race; the vocalist who voluntarily sings flat is better *qua* vocalist, but not *qua* musical performer; and so on. However, from the fact that runners, wrestlers, musicians, and archers who voluntarily misuse their respective *technai* are better *qua* runners, wrestlers, musicians, and archers than their less skilled and involuntary counterparts, it does not follow that they are better *qua* human beings. It is only by blatant equivocation that anyone could argue that since the former are *better at* what they do, they are, therefore, *better*, that is *morally* better.

---

[42] See Guthrie, 1975: 195; Hoerber, 1962: 127; Mulhern, 1968: 288; and Sprague, 1962: 72. For a vigorous – but, to my mind, unconvincing – rebuttal, see Weiss, 1981: 298–304, according to whom ἀγαθός, as employed by Socrates throughout the *Hippias Minor*, does not mean "morally good"; ὁ ἀγαθός is "an incomplete expression" which becomes "complete" by specifying the *technē* in which he is skilled, e.g., the just man is good *at* justice. See also Penner, 1973a: 141–43.

This brings us to the second logical flaw. Throughout the argument, Socrates implies that insofar as a person voluntarily fails to do what he is capable of doing, he voluntarily misuses his *technē*. However, in implying this, he overlooks an important distinction. It is true of the doctor who voluntarily poisons a patient, thereby misusing the *technē* of medicine, but it is not true of the runner who voluntarily loses a race, the wrestler who voluntarily loses a match, the vocalist who voluntarily sings flat, or the archer who voluntarily misses the target. Unlike the former, the latter do not *mis*use their *technai*; on the contrary, they do not use them at all.

I conclude that Socrates is wrong on four counts: (i) in defining the "false man" as "the man who is capable of speaking falsely"; (ii) in claiming that the true and false man are one and the same; (iii) in arguing that "A is *good at* X-ing" entails that "A is *good*"; and (iv) in suggesting – however tentatively or vacillatingly – that the voluntary wrongdoer is (morally) better than the involuntary one. Hippias, on the other hand, is right on three counts: (i) in denying that the true and false man are one and the same; (ii) in denying – or, at least, in doubting – that "A is *good at* X-ing" entails that "A is *good*"; and (iii) in denying that the voluntary wrongdoer is (morally) better than the involuntary one.

Not only is Socrates "in a muddle" about the problem of voluntary wrongdoing; the whole dialogue is something of a muddle. Furthermore, it is not Hippias' false (or confused) beliefs that account for the dialectical impasse with which the discussion concludes. The blame is wholly traceable to Socrates. It is he who contributes all the false (or dubious) premises.[43] It is also he who draws (or is inclined to draw) all the fallacious inferences. Hippias, on the other hand, does not endorse them: and it is to his credit that he does not. Although far from astute and unable to diagnose what is wrong with Socrates' arguments, he perceives that something is wrong with them and finally pronounces the conclusion of the dialogue "monstrous." The legitimacy of his protest – the product of a robust common sense and a Socratically uncontaminated linguistic sensitivity – is attested to by Plato's and Aristotle's subsequent acknowledgments of the possibility of *akrasia*.

[43] This is sufficient to discredit Vlastos's contention, 1983a: 57 – endorsed by Stokes, 1986: 29–30 – that the theses investigated by Socrates in the early dialogues are, without exception, advanced by his interlocutors.

On the other hand, there is no textual basis for accusing Socrates of deliberate sophistry in the *Hippias Minor*. The conceptual thicket in which he finds himself may very well be symptomatic of "honest perplexity." However, in view of the false premises and fallacious inferences which generate it, the perplexity is self-induced. And its magnitude is intensified by the realization that the solution finally arrived at – the doctrine that all wrongdoing is involuntary – is every bit as counterintuitive and paradoxical as the perplexity it is intended to dispel.

Has Socrates cared for the soul of Hippias? He has not. It is hard to believe that he has even tried. Although we should hesitate before endorsing I. F. Stone's contention that the *Hippias Minor* is a satire of Socrates who "outdoes the Sophists in sophistry,"[44] it remains true one searches the dialogue in vain for the moral seriousness and concern for the souls of his fellows for which Socrates has traditionally been revered.

[44] 1988: 56–57.

CHAPTER 6

Laches and Nicias

In the *Meno*, after uncharacteristically acknowledging that Athenian history provides many examples of good politicians who were also good men, Socrates asks:

[B]ut have they been good teachers of their own virtue? That is the point we are discussing, not whether there are good men here or not, but ... whether virtue (ἀρετή) can be taught ... whether the good men of today and of the past knew how to pass on to another the virtue they themselves possessed, or whether a man cannot pass it on or receive it from another. (*M.* 93a6–b5)

His doubts are prompted by the fact that good men like Themistocles and Pericles, who spared no expense to teach their sons everything else, did not teach them to be virtuous.

In the *Laches*, no one ventures the opinion that virtue cannot be taught; the presumption throughout is that it can. The dialogue depicts a conversation whose dramatic date falls somewhere between the retreat from Delium (424) – a humiliating Athenian defeat which, according to Laches, could have been avoided had everyone fought as bravely as Socrates (*La.* 181b1–4) – and the Battle of Mantinaea (418) in which the historical Laches perished. The scene is an unidentified palaestra where Stesilaus, a teacher of the art of fighting in heavy armor, has just completed a demonstration. Among those present are Socrates, Lysimachus, and Melesias, the sons of Aristides the Just and Thucycides the Elder; they are accompanied by their sons, also named Aristides[1] and Thucydides, for whose benefit the ensuing discussion is ostensibly conducted. Acknowledged nonentities in Athenian public life, Lysi-

---

[1] At *Th.* 150e1–151a2 "Socrates" numbers Aristides among those who had forsaken him too early. Having taken up with evil companions, he suffered a miscarriage of the ideas with which he was pregnant and neglected the intellectual offspring to which he had given birth through the agency of Socratic midwifery.

machus and Melesias blame their fathers for neglecting their education. Ashamed in their sons' eyes and determined to be better fathers themselves, they have invited Laches and Nicias,[2] two celebrated Athenian generals with sons of their own,[3] to solicit their advice about whether the boys should acquire Stesilaus' art as part of an education designed to make them as good as possible.

That Lysimachus and Melesias are genuinely concerned about their sons is beyond dispute. However, their views about what they should learn and why they should learn it leave something to be desired. Even if we reject Stokes's overly harsh judgment that their values are "of the utmost banality,"[4] the fact remains that they are rather superficial. Although brimming over with good intentions, they are chiefly concerned that their sons receive an education which will equip them to perform noble deeds (καλὰ ἔργα) and thereby become worthy of their illustrious names.

Nicias warmly endorses this heartfelt display of parental concern. So does Laches, but he wonders why Lysimachus and Melesias have not solicited the opinion of Socrates who is of the same deme, whose every waking hour is spent discussing the education of the youth, and whose military prowess at Delium attests to the fact that he is eminently qualified to give advice about strategic tactics. The somewhat out-of-touch Lysimachus, who had not realized that Socrates is the son of his old friend Sophronicus, is elated and immediately turns to Socrates for advice.

We expect Socrates to challenge this preoccupation with curricular trivia. But he does not. Although he will later raise issues of greater moment than whether the acquisition of the art of fighting in heavy armor should rank high on the diligent parent's list of educational *desiderata,* for the present he defers to the older and more experienced generals.

Nicias enthusiastically recommends the acquisition of this art. His reasons, unimportant in themselves, are worth noticing for the light they shed on his character and on the petty and increasingly mean-spirited rivalry which quickly develops between him and

---

[2] The historical Nicias was executed in 413 for incompetence which undermined the Sicilian expedition and led to the downfall of Athens.

[3] At *La.* 180c8–d3 Nicias credits Socrates with having secured the services of Damon of Oa as a music teacher for his son Niceratus. Although Damon was a sophist and a pupil of Prodicus, he is Socrates' musical authority throughout the Platonic corpus. In Xenophon's *Symposium* (3.5), Niceratus reports that his father was so intent on his becoming a good man that he made him memorize the entire *Iliad* and *Odyssey.*

[4] 1986: 42.

Laches. According to Nicias, the art of fighting in heavy armor is an excellent form of exercise and self-discipline. It is also militarily advantageous. Its acquisition leads to a mastery of the whole art of military science and thus enables its possessor to ascend naturally to the rank of general. Above all, it makes him bolder and more courageous (θαρραλεώτερον καὶ ἀνδρειότερον, 182c6) in battle, not to mention more impressive to his peers and more intimidating to his enemies – a revealing afterthought which shows how much reputation matters to Nicias.

Laches disagrees. Prefacing his rebuttal with elaborate assurances that he is loathe to dissuade anyone from acquiring a *bona fide* art and even more loathe to contradict a colleague, he immediately proceeds to do both with a gusto which reveals that his apparent civility towards Nicias was actually the preamble to a scathing critique of his views about military tactics and an implicit slur on his professional judgment. In Laches' opinion, Nicias has greatly exaggerated the usefulness of the art of fighting in heavy armor. For one thing, it is not cultivated in Sparta where nothing militarily advantageous is overlooked. Nor can he recall anyone who ever distinguished himself by means of it. In fact, Stesilaus is living proof of its uselessness. Once during a naval battle, his spear accidentally became entangled in the rigging of an enemy ship moving in the opposite direction – a mishap which required him to run the entire length of his own vessel in a futile effort to extricate it, thereby rendering himself strategically vulnerable and reducing himself to a laughing stock – an indication of the importance that Laches ascribes to reputation and a tell-tale sign that, in addition to being very competitive and prone to rhetorical overkill, he is something of a gossip. He concludes by noting that Nicias is also wrong in thinking that the possession of this art makes one more courageous in battle. On the contrary, if one is cowardly, it will make him rash; and if one is already courageous, it will prompt jealous colleagues – of whom Laches appears to be one – to scrutinize him all the more closely in search of the slightest slip.[5]

---

[5] "Courage" and "courageous" are sometimes infelicitous translations of ἀνδρεία and ἀνδρεῖος (see Méron, 1979: 185–203; and Stokes, 1986: 36, 44–45, 55–57). Laches' speech is a case in point. By "courage" he does not mean a moral quality which enables its possessor to perform heroic actions from which the faint-hearted shrink; in employing the terms ἀνδρεῖος and δειλός (184b3–6), he is not so much distinguishing the courageous from the cowardly as the skilled from the unskilled. Stesilaus' behavior is laughable: not because he is a coward, but because he is inept. If we translate ἀνδρεία as "courage," the anecdote becomes contextually irrelevant.

Confronted with this disagreement between two experts, Lysimachus implores Socrates to cast the tie-breaking vote.[6] Sardonically asked whether he thinks truth is ascertained by counting heads, Lysimachus confesses that he knows of no other way. Although he is universally disparaged for this reply, it is perfectly reasonable given the mildly Kafkaesque situation in which he finds himself. Having initially solicited the advice of Nicias and Laches, he had been urged to consult Socrates, who had agreed to shed whatever light he could but only after hearing what the generals had to say. Finding them hopelessly at odds, he repairs once again to Socrates, only to be ridiculed for his Democratic Theory of Truth – a hectoring tactic which is not only unfair but unkind. This is not mere sentimentalism on my part elicited by the fact that Lysimachus is an old man. In soliciting Socrates' opinion, he is not consulting just any third person, but someone who just minutes ago had been recommended to him as another expert – indeed, as the foremost expert. In fact, Lysimachus' behavior is eminently sensible. Confronted with a disagreement between two experts, what else can a non-expert do but consult another expert?

To prevent Melesias from endorsing Lysimachus' theory of truth, Socrates provides him with a bit of coaching. If in doubt as to how his son should go about preparing for an athletic contest, would he put the matter to a popular vote or consult a competent trainer? "The latter," replies Lysimachus. Socrates concurs on the ground that such decisions require expertise, and the opinion of an expert should prevail even if he is outvoted by many non-experts (184e11–185a3).[7] Furthermore, before consulting an expert, one needs to know what one is consulting him about. The non-plussed Nicias retorts that Lysimachus and Melesias know perfectly well what they are consulting Laches and him about, namely, the advisability of acquiring the art of fighting in heavy armor. Socrates disagrees: what they are chiefly concerned about is how to make their sons as good as possible. Accordingly, what they really need is not someone skilled in this or that military tactic but someone skilled in caring for the soul (τεχνικὸς περὶ ψυχῆς θεραπείαν, 185e4). In thus changing the subject from education as

---

[6] A feeble response, according to Arieti, 1991: 56, which reveals "the shallowness of [Lysimachus'] mind" and "the popular insipidity" of entrusting young minds to "democratic mechanisms."

[7] Cf. *Cr.* 44c6–9, 47a2–c3, 48a5–7; and *G.* 471e2–472a1.

preparation for noble deeds to education as care of the soul, Socrates leads the discussion in a very different direction and, in the process, deprives the specifically military expertise of Nicias and Laches of whatever authority it may have had.

Socrates thereupon lays down an important (and characteristically Socratic) procedural stipulation: professions of expertise should not be accepted at face value; every claimant must produce his credentials either by identifying the teacher(s) who have improved him or by identifying people he has improved (186e3–187a8). Any candidate who fails to satisfy one (or both) of these conditions disqualifies himself as an expert.

Although it is understandable that Socrates should want to expose the superficiality of Lysimachus' and Melesias' educational goals, his method of going about it is somewhat devious. Having agreed, as military experts, to serve as consultants about the advisability of acquiring the art of fighting in heavy armor, Nicias and Laches suddenly find themselves cast in the unsought – and unprofessed – role of moral experts and required either to justify their claim to moral expertise or withdraw it. Their already diminished authority is undermined still further when Socrates expresses his "surprise" upon finding them in disagreement; for there can be no disagreement between real experts. Having laid down his criteria of expertise and having implied that, in view of their disagreement, Nicias and Laches cannot both be experts, he urges Lysimachus to question them in an effort to determine which of them is. Predictably, Lysimachus begs off and implores Socrates to question them in his stead.

Before undergoing Socratic cross-examination,[8] Nicias reveals that he is aware of what he is letting himself in for. Addressing Lysimachus, he says:

> You don't appear ... to know that whoever comes into close contact with Socrates and associates with him in conversation must necessarily, even if he begins by conversing about something quite different ... keep on being led about by the man's arguments until he submits to answering questions about himself concerning both his present manner of life and the life he has lived hitherto. And when he does submit to this questioning, you don't realize that Socrates will not let him go before he has well and truly tested (βασανίσῃ) every last detail. (187e6–188a3)

---

[8] As always, participation in elenctic debate is voluntary (see *La.* 188a6–c3, 189a1–3; and *Ch.* 158e4–5).

Viewed philosophically, Nicias' speech is an astute commentary on the *ad hominem* character of the Socratic elenchus and an "ominous hint"[9] that Socrates is about to examine his interlocutor's life as well as his thesis. Viewed dramatically, however, it is a condescending gesture towards Laches calculated to convey the message that, so far as Socrates is concerned, Nicias is in-the-know. Having advised his dialectically uninitiated colleague of the rigors of the Socratic elenchus, Nicias announces that he is willing to be tested. He offers several reasons – all of them self-congratulatory: first, he is accustomed to these discussions and knows what to expect; second, there is no harm in being reminded of one's past misdeeds; and, third, conversations with Socrates always make him think harder.[10] He concludes by expansively noting that not everyone is so refreshingly eager for correction and reproof; indeed, many find the experience unpleasant, and he fears that Laches might be one of them.

Not about to be upstaged, Laches responds with a rhetorical flourish of his own. He, too, is a lover of discussion (φιλόλογος) – albeit with a low tolerance for moral hypocrites whose behavior is at variance with their principles. Accordingly, he has a condition: his conversational partners must be worthy of him. Their deeds must be consistent with their words, that is, they must practice what they preach. If this condition is not satisfied, he becomes a hater of discussion (μισόλογος); and the greater the discrepancy, the greater his hatred. Fortunately, Socrates measures up to his lofty standards. He would, therefore, be happy to be examined and, if need be, refuted by this true musician (μουσικός) whose behavior at Delium testifies to his courage and whose life bespeaks so complete a harmony between his words and deeds that it may without exaggeration be described as the paradigmatic embodiment of the authentically Greek mode – the Dorian (188d2–8).[11]

This long introduction (178a1–190d2) – if "introduction" is not a misnomer for what is, in fact, almost half of the dialogue – accomplishes several important philosophical purposes. Ostensibly

---

[9] The terminology, admirably apposite, is O'Brien's (1963: 136).

[10] Although Xenophon's writings abound with testimonials about Socrates' salutary effects on his interlocutors, such tributes are rare in Plato. This is one of them.

[11] The mode which "suitably imitate(s) the tone and rhythm of a courageous person who is . . . facing wounds, death, or some other misfortune, and who, in all these circumstances, is fighting off his fate steadily and with self-control" (*R.* 399a5–b3).

concerned with the advisability of acquiring the art of fighting in heavy armor, it actually provides what is perhaps the clearest statement in the early dialogues of the announced purpose of the Socratic elenchus – to test the interlocutor "well and truly" about "every last detail." It also provides a correspondingly clear description of the ideal interlocutor – someone who is willing to be tested and, if need be, refuted. Judged solely by their speeches, Nicias and Laches admirably embody this ideal. Unlike most Socratic interlocutors, both know from the start what will be required of them, and both are willing to submit. Judged by their behavior, however, both fall far short and fail to comport themselves like the ideal interlocutors they purport to be.

Having inherited control of the discussion, Socrates substitutes a different line of questioning. Instead of requiring Nicias and Laches either to justify their claim to moral expertise or withdraw it, he proposes another strategy which will achieve the same result but enable them to proceed at a more fundamental level. He introduces it with uncharacteristic laboriousness:

Suppose we know, about anything whatsoever, that if it is added to another thing, it makes that thing better, and furthermore, we are able to make the addition, then clearly we know the very thing about which we should be consulting as to how one might obtain it most easily and best. (189e3–7)

Having delivered himself of this obscure utterance, Socrates clarifies it as follows:

[S]uppose we know that sight, when added to the eyes, makes better those eyes to which it is added, and furthermore, we are able to add it to the eyes, then clearly we know what this very thing sight is, about which we should be consulting as to how one might obtain it most easily and best. (190a1–5)

Knowing what sight is, ophthalmologists do not tell their patients that it is good; they enable them to see. Analogously, knowing what virtue is, moral experts do not tell their pupils that certain actions are good; they enable them to *be* good.[12] So if Nicias and Laches are to be of any help to the sons of Lysimachus and Melesias, they must know what virtue is and how to inculcate it in

---

[12] As Woodruff, 1988: 96, aptly puts it: "An expert on Courage should be like a doctor who knows how to perform a courage-implant and guarantee that the implant will never fail to cause the recipient to act in courageous ways."

others; and if they know what it is, they must be able to say what it is (190c3–7). To make the discussion more manageable, Socrates narrows the topic from the "whole" of virtue to the specific "part" with which they are presently concerned, namely, courage (ἀνδρεία).[13] The question, then, is: What is courage?

Laches thinks the question is easily answered: anyone is courageous who stays at his post and faces the enemy (190e4–6). Socrates agrees, but complains that Laches has not answered his question: instead of defining courage, he has merely produced an example of a courageous action. But many counterexamples come to mind. Can a soldier not display courage in retreating (191a5–6),[14] as well as in many other situations, for example, amid perils at sea, in illness, in poverty, in politics, and so on (191c7–e8)? Laches concurs. Socrates thereupon explains that what he wants is not an example of one or two courageous actions, but a definition of courage which explains what is the same in all these cases (τί ὂν ἐν πᾶσι τούτοις ταὐτόν ἐστιν, 191e10–11) – the power (δύναμιν) which is denoted by the term "courage" and which is common to all actions called by that name (192b5–8).[15]

Vlastos thinks that, in supplying this list of diverse examples, Socrates is able to "extend enormously the range of [the] application" of the term "courage,"[16] thereby affecting "a radical revision" of the meaning that attaches to it in conventional usage and stretching its application so as "to break the traditional moral dogma that had kept courage a class-bound, sex-bound, virtue."[17] Laches thinks of courage in primarily military terms – as paradigmatically the virtue of a soldier. Under Socrates' guidance – with its characteristic "tendency towards greater generality and abstraction"[18] – he gradually realizes that its scope is wider.

But Socrates' "guidance" admits of another interpretation. Al-

---

[13] Albeit without explaining what he means by a "part" of virtue – the very thing for which he faults Protagoras (*Pr.* 329b5–331a4).

[14] "[A] nice touch" on Plato's part (Santas, 1971: 185), since Laches had previously praised Socrates' courage during the *retreat* from Delium. At *Sym.* 221a5–b1 Alcibiades reports that during that battle Socrates was much cooler under pressure than Laches – an untimely truth discreetly suppressed here.

[15] Although the *Laches* and the *Charmides* are both definitional dialogues in which the "What-is-*F*?" question is prominent, in neither are the objects of Socrates' search described as *eidē* or *ideai*, as they are in the *Euthyphro*. See Vlastos, 1991: 93, n. 46.

[16] 1956: 1. See also Stokes, 1986: 71–74; and Penner, 1992a: 2.

[17] Vlastos, 1981b: 411, n. 3.

[18] The terminology is Santas's (1971: 187).

though diverse examples can be employed to "extend enormously" the applicational range of a term, they can also be employed for other, less salutary purposes. This passage is a case in point. Socrates introduces his diverse examples: not as illuminating supplements designed to make it easier for Laches to discover the defining characteristic common to all those actions and persons to which the term "courage" is correctly applied, but as gratuitous complications designed to make it harder for him to discover it. Anticipating trouble, Laches asks whether it is really necessary to state "what is the same" in all these examples (192b9–c1). His question is a good one, but Socrates ignores it. Instead of dispelling Laches' doubts by explaining why it is necessary, he requires him to accept this doctrine on authority and merely assures him that it is necessary if they are to answer "their" question.[19]

Laches thereupon defines courage as "a certain endurance of the soul" (καρτερία τις ... τῆς ψυχῆς, 192b9). Socrates is again dissatisfied. Having rejected Laches' first answer by producing examples of the *definiendum* which are not covered by the *definiens*, thereby showing that it is too narrow, he rejects his second by producing examples which are covered by the *definiens* but which are not examples of the *definiendum*, thereby showing that it is too broad. His argument – 192c4–193d12 – is as follows:

(i)   Courage is noble (καλῶν).
(ii) When conjoined with wisdom (φρονήσεως), endurance is noble and good; but when conjoined with foolishness (ἀφροσύνης), it is harmful and bad (βλαβερὰ καὶ κακοῦργος).
(iii) What is harmful and bad cannot be noble.
(iv) Since courage is noble, harmful and bad endurance cannot be courage.
(v)   Hence only wise endurance is courage.

"So it seems" (Ἔοικεν), replies Laches.[20]

---

[19] This is the closest Socrates ever comes to "explaining" why, in defining a term, it is necessary to state the character *F*-ness common to all *F*s. It is, of course, no explanation at all.

[20] In inducing Laches to affirm that courage is wise endurance, Socrates elicits his assent to a thesis which, in view of the counterexamples that follow, he himself rejects. This single passage is sufficient to discredit Vlastos's contention that Socrates would ever "(knowingly, and in a serious vein) assert categorically a false premise or endorse a fallacious argument" (1981b: 223, n. 5).

Here, then, is a new definition to examine. Whose definition is
it? According to Socrates, it is Laches'. Most commentators agree:
first, because Laches had agreed to each step of the argument;
second, because he had also agreed that the definition – courage
is wise endurance – follows from what he said (κατὰ τὸν σὸν
λόγον, 192d10). Commenting on Socrates' procedure, Vlastos says:

> By exploring relations of implication and incompatibility between the
> proposed statement and all sorts of others ... Socrates' method makes
> you see how big in their consequences are matters that seem so picayune
> and piddling by themselves, and thus how worthy of serious inquiry are
> things which otherwise would have passed unnoticed ... And the very
> fact that you are required to say whether or not you agree to each prop-
> osition as it is put before you, one at a time, gives you a high incentive to
> press for clarification, for you may soon look like a fool if you agree to
> something without understanding what exactly you agreed to.[21]

Vlastos's remarks make Socrates' every move seem perfectly
straightforward and eminently fair. At every stage of the argument, the interlocutor is pointedly asked whether he assents to the
proposition posed for his assent. He is invited to dissent or to
"press for clarification" so that later on he will not "look like a
fool." He need not assent. But if he does, he is expected to abide
by his logical commitments and to acknowledge that he has been
refuted "from his own beliefs." What could be more reasonable?
The only thing Vlastos neglects to mention is that by the end of
the discussion the interlocutor will probably "look like a fool"
anyway.

Why? Because in spite of Socrates' "guidance" he still manages
to commit some fatal logical blunder? Or because Socrates' "guidance" is designed to ensure that he will commit it? In Laches'
case, the latter is closer to the truth. A general whose understanding of courage is confined to examples drawn from the battlefield
and who can elucidate it in only the vaguest of terms as "a certain
endurance of the soul," Laches has said nothing to suggest that he
thinks courage has anything to do with wisdom. Having stated
his "view" of courage, he is presented with a series of propositions phrased in such a way as to make dissent virtually impossible, informed that they entail that courage is wise endurance, and
thereupon identified as the proponent of this definition which, al-

---

[21] 1956: xlv–xlvii *passim*.

though it never entered into his head, is said to follow from "his" account.[22]

Returning to the discussion, it has apparently come to light that courage is not endurance *simpliciter* but *wise* endurance. No student of the early dialogues will be surprised by the next question: Wise *about what* (εἰς τί, 192e1)? About all things – great and small?[23] Surely not. An investor is not courageous because he wisely endures in investing his money. Nor is a doctor courageous because he wisely endures in withholding food and water from patients whose condition they would aggravate. Curiously, Socrates does not explain (and Laches does not ask) why these wise endurers are not courageous. But the foregoing argument provides a clue. Since Socrates and Laches have agreed that courage is noble and since the end for the sake of which the wise investor invests – financial gain – is not noble, neither is the endurance he displays in pursuing it. Hence, however wise his endurance, it is not courageous. But this is not true of the doctor whose end – the well-being of his patient – *is* noble. So why is *his* wise endurance not courageous? Here the foregoing argument is of no help. Lacking definitive textual evidence, we must settle for an answer that is compatible with the text.

I suggest the following. Since the obstacles which the doctor must endure – the complaints of his disgruntled patients – are comparatively trivial, they invest his wise endurance with a corresponding triviality which prohibits his behavior from being described as courageous. For an action to be courageous, it is not sufficient that it manifest wise endurance. Two further conditions must be satisfied: first, the end at which it aims must be noble; second, in pursuing that end, the agent must incur and endure

[22] Penner, 1992a: 16–18, acknowledges that Socrates – "deliberately" and even "wickedly" – induces Laches and Nicias to endorse deficient views of courage. He does the same thing to Euthyphro. If we complain that this is unfair, Penner disagrees: "Whatever the strict rights and wrongs, fairnesses or unfairnesses, of Socrates' treatment of Euthyphro," it is "justified" because he has not "thought out" his position (18, n. 30). Presumably, he would say the same thing about Socrates' treatment of Laches and Nicias.

[23] Commentators differ about what Socrates means by "great" and "small." Santas, 1971: 192–93, thinks he is making a distinction between being wise in the sense of knowing one's alternatives and their likely consequences, and being wise in the sense of knowing the comparative worth of those consequences. Vlastos, 1994: 110–12, thinks he is making a distinction between moral knowledge and technical expertise. Stokes, 1986: 82–83, disagrees with both and argues – rightly, in my opinion – that he is making a distinction between the magnitudes of the respective endurances involved.

some significant risk(s). Although Socrates' counterexamples do not show that Laches' definition of courage as wise endurance is false, they do show that it is defectively incomplete.

But what is incomplete about it? Here we are in for a surprise. Since Socrates has argued that courage is neither endurance *simpliciter* nor wise endurance *simpliciter*, we expect him to pursue his original question: Wise *about what?* and thereby try to remedy the vagueness of Laches' definition.[24] But he does not. Instead, he produces a counterexample designed to show that courage does not require wisdom at all. Laches is asked to imagine two soldiers on opposing armies who endure in battle: the first, knowing on the basis of a wise calculation (φρονίμως λογιζόμενον) that his army is superior, that it outnumbers the enemy's, that it is advantageously positioned, and that reinforcements are on the way; the second, knowing that his army is inferior, that it is outnumbered by the enemy's, that it is precariously positioned, and that no reinforcements will arrive. Asked which soldier is more courageous, Laches unhesitatingly opts for the latter – in spite of the fact that his endurance is more foolish (193b1).

More counterexamples follow. What about cavalry-riders, archers, and divers who incur and endure grave risks without possessing knowledge and/or the requisite skills? Are they also more courageous than their more knowledgeable and skilled counterparts? Laches thinks so – in spite of the fact that they are also more foolish (193c8).[25] Socrates thereupon concludes that this claim, taken in conjunction with Laches' previous admission that foolish endurance is harmful and bad, is inconsistent with his original assertion that courage is noble and entails that courage is not wise, but foolish endurance (193d6–7). Laches reluctantly agrees.

---

[24] Thus Devereux, 1977: 135–36, declares that if Laches had been able to specify the *kind* of wisdom that is involved in courage, his definition would presumably have been accepted by Socrates who all along seems to imply that some important, albeit highly elusive, kind of wisdom is a necessary (and perhaps also a sufficient) condition of courage.

[25] At *Pr.* 349e8–350c5 Socrates employs the same counterexamples to prove the opposite conclusion: those who do such things are not more courageous. Indeed, they are not courageous at all; they are mad (μαίνομενοι). Devereux, 1977: 136–37, thinks this shows that Plato has come to recognize that someone who lacks knowledge and/or the requisite skills can be more courageous than someone who possesses them and that he employs the character "Socrates" to criticize the historical Socrates who denied this. So, too, Vlastos, 1994: 117, according to whom Socrates' refutation in the *Laches* of the very definition of courage that he himself had endorsed in the *Protagoras* suggests that the former post-dates the latter and represents an advance in Plato's understanding of courage.

Has Socrates refuted the definition of courage as wise endurance? He has not. It is true that one cannot consistently affirm:

(i) Courage is wise endurance,

and:

(ii) The soldier who foolishly endures in the face of overwhelming odds is more courageous than his more fortunate opponent;

or:

(i) Courage is wise endurance,

and:

(iia) Horsemen, archers, divers, etc., who foolishly endure without knowledge and/or the requisite skills are more courageous than their more knowledgeable and skilled counterparts.

It is also true that Laches has affirmed both pairs of inconsistent conjunctions. Having done so, he is informed that he must withdraw (i). Which he does. But needlessly. "Courage is wise endurance" is false only if it is possible for a person to be both courageous and foolish. That is, (i) is false only if (ii) and (iia) are true. But the truth of each can be disputed: first, by denying that those who endure in the face of overwhelming odds without knowledge and/or the requisite skills are more courageous than those who do not; second, by denying that they are more foolish – or, for that matter – that they are foolish at all. Although Laches avails himself of neither strategy, he should have opted for the second. "A does not know X" entails "A is ignorant of X," but it does not entail "A is foolish." No one can know everything, and it is possible to be ignorant of something without being foolish. If I do not know that Lincoln is the capital of Nebraska, I am ignorant of that fact. But I am not necessarily foolish. Whether one is or is not foolish depends on considerations other than what one knows and does not know. A life-long resident of the Arctic Circle would not be judged foolish for failing to know that Lincoln is the capital of Nebraska, but a life-long resident of Lincoln presumably would.

Laches could also have invoked the distinction between not *knowing that* and not *knowing how*. Unlike the former, which signals ignorance, the latter signals inability. We do not judge people ignorant because they do not know how to compose sonatas or repair air-conditioners. Unlike *not knowing that* and *being ignorant*, which are symmetrical and inter-entailing, *not knowing how* and *being unskilled* are neither. "A is skilled at X-ing" entails "A knows how to X," but "A knows how to do X" does not entail "A is skilled at X-ing." Not every case of knowing how is a skill. We do not speak of diners skilled at wielding forks or of pedestrians skilled at walking upright. These abilities are too fundamental to be called skills. To lack them is not to be unskilled, but to be handicapped. Nor does lacking certain skills necessarily render one foolish. If, lacking musical training and incapable of reading a score, I apply for the post of conductor of a major orchestra, I am a fool. However, if, being a poor swimmer or no swimmer at all, I dive into the raging surf to save my drowning daughter, I am not – even if it costs me my life. On the contrary, I perish performing an action which my obituary might describe as heroic. Since it is possible to be both ignorant and unskilled without being foolish, Socrates' counterexamples do not demonstrate what they are intended to demonstrate.

In fact, the counterexamples are importantly different. In the first, the soldier who is judged more courageous does not lack knowledge; he has exactly the same knowledge as the soldier who is judged less courageous. They differ: not because one has knowledge which the other lacks, but because the first has knowledge which is reassuring and confidence-enhancing whereas the second has knowledge which is discouraging and confidence-diminishing. So their respective courage (or lack of it) cannot be ascribed (or withheld) on the basis of their knowledge (or lack of it); it must be ascribed on the very different basis of how they are prepared to act and what they are prepared to risk and to endure in light of the knowledge they have – which is the same in both cases. Since this is so, it is hard to understand why Socrates thinks the endurance of the one is more foolish than that of the other or, for that matter, why he thinks it is foolish at all. Unless it is because he does not retreat. But surely Socrates is not suggesting *that*. It is precisely because he does *not* retreat but stays at his post in the full knowledge of his precarious circumstances that he is judged more courageous.

The epistemic situation is very different in the second counterexample. Here, too, unskilled (or less skilled) cavalry-riders, archers, divers, and so on are judged more courageous, albeit also more foolish, than their more knowledgeable and skilled counterparts. However, unlike the alleged foolishness of the badly positioned and outnumbered soldier, their alleged foolishness is not traceable to their willingness to act or to endure in the face of confidence-diminishing knowledge, but rather to their willingness to act and to endure without knowledge and/or the requisite skills. Again it is hard to understand why Socrates thinks their endurance is more foolish or, for that matter, why he thinks it is foolish at all. Unless it is because they do not refrain from incurring and enduring these risks. But surely he is not suggesting *that* either. It is precisely because they *do* incur and endure them that they are judged more courageous. In short, it is beginning to look like the proposition "All who endure in the face of confidence-diminishing knowledge and without the requisite skills are foolish" is false.

There is a more fundamental question. Why does Socrates ask Laches which soldier is more courageous in the first place? Clearly, because he wants him to say that it is the soldier answering to the description of (ii) or (iia). That is, wishing to refute Laches' definition of courage as wise endurance, Socrates feeds him a premise which he – Socrates – thinks is false, but which he suspects Laches thinks is true and to which he will assent. And he does. It might even be said that he sincerely assents. But what is such assent worth?[26] This raises awkward questions about the whole exchange. If courage is neither endurance *simpliciter* nor wise endurance *simpliciter*, and if there is no necessary connection between it and wisdom (knowledge, possessing the requisite skills, etc.), then the foregoing search for the specific *kind* of wisdom possessed by the courageous man was a pointless digression, as Socrates implicitly acknowledges a few minutes later when he abruptly drops the whole subject. All of which makes one wonder why he introduced the concept of wisdom in the first place and ascribed such importance to the seemingly crucial, but in fact irrelevant, question: Wise *about what*?

Having jettisoned the apparently superfluous component of wisdom, Socrates suggests that he and Laches allow themselves to be persuaded by the foregoing argument "to a certain extent" (τό γε

---

[26] This passage provides further textual evidence against Vlastos's contention that "*when Socrates is searching for the right way to live, in circumstances in which it is reasonable for him to think of the search as obedience to divine command*, his argument cannot involve wilful untruth" (1991: 134).

τοσοῦτον, 193e8), namely, to the extent that courage enjoins endurance. Some commentators think this is a "hint" that Laches is
"on the right track,"[27] i.e., that Socrates thinks endurance is an
essential component of courage which should be retained as part
of its definition. This is disputed by others[28] and, above all, by
Stokes,[29] according to whom Socrates' remark is merely "a piece
of urbanity, suggesting the continuance of the discussion ... in
terms which the soldierly Laches can be expected to appreciate
and understand."

At this point, Laches confesses that a certain contentiousness
(τίς ... φιλονικία, 194a7–8) has taken hold of him. The malady
from which he is suffering – highly contagious, as things turn out –
should not be confounded with the "hatred of discussion" to
which he alluded earlier. Although symptomatically similar, they
are distinct. Unlike the latter, which is psychological, contracted
through exposure to moral hypocrites, and medically analogous to
an allergic reaction, the former is logical, symptomatic of conceptual impotence, and medically analogous to a constitutional deficiency. Laches' contentiousness manifests itself as a conflict within
himself. Convinced that he knows what courage is, he is vexed because he cannot say what it is – a rueful allusion to Socrates' earlier contention that anyone who knows what virtue (or a virtue) is
can say what it is (190c6) – a contention Laches had confidently
endorsed (190c7).[30]

Grote[31] thinks Laches' vexation is symptomatic of the "intellectual deficiency which Sokrates seeks to render conspicuous to the
consciousness ... and which he impugns as the false persuasion
of knowledge." But this contention is not supported by the text.
No "intellectual deficiency" has been "rendered conspicuous" to
anyone's consciousness – certainly not to Laches' consciousness.
Laches is vexed: not because he has been convicted of "the false
persuasion of knowledge," but because he is having trouble putting his thoughts into words. The correct definition of courage is
on the tip of his tongue. In short, being examined by the sublime

---

[27] Devereux, 1977: 136, n. 20. See also Grote, 1867, 1: 478–80; Shorey, 1903: 12–13;
O'Brien, 1958: 124, 1967: 113; and, by implication, Santas, 1971: 195.

[28] Among them, Pohlenz, 1913: 28; and Irwin, 1977: 302, n. 59.

[29] 1986: 89.

[30] See Stokes, 1986: 66, Socrates is unwaveringly committed to the principle that "If one
knows what something is, one can explain what it is."

[31] 1867, 1: 477.

incarnation of the Dorian mode called "Socrates" is not proving to be the exhilarating experience he thought it would be.

Neither noticeably surprised by nor noticeably sympathetic to Laches' discomfiture – *aporia* is, after all, the intended result of all this – Socrates adds insult to injury by suggesting that he continue the discussion with Nicias who might be more adept at giving his thoughts the stability of speech (194c4–6). The palpably delighted Nicias jumps at the chance to outshine his colleague – now turned rival. Ignoring the notion of endurance altogether, he suggests a way out of the impasse: in his opinion, Socrates' and Laches' difficulties are traceable to the fact that they are overlooking a remark which Socrates has often made in Nicias' presence to the effect that a man is good in the things about which he is wise and bad in the things about which he is foolish – a remark which implies that if the courageous man is good, he must also be wise (194d1–2).

Socrates acknowledges that what Nicias says is true. But his reply is ambiguous. Does he mean that the thesis which Nicias has often heard him assert is true? Or does he merely mean that it is true that Nicias has often heard him assert it? Nicias takes him to mean the former. And with good reason. For Nicias' next definition of courage as knowledge of what is to be feared and not feared (194e11–195a1) is identical with Socrates' definition at *Pr.* 360d1–5, except that Socrates' substitutes "wisdom" (σοφία) for "knowledge" (ἐπιστήμη).[32] Socrates neither agrees nor disagrees with Nicias' definition; he simply alerts Laches to the fact that Nicias seems to be saying that courage is a kind of wisdom (σοφίαν τινά, 194d9).[33] When Laches vacantly wonders *what* kind, Socrates urges him to ask Nicias – which he does, albeit with icy brevity: "All right" (Ἔγωγε, 194e2), that is, Nicias may consider himself asked. However, before Nicias can reply, Socrates intervenes and asks the same question more pointedly. Since the kind of knowledge (or wisdom) Nicias has in mind does not consist in being skilled at playing the flute or the lyre, what does it consist in? What is this knowledge knowledge of?

---

[32] As Vlastos, 1981b: 230, n. 24, rightly points out, "The allegation one meets frequently in the scholarly literature that no acceptable definition of a virtue is ever reached in the Socratic dialogues is false."

[33] As Stokes, 1986: 56, rightly observes, Nicias' definition implies that he has changed his mind and no longer thinks that the acquisition of the art of fighting in heavy armor is sufficient to induce courage, although he may still think it is sufficient to induce boldness.

Having just failed to answer this question himself and growing more competitive by the minute, Laches applauds this line of questioning and demands that Nicias answer. Gallingly unflustered, Nicias replies that courage is knowledge of what is to be feared and not feared, whether in war or in anything else (194e11–195a1) – a definition which Laches judges strange (ἄτοπα) on the ground that wisdom is distinct from courage. But, as Socrates frustratingly points out, that is precisely what Nicias is denying. Laches interprets this remark as a call to arms and accuses Nicias of talking nonsense – an insult which Nicias dismisses as a mere *tu quoque* traceable to the fact that Laches had just been accused of the same thing. Irked that Socrates is siding so openly with Nicias, who had previously flaunted his familiarity with Socrates and his ways, Laches sets out to prove that it is Nicias who is talking nonsense. A piece of amateur elenchus follows.

How can Nicias define courage as knowledge of what is to be feared and not feared? Doctors, farmers, and other experts know what is to be feared and not feared in their respective *technai*; but that does not make them courageous. Socrates now taunts Nicias by observing that there seems to be something in what Laches is saying. Perhaps suffering from a touch of *philonikia* himself, Nicias abrasively agrees that there may be something in it, but nothing true. Doctors are experts about health and disease, but that is the extent of their expertise. *Qua* doctors they do not know in particular cases whether health is preferable to disease or whether life is preferable to death.[34] A speedy death is sometimes preferable to a lingering illness, and about such matters a doctor's judgment is no better than anyone else's. Competent judgments of this kind require a unique kind of wisdom, namely, the kind possessed by the courageous man. Courage is not just knowledge (or wisdom), but knowledge of a unique kind: knowledge of what is *truly* to be feared and not feared (195d7–9).

Laches trivializes Nicias' distinction by misinterpreting it: he is obviously talking about prophets who can foresee the future and claiming that they alone are courageous, since they alone know in particular cases when life is preferable to death. Although Laches thinks this is patent nonsense, Socrates disappoints him by saying

---

[34] "[O]ne of the best moves of any Socratic interlocutor in the whole of the early dialogues" (Penner, 1992a: 20).

that there seems to be something in what Nicias is saying. He adds:

Let us find out more clearly what he means (τί ποτε νοεῖ), and if he is really saying something, we will agree with him (196c1–4).[35]

Resuming the role of questioner, Socrates wonders whether Nicias still thinks that courage is knowledge of what is to be feared and not feared, and that such knowledge is a necessary – and perhaps a sufficient – condition for being courageous. Assured that he does, Socrates confronts him with a dilemma: in that case, he must either withhold courage from wild animals or credit them with a kind of wisdom possessed by few human beings. Laches explodes with glee and can hardly wait for Nicias to impale himself on one of the horns of this dilemma. But Nicias has a card up his sleeve. He opts for the first horn, but immediately distinguishes courage from boldness, thereby divesting the claim of its absurdity and depriving Laches of his triumph.[36] Animals are not courageous and wise, they are bold and foolish (ἄφοβον καὶ μῶρον, 197a8).[37]

The dialectically-outclassed Laches accuses Nicias of splitting hairs. But Socrates again takes up Nicias' cause, tracing his deftness at drawing distinctions to his association with Prodicus[38] and insisting that his view warrants serious consideration. Dripping

---

[35] Although it would be an exaggeration to say that this passage is an anticipation of the concept of Socratic midwifery set forth for the first time at *Th.* 148e6–151d6, some commentators think it is a good example of the sort of thing that makes midwifery an apt image for what Socrates claims to do for his "intellectually pregnant" interlocutors in the early dialogues – i.e., to assist them in giving birth to the ideas that are in their minds. See Burnyeat, 1977b.

[36] Another example of Nicias' "astuteness," according to Penner, 1992a: 21. In fact, this distinction was already implicit in Nicias' earlier contention that the art of fighting in heavy armor induces boldness *and* courage (182c6).

[37] Although at 184b3–c4 Laches objects to Nicias' distinction between courage and boldness and accuses him of flouting ordinary language, his criticism of Nicias' claim that the art of fighting in heavy armor induces courage is based on (what amounts to) the same distinction.

[38] Prodicus of Ceos was famous for his subtle distinctions – a technique which Socrates admires in spite of its possible abuses (*La.* 197d1–5, *Ch.* 163d1–4) and which, as Prodicus' "disciple" (*Pr.* 341a4), he periodically employs with an ingenuity bordering on the perverse (see, e.g., *Pr.* 340e5–347a3). The J. L. Austin of classical antiquity, Prodicus' linguistic sensitivity bespeaks an attentiveness to and respect for "our common stock of words [which] embodies all the distinctions men have found worth drawing, and the connexions they have found worth making, in the lifetimes of many generations..., [and which] are likely to be more numerous, more sound ... and more subtle, at least in all ordinary and reasonably practical matters, than any that you and I are likely to think up in our arm-chairs of an afternoon" (Austin, 1961: 130).

with acrimony, Laches tries to extricate himself from the discussion, but is prevailed upon to stay. Assured that Nicias still thinks courage is a "part" of virtue, Socrates argues that his definition of courage as knowledge of what is to be feared and not feared is not satisfactory. His argument – 197e10–199e12 – is as follows:

(i)   Courage is a "part" of virtue.[39]
(ii)   What is dreaded is what causes fear and what is not dreaded is what may be safely dared.
(iii)   Fear is of expected evils and hence of what is future.
(iv)   Things are dreaded because they are future evils.
(v)   Hence courage is knowledge of future evils and future goods.
(vi)   But knowledge of what is to be feared and not feared is not just knowledge of the future, but also of the past and present and, therefore, knowledge of all evils and goods.
(vii)   Hence since courage is knowledge, it too is knowledge of all evils and goods.
(viii) But then it is not a "part" of virtue, but the whole of it.
(ix)   Hence courage cannot be defined as knowledge of what is to be feared and not feared.

Nicias reluctantly concurs.[40]

Some commentators[41] are very critical of this argument while others[42] find it completely convincing. The crucial step is (vi). Here Socrates argues that, unlike *things* that induce fear, which are necessarily future, *knowledge of* things that induce fear is not divisible into temporal categories. Knowledge of fearful things past, present, and future is not three different kinds of knowledge. Knowledge is universal, i.e., it is knowledge of everything that is to be feared (and hence evil) and not feared (and hence good) – whether past, present, or future.

But the conclusion does not follow. "Whatever need not be

---

[39] A problematic claim which, according to Santas, 1971: 202, Socrates abandons in the *Protagoras* in favor of the Doctrine of the Unity of the Virtues. At *Eu.* 11e7–12e8 piety and justice are also said to be "parts" of virtue.

[40] Since the definition under scrutiny is not Nicias' but Socrates', it seems that the foregoing criticism is self-criticism. Thus Vlastos, 1991: 113, n. 28 declares that in the *Laches* Plato portrays Socrates attacking a Socratic thesis which is defended by Nicias who is left "holding the bag."

[41] See, e.g., Santas, 1971: 203–5; Penner, 1973b: 60–62; C. C. W. Taylor, 1976: 107; and Irwin, 1977: 88–89, 302, n. 62.

[42] See, e.g., Vlastos, 1981b: 266–69, and 1994: 117–24; and Allen, 1996: 58.

feared (and hence may be safely dared) is a future good" does not entail "Whatever is a future good need not be feared (and hence may be safely dared)." Socrates is guilty of illicit conversion. Many future goods, for example, health, involve no risks whatever and, therefore, do not fall into the category of actions that may be safely dared. Accordingly, a person who has knowledge of what is to be feared and not feared need not have knowledge of *all* goods and evils, but only of those which are relevant to his legitimate fears. Neither does it follow that insofar as Nicias' definition encompasses only future goods and evils and ignores past and present ones, it only accounts for a third of courage. Nor is it the case that Nicias' definition turns out to be the definition of the whole of virtue rather than merely of a "part" of it.[43] In short, Nicias' definition has not been refuted. But the discussion proceeds as if it had been.

Nicias' apparent defeat sets his reputation back light years in the eyes of Laches, miraculously cured of *philonikia* and back on his feet. The gratifying spectacle of his humbled colleague elicits a torrent of withering irony reminiscent of Socrates in the *Euthyphro*: "What? Dropping out of the discussion just when you were about to instruct me about the nature of courage so I could live a better life?" Having previously advertised himself as a serious inquirer whose voluntary submission to Socratic cross-examination is a testimony to his moral earnestness and a source of endless benefits, Nicias suddenly shows a different face. Smarting from his apparent defeat and licking his dialectical wounds, he officiously chirps that he has said all that anyone could reasonably be expected to say on the difficult subject of courage. He solemnly adds that he has every intention of remedying whatever deficiencies he may have exhibited by consulting with Damon "and others" – after which he will return to enlighten Socrates and Laches (200b2–c1). After a terminal exchange of insults by Laches and Nicias, the dialogue concludes with a bit of post-elenctic chit-chat. Laches advises Lysimachus and Melesias to dismiss himself and Nicias, and to secure the educational services of Socrates. Socrates reaffirms his advisory incompetence and unhelpfully urges everyone

---

[43] In fact, as Kahn, 1996: 167, rightly points out, even if it did, this should be counted a success rather than a failure, since the original project was to define virtue, i.e., the "whole" of virtue – a project which had been shelved on the ground that it would be easier to define one of its "parts."

to seek out the best teachers they can find. Lysimachus thinks this is a splendid idea and suggests that they all reconvene the next day.

I said earlier that, when judged solely by their speeches, Nicias and Laches are admirable embodiments of the ideal Socratic interlocutor, but, when judged by their behavior, both fall far short. I will conclude this chapter with a few remarks about how and why.

Initially, Laches' deficiencies seem more glaring and more grievous. Highly competitive and dripping with superiority, he gets off to a bad start. Impatient with logical details and quickly out of his depth, he has soon had his fill of argumentation. Unable to define courage, he becomes touchy and inclined to over-statement and over-reaction. When Nicias succeeds him as interlocutor and experiences similar difficulties, he rejoices and eagerly anticipates the demise of his colleague's equally doomed and slowly expiring definition of courage over which he circles like a vulture.

But we should not be too hard on Laches for his poor showing. Socrates is deeply implicated. Having dubiously disposed of Laches' attempts to define courage, he deliberately provokes him by transforming him into an inverted instantiation of his own metaphor – his words are not consistent with his deeds – and by repeatedly and openly siding with Nicias. The escalating rivalry between the two is deliberately exacerbated by an uncommonly divisive Socrates who magnifies their slightest disagreement and exploits their increasingly acrimonious one-upmanship to drive a wedge between them while simultaneously issuing periodic reminders that they are not individuals in competition with each other, but a company of truth-seekers embarked on a "joint" inquiry.

Initially, Nicias makes a better impression. More familiar with Socrates and his method, he seems less intimidated by philosophical discussion and more willing to profit from it. Although Penner may overestimate his logical acumen, he is certainly more astute than many of Socrates' interlocutors; and he is infinitely more astute than Laches. Eager to assure everyone that he is far from perfect (though not nearly so far as some of his colleagues), he revels in his self-appointed role of media-analyst providing on-the-scene, pre-debate coverage buttressed with evangelical-like personal "testimonies" about the Socratic elenchus and its power to produce "changed lives." An experienced participant and grateful beneficiary, he has taken time out of his busy schedule to serve as educational consultant and to instruct the dialectically uninitiated about the joys of refutation.

However, in spite of his shortcomings, Laches has qualities that Nicias lacks. Although capable of monumental pettiness and uncommonly eager to see others suffer as he has suffered, he is neither so self-absorbed nor so self-indulgent. He also has a certain psychological resilience. Every time we think we have had about enough of him, he reengages us by bouncing back and resolving to follow the discussion to its conclusion. If his later contributions are negligible and largely negative, he at least remains an active participant in the discussion.

That cannot be said of Nicias. Initially more impressive, he does not wear nearly so well and, in the end, proves to be little more than a military celebrity doing a Socratic commercial – someone who would rather chatter about the joys of refutation than experience them. By the end of the dialogue, we have seen through him and realized that his superficially impressive speech about the benefits of submitting to Socratic cross-examination was a bit unctuous and mostly talk. Unlike Laches, who had no idea of what he was getting into but weathered the ordeal surprisingly well, Nicias claims to be an insider, but inadvertently betrays that he is actually impervious to Socratic cross-examination and ineligible for its alleged benefits. Like his military uniform, his Socratic rhetoric is something to be slipped into whenever he wants to cut an impressive figure but discarded as soon as the mood has passed. Ostensibly a living advertisement for Socrates, he is actually a fraud. Pit him in debate with Socrates and he can do little more than quote him and produce clever, *ad hoc* distinctions. Upon being refuted, he pouts, extricates himself from the discussion, and books an appointment with Damon – his real but hitherto undisclosed authority who will remedy his deficient intellectual grasp and presumably make further Socratic conversations superfluous.

What shall we say about this dialogue? Do Socrates' arguments persuade anyone of anything? Does the *aporia* to which they lead infuse anyone with self-knowledge? If so, it has eluded me.[44] The

---

[44] Even the usually instructive Guthrie makes surprisingly little of the *Laches*. Initially commending it as "a model of Socratic dialectic," he is finally reduced to praising its "considerable value as entertaining literature" (1975: 131).

Laches reveals that although the Socratic elenchus can expose ignorance, defined in Socratic terms, it can neither provide knowledge
nor motivate the ignorant, again defined in Socratic terms, to
search for it. In the end, everyone remains exactly as they were.
All they can do is marvel at the time they have wasted and, with
their appetites inexplicably whetted for more of the same, resolve
to reconvene the next day – albeit with no specific agenda to pursue, no experts with whom to pursue it, and nothing better to look
forward to than the overnight "enlightenment" that Nicias will
have absorbed from Damon. Why bother?

CHAPTER 7

Charmides and Critias

The *Charmides* is one of three early dialogues in which relatives of Plato appear. The historical Charmides was Plato's maternal uncle, and the historical Critias[1] was Charmides' cousin and guardian. Later members of the Thirty, both perished fighting against the Athenian democracy.[2] The dramatic date of the dialogue, narrated by Socrates, is 432.

Having just returned from the Battle of Potidaea in which he had displayed great courage and saved the life of Alcibiades (*Sym.* 220d5–221b1), Socrates repairs to the palaestra of Taureas to find out how philosophy has fared during his absence and whether anyone has distinguished himself in wisdom or beauty or both. His attention is directed to Charmides, a beautiful youth[3] full of promise who has just arrived accompanied by his court of flushed and panting lovers. Assured by Critias that he is equally beautiful in soul and already a poet and a philosopher (φιλόσοφος, *Ch.* 154e8–155a1), the momentarily smitten Socrates pulls himself together and sets out to examine him.

Like many Socratic interlocutors, Charmides is lured into the discussion on false pretenses. Informed by Critias that there is a doctor on the premises who can cure his morning headaches, Charmides dutifully appears before "Dr. Socrates" who authoritatively explains that he is in possession of a leaf the application of which, if accompanied by an incantation, cures a person of his

---

[1] According to Xenophon, the historical Critias was an ambitious and violent man who grievously harmed the city (*Mem.* 1.2.12). He did not profit from his association with Socrates because people learn nothing from a teacher with whom they are out of sympathy (1.2.39).

[2] They are anonymously alluded to in the *Seventh Letter* (324d1–2) as "relatives and acquaintances" of Plato's.

[3] Although most commentators think Charmides is a teenager, Méron, 1979: 99, n. 74, points out that both the terminology Socrates uses to describe him – μειράκιον (154b5), νεανίσκος (154d1), and νεανίαν (155a4) – and the examples he uses to refute him – copying letters (159c3–4), running and jumping (159c13–d2) – suggest that he is younger.

bodily ailments. However, there are two strings attached: the treatment cannot cure one part of the body without curing the whole, and it cannot cure the body without first curing the soul. It affects this double cure by causing temperance (σωφροσύνη)[4] to be implanted (ἐγγίγνεσθαι) in the soul which is the ultimate source both of bodily health and bodily illness (155e5–157b1). So if Charmides wants to be cured of his headaches, he must submit his soul for treatment. The charade ends abruptly when Charmides reveals that he knows perfectly well that the "doctor" is Socrates.

Critias thereupon declares that Charmides is not only the most beautiful youth he knows but also the most temperate – a remark which confronts the blushing Charmides with an awkward dilemma: he must either deny that he is temperate, thereby contradicting Critias and "many others," or agree that he is, thereby praising himself. Socrates comes to the rescue by proposing that they jointly investigate whether he is temperate. Having secured Charmides' agreement,[5] he explains what seems to him the best method. If temperance is present in (πάρεστιν)[6] Charmides (158e7), he must have some opinion about *what* it is (ὅτι ἐστίν) and what *kind* of thing it is (ὁποῖόν τι, 159a3); for temperance necessarily (ἀνάγκη) gives some intimation of its nature which enables its possessor to form an idea of it (159a1–3). And if Charmides has an idea of what it is, he must be able to say what it is (159a6–7). So: what is temperance?[7]

Charmides replies that, in his opinion, temperance is doing

---

[4] Temperance was, together with courage (ἀνδρεία), justice (δικαιοσύνη), and wisdom (σοφία), one of the four so-called "cardinal" virtues. A term with no exact English equivalent, σωφροσύνη is sometimes translated as "moderation" or "self-control." Burnyeat, 1971: 216, thinks it is actually untranslatable "because the phenomena it grouped together for Greek culture do not form a whole to our outlook." So, too, Hazebroucq, 1997: 10–12; and Cooper, 1997: 639.

[5] As always, participation in the Socratic elenchus is voluntary. See *La.* 187c1–d5, 188a6–c3, and 189a1–3.

[6] Plato often speaks of properties as being "in" persons rather than of persons having those properties. Unlike the *Euthyphro*, in which Socrates treats piety almost exclusively as a property of actions, in the *Charmides* he treats temperance as a property both of actions and persons and implies that the latter is prior to the former, i.e., that a person can perform temperate actions if and only if he is temperate. He implies the same thing about courage in the *Laches*.

[7] Although the *Charmides* concludes with a long discussion of self-knowledge, I cannot accept Saunders's contention, 1987: 165, that what is actually under investigation in this dialogue is not temperance but knowledge – in particular, "the strange and problematic concept of 'knowledge of knowledge'." Even after the discussion takes this quasi-epistemological turn, the fundamental question is whether "knowledge of knowledge" is a satisfactory definition of temperance.

everything orderly and quietly, for example, walking in the streets, talking, and so on – in sum (συλλήβδην), that it is a kind of quietness (ἡσυχιότης τις, 159b2–6). A. E. Taylor somewhat patronizingly remarks:

As is natural in a mere lad, Charmides fixes first of all on an exterior characteristic ... in the form which would be most familiar to a boy – the form of decent and modest bearing towards one's elders and "good behaviour" generally.[8]

However, in his haste to disparage Charmides' superficial understanding of temperance, Taylor overlooks the fact that he avoids the error – common in the early dialogues – of defining a moral term by means of examples, thereby confusing definition with enumeration of instances. Although Charmides gives several examples of temperate actions, he immediately brings them under a single definition[9] without having to be coached by Socrates – a conceptual feat which lends some (but not much) credence to Critias' claim that he is "already a philosopher."

Instead of complimenting Charmides for avoiding this blunder, Socrates finds fault with his definition. Although some might say that the quiet are temperate, Socrates thinks they are wrong. His argument – 159b8–160d4 – is as follows:

(i)   Temperance is admirable (καλῶν).
(ii) It is more admirable to write quickly than quietly, to read quickly than slowly, to play the lyre quickly and brilliantly than quietly and slowly, etc.; and the same is true of bodily actions generally.
(iii) Agility and quickness are admirable, but slowness and quietness are shameful (αἰσχροῦ).
(iv) Therefore, since temperance is admirable, it follows that quickness is more temperate than quietness – at least with respect to bodily actions.

The same is true of all "mental" actions:

(i)   Facility in learning is more admirable than difficulty.
(ii) Facility consists in learning quickly whereas difficulty consists in learning quietly and slowly.
(iii) It is better to teach, and to understand, and to remember

---

[8] 1929: 50. So, too, Tuckey, 1951: 19. Santas, 1973: 107, is much less condescending.
[9] See ch. 6, n. 15.

quickly and energetically than quietly and slowly; and the same is true of "mental" actions generally.

(iv) Therefore, in everything that concerns body and mind, temperance is not quietness – at least not by this argument (ἔκ γε τούτου τοῦ λόγου).

Although Charmides instantly concurs, both arguments are faulty. For one thing, both depend on bizarre contrasts. Asked whether it is better to write quickly or quietly, Charmides opts for the former. This is a curious response. The opposite of "quickly" is not "quietly" but "slowly," and the opposite of "quietly" is not "quickly" but "noisily." Asked whether it is better to read quickly or slowly, he again opts for the former. His answer is equally ill-advised. He should have replied that the question cannot be answered *in general*; it all depends on the book one is reading. *Sein und Zeit* should be perused slowly whereas *Ken Bails Out* may be devoured at a faster pace. Nor are there any general musical reasons for thinking that it is better to play the lyre quickly and brilliantly than quietly and slowly. It all depends on the piece one is playing. A *vivace* should be played quickly and brilliantly whereas an *adagio* should be played quietly and slowly. But even if Socrates' questions had been more carefully formulated and his examples more judiciously chosen, there are far too few of them. Every *epagōgē* is necessarily incomplete, but this tiny Socratic sample does not even begin to warrant the universal conclusion that, in "everything" that concerns body and mind, quickness is more temperate than quietness.

Both arguments are also fallacious. Each concludes that temperance is not quietness (or a kind of quietness) on the ground that temperance is admirable and quick actions are more admirable than quiet ones. More precisely:

(i)   If an action is temperate, it is admirable.
(ii) Actions a, b, and c (which are quick) are more admirable than actions d, e, and f (which are quiet).
(iii) Therefore actions a, b, and c are more temperate than actions d, e, and f.

This argument affirms the consequent.[10] According to Aristotle, fallacies "connected with the consequent" (παρὰ τὸ ἑπόμενον) are

---

[10] Of course, the argument affirms the consequent only if it is formulated hypothetically. But even if it is formulated categorically, as Socrates formulates it here, the argument

"due to the idea that the consequent is convertible. For whenever, if A is, B necessarily is, men also fancy that, if B is, A necessarily is" (*S.E.* 167b2–4). These fallacies comprise part of the class of fallacies "due to accident" (τοῦ συμβεβηκότος):

> For the consequent is an accident but differs from the accident because the accident can be secured in the case of a single thing by itself, for example ... a white thing and a swan, whereas the consequent always exists in more than one thing; for we claim that things which are the same as one and the same thing are the same as one another. (*S.E.* 168b28–34)

But, as Aristotle rightly points out, this is not always true in the case of accidental properties: from the fact that snow and swans are both white, it does not follow that snow is more swanlike than rain (*S.E.* 168b34–35). In arguing that since temperance and quickness are both admirable, and since quick actions are more admirable than quiet ones, it follows that they are also more temperate, Socrates fallaciously fastens upon (what Aristotle calls) an "accidental" (συμβεβηκός) property common to both. Aristotle calls such arguments "sophistical" (σοφιστικῶν) because they "appear to be refutations but are really fallacies" (*S.E.* 164a20–22), they "do not affect their object but only appear to do so" (*S.E.* 165a4–5), and they succeed only because of their victims' inexperience and lack of argumentative skill (*S.E.* 164b25–28).[11]

Socrates further complicates matters by confronting Charmides with a puzzling dilemma: Either, as he himself is inclined to think, there are no (or very few) quiet actions which are more admirable

---

remains invalid: "All temperate actions are admirable" does not entail "All admirable actions are temperate." This is illicit conversion. Interestingly, when Laches defines courage as a certain endurance of the soul (καρτερία τις ... τῆς ψυχῆς, *La.* 192b9), Socrates rejects his definition for precisely this reason: from the fact that courageous actions exhibit endurance, it does not follow that all actions which exhibit endurance are courageous (193a3–d9). Of course, Socrates never talks about valid and invalid *inferences*, much less about *patterns* of valid and invalid inference.

11 Commentators say strange things about Socrates' argument. Tuckey, 1951: 19, n. 1, concedes that it is "vitiated by a paralogism," but thinks that it "exposes the inadequacy" of Charmides' definition. Santas, 1973: 113, concedes that it "seems full of logical faults," but thinks that it "comes very close to doing its job." Neither explains how a fallacious argument can "expose" anything or "do its job." Lamb, 1925: 7, thinks the argument commits the fallacy of undistributed middle and speculates that Charmides' "failure to protest ... was brought out in the discussion at the Academy." He adds that Plato "would perhaps excuse himself by saying that when he wrote the *Charmides* he was more intent on intellectual drama than on logical accuracy." For a recent defense of Socrates against the charge of fallacious reasoning, see Hazebroucq, 1997: 156–66.

than quick ones or there are many quiet and quick actions which
are equally admirable; however, even if the latter were true, it
would still be incorrect to define temperance as quietness since, as
the foregoing argument has demonstrated, quick actions are no
less (οὐχ ἧττον) admirable, and therefore no less temperate, than
quiet ones (160d1–3).

He is, of course, wrong about this. The foregoing argument did
not demonstrate that at all. What it purported to demonstrate was
not that quick actions are *no less* admirable, and, therefore, *no less*
temperate, than quiet ones, but rather that they are *more* admirable, and, therefore, *more* temperate, than quiet ones. In addition to
arguing fallaciously, Socrates has misrepresented the conclusion
of his own argument. For even if there are many quiet and quick
actions which are equally admirable, the proposition:

(i) Actions a, b, and c (which are quick) are more admirable, and
    therefore more temperate, than actions d, e, and f (which are
    quiet).

is incompatible with the proposition:

(ii) Actions d, e, and f (which are quiet) are no less admirable, and
     therefore no less temperate, than actions a, b, and c (which are
     quick).

Since (i) and (ii) are incompatible, no single argument can establish both.[12]

In fact, Charmides could have undercut both arguments by
lodging a methodological objection. Asked whether temperance is
admirable, he should have replied: "I have no way of knowing
that, Socrates; for, as you yourself constantly imply, one cannot
know what properties are predicable of a virtue until one knows
what that virtue is. And we have not yet discovered what temper-

---

[12] Santas, 1973: 116–17, defends Socrates on the (to my mind) unconvincing ground that
he is not trying to show that quietness is *contrary* to the nature of temperance, but
that it is *irrelevant* to it; "[l]ooked at this way, Socrates' argument is ... convincing,
though from the point of view of impeccable logic it still remains faulty." Irwin, 1995:
36, and Kahn, 1996: 189, think Socrates' criticisms of Charmides' first two definitions of
temperance are intended to show that temperance cannot be defined in terms of external
actions without reference to motivation. Chrétien, 1987: 12–13, defends Socrates on the
very different ground that, as a matter of fact, temperance is not the same thing as
quietness, thereby apparently endorsing Socrates' argument on the ground that its conclusion is true.

ance is."[13] I conclude that Socrates has not refuted Charmides' definition of temperance.[14]

But the discussion proceeds as if he had. Again exhorted to say what temperance is, Charmides asserts that insofar as temperance makes men ashamed or modest, it is the same as modesty (αἰδώς, 160e4). Socrates thereupon lodges another objection. His argument – 160e6–161b2 – is as follows:

(i) Temperance is admirable.
(ii) Temperate men are good.
(iii) Whatever is good makes men good.
(iv) Temperance is always good.
(v) But modesty is not always good; for, as Homer observes, it is not good for a beggar to be modest.
(vi) Insofar as modesty is both good and not good, it is no more (οὐδὲν μᾶλλον) good than evil.
(vii) Therefore, since temperance is always good and always makes men good, it cannot be the same as modesty.

Although this is one of the lamest arguments in the early dialogues, Charmides is undone by it.[15] But again there is an obvious reply. Charmides should have explained that he does not accept things on Homeric authority. He should have added that, in view of the fact that Socrates always objects when his interlocutors appeal to poetic authority, he is surprised to find him doing the same thing.[16]

Of course, Charmides says no such thing. Instead, he announces that he has just recalled another definition which seems to him more promising, namely, that temperance is minding one's own business (τὸ τὰ ἑαυτοῦ πράττειν, 161b6). When Socrates suggests that Critias is the originator of this definition, Critias vigorously

---

[13] At G. 448e2–4 Socrates faults Polus for saying that rhetoric is the most admirable (τῆς καλλίστης) of all the *technai* without having defined rhetoric – an error which reveals that he is unequipped for dialectic. See Robinson, 1953: 51: "[T]he impression vaguely given by the early dialogues as a whole is that Socrates thinks there is no truth whatever about X [the concept or term under discussion] that can be known before we know what X is."

[14] As Chambry, 1967: 266, justly observes: "L'argumentation de Platon ressemble plus d'une fois à celles des sophistes, plus préoccupés d'avoir le dessus que d'avoir raison." Cf. Méron, 1979: 99–100, who characterizes Socrates' arguments as "les réfutations ... faibles."

[15] With good reason, according to Saunders, 1987: 168: "One negative case is enough to dispatch the proposed definition."

[16] "[C]omme si Homère était un oracle infaillible" (Chambry, 1967: 267).

denies the allegation.[17] Ignoring his protest, Socrates focuses on the definition itself and pronounces it "a kind of riddle" (αἰνίγματι ... τινι, 161c9): surely its originator did not mean that a temperate person should write only his own name, build only his own house, weave only his own clothes, and so on. No city based on that principle would be well governed, and surely a temperate city would be a well-governed one. So temperance cannot be "minding one's own business" in *that* sense. Only an idiot (ἠλιθίου) would say such a thing (162b1–2). But then what *did* the originator of the definition mean? Charmides does not know and, looking straight at Critias, divulges that he would not be surprised if the originator himself did not know what he meant. Irritated by Charmides' remark, Critias grudgingly acknowledges that the definition is his.

Before proceeding further, it is worth pausing to notice that Critias' irritation is misplaced; it was not Charmides but Socrates who parodied his definition beyond recognition and made him look like a fool. Although many commentators are put off by Critias' irritation,[18] it is perfectly understandable. Having been lured into the discussion and asked to improve on sheer idiocy, he has fallen victim to a typical Socratic tactic which should not be euphemistically described as an attempt to help him "make his meaning clearer."[19] Determined to reinstate himself as a thinker of consequence, he agrees to succeed Charmides as Socrates' interlocutor.

What is going on here? Why does Socrates pronounce Critias' definition "a kind of riddle"? His ostensible reason is that "minding one's own business" cannot mean writing only one's own name, building only one's own house, and so on. He is, of course, right. But that is not a sufficient reason for pronouncing the definition a riddle. Its apparent obscurity is not traceable to Critias' actual view but to Socrates' tendentious interpretation of it – an

---

[17] Horneffer, 1904: 56–57, thinks the true originator is Socrates. Having noted that Nicias advances a definition of courage which he ascribes to Socrates (*La.* 194d1–2), Horneffer suggests that in both dialogues Plato is criticizing Socratic doctrine by putting it into the mouth of an interlocutor. See also Vlastos, 1991: 113, n. 28: "[T]he procedural form of elenctic argument prevents [Socrates] from making any of his own doctrines the target of elenctic refutation by himself"; hence "when Plato "wants to show Socrates attacking a Socratic thesis he hands that thesis over to an interlocutor, making him its proponent *pro tem.*"

[18] Friedländer, 1964, II: 67–68, thinks it reveals his intemperance and marks him as a future tyrant.

[19] Teloh's gloss is representative: "Socrates' ironical misinterpretations have an important function: they force the author of the account to clarify it" (1986: 62).

interpretation which is all the more strange in view of the fact that at *R*. 369e6ff. "Socrates" bases his ideal society on the very same principle, that is, the so-called Principle of the Division of Labor according to which everyone must "mind his own business" by doing that particular work (ἔργον) for which he is best suited by nature. From the moment that principle is introduced, its meaning is treated as luminously self-evident; and everyone is expected to give his immediate and unqualified assent. And everyone does. It never occurs to Adeimantus or Glaucon to pronounce the principle a "riddle" and to ask whether "Socrates" means that everyone should write only his own name, build only his own house, and so on. Why, then, does it occur to Socrates?

The answer, I think, is this. Socrates' request for "clarification" enables him, like an expert hunter with a well-trained bird-dog, to flush a new interlocutor out of the protective social shrubbery. Unable to sit by and allow himself to be reduced to a laughingstock, Critias is manipulated into entering the discussion in self-defense.

Having assented to the truism that craftsmen make (ποιεῖν) things for other people, he is asked how they can be temperate. Critias fails to see the problem. And with good reason – there is none. However, Socrates begs to differ and explains the "difficulty" as follows. If, as Critias has suggested, temperance is "minding one's own business" and if craftsmen do (πράττειν) other people's business, does it not follow that they are intemperate (163a1–4)? The answer, of course, is that this does not follow at all; Socrates has confounded making with doing.[20] Critias spots the mistake at once and rightly points out that making and doing are two very different things. Craftsmen can *make* things for other people without *doing* their business. Indeed, in making good and useful things for others, they *are* "minding their own business" (163b3–c8).

Although Critias is obviously right, Socrates accuses him of oversubtlety – a technique he has learned from Prodicus – and unhelpfully asserts that the things we refer to are more important than the terminology we use in referring to them (163d1–e3), thereby diverting attention from his own mistake and falsely implying that

---

[20] A piece of "shameless sophistry" (Guthrie, 1975: 159). "A sophistic trick" by which Socrates "perverts" the obvious meaning of Critias' statement and invests it with a "ludicrous" meaning of his own (Saunders, 1987: 169). Similar criticisms are made by Friedländer, 1964, II: 72; Santas, 1973: 108; and Hyland, 1981: 73.

Critias is taking refuge in mere verbal quibbling. However, he thereupon proceeds to trivialize his own objection. Having just faulted Critias for his preoccupation with inconsequential linguistic niceties, he now demands *more* precise definitions of "making" and "doing" – the very niceties just disparaged. Does Critias think that this "doing" or "making" – or whatever he wishes to call it – is temperance? He does. He also thinks that temperance is the doing of good things (163e10–11).

Having set forth his view of temperance, Critias asks whether Socrates agrees with it. Socrates' response is noteworthy: Critias is not to worry about that *yet* (πω); what matters is not what *he* – Socrates – thinks, but what Critias thinks (163e6–7). That little word "yet" – so tantalizing but so misleading – implies that although it is presently Critias' turn to say what he thinks, it will soon be Socrates' turn. The implication is false, as we discover a few Stephanus pages later, when in response to Critias' question as to whether Socrates agrees that temperance is self-knowledge, Socrates replies:

[Y]ou are talking ... as though I professed to know the answers to my own questions and as though I could agree with you if I really wished. This is not the case – rather, because of my own ignorance, I am continually investigating in your company whatever is put forward. (165b5–c1)

This is a surprising response from someone who just minutes ago had said that it was not his turn to say what he thought *yet*.[21]

Critias is in for another disappointment. Having just defined temperance, he now finds that Socrates has no intention of examining his definition. Apparently no longer interested in discovering what temperance is, Socrates abruptly changes the subject and confesses that he is surprised to learn that Critias believes that it is possible for a temperate person to be ignorant of his own temperance, i.e., that a person can be temperate without knowing it (164a1–3) – a remark which leads the discussion in a very different direction.

Critias is puzzled by the remark and explains that he does not believe this at all. Socrates retorts that he is logically committed to believing it by his previous admission that craftsmen can be tem-

---

[21] As usual, commentators rush to Socrates' defense. Hyland's opinion is representative: Socrates refuses to say what *he* thinks because he wants "to penetrate to the very core of" Critias' position (1981: 86).

perate in doing (ποιοῦντας) other people's business (164a5–7). His argument – 164a9–c6 – is as follows:

(i)   In curing his patient, a doctor does what is beneficial (ὠφέλιμα) for himself and for his patient, thereby doing what he ought (τὰ δέοντα πράττει).
(ii) He who does what he ought is temperate.
(iii) But a doctor cannot know in advance whether his patient will be cured and, therefore, cannot know in advance whether what he has done is beneficial.
(iv) Therefore if a doctor can cure his patient (and thereby do what is beneficial for him) without knowing it in advance, and if he is temperate insofar as he does what is beneficial, then it follows that he can be temperate without knowing it.

Obviously alarmed, Critias replies that if this conclusion really does follow from his previous admission, he will retract it.[22] For he would almost say that temperance is the same thing (αὐτὸ τοῦτό ... εἶναι) as self-knowledge (164d3–4)[23] and that the Delphic inscription "Know yourself" is an exhortation to be temperate.[24]

Socrates has not, of course, shown that Critias is logically committed to believing that a person can be temperate without knowing it. The aporetic impasse to which he has been reduced is not traceable to his actual position but to Socrates' misrepresentation of it. However, this time Critias does not realize what is going on and does not protest. Asked whether he remembers saying that craftsmen can be temperate in doing other people's business (164a8), he says he does. But his memory is faulty. He did not say that at all, indeed, that is exactly what he denied:

[H]ave I agreed that those who *do* other people's business are temperate by admitting that those *making* other people's things are temperate? (163a10–12)

22 According to Kraut, 1983: 66; and Vlastos, 1983b: 73, Socrates' interlocutors never renege on their previous admissions, i.e., they never retract propositions to which they previously assented. Perhaps not. But the possibility is envisaged here.
23 Irwin, 1995: 39, notes that this definition is "surprising" because it makes no mention of the non-cognitive component of self-control which figures so prominently in the Socratic concept of temperance in other early dialogues and which Socrates himself previously manifested in this one when he resisted the powerful sexual urge elicited by Charmides' beauty.
24 Horneffer, 1904: 62, thinks this allusion to the Delphic oracle constitutes further textual evidence for ascribing the definition of temperance as "minding one's own business" to Socrates.

What Critias actually said was that craftsmen can *make* things for other people without *doing* their business; he added that making and doing are two very different things. However, Socrates ignores what he actually said, puts words into his mouth, and then "refutes" him. Although he claims to be refuting Critias "from his own beliefs" (ὡς ὁ σὸς λόγος, 164c2), his refutation depends on his tendentious interpretation of Critias' actual position.[25]

Even if Critias had said what Socrates claims he said, he would still not be logically committed to believing that a person can be temperate without knowing it. From the fact a doctor cannot know in advance whether his patient will be cured, it does not follow that if he is cured, the doctor was temperate all along without knowing it. Whether a doctor is temperate is not contingent upon the recovery of his patients. A temperate doctor is not one who *cures* his patients but one who *does his best* to cure them by conscientiously doing what is in their best medical interests. Although he cannot know in advance that he has done the former, he *can* know that he has done the latter and that he is, therefore, temperate.

Socrates' argument is problematic for a second reason. In claiming that it is possible for a person to be temperate without knowing it, Socrates contradicts his earlier contention that if a person is temperate, he must have some opinion about it, since temperance necessarily gives some intimation of its nature which enables its possessor to form an idea of it (159a1–3). If this is true, as he previously assured Charmides, then it cannot be true, as he now assures Critias, that a person can be temperate without knowing it; on the other hand, if a person can be temperate without knowing it, then from the mere fact that Charmides cannot define temperance it does not follow that he is not temperate. Socrates cannot have it both ways.

Having identified temperance with self-knowledge, Critias again asks whether Socrates agrees. Socrates coyly replies that before divulging his opinion, he needs time to reflect. However, the ensuing interlude of Socratic "reflection" is not the prelude to a momentous revelation. Having "reflected," Socrates merely invokes the *technē*-analogy and introduces another gratuitous complication. If

---

[25] A. E. Taylor, 1929: 52, is wrong in claiming that Critias "has not ... thought out the implications of his own distinction." So is Vlastos, 1981b: 207, n. 7, according to whom Critias is "a pretentious and unclear thinker."

temperance is knowing something (γιγνώσκειν ... τί), it must be a kind of knowledge (ἐπιστήμη τις); and, like all knowledge, it must be knowledge *of* something (τινός, 165c4–6). But of what? "Of oneself" (ἑαυτοῦ, 165c7), replies Critias. Socrates neither agrees nor disagrees; instead, he exploits the logic of the *technē*-analogy. Medicine is knowledge of health, carpentry is knowledge of building, and so on. Indeed, every *technē* is knowledge of something and invests its possessor with a unique expertise which enables him to produce some fine result (καλὸν ... ἔργον, 165d1–2). So if temperance is knowledge, it too must produce some fine result. What is it?

At this point, Critias registers a protest: Socrates is not inquiring rightly (οὐκ ὀρθῶς ζητεῖς, 165e3). Previously he had asked how temperance is different from all other knowledge; now he is asking how it is the same,[26] thereby overlooking the fact that temperance is different from medicine and carpentry in that it does *not* produce some fine result. Arithmetic and geometry differ from them in the same way. In short, although every *technē* is knowledge *of* something and invests its possessor with a unique expertise, it is not the case that every *technē* necessarily produces some fine result (165e3–166a2).

Commentators differ about how this exchange should be read. Some think that Critias' objection is symptomatic of Plato's own growing misgivings about the *technē*-analogy.[27] Thus Kahn declares:

Critias succeeds in blocking Socrates' use of *epagōgē* by twice challenging the tacit assumption of similarity on which the argument from analogy must rely ... [Plato] has now made the reader aware of the weakness of any argument from *epagōgē*, in its implicit assumption of relevant similarity between the cases cited and the item under dispute. The reader may now expect greater rigor in the method of argumentation.[28]

Perhaps. But if "the reader" does expect this, the expectation is quickly disappointed. For Socrates continues to make copious use

---

[26] Friedländer, 1964, II: 73, defends Socrates on the ground that, in asking both how temperance differs from and resembles other kinds of knowledge, he is searching for "the *genus proximum* and the *differentia specifica*." But this is nothing more than an *ad hoc* rescue operation conducted under the dubious auspices of Aristotelian logical categories alien to Socratic thought.

[27] See, e.g., Guthrie, 1975: 168; Irwin, 1977: 75–76; Saunders, 1987: 170–71; and Kahn, 1996: 191–203.

[28] 1996: 194.

of arguments from *epagōgē* and with the same cavalier disregard of dissimilarities. The only discernible difference between his previous and subsequent use of them is that before deducing his next inference – that, like other kinds of knowledge, temperance has a distinct object – he acknowledges that this conclusion cannot be known to be true with complete certainty. But he clearly thinks that it is eminently reasonable – so reasonable, in fact, that he pronounces the opposite view – Critias' – "strange" (ἄτοπον). The upshot is that Critias' "challenge" is largely ignored and Socrates' method of argumentation remains largely the same.

Whether Plato actually employs Critias as a mouthpiece for his own growing misgivings about the *technē*-analogy is a question which lies beyond the scope of this book. For our purposes, it is sufficient to notice that Socrates does not dispute Critias' complaint that he is not inquiring rightly; on the contrary, he concedes the point: "You are right" (166a3). However, his concession is hedged with qualifications. Having just been refuted (or, at least, corrected) about a matter of considerable importance, Socrates does not respond to Critias as he routinely expects his interlocutors to respond to him. He neither bemoans the fact that he had previously been the unwitting victim of a false belief – the greatest evil that can befall a human being (*G.* 458a8–b1) – nor applauds Critias as his greatest benefactor – the appropriate response on the part of someone who has just undergone the beneficial experience of refutation (*G.* 506c2). Instead, he shifts his ground and tries to salvage whatever he can: "You are right. But ..." (166a3).

But what? Having acknowledged that he was wrong in thinking that temperance produces some fine result, Socrates insists that he was right about two other things: first, although arithmetic and geometry do not produce a unique result, they do have a unique subject matter; second, their subject matter, like that of every science, is distinct from the science itself. In short, knowledge is always distinct from its object. So if temperance is a kind of knowledge, the same must be true of it.

Critias disagrees. Unlike all other knowledge, which is knowledge of something other than itself, temperance is knowledge both of other things and of itself (τε ἄλλων ἐπιστημῶν ἐπιστήμη ἐστὶ καὶ αὐτὴ ἑαυτῆς, 166c2–3); furthermore, he thinks Socrates is well aware of this, but is ignoring it because he is only interested in refuting him. Socrates does not deny that refuting Critias is one of his objectives, but he does deny that it is his only one:

[H]ow could you possibly think that even if I were to refute everything you say, I would be doing it for any other reasons than the one I would give for a thorough investigation of my own statements – the fear of unconsciously thinking I know something when I do not. And this is what I claim to be doing now, examining the argument for my own sake primarily, but perhaps also for the sake of my friends. (166c7–d4)

Wrenched from context, as it usually is, this assurance that elenctic examination is always *self*-examination seems to underscore Socrates' philosophical seriousness.[29] In fact, it reveals his lack of seriousness. First, it is a mere diversionary maneuver which enables Socrates to conceal his flawed methodology by appealing to his (allegedly) salutary intentions. Second, it is patently insincere. That this is so is borne out both by what precedes and by what follows it. Coming, as it does, from someone who had just been refuted and who had responded to refutation by shifting his ground, the solemn announcement, "I examine arguments primarily for my own sake," becomes singularly unconvincing. And it is even more unconvincing when he proceeds to transfer the argumentative burden from his own shoulders to those of his interlocutor and thereupon exhorts him to attend to the argument instead of worrying about who is refuting whom. The evasion works. Critias drops his protest.

Called upon to clarify his contention that temperance is self-knowledge, Critias repeats that it is a unique kind of knowledge which is both of other things and of itself, that is, it is knowledge of knowledge. Prompted by Socrates, he agrees that it is also knowledge of lack of knowledge; for if temperance is knowledge of what one knows (ἐπιστημῶν ἐπιστήμη), it must also be knowledge of what one does not know (ἀνεπιστημοσύνης ἐπιστήμη, 166e6–7). Socrates thereupon points out that if this is true, then two important epistemic consequences follow: first, only the temperate man will know himself (ἑαυτόν) and be able to examine

---

[29] Commenting on this passage, Vlastos writes: "Moments of self-revelation like these are rare in the early dialogues" and "Socrates means to be taken at his word" (1971: 9–10).

what he knows and does not know;[30] second, only he will be able to examine other people to determine what they know and do not know (167a1–4).

Socrates finds both claims problematic. His reasoning – tortuous in the extreme – is as follows. If there is a kind of knowledge which is both knowledge of other things and of itself, it must differ from every other cognitive or perceptual capacity (δύναμις). For if such knowledge exists, it must not only be knowledge *of* something; it must also be *of a nature to be* (ἔχει τινὰ τοιαύτην δύναμιν ὥστε τινὸς εἶναι, 168b3) knowledge of something, just as that which is greater *than* something else is not only greater than it, but also *of a nature to be* greater than it. The question, then, is: Is there anything of which it may be truly said that when a property by virtue of which that thing is related to some other thing is applied to that thing itself, the same reflexivity invests it with the "being" (τὴν οὐσίαν) of the thing to which it is related? It does not seem so. For example, if vision were both of other things, i.e., of color, and of itself, then there would be a kind of vision which is not of color, but of vision and lack of vision; if hearing were both of other things, i.e., of sound, and of itself, then there would be a kind of hearing which is not of sound, but of hearing and lack of hearing. The same is true of magnitude and number and similar things: "[If] we should discover something greater that is greater than the greater things and than itself, but greater than nothing than which the other greater things are greater," then "if it were actually greater than itself, it would also be less than itself." Similarly, "anything that was the double of other doubles and of itself would ... be half of itself and of the other doubles." Similarly, anything that is more than itself will also be less; anything heavier will also be lighter; anything older will also be younger; and so on. But it seems absurd to say this about vision, hearing, and magnitude. And it seems equally absurd to say it about knowledge. It would seem that knowledge can no more know itself than vision can see itself, or hearing hear itself, or desire desire itself, or wish wish itself, or love love itself, or fear fear itself, or belief believe itself (167c8–168a4).

---

[30] The shift from temperance as knowledge of one*self* to knowledge of one's *knowledge* is sometimes judged fallacious (see, e.g., Tuckey, 1951: 33–37; and Saunders, 1987: 169–70, 192). For rebuttals, see Brun, 1960: 63–64; Santas, 1973: 119, n. 12; Guthrie, 1975: 169; and Chrétien, 1987: 22.

For reasons which I cannot fathom, Critias claims to understand this argument and thinks that its conclusion follows necessarily. Socrates seems pleased with the argument too and thinks it shows that it is highly unlikely that such knowledge exists. However, he is unwilling categorically to deny that it does. It would take "some great man" to determine whether "there are things that apply to themselves," and, if so, whether temperance is one of them (169a1). Having suggested that they investigate this difficult matter on some future occasion, he proposes that they assume for the sake of the discussion that such knowledge does exist and asks Critias to explain how it would be beneficial (ὠφέλιμον, 169c1), that is, how it would enable its possessor to know what he knows and does not know (169d5–8).

Methodologically speaking, this is a very puzzling passage. Having just acknowledged the limits of analogical argumentation, with "its implicit assumption of relevant similarity between the cases cited and the item under dispute," Socrates proceeds to refute Critias' definition of temperance with an analogical argument. Although Critias concedes that Socrates' conclusion follows, his previous remarks about relevant dissimilarities provide him with a cogent rejoinder. In response to Socrates' contention that it is "strange" (ἄτοπον) to say that temperance is knowledge both of something else and of itself – a claim which makes temperance different from every other kind of knowledge – Critias should have said: "Of course it is strange. Temperance *is* different from every other kind of knowledge. That was precisely my point. You cannot hope to persuade me that I am mistaken in believing that temperance is different from every other kind of knowledge by means of an *epagōgē* designed to show that temperance is different from every other kind of knowledge!"

Of course, Critias does not lodge this objection. Instead, in reply to Socrates' query about how knowledge which is both of other things and of itself would be beneficial, he produces a series of analogies which tell against his repeated assurances that temperance is different from every other kind of knowledge: just as a person who has swiftness and beauty will be swift and beautiful, so also a person who has self-knowledge will know himself. Socrates does not dispute the tautological claim that a person who has self-knowledge knows himself; what he wants to know, however, is how this (alleged) knowledge would be beneficial in the sense of enabling its possessor to know what he knows and does not know (169e6–8). Critias thinks the answer is obvious: it is because self-knowledge and knowing what one knows and does not know are the same (ταὐτόν, 170a1).

Socrates is inclined to disagree. His reasoning – 170a6–171c10 – is as follows:

(i)   If there is such a thing as knowledge of knowledge, its subject matter (or content) is confined to what is and what is not knowledge.

(ii)   But the knowledge that something is knowledge is not the same as the knowledge that something is healthy or musical; the latter are known by the *technai* of medicine and music whereas the former is known by knowledge.

(iii)   Therefore if a person has no knowledge of medicine or music but only knowledge of knowledge, he will know *that* he knows something, but not *what* he knows.

(iv)   So if temperance is knowledge of knowledge, the temperate man will not know what he knows and does not know; he will only know that he knows and does not know something.

(v)   Nor will he know what other people know and do not know; he will know only that they have some knowledge.

(vi)   So the temperate man will not be able to distinguish a competent doctor from a quack (or any other genuine practitioner of a *technē* from an imposter). To do that, he must be a doctor himself.

(vii)   Therefore, if temperance is knowledge of knowledge and lack of knowledge, then insofar as it enables its possessor to know only *that* he and other people know something but not *what* they know and do not know, it is not beneficial but useless.[31]

---

[31] This argument has recently been championed by Kahn, 1996: 199, who agrees that "one cannot test the credentials of others in regard to a subject in which the tester himself lacks expertise." Kahn thinks the argument has "serious consequences" for the Socratic enterprise of testing the wisdom of others: for if one cannot distinguish a doctor from a quack (or any other genuine practitioner of a *technē* from an imposter) unless one is a doctor (or a practitioner of the relevant *technē*) oneself, how can Socrates, who is a practitioner of none of these *technai*, expose false claimants of knowledge? According to Kahn, he cannot. A similar objection is raised by Tuckey, 1951: 66–67, who acknowledges that Socrates' claim that a non-expert cannot distinguish genuine practitioners from imposters seems inconsistent with his claim that the craftsmen knew many fine things (*Ap.* 22d1–2) – a claim which presupposes that Socrates *can* recognize genuine practitioners. However, Tuckey thinks the inconsistency is only apparent and easily re-

This argument is intended to show that the second-order knowledge (or meta-knowledge) under examination – knowledge of knowledge – cannot enable its possessor to know what he and other people know and do not know unless he also has some first-order knowledge, that is, unless, in addition to knowing what is and is not knowledge, he knows some specific subject matter. For it is its specific subject matter which distinguishes each kind of knowledge (and each *technē*) from every other.

Before examining this argument, it is worth noticing a preliminary point. There is no analogy between knowledge of medicine or music, on the one hand, and knowledge of knowledge, on the other, unless we assume that, like medicine and music, virtue – and, therefore, temperance, which is one of its "parts" – is a *technē*; and that, like the possessor of the former, the doctor and the musician, the possessor of the latter, the temperate man, is a practitioner of a *technē*. However, to assume this is to reinstate the very *technē*-analogy which, according to some commentators,[32] had just been criticized (by Plato with Critias serving as his mouthpiece) on the ground that it relies too heavily on the similarities between virtue and the *technai* and is insufficiently sensitive to the dissimilarities between them. Of course, this is more a criticism of Critias' definition of temperance than of Socrates' criticism of it. But if Plato really is criticizing (or having second thoughts about) the *technē*-analogy in the *Charmides*, this is surely one of the criticisms he would have made. Instead, he makes a very different criticism. The foregoing argument is intended to demonstrate that if Critias is right in thinking that temperance is knowledge of knowledge, then the temperate man cannot know *what* he or anyone else knows and does not know; he can only know *that* he and they know something.

But the argument is unsound. In order to distinguish a competent doctor from a quack (or any other genuine practitioner of a *technē* from an imposter), one need not be a doctor oneself. It is, of course, true that anyone who can make such distinctions must

moved. Following Pohlenz, 1913: 54, he removes it by arguing that Socrates' assessments of technical expertise are based on the application of the elenchus and, therefore, do not require that he himself possess the relevant expertise. Kahn rejects this solution on the ground that there is no such thing as elenctic knowledge, there is only knowledge of medicine, carpentry, etc. (199–200).

[32] See n. 27.

know, in some sense of "know," what a doctor knows. But "knowing what a doctor knows" is ambiguous. It could mean either that one *knows the same things* that doctors know or that one knows the *kinds of things* that doctors know. Although the first sense of "knowing what a doctor knows" requires that one be a doctor oneself, the second does not. All it requires is that one has some broad but nevertheless genuine understanding of the knowledge and abilities which constitute medical expertise. Only by overlooking this distinction could anyone claim that it takes an expert to recognize an expert. In fact, Socrates has greatly overestimated the difficulty of identifying experts and distinguishing them from non-experts.

To be sure, there are some technical and highly specialized situations in which only an expert can assess someone else's claim to expertise: only a legal expert can assess the expertise of a law student taking a bar exam, only an expert historian can assess the expertise of a candidate for an advanced degree in history, and so on. But there are many other situations which do not require this kind of expertise. Many assessments of expertise (or lack of it) are made, not by determining what someone does (and does not) know, but by observing what he can (and cannot) do. Vacationing in the tropics, I develop a fever and break out in a generalized rash. I book an appointment with the first available doctor who examines me, fails to notice the rash, and concludes that I have the flu. Skeptical, I call his attention to my rash covered body and humbly suggest that I have the measles. Astonished by this hitherto unnoticed symptom, he concurs. I do not need a medical degree to realize that I am not in the presence of a brilliant diagnostician. In other situations, assessments of expertise (or lack of it) are made by inspecting the alleged expert's product. Unhandy with tools and ignorant of the principles of engineering, I hire a carpenter to build a house. Upon moving in, I notice that the walls are sagging and that part of the roof has collapsed. I do not need an engineering degree to realize that my contractor is not a skilled practitioner of the *technē* of carpentry. Such judgments need not be withheld on the ground that I am neither a doctor nor a carpenter. Assessments of expertise (or lack of it) can also be made in many other ways. Sometimes a non-expert need only collect a few bits of obscure or highly technical information which only an expert would be likely to know and then query the alleged expert to determine whether he knows them. Other determinations of expertise (or lack of it) are easier still. To determine whether you know Greek, I need not know the language myself; I need only hand you a Greek text, ask you to translate, and observe your embarrassment at being unable to make head or tail of it.

Socrates' argument can be faulted on another ground. The argument tries to show that if temperance is knowledge of knowledge and lack of knowledge, then the temperate man can only know *that* he (or someone else) knows something; he cannot know *what* he (or someone else) knows. To know that, he must be an expert himself. The unanswered question is: How can the temperate man know *that* he (or someone else) knows something unless he knows *what* that knowledge is? The answer is, of course, that he cannot. The same fact (if it is a fact) which prevents the temperate man from knowing *what* someone knows unless he knows it himself also prevents him from knowing *that* someone else knows something. Knowing only the criteria which must be satisfied if something is to count as knowledge, how can the temperate man know *that* someone's purported knowledge-claims satisfy them unless he knows *what* he claims to know? Second-order knowledge that someone has knowledge is parasitic on first-order knowledge of what it is. Indeed, to say that someone knows something, for example, carpentry, *is* to say what he knows.

Socrates advances one final argument again Critias' definition of temperance. It has been agreed that if temperance is knowing what one knows and does not know, it is beneficial for its possessor. Equipped with this knowledge (and the knowledge of what other people know and do not know), it would seem that a person could live his life unerringly, doing only that about which he has knowledge and assigning all else to others with the requisite expertise. It would also seem that a city based on that principle would conduct itself admirably and well (καλῶς καὶ εὖ πράττειν), and those who live admirably and well are happy (εὐδαίμονας, 172a1–3). According to Socrates, however, this is an illusion. Such an arrangement would not be beneficial in the deepest and most important sense. It is true that in such a state of affairs everything would be done in accordance with knowledge, that is, in accordance with the relevant *technai* and under the direction of acknowledged experts. But this would not be sufficient for happiness.

Critias is astonished by the curious turn the argument has taken

– apparently with good reason. For the philosopher who believes that virtue is knowledge to suggest that those whose lives are completely governed by knowledge would not necessarily be either virtuous or happy seems bizarre and utterly un-Socratic.

But this initial impression is unfounded. Socrates is not rejecting the rule of knowledge *simpliciter*, but only of a certain *kind* of knowledge. That this is so is borne out by his response to Critias' next question: If we reject the rule of knowledge, what will we put in its place? Critias thinks human happiness is contingent on behaving as knowledge directs. Socrates agrees, but he sees a further problem: knowledge of what? Surely not of shoe-making or working with bronze or wood? So it is not knowledge *simpliciter* that leads to happiness but knowledge of a certain kind, namely, knowledge of good and evil (τὸ ἀγαθόν ... καὶ τὸ κακόν, 174b10). Lacking this, medicine would still produce health, weaving would still produce clothing, and so on; however, this is not sufficient to insure the kind of happiness Socrates is talking about which is not contingent on *having* these things but in *using them properly* (174c9–d7).[33] So even if there is such a thing as knowledge of knowledge and lack of knowledge, it would not necessarily be beneficial to its possessor. Socrates thereupon concludes that his (and Critias') previous assumption that temperance is beneficial now seems hasty and ill-advised. For how can something be beneficial if it produces no benefits? So the discussion has been in vain.

At the same time, Socrates cannot bring himself to believe that temperance is not beneficial; indeed, he thinks it is a great good. It is only because he is such a poor investigator that he has failed to understand its nature and to discover its benefits. Not only have Critias and he failed to discover the nature of temperance; they also made many wrong concessions along the way. They did so in order to maintain the thesis that the temperate man knows what he knows and does not know – a thesis now seen to be absurd. For nothing can be more irrational (ἀλογώτερον) than to believe that one can know in a sort of way (ἀμῶς γέ πως) what one does not know at all. As a result, the inquiry (ἡ ζήτησις) is mocking them (175c3–d6). What troubles Socrates most of all, however, is that Charmides will derive no benefit from his temperance.

---

[33] This doctrine is elaborated more fully in the *Euthydemus* where Socrates speaks of "the royal art" (τὴν βασιλικὴν ... τέχνην, 291b5) which, by regulating the subordinate arts by directing them to their proper ends, insures happiness.

Charmides again confesses that he does not know whether he is temperate; indeed, in view of Socrates' and Critias' failure to discover what temperance is, how could he know? Nevertheless, he is willing to be "charmed" by Socrates every day for as long as he thinks necessary. Critias thinks this is sufficient proof of Charmides' temperance and urges him never to forsake Socrates. Charmides promises to obey his guardian – even if has to resort to force – an ominous forecast of his later willingness to employ force to achieve his political ends. And with this the dialogue concludes.

In studying the *Charmides*, it is important to remember that Charmides and Critias later became members of the Thirty. It is also important to remember that many Athenians attributed their downfall to their association with Socrates. Since the dialogue provides no reason for thinking that Plato agreed,[34] we must assume that he accounted for their downfall in some other way. The opening pages of the dialogue provide several clues.

Here is Charmides – a beautiful youth full of promise. Although (allegedly) enamored of temperance, he is also highly susceptible to flattery and luxuriates in the attention of his admirers. He is also an intimate of Critias – a disrespecter of morality and a future tyrant. He thus combines in his person the two deadly ingredients against which the "Socrates" of the *Republic* warns: the capacity to be corrupted and the company of a potential corrupter.

Enter Socrates. Momentarily stunned by Charmides' physical beauty, he quickly recovers and asks whether he is equally beautiful in soul. Critias thinks so and adds that he is also the most temperate youth he knows. But Charmides is not so sure and agrees to be questioned. Surely if temperance is in him, he can say what it is. But he cannot and is quickly reduced to *aporia*. Having taxed Charmides' meager dialectical ability to the limits, Socrates enlists the services of Critias. Although somewhat better equipped than Charmides, he too soon founders and finds himself agreeing that although temperance is universally praised as the most admirable thing in the world, this assessment is wildly premature in view of the foregoing discussion which seems to suggest that it is not beneficial but useless. Socrates expresses concern for Charmides, albeit not for Critias, and Charmides agrees to participate in future discussions, unproductive though they are.

---

[34] In fact, many commentators think Plato wrote the *Charmides*, at least in part, to defend Socrates against this charge.

Many commentators have been baffled by the *Charmides* – a "curious and difficult"[35] dialogue "whose point is very hard to see."[36] The more radical question, of course, is: Does it have a point?

Anyone who ventures an answer to this question is obliged to ponder some hard questions: Has Socrates really conducted a serious investigation into the nature of temperance? Or has he merely tried to persuade his interlocutors that they do not know what it is and that every attempt to find out will inevitably end in failure? Has he really tried to persuade them that temperance is beneficial and worthy of being cultivated? Or has he merely tried to confuse them? Has he made a genuine effort to discover what they really believe? When they advance their opinions, does he take them seriously and examine them honestly and in good faith? Or does he distort what they say and even put words into their mouths so he can refute them more easily? Has he conducted the argument chiefly (or solely) for his own benefit? Or has he also conducted it partly for his interlocutors' benefit? More radically, has he conducted it for anyone's benefit?

The dialogue provides no reason for thinking that Socrates has conducted a serious investigation into anything. His purpose throughout does not seem to be truth, but victory. In the process, he employs many arguments which are demonstrably fallacious or unsound. *Aporia* there is, but its effects are the very opposite of those envisaged in the *Apology*. No one is seized by his ignorance and impelled to take up the philosophical quest. Although more than a third of the dialogue is concerned with self-knowledge, no one achieves it; on the contrary, if the dialogue proves anything, it proves that self-knowledge is difficult to define, even more difficult to achieve, and, in the end, probably not worth achieving. By the end of the discussion, Charmides is as confused as he was at the beginning. Perhaps more so. Instead of emerging with his soul improved, he is reduced to incoherent stammering about "improvement" and the Socratic "charm" in which he does not believe but which allegedly produces it. In the meantime, Critias looks on, like a helpless parent unsure of what his child needs but sure that he needs something, vacantly praising temperance and inexplicably urging Charmides to cultivate it by attaching himself to Socrates.

---

[35] Guthrie, 1975: 163.   [36] Crombie, 1962, I: 211.

Even if Plato did write the *Charmides* partly to absolve Socrates of all responsibility for the crimes of his former companions, conversations like the one depicted in it might very well have unintentionally undermined the morality of (some of) his interlocutors. On this subject, Edward Meyrick Goulburn has written well:

[Socrates'] *design* was to point out to men that they had no clear and consistent notions of moral subjects, and to lead them to form such notions. The *result*, it may be feared, was to puzzle them as to right and wrong, and make them question what their moral sense told them ... Socrates *did* raise questions ... without setting them at rest; and though ... he did this from his thorough honesty of mind, and with a view to make his countrymen honest-minded, one can quite conceive that in many instances the effect was to make them skeptical ... Where a few minds were touched and improved, a greater number would accept the difficulties as an excuse for throwing overboard altogether all care for virtue.[37]

The clear implication seems to be that this may very well have happened to Charmides. In any event, before denouncing him, we should ponder Goulburn's sobering words.

We should also ponder the middle-period Plato's arresting claim that the greater the initial promise, the more lamentable its corruption. The very qualities that make up the "philosophical nature" (τῆς φιλοσόφου φύσεως) are the principal causes of its corruption and destruction when the person is poorly educated and badly brought up, and it is such men who do the greatest harm to cities and individuals (*R.* 495a4–b6). Although unsparing in his criticism of cities and institutions, Plato is often surprisingly gentle towards the very persons whose views and behavior he most deplores. His criticism is often tempered by his perception of the fragility of youth's firm but untested resolve. Viewed in the light of once bright but now faded promise, apparently unredeemable character flaws elicit criticism tinged with compassion and regret for what might have been. Such understanding, typical of middle-period Plato, is unavailable to those whose criticism springs solely from moral outrage and can only be achieved by those who are willing to look long and hard in the most unlikely places. Charmides' end is all the more regrettable in light of his promising beginnings.

[37] 1858: 51, 60–61.

CHAPTER 8

Euthyphro

Of all the interlocutors encountered in the early dialogues, few are more interesting than Euthyphro.[1] A diviner (μάντις) by profession, he is a claimant to esoteric theological knowledge which enables him to unravel even the knottiest moral issues, and remarkable prophetic powers which enable him to predict the future with universal accuracy. Although much younger than Socrates, he is not a youth;[2] his father is an old man and he himself is a familiar figure in the Assembly. Convinced that his knowledge of things divine uniquely qualifies him as a theological and moral expert, he seems a made-to-order target for the transparently skeptical and irony drenched Socrates with whom he becomes embroiled in debate about piety (τὸ ὅσιον)[3] on the royal porch of the King Archon after announcing that he is prosecuting his father for murder – a morally controversial and socially scandalous course of action which has outraged his relatives and infuses the discussion with a sense of practical urgency. The ensuing search for a definition of piety is no disinterested academic exercise. Euthyphro's dogged attempt to define this familiar but unexpectedly elusive term is an exercise in self-justification on the part of a zealous moralist determined to prove that he knows what he is doing. Plato often

---

[1] Unknown outside the pages of Plato, Euthyphro is generally believed to have been an historical person. His historicity is implied at *Crat.* 396d4–397a1 where he is traced to the deme of Prospalte and credited with having inspired Socrates to study the etymology of names. He is also alluded to at *Crat.* 399a1, 407d8, 409d1–2, and 428c7.

[2] Estimates of his age range from fairly young (Allen, 1970: 20) to middle-aged (A. E. Taylor, 1929: 146).

[3] The Greek term has no exact English equivalent. "Holiness" has Judeo-Christian overtones which are foreign to it, whereas "piety" sounds quaint and conjures up dreary images of Victorian prudery at which modern readers smile. An action is pious (ὅσιον) if it is sanctioned by divine (as opposed to human) law (Allen, 1970: 25). The term connotes a religious duty – that part of justice which has to do with the gods rather than with men (*Eu.* 12e5–8). I will retain the term "piety" for lack of a better one.

plays on proper names, and most commentators think the title "straight thinker" (from εὐθύς and φρονέω) is ironic.[4]

Euthyphro is often cited as the paradigmatic example of the puffed-up know-it-all ripe for dialectical deflation, and even the most charitable reader must admit that there is truth in the charge. His superior air and prodigious self-confidence are evident in his every utterance. He flaunts his theological credentials and adopts a patronizing tone towards Socrates – a mere layman in Euthyphro's opinion – and towards people generally. His overconfidence is matched by his insensitivity which borders on the monumental and blinds him to the fact that he is not being taken seriously – either by Socrates, who is merely amused by him, or by his family, who think he is a religious fanatic and possibly even insane (μαίνεσθαι, 4a1).

According to J. Adam, Euthyphro is "the incarnation of Plato's view of Athenian orthodoxy carried consistently into practice" and, by implication, a representative of the traditional mind-set that was responsible for Socrates' death.[5] Both contentions are contradicted by the facts. Athenian religion was based on ritual observance, not on credal allegiance, and it required no doctrinal orthodoxy of its adherents. Furthermore, Euthyphro's brand of religion, with its "fundamentalist" belief in the literal truth of Homeric theology, was not taken seriously by most educated Athenians.[6] Both contentions are also contradicted by the texts. When Socrates divulges that he is being prosecuted, *inter alia*, for not believing in the gods of the city and for introducing new ones, Euthyphro is surprised and responds as a kindred spirit, tracing the charge to Socrates' well-known claim to be guided by his *daimonion* – a claim which his enemies have misconstrued as a religious innovation (3b5–6). The fact that Socrates' legal predicament comes as news to Euthyphro reveals that, although he knows him by reputation and personal acquaintance, he knows nothing about his escalating problems with Athens.

As is abundantly clear from the conversation that follows, he also

---

[4] A notable dissenter is Geach, 1966: 382, who calls Euthyphro "Mr. Right-Mind" and applauds both what he is doing and his reasons for doing it.

[5] 1890: xxiv. So, too, Croiset, 1949: 183: "Euthyphron est en quelque sorte le type de cette ignorance naïve et incurable qui avait condamné Socrate."

[6] See Burnet, 1924: 85–86; A. E. Taylor, 1929: 147; Allen, 1970: 62; Guthrie, 1975: 103; and Dorion, 1997: 180–85.

knows nothing about the Socratic elenchus. His first (and probably last) taste of it is a bitter one. Capable neither of setting forth a coherent case nor of following a sustained argument, Euthyphro is hopelessly unequipped for discussion with the likes of Socrates and almost immediately out of his depth. The helplessness to which he is reduced at the end of the dialogue is a predictable sequel to the confidence which he exudes at the beginning. Predictable to the reader, that is. Euthyphro himself has no idea of what he is in for. He thinks – and is encouraged to think – that he can shed light on the nature of piety and thereby instruct the lamentably ignorant Socrates who is "eager" to become his disciple.

In defense of this policy of ironic flattery and deliberate concealment of purpose, it might be argued that if Socrates had laid his cards on the table and announced that during the next few hours Euthyphro's whole theological *Weltanschauung* would come crashing down like a house of cards, he would have extricated himself from the discussion and fled. But however the policy is to be explained, it can only be described as a form of intellectual ambush.

Commentators are repelled, to varying degrees, by all Socrates' interlocutors, but they are particularly repelled by Euthyphro. According to A. E. Taylor[7] and R. E. Allen,[8] he had no legal case against his father and knew it; Taylor thinks his litigation was motivated purely by self-interest: the desire to purge himself of the pollution (τὸ μίασμα) which attached to him as the relative of a murderer. T. F. Morris[9] thinks his litigation was motivated primarily by resentment: in dire need of competent legal advice, his father had not consulted Euthyphro, who lived in the same city and perhaps in the same home, but solicited the opinion of a stranger in faraway Athens. As for Euthyphro himself, no pejorative is too extreme: he is "dogmatic" and "not very bright,"[10] a "spoiled child,"[11] a person of "pseudo-piety"[12] and "ultra-pious pretensions,"[13] who "combines [within himself] the worst features of a sciolist and a prig,"[14] a "comic figure" whose "pretended elevation above [his contemporaries] is pure imposture and alazony,"[15] an exponent of "crackpot theology,"[16] a "pig-

---

[7] 1929: 146–47.   [8] 1970: 20–21.   [9] 1990: 316.   [10] Teloh, 1986: 27.
[11] Shorey, 1933: 77.   [12] Friedländer, 1964, II: 82.   [13] Grote, 1867, I: 310.
[14] J. Adam, 1890: xxiv.   [15] Versényi, 1982: 38.   [16] McPherran, 1996: 182.

headed professional" and "superhypocrite,"[17] and a "complacent fanatic" who "[f]or sheer sluggishness of intellect it would be hard to beat."[18] One critic has gone so far as to suggest that he "would have done well in the Nazi Youth Movement."[19]

This extraordinary torrent of invective is prompted by the tenacity with which Euthyphro clings to the belief that it is pious to prosecute his father in spite of the fact that he cannot define piety. From it, we can reconstruct the standard picture's estimate of him: whereas a reasonable man would have been stopped dead in his tracks by Socrates' arguments, abandoned his "divine command" theory of ethics, and dropped (or, at least, reconsidered) his litigation against his father, Euthyphro learns nothing. Although momentarily perplexed, he is not seriously shaken. His inner core has not been touched, his confidence has not been undermined, and his behavior has not been rendered problematic. He is not interested in achieving deeper understanding, but in displaying that he already has it and that Socratic criticism is wasted on him. The religion to which he subscribes solves the only problems he has. Or wants. He participates in the discussion but not in the quest. In spite of his pious facade, he is actually an impenetrable dogmatist who catches no glimpse of what the shameless Callicles perceives very clearly when he declares that Socrates' views, if taken seriously, would turn the life of mortals on its head (*G.* 481c1–4). Unlike Callicles, who recoils from the prospect, Euthyphro is oblivious to it.

But Socrates' interlocutors are seldom as bad as their publicity. And Euthyphro is no exception. In saying this, I am not overlooking his deficient intellectual grasp and off-putting character traits. But if we are not completely to approve of him, neither are we at liberty completely to disapprove of him. As Jowett humanely – and rightly – observes, whatever his intellectual and personal shortcomings, Euthyphro "is not a bad man."[20] Accordingly, instead of evaluating him in Socratic terms and adding our voices to the already deafening chorus of his detractors, we need to evaluate him on his own terms. Two questions cry out for answers: first,

---

[17] Cook, 1996: 36, 144.
[18] Vlastos, 1971: 13.
[19] Holland, 1981–82: 5.
[20] 1872, I: 298 – a judgment endorsed by Guthrie, 1975: 103.

exactly what kind of expertise does Euthyphro claim to have?; second, does Socrates demonstrate that he does not have it? I will argue that an accurate answer to the first question requires a negative answer to the second.

A dramatic dialogue – and, by common consent, one of Plato's earliest works – the *Euthyphro* begins *in medias res*. The scene is Athens; the year is 399.

Having learned that Socrates is being prosecuted, *inter alia*, for religious innovations, Euthyphro attributes the charge to jealousy and love of slander, and thereupon draws a parallel between Socrates and himself. Superior people like themselves must always endure the petty criticism of inferior ones. His litigation against his father has elicited similar criticism. Even his infallibly accurate prophecies are laughed at in the Assembly. But these critics are inconsequential and should be ignored. In thus urging Socrates to disregard the opinions of "the Many" – the same advice Socrates gives Crito – Euthyphro reveals that he is an independent thinker with the courage of his convictions who will not allow the disapproval of his theologically benighted relatives to dissuade him from doing what he thinks right.[21]

Inexplicably, Socrates taunts him on this point. Instead of rejoicing that in Euthyphro he has finally found an interlocutor who, whether right or wrong,[22] has at least managed to transcend the unstable opinions of "the Many," he feigns shock and observes that most people would strongly disapprove of a son who prosecuted his own father. He adds that he himself is inclined to agree that it would not be right for just anyone (τοῦ ἐπιτυχόντος, 4a11–b2) to do such a thing, but only someone far advanced in wisdom. Assured that Euthyphro is *not* just anyone and that he *is* far advanced in wisdom, Socrates asks a puzzling – and very un-Socratic – question to which he gives an equally puzzling – and equally un-Socratic – answer: Was the deceased a relative? Surely he was, for no one would risk displeasing the gods by prosecuting his father

---

[21] Actually, Euthyphro's relatives do not object to his litigation on the ground that it is wrong to prosecute one's father, but on the very different ground that his father is probably innocent of the charge of murder and, even if he is not, should not be prosecuted because the deceased was himself a murderer (4d5–e3).

[22] As Allen, 1970: 22, points out, Socrates' chief purpose is not to determine whether Euthyphro is right or wrong in prosecuting his father, but to determine whether he can justify his conduct by producing the standard to which he appeals in making his first-order moral judgments.

for the death of a stranger (4b4–6) – much less a mere hired man (θητός, 15d5–6).[23]

Euthyphro is appalled by this absurd (γελοῖον) line of reasoning. Whether the deceased was a relative is irrelevant, he explains; what matters is whether he is a wrongdoer.[24] If he is, he should be prosecuted – even if he shares one's hearth and table. The pollution is the same if one does not purge oneself *and him* (τε καὶ ἐκεῖνον, 4c1–3) of the corrupting effects of his wrongdoing.[25] In fact, the deceased was a day-laborer on his father's farm in Naxos. Having killed a slave in a drunken rage, he had been bound hand and foot and cast into a ditch by Euthyphro's father whose subsequent negligence resulted in his death.

Socrates again marvels at Euthyphro's boldness and blatant disregard of public opinion. Is his knowledge of piety so exact that, in prosecuting his father, he is not afraid that he might be doing something impious himself?

These Socratic appeals to *endoxa* are puzzling. It is true that prosecuting one's father is an action which would have struck Euthyphro's contemporaries as abhorrent.[26] But of what relevance is this sociological fact about Athenian *mores*? Socrates never attaches any epistemic weight to the opinions of "the Many"; on the contrary, he habitually disregards them and urges his interlocutors to do the same. Of the many passages that could be cited, two must suffice. In response to Crito's worries about how his reputation would suffer if "people" were to think that he had been unwilling to provide the funds necessary for Socrates' escape from prison, he asks:

[S]hould we follow the opinion of the many and fear it, or that of the one, if there is one who has knowledge of these things and before whom we feel fear and shame more than before all the others? (*Cr.* 47c11–d2)

---

[23] A remark which, according to the politically offended Stone, 1988: 150, reveals that these humble folk never entered "the field of Socratic vision" because they "did not 'count'." It is true that the typical Athenian had a low view of the *banausia*. However, before ascribing this attitude to Socrates, it should be remembered that the typical Athenian also made a sharp distinction between manual laborers (μισθωτοί) and craftsmen (δημιουργοί). See Roberts, 1984: 69–71; and Mazel, 1987: 120–23. As is evident from Socrates' many allusions to the craftsmen, he had a deep respect for them and for the understanding which they brought to their work.

[24] A "very Socratic-sounding" rebuke, as Arieti, 1991: 144, aptly observes.

[25] An *addendum* which contradicts A. E. Taylor's contention (see n. 7 above) that Euthyphro was motivated purely by self-interest. Even the highly critical Allen, 1970: 23, concedes that Euthphro's motivation is "to some degree" unselfish.

[26] See Grote, 1867, I: 315; and Allen, 1970: 22–23.

Similarly, when Polus ridicules the Socratic thesis that it is better to suffer injustice than to commit it and assures him that it would be rejected out of hand by everyone, Socrates replies:

[Y]ou're trying to refute me in oratorical style, the way people in law-courts do when they think they're refuting some claim. There, too, one side thinks it's refuting the other when it produces many reputable witnesses on behalf of the arguments it presents, while the person who asserts the opposite produces only one witness, or none at all. This "refutation" is worthless, as far as truth is concerned. (*G.* 471e2–472a1)

Why, then, does he disagree when Euthyphro tells him the same thing? A curious inconsistency is in evidence here. Having rebuked Crito and Polus for taking the opinions of "the Many" too seriously, he rebukes Euthyphro for not taking them seriously enough. Clearly, he cannot have it both ways. How nice it would have been if Euthyphro had replied: "You surprise me, Socrates. I do not think one should base one's moral beliefs on the unstable opinions of 'the Many'. Nor do I think one should try to refute people in oratorical style, as they do in the lawcourts, by producing many witnesses. Such refutations are worthless as far as truth is concerned."

But what if Euthyphro had opted for the opposite point of view? What if he had not flouted the opinions of "the Many," sided with his relatives, and asserted that although, generally speaking, one ought to prosecute wrongdoers – murderers, in particular – one ought not prosecute if the wrongdoer is one's father? Would this thesis have fared any better? I cannot believe it. Had Euthyphro asserted this, Socrates would surely have objected on the ground that it makes no difference whether the wrongdoer is a relative; all that matters is whether he is a wrongdoer – precisely the ground here used by Euthyphro.

That this is not idle speculation is borne out by the fact that this is exactly what Socrates does say in the *Gorgias*:

[W]hoever avoids paying his due for his wrongdoing ... deserves to be miserable beyond all other men ... and the one who avoids paying what's due is always more miserable than the one who does pay it ... [I]f he or anyone else he cares about acts unjustly, he should voluntarily go to the place where he'll pay his due as soon as possible; he should go to the judge as though he were going to a doctor, anxious that the disease of injustice shouldn't be protracted and cause his soul to fester incurably ... [H]e should not keep his wrongdoing hidden but bring it out into the open, so that he may pay his due and get well … He should be his own chief accuser, and the accuser of other members of his family.[27] (*G.* 479e1–480d4)

In this passage, Socrates is in full agreement with Euthyphro: all wrongdoers should be punished – including friends and relatives. And if the wrongdoer will not turn himself in voluntarily, he should be compelled to do so *by members of his own family*. This is not the behavior of the religious fanatic, but of the virtuous man.[28]

The only possible conclusion that can be drawn from all this is that, given Socrates' views about the duties of people *vis-à-vis* wrongdoers, as set forth in the *Gorgias*, there is nothing outrageous or even mildly dubious about Euthyphro's litigation against his father; on the contrary, he is doing exactly what he ought to be doing. Insofar as Socrates denies (or questions) this in the *Euthyphro*, he contradicts himself. He also does Euthyphro the grave disservice of diverting him from doing what he himself believes is the right thing. These considerations throw a very different light on the whole discussion and the purpose for which it is being conducted. *Aporia* induced to make a person question beliefs that one thinks false or to deter him from conduct that one thinks wrong needs to be distinguished from *aporia* induced to make a person question beliefs that one thinks true or to deter him from conduct one thinks right. Knowingly to induce the latter renders one vulnerable to the charge of inducing *aporia* not as a means to the salutary ends of convicting him of ignorance and improving his soul, but as an end in itself and, therefore, of arguing for victory instead of truth.

Having expressed these general doubts about the morality of Euthyphro's conduct, Socrates becomes more specific. To determine whether Euthyphro can justify his contention that it is pious for him to prosecute his father, Socrates asks him to define piety. Of course, Euthyphro cannot define this term to Socrates' satis-

---

[27] Although most commentators dismiss Euthyphro's view of "pollution" as a piece of superstition (see, e.g., Vlastos, 1971: 12–13), it is, in fact, a distant relative of the Socratic view, set forth repeatedly in the *Gorgias*, that the wrongdoer's soul is a diseased soul which can only be restored to health by undergoing remedial punishment.

[28] See Méron, 1979: 182: "Il est très important de renoncer à l'interprétation usuelle mais étrange … qui veut faire de Socrate un champion de la solidarité familiale ou tribale au mépris du grand principe abstrait de justice."

faction; and for this reason his professed theological expertise is dismissed by Socrates (and legions of commentators) as a ludicrous pretension. However, this is not a textual claim; it is a philosophical thesis which begs the question of the correctness of the Socratic approach to moral philosophy and evaluates Euthyphro in light of it. More exactly, it signals a tacit endorsement of the so-called principle of "the priority of definition" according to which knowing the definition of a term is a necessary condition for applying it correctly.[29]

Before proceeding further, it is worth pointing out that Euthyphro need not have become embroiled in this search for a definition at all. In asking for a definition of piety, Socrates is asking for a standard (παραδείγματι) by which to identify pious actions and to distinguish them from impious ones (6e3–6). The implication is that, without such a standard, Euthyphro cannot justify his litigation against his father. More precisely, he cannot know that it is pious to prosecute his father unless he knows what piety is. The fact is, however, that Euthyphro has *already* justified his litigation by invoking the principle that wrongdoers ought to be prosecuted, including friends and relatives – a principle Socrates accepts. So if Euthyphro's father is a wrongdoer, the morally required course of action seems crystal clear: he ought to be prosecuted. So why does Euthyphro need a definition of piety? The answer cannot be: in order to determine whether it is pious to prosecute his father. Although having an airtight definition of "piety" may be the most reliable way of distinguishing pious actions from impious ones, clearly it is not the only way. In the *Gorgias*, Socrates has no definition of justice; but that does not prevent him from arguing that it is just to prosecute wrongdoers – all wrongdoers, including members of one's own family. If the absence of a definition of the relevant moral term poses no problems for Socrates, why should it pose any for Euthyphro? Furthermore, since Socrates himself views filial piety as a *prima facie* duty which can be (and often is) overridden by other duties, his professed skepticism about the morality of Euthyphro's conduct is not sincere but bogus. Lacking a defi-

---

[29] Although this principle is routinely ascribed to Socrates (see, e.g., Robinson, 1953: 51–52; Geach, 1966: 371; Santas, 1972: 127–41; Irwin, 1977a: 40–41; Burnyeat, 1977a: 381–98; Benson, 1990: 19–65; and Brickhouse and Smith, 1994: 45–55), he nowhere unambiguously affirms it and, therefore, nowhere clearly commits the so-called "Socratic fallacy" (see Geach, 1966: 371; Beversluis, 1987: 211–23; and Vlastos, 1990: 1–15, and 1994: 67–86).

nition of piety himself, a serious inquirer would have accepted Euthyphro's appeal to the principle that wrongdoers should be prosecuted as the best justification available under the circumstances. But Socrates is not a serious inquirer who is willing to play fair with his interlocutor; he is a "moral gadfly" who is determined to find fault – even if he agrees with him.

The arguments that Socrates advances against Euthyphro's definitions of piety are well known, and there is no need to belabor the obvious by dwelling on his lack of success. But what follows? According to Socrates, the epistemic consequences are momentous. Although he does not unambiguously assert that without a definition of piety Euthyphro cannot know that any action whatever is pious, he strongly implies that he cannot know that it is pious to prosecute his father.

The request for a definition is prefaced by a very technical explanation of the kind of answer Socrates wants:

Tell me ... what kind of thing do you say that [piety and impiety] are, both as regards murder and other things ... [I]s the pious not the same and alike (ταὐτόν) in every action, and the impious the opposite of all that is pious and like itself, and everything that is to be impious presents us with one form or appearance (μίαν τινὰ ἰδέαν) in so far as it is impious?. (5c8–d5)

Unaware that, in endorsing this piece of Socratic metaphysics, he is committing himself to an extraordinarily rigorous criterion of knowledge, Euthyphro concurs. The "What-is-*F*?" question follows:

Tell me then, what is the pious, and what the impious, do you say? (5d7)

According to Burnet,[30] Euthyphro "appears to be quite familiar" with Socrates' terminology and "accepts it without demur." He adds that Plato "always represents the matter in this way. No one ever hesitates for a moment when Socrates talks of ἰδέαι and εἴδη, and Socrates never finds it necessary to explain the terms." Neither claim can withstand textual scrutiny. Like many commentators, Burnet mistakes verbal assent for real assent.

It is true that Euthyphro "accepts" Socrates' terminology "without demur." But he does not have the faintest idea what he

---

[30] 1924: 112.

has "accepted." That this is so is borne out by his first response. Asked what piety is, he instantly betrays his lack of understanding:

> I say that the pious is to do what I am doing now, to prosecute the wrong-doer, be it about murder or temple robbery or anything else, whether the murderer is your father or your mother or anyone else; not to prosecute is impious. (5d8–e2)

As evidence for this contention, Euthyphro cites the case of Zeus, the best and most just of the gods, who punished his father for his misdeeds, just as he had punished his father for similar crimes. Euthyphro knows his Homer and thinks he is on solid theological and moral ground. In prosecuting his father, he is patterning his conduct on that of the gods. His life is an *imitatio deorum*. In approving of Zeus but disapproving of him, his relatives contradict themselves (5e2–6a5).

Before criticizing Euthyphro's first definition of piety, Socrates confesses that he finds it hard to believe that the gods disagree about what is pious and impious and that they behave impiously themselves.[31] But instead of explaining why he finds it hard to believe these things and presenting his moral critique of Homeric theology, thereby being of real help to Euthyphro, he drops the point and lapses into ironic self-deprecation, "acknowledging" that he is probably as wrong about this as he is about practically everything else and "deferring" to wiser heads like Euthyphro. This is as unfortunate as it is dishonest. In concealing his objections, he trivializes them and, in the process, shortchanges Euthyphro who understands neither what Socrates' misgivings about Homeric theology are nor what is really at issue between them.[32] In short, having explicitly questioned the morality of Euthyphro's litigation against his father, an action he thinks right, Socrates now implicitly endorses the truth of his theology, a belief-set he thinks largely false.

It is only after this pointless digression – and missed opportunity – that he faults Euthyphro for having produced an example of a

---

[31] He adds that he suspects this is the real reason he has been charged with atheism – a much more candid explanation than the one given at *Ap.* 27e3–28a1 where he dismisses the charge as a mere fabrication based on prejudice and hostility. J. Adam's contention, 1890: xiv, that Socrates' refusal to allow that the gods quarrel among themselves seems to suggest "an underlying note of monotheism" in his thought is textually indefensible.

[32] In *Republic* II–III "Socrates" deplores Homer's misrepresentation of the gods and sets forth the moral critique of Homeric theology implicit in the *Euthyphro*.

pious action instead of a definition of piety.[33] He thereupon proceeds to explain the terminology which, according to Burnet, never needs to be explained:

Bear in mind ... that I did not bid you tell me one or two of the many pious actions but that form itself (αὐτὸ τὸ εἶδος) that makes all pious actions pious, for you agreed that all impious actions are impious and all pious actions pious through one form (μιᾷ ἰδέᾳ), or don't you remember? ... Tell me then what this form itself is, so that I may look upon it, and using it as a model (παραδείγματι), say that any action ... that is of that kind is pious, and if it is not that it is not. (6d9–e6)

Euthyphro says he does remember saying that. But his memory is faulty. It was Socrates who said it. Of course, he did not *assert* that there is "one form" which is the same in all pious actions and "by which" they are pious; he merely "asked" whether Euthyphro was prepared to assert it. But he obviously believes it, and he wants Euthyphro to believe it, too – or to *say* he does. That this is so is clear from the language in which the question is couched. Socrates does not ask: *Is* the pious the same in every action? – a straightforward question which leaves the answer open and allows his interlocutor to say what he really believes – but rather: *Is not* (ἢ οὔ), i.e., *is it not the case that,* the pious is the same in every action? (5d1–2) – a leading question which invites an affirmative answer and, in fact, solicits agreement. And Euthyphro did "agree," that is, he said, "Most certainly" (5d6). But he "agreed" without the slightest idea of what he was agreeing to. If he had understood, he would not have produced an example of a pious action instead of a definition of piety. Anyone who calls this "sincere assent" is stretching the meanings of "sincere" and "assent" to the breaking point.

Having "reminded" Euthyphro of his previous "admission," Socrates again implores him to elucidate the nature of piety. Completely at sea but still eager to display his theological expertise, Euthyphro tries again:

If that (οὕτω) is how you want it, Socrates, that (οὕτω) is how I will tell you. (6e7–8)

The repetition of οὕτω is the linguistic tip-off: if *that* is the kind of explanation you want – whatever "that" may be – then *that* is the

---

[33] This is a common mistake in the early dialogues, but it is especially noteworthy here because, in having previously alluded to the "essential nature" which is the same in all pious actions and "by which" they are pious (5d1–5), Socrates had taken steps to prevent it.

kind of explanation you will get. Clearly, Socrates' terminology is not "quite familiar" to Euthyphro who by this time is groping in the dark.

His next definition follows:

Well then, what is dear to the gods is pious, what is not is impious. (6e10–7a1)

R. E. Allen[34] labels this a species of theological voluntarism – "the view that whatever is good is good because God wills it." Although the terminology is anachronistic – the Greeks were not monotheists and they had no concept of "the will" – it is accurate to describe Euthyphro as a philosophical ancestor of the theological voluntarism which surfaced in late medieval philosophers like William of Ockham and post-Reformation theologians like Richard Hooker and John Calvin:

The will of God is the highest rule of justice; so that what he wills must be considered just, for this very reason, because he wills it ... [I]f you go further, and ask why he so determined, you are in search of something greater and higher than the will of God, which can never be found.[35]

Unlike theological intellectualism – of which Socrates is a philosophical ancestor – according to which God wills those things which his intellect judges good, theological voluntarism maintains that the divine will is constrained by nothing – not even by the divine intellect: things are not loved by God because they are pious, they are pious because they are loved by God.

However, Euthyphro is a polytheist whose gods love different things; and Socrates will shortly object to his definition on precisely that ground. Before doing so, however, he elicits two damaging admissions: first, the gods disagree not only about what is pious, but also about what is just, beautiful, and good; second, they love things insofar as they possess these properties. He thereupon argues that Euthyphro's contention that the gods disagree about these matters, conjoined with his previous admission that the pious is the opposite of the impious, entails that insofar as the same actions are both loved and not loved by the gods, they are both pious and impious (7e1–8a9). Grasping at straws, Euthyphro insists that there are some things about which the gods do not dis-

---

[34] 1970: 44.   [35] 1949, III: 23.2.

agree. That murderers should be prosecuted is one of them. Socrates thereupon amends Euthyphro's definition so that it reads:

[W]hat all the gods hate is impious, and what they all love is pious. (10d2–3)

Euthyphro accepts the amendment.

Socrates' next objection follows. Like many of his objections, it takes the form of a question: Is the pious pious because it is loved by all the gods or do they love it because it is pious? (10a1–3). Although the question is perfectly clear, Euthyphro does not understand it – another indication of the galactic distance between their respective theologies. Socrates explains by means of analogies: we speak of carrying and of being carried, of leading and of being led, of seeing and of being seen. In each case, the former is prior to the latter: that is, a thing is in a state of being carried because it is carried, in a state of being led because it is led, in a state of being seen because it is seen. Formulated with complete generality:

[I]f anything is being changed or being affected in any way, it is not being changed because it is something changed, but rather it is something changed because it is being changed; nor is it being affected because it is something affected, but it is something affected because it is being affected. (10c1–4)

The same is true of loving and being loved: a thing is in a state of being loved because it is loved (10c6–11). Euthyphro again concurs.

Socrates elicits these seemingly innocuous admissions as a preliminary to refuting Euthyphro's amended definition of piety. However, before he can refute it, he must elicit one more admission. Euthyphro has said that piety is what is loved by all the gods. But why do they love it? Because it is pious or for some other reason (δι' ἄλλο τι, 10d4)? Surprisingly, given his theological voluntarism, Euthyphro opts for the former. Socrates savors this fatal admission before demonstrating its fatality: so piety is loved by all the gods because it is pious, not pious because it is loved by all the gods? "Apparently," replies Euthyphro, thereby contradicting himself.

R. E. Allen[36] finds it "odd" that Euthyphro should affirm this thesis: no theological voluntarist "who knew what he was about"

---

[36] 1970: 44.

would ever say such a thing. Allen is right. Why, then, does Euthyphro say it?

Allen thinks he says it because he misunderstands his own position. That is true, but it is also very general. The text provides a
better explanation. Euthyphro says that piety is loved by all the
gods because it is pious because saying that seems preferable to
saying that they love it "for some other reason" – the only alternative Socrates gives him. It also relieves him of the unenviable
task – sure to be assigned – of having to explain what that "other
reason" is. If Euthyphro had understood his own position, he
would also have understood that theological voluntarism provides
him with a way out: there *is* no "other reason." It is the fact that
the gods love something that makes it pious, not some reason independent of, and prior to, their loving it. But Euthyphro cannot
avail himself of this solution. Socrates had blocked this move a
few Stephanus pages earlier by getting him to agree that the gods
love things insofar as they are just, beautiful, and good (7e6–7). Of
course, no theological voluntarist "who knew what he was about"
would ever say that either. It is this more general admission which
is the real source of his difficulties. In making it, Euthyphro
walked into the Socratic trap which now springs shut.

Socrates' analogies suddenly take their toll. Euthyphro is informed that it follows from "his" account (ὡς σὺ λέγεις) that what
is pious and what is loved by the gods are not the same. Socrates'
argument – one of the most torturously complex in the Platonic
corpus – is as follows (10d1–11b1):

(i)   What is pious is loved by the gods because it is pious, it is not
      pious because it is loved by the gods.
(ii) But what is loved by the gods is loved because they love it;
      they do not love it because it is loved.
(iii) If what is loved by the gods and what is pious were the same,
      then since the pious is loved because it is pious, what is loved
      by the gods would be loved because it is loved; and if what is
      loved by the gods is loved because they love it, then the pious
      would also be pious because they love it.
(iv) However, precisely the opposite is the case: the one (what is
      loved by the gods) is of a sort to be loved because it is loved,
      whereas the other (what is pious) is loved because it is of a
      sort to be loved.

(v) Therefore the pious cannot be defined as what is loved by all
     the gods.

In short, instead of explaining what piety *is* (τὸ ὅσιον ὅτι ...
ἐστιν, 11a7), Euthyphro has merely mentioned one of its properties
– it is loved by all the gods (11a6–b1). So will he please stop concealing his view and answer the question he was asked?

The exasperated Euthyphro exclaims:

But Socrates, I have no way of telling you what I have in mind, for
whatever proposition we put forward goes around and refuses to stay
where we establish it. (11b6–8)

Characteristically, Socrates objects to Euthyphro's use of "we" on
the ground that all the foregoing statements were Euthyphro's
(11c4–5); so the blame is also his. Euthyphro begs to differ:

I am not the one who makes [every proposition we put forward] go
round and not remain in the same place; it is you. (11c8–d2)

Interestingly, Socrates does not deny the allegation; he merely says
that *if* he is to blame, he is clever against his will (ἄκων, 11d7); for
he, too, would like their statements to stay in place. Although
every commentator I have consulted agrees with Socrates, I think
Euthyphro is right.

This is a minority opinion if there ever was one. Of all the arguments in the early dialogues, this has traditionally been thought
to be one of the most cogent and philosophically important. Indeed, if Kai Nielsen[37] is right, in demonstrating that piety cannot
be defined as what is loved by the gods, Socrates proved once-and-
for-all "that morality and religion are logically independent and
that it is impossible to base a morality (any morality) on religion."
But that is to claim too much for the argument. Socrates has not
proved that piety cannot be defined as what is loved by all the
gods.

But he has proved something else, namely, that piety cannot be
defined as what is loved by all the gods *if* their reason for loving it
is because it is pious.[38] To say that is to say that piety is pious independently of the gods' loving it – which is precisely what the
theological voluntarist denies: being loved by the gods is not a

----

[37] 1961: 175.
[38] This point is powerfully argued by Cohen, 1971: 175.

consequential property of piety, that is, piety is not loved by the gods because of some intrinsic character which elicits their love and on which it is parasitic; piety is pious because they love it. "What is loved by all the gods is pious" is true by definition. It is logically impossible for something to be loved by all the gods and not pious or to be pious and not loved by all the gods. Socrates' argument does not touch this position. It does not refute consistent theological voluntarism; it only refutes the inconsistent voluntarist who asserts both that piety is what is loved by all the gods and that they love it because it is pious.

But surely, it will be said, Euthyphro's theological voluntarism is one of the inconsistent varieties; for he unambiguously affirms this inconsistent conjunction. Yes, he does. But before making too much of this, we need to ask why.

As we have seen, Euthyphro's admission that the gods love piety because it is pious is a fatal one based on a misunderstanding of his own position. But it is a Socratically induced misunderstanding.[39] Socrates does not *discover* an inconsistency in Euthyphro's belief-set; he *supplies* the conjunct which generates the inconsistency by getting Euthyphro to say that the gods love piety because it is pious – a thesis which he does not believe and which, given the foregoing discussion, Socrates knows he does not believe. In short, Socrates *leads* Euthyphro into inconsistency. But although the theses he induces Euthyphro to affirm are inconsistent, Euthyphro's belief-set is not. The assertion of an inconsistent conjunction bespeaks inconsistency in the assertor's belief-set if and only if he believes both conjuncts. But Euthyphro does not. Like many other Socratic interlocutors, he has not been refuted "from his own beliefs."

After several more, equally futile attempts to define piety, Euthyphro extricates himself from the discussion and hurries off, leaving Socrates to express his "disappointment" at having failed to discover the nature of piety. And with this the dialogue concludes. The text provides no support for Diogenes Laertius' contention that Socrates diverted Euthyphro from prosecuting his father (2.29).

---

[39] Shorey saw this very clearly: "Euthyphro incautiously admits that God loves the holy because it is holy ... He ought to have said, No, God does not love it because it is holy, but his loving it makes it holy" (1933: 76). So, too, Teloh, 1987: 32: "Socrates ... throws a cloud of dust at Euthyphro and confuses him into reversing his position."

The *Euthyphro* corroborates Xenophon's claim that Socrates "could do what he liked with any disputant" (*Mem.* 1.2.14). However, it is idle for him to disclaim responsibility for the conclusions arrived at on the patently false ground that the statements which generated them were all Euthyphro's. Far from being clever "against his will," Socrates marshals his arguments with an ingenuity that often borders on the perverse, feeding his interlocutor exactly the premises needed to "refute" him and making sure that he "assents" to them. However, the ensuing aporetic impasse shows neither that Euthyphro's position is indefensible nor that his claim to theological expertise is a ludicrous pretension. Of course, if we approach the early dialogues with the assumption that the Socratic theory of definition is correct and that a knowledge-claim is justified if and only if the claimant can produce a definition of the term under discussion which states what is common to all and only the members of the class to which that term is correctly applied and thus serves as the necessary and sufficient conditions governing its application, then Euthyphro fails miserably. But why make that assumption? Before judging Euthyphro too harshly, several points should be noted.

First, in requiring Euthyphro to demonstrate his theological expertise by stating the *eidos* which is common to all (and only) pious actions and "by which" they are pious, Socrates introduces a criterion of piety which is alien to Euthyphro's belief-system. Euthyphro's criterion is theological: piety is what is loved by the gods. At first insufficiently attentive to their alleged[40] moral disagreements, he is pushed to the unwelcome conclusion that, insofar as the same things are both loved and not loved by the gods, they are both pious and impious. To avoid self-contradiction he invokes universal agreement among the gods, but is then pushed to the equally unwelcome conclusion that, insofar as being pious and being loved are not the same, being loved by all the gods is not the definition of piety. But although Socrates embroils Euthyphro in one logical difficulty after another, his refutation ultimately fails: not because Euthyphro is intellectually dishonest and refuses to accept the inferences which Socrates deduces from his assertions, but because the two crucial premises from which they are deduced

---

[40] The qualification is important. Socrates nowhere agrees that the gods actually disagree and more than once implies that he thinks they do not.

are propositions which Euthyphro does not believe, namely, that the gods love things insofar as they are just, beautiful, and good, and that they, therefore, also love things insofar as they are pious.

Second, in addition to introducing an alien criterion of piety, Socrates introduces an equally alien criterion of theological expertise. Euthyphro's expertise is based on his knowledge of the Homeric texts. With them at his fingertips, he has no difficulty finding authoritative precedents for his conduct. It is his knowledge of these texts, not his knowledge of the *eidos* of piety, which makes him a theological expert. Knowledge of the *eidos* is Socrates' criterion of theological expertise – a criterion which he smuggles into the discussion without ever explaining *how*, or even *that*, it differs from Euthyphro's. Having imprudently endorsed this criterion, Euthyphro painfully discovers that he cannot comply with (what he thought was) the simple request of defining piety. But while this shows that he is not a theological expert in Socrates' sense of "expert," it does not show that he is not a theological expert in his own very different sense. Socrates obscures this all-important distinction by periodically "reminding" him that knowledge of the *eidos* of piety is precisely what, *qua* expert, he claims to have. But he is wrong. Euthyphro claimed no such thing. Hence when Socrates denies that Euthyphro is a theological expert, he is right – in his sense of "expert." But he is not contradicting Euthyphro's claim that he is – in *his* sense of "expert." "I am a theological expert" is contradicted by "You are not a theological expert" if and only if both speakers mean the same thing by "expert." But Socrates and Euthyphro do not. Ostensibly contradictory, their claims are, in fact, compatible. What Socrates proves beyond all doubt that Euthyphro does not have is something he never claimed to have.

Third, Socrates never gives Euthyphro a convincing reason for abandoning his theological voluntarism. In fact, he never gives him the slightest hint of what, according to Socrates, he desperately needs to know if he is ever to see the (alleged) error of his way, namely, *that* – and *why* – the collective love of the gods is not a satisfactory definition of piety. The only reason Euthyphro is given for abandoning this definition is that it is inconsistent with two other statements to which he has verbally assented but which he does not believe – surely an inadequate reason for anyone to abandon any position.

Finally, given the torturous complexity of Socrates' central argument and the technical and unfamiliar language in which it is couched, it is hardly surprising that Euthyphro fails to understand it and is ultimately reduced to a cry of despair. It would have been astonishing if he had understood it. And it would have been even more astonishing if, having understood it, he had abandoned his theological voluntarism forthwith – right there on the Royal Porch. Extended quotation is always tedious, but it is sometimes very useful. To see what Euthyphro is being asked to understand, ponder R. E. Allen's elegant formulation of Socrates' argument:

Assume that what is dear to the gods and the holy are the same. Then (i) if the holy is loved because it is holy, what is dear to the gods is loved because it is dear to the gods. Consequent follows from antecedent by substitution. But it has been agreed that the consequent is false (10c). Therefore, either the antecedent is false or the substitution impossible. But it has been agreed that the antecedent is true (10d). Therefore, the substitution is impossible: what is dear to the gods and the holy are not the same. Again, (ii) if what is dear to the gods is dear to the gods because they love it, the holy is holy because it is loved. Once more, consequent follows from antecedent by substitution. But it has been agreed that the consequent is false (10d). Therefore, either the antecedent is false or the substitution impossible. But it has been agreed that the antecedent is true (10c). Therefore, the substitution is impossible: what is dear to the gods and the holy are not the same. In short, Euthyphro's definition implies an equivalence. But if either side of that equivalence is true, the other side is false. Thus the equivalence, and both of its component implications, are false, The definition must be rejected.[41]

What could be simpler than that?

However, the problem is not simply that Socrates' argument is complex and highly technical. The real problem lies deeper.

One cannot hope to refute a religious person by extracting one or two beliefs from his belief-system and set of religious and linguistic practices and subjecting them to contextually isolated philosophical scrutiny. The religious mentality is not inculcated piecemeal, one belief at a time, and it cannot be refuted piecemeal either. Such "refutations" only confirm the believer's suspicion that philosophical criticism is wrongheaded and beside the point. That is exactly what happens to Euthyphro. He comes into the discussion believing that piety is what is loved by the gods, and he

---

[41] 1970: 43.

leaves believing the same thing. Although his sudden exit is routinely described as a face-saving strategy motivated by intellectual
dishonesty, that is neither the only nor the most convincing assessment. It is not as if, during the course of the discussion, Euthyphro discovers to his horror that he is devoid of theological expertise but suppresses this bitter truth because he is determined to
prosecute his father in the name of the very virtue about which he
has just revealed that he knows nothing. On the contrary, the only
thing he seems to have learned is that, when pitted against logical
nit-pickers like Socrates, one must remember to preface one's assertions about the gods with the universal quantifier "all."

If, with proponents of the standard picture, we read the dialogue straight, we will miss its many (perhaps inadvertent) comic
touches: on the one hand is the dialectically expert Socrates, spinning out arguments of increasing complexity in hopes of persuading Euthyphro that he does not know what he thinks he knows; on
the other hand is the dialectically inept Euthyphro, trying to survive the ordeal by answering questions which he does not understand and by assenting to propositions which he does not believe
and which only lead him into deeper logical quicksand. Whether
intentional or not, the disparity between the two is high comedy –
a philosophical spoof which depicts both the intellectual inability
of Euthyphro and the psychological naivete of Socrates who fails
to perceive the futility, not to mention the absurdity, of applying
the elenchus to the likes of him. The crowning absurdity is the
central argument itself.

Socrates fails to dissuade Euthyphro from prosecuting his
father: not because he is an impenetrable dogmatist, but because
they share no common ground. Not only do they have different
beliefs about morality, the gods, and the connection (or lack of
connection) between them; they also have different *criteria* for arriving at, and assessing the adequacy of, those beliefs. These crucially important differences are never made explicit; they are, for
the most part, minimized and even swept under the rug. As a
result, Euthyphro neither understands Socrates' criticism nor perceives its relevance to his theology. To make matters worse, Socrates does not seem to care whether he understands and largely
ignores his actual views as well as his actual reasons for holding
them.

But that is only part of the story – and not the most important part. In focusing exclusively on the truth-value of Euthyphro's beliefs and his ability to defend them, Socrates bypasses the psychologically formative role that the Homeric world-view plays in Euthyphro's life: the process by which he acquired his beliefs, how they shape his sensibilities, and how they illuminate his experience – in particular, his concept of religious and moral obligation. Euthyphro not only espouses religious beliefs; his affectional responses have also been decisively shaped by religion. He looks at life in religious terms. Like many believers, before and since, he resists, and finds it natural to resist, the suggestion that the behavior of deities must conform to moral standards which transcend them and to which they themselves are subject. Obeying the gods, doing what they love, "doing their will" – all this is part and parcel of the religious life. It never occurs to the theological voluntarist to wonder whether the commands he obeys are good when judged independently of the divinity (or divinities) who command them; and when the question is put to him, he typically rejects it out of hand as illegitimate and, perhaps, even as blasphemous. The arguments of the *Euthyphro* luminously reveal the impotence of philosophical criticism directed at these kinds of beliefs as held by these kinds of believers. In the final analysis, nothing has been achieved. Euthyphro can only marvel at Socrates' inexplicable misgivings about Homeric theology, and Socrates can only marvel at Euthyphro's inexplicable credulity. Euthyphro leaves the discussion as convinced of his theology and his theological expertise as when he entered it. Instead of concluding that he does not know what he thought he knew, he concludes that Socrates has been toying with him and merely trying to confuse him. He is largely right.

According to his "official" explanation in the *Apology*, Socrates embarked on his divine mission in obedience to the god at Delphi who had commanded him to live the life of a philosopher, examining himself and others, thereby caring for their souls. This is not borne out by the *Euthyphro*. Of all the characteristics displayed by Socrates in this dialogue, soul-care is not one of them. This salutary goal must be imported into the dialogue from the *Apology*. In the *Euthyphro*, Socrates' dialectical performance suggests that his sole concern is to refute whatever thesis his interlocutor advances – even if it is one with which he himself agrees or one which he himself has supplied. Having done so, he luxuriates in his victory and waxes ironic: "What? Leaving just when you were about to instruct me about piety and impiety so that I can defend myself against Meletus and live a better life?"

The whole encounter is a revealing commentary on his explanation of why he is perpetually surrounded by clever young men:

> Why ... do some people enjoy spending considerable time in my company? You have heard why, gentlemen of the jury, I have told you the whole truth. They enjoy hearing those being questioned who think they are wise, but are not. And this is not unpleasant. (οὐκ ἀηδές, *Ap.* 33b9–c4)

Not unpleasant! i.e., amusing! That is a much better description of what is going on. It is fun to refute people. And Socrates is clearly having fun in the *Euthyphro*. Although the conversation is a private one unwitnessed by those clever young men who enjoy watching Socrates refute his interlocutors and who laugh at them in imitation of their mentor, the fact remains that for a person allegedly operating with such lofty purposes, Socrates seems to be enjoying himself a bit too much at Euthyphro's expense. Nor can his dialectical tactics be vindicated by invoking something called "irony" – that blessed term of genuine but limited applicability which has been employed by generations of commentators to cover a multitude of Socratic sins. Employed for partisan purposes, the appeal to irony is little more than an *a priori* device by which *prima facie* offensive behavior is redescribed so as to render it compatible with announced seriousness and nobility of purpose.

Does Socrates care about Euthyphro's soul? If so, it has eluded me. Gregory Vlastos is very sensitive to the complaint:

> As you watch Euthyphro hurry off, this is what you feel like telling Socrates: "I don't believe you really care for that man's soul, for if you did, how could you have let him go with his head still stuffed with his superstitions? ... Why then not tell him this, and show him the difference between religion and magic?" But if you go back and re-read the dialogue more carefully, you can figure out Socrates' reply: "That is what I did try to show him. But I wanted him to find it out for himself."[42]

---

[42] 1971: 13. See Vlastos, 1991, in which the claim that the interlocutor must find the truth by himself is repeated three times within the space of eight pages: 36, 42, 44. Although Vlastos thinks Socrates cares for the souls of his fellows, he also thinks that his care "is limited and conditional" and that his greatest failure was "a failure of love" (1971: 16) – a contention contested by Penner, 1992b: 144. See also Goulburn, 1858: 84: "When [Socrates] spoke *minds* responded to him, and not infrequently *consciences* responded also; but as the heart did not speak in him, hearts *never* responded ... The great lack of the character of Socrates was love."

The same explanation is given by Terry Penner:

Socrates does not think giving someone a formula, such as "Courage is the knowledge of the fearful and the hopeful," will be of any help at all to them if they don't understand – and understand *for themselves* – what that broad *thing to be known* is that that sentence makes reference to.[43]

And by Michael Frede:

[I]t is crucial that one arrive at the right view by one's own thought, rather than on the authority of somebody else, e.g. the questioner.[44]

How do these commentators know this? Socrates never says anything like it. What he does say is that *he* cannot impart knowledge because he has none. And neither, he suspects, does anyone else. However, if they did, he would certainly want them to impart it. The early dialogues abound with this request. Assured that Euthyphro has a firm grasp of the nature of piety, Socrates does not implore him to seal his lips on the ground that he – Socrates – must "find it out for himself"; he implores him to impart his (alleged) knowledge (*Eu.* 6e3–6). Charmides, Critias, Laches, Nicias, Cephalus, Polemarchus, and Thrasymachus are also implored to impart their (alleged) knowledge of temperance, courage, and justice.

It is possible to discount all these passages on the ground that, in making these requests, Socrates is being "ironic." But it is not possible to discount a parallel passage in the *Crito* in which he unambiguously and emphatically exhorts Crito to attend to the moral expert, that is, the person who knows about justice and injustice and who represents truth itself (ὁ εἷς καὶ αὐτὴ ἡ ἀλήθεια) – if such a person exists – and who should be respected and feared above all others (*Cr.* 48a5–10). The fact that, in all likelihood, such a person does not exist does not change the fact that he would be the person to consult if he did. There is not the slightest suggestion in this passage (or anywhere else in the early dialogues) that moral knowledge is incommunicable and that everyone must "find it for themselves."[45]

[43] 1992b: 144.
[44] 1992: 217.
[45] As usual, Vlastos has anticipated the objection: "That each of us must find out moral truth for ourselves is itself something which Socrates wants us to find out for ourselves" (1991: 110, n. 16) – a reply which makes the incommunicability thesis textually unfalsifiable.

The *Euthyphro* provides no reason for thinking that Socrates cares about Euthyphro's soul – unless we define "cares" in such a way that it is compatible with any behavior whatever, however uncaring it may seem to the casual observer who is insensitive to the nuances of Socratic "irony" and unaware of the incommunicability of moral knowledge. As for Euthyphro himself, it never seems to occur to him that Socrates does not care about his soul. So far as he is concerned, his soul is in good hands – the hands of the gods – and he has no need of Socrates or of moral gadflies generally. Nor does he give any indication of thinking that he has sustained a humbling intellectual defeat – much less a defeat of the magnitude which proponents of the standard picture have been celebrating for the past two-and-a-half millennia. His discussion with Socrates was an inconsequential incident in a busy day and soon forgotten among the hustle and bustle of the courthouse. What, from Socrates' "official" point of view, should have been a shattering existential confrontation culminating in the discovery of his appalling ignorance was, from Euthyphro's point of view, a mere interlude, a way of passing the time, until court is in session and the important business of the day begins. Little wonder that he excuses himself and hurries off – an eminently sensible thing to do in view of the charade he has just been compelled to endure.

CHAPTER 9

Cephalus

The aging Cephalus makes his brief appearance in *Republic* I. Although the *Republic* is a middle dialogue, there is a long scholarly precedent for making a fairly sharp distinction between Book I and Books II–X. Unlike the latter, in which the Socratic elenchus is wholly absent, the dialogue form only nominally retained, and the interlocutors largely reduced to concurring listeners, the former reads like a typical early dialogue. Although not immediately apparent, the subject is justice, and Cephalus is the first of three interlocutors. The discussion ends inconclusively. No acceptable definition is forthcoming, and it is partly for this reason that some commentators[1] think Book I was originally an early dialogue or dialogue fragment (entitled *Thrasymachus*, according to Dümmler),[2] which Plato later used as an introduction. Whether or not one accepts this view,[3] the fact remains that most commentators spend little time on Book I and treat it as a mere preliminary.[4] And if Book I receives very short shrift, Cephalus receives the shortest of all.[5]

In defense of this policy, it might be argued that Socrates also makes short work of Cephalus. Their encounter is the shortest on record – barely three Stephanus pages (*R.* 328c5–331d7) – and most

---

[1] See, e.g., Field, 1930: 67; Friedländer, 1964, II: 50, 63; Ryle, 1966: 244; Gosling, 1973: 18; and Guthrie, 1975: 437.

[2] 1889: 237. Grote, 1867, III: 24–25, thinks Plato originally intended to use the *Cleitophon* as an introduction to the *Republic*, but abandoned the idea because Cleitophon's case against Socrates was too hard to answer and opted for the easier task of answering Thrasymachus.

[3] Many do not. See, e.g., A. E. Taylor, 1929: 264; Shorey, 1933: 215; Kahn, 1968: 368; Irwin, 1977: 178–84; Annas, 1981: 16–17; and Lycos, 1987: 1.

[4] Notable exceptions include Annas, 1981: 16–18; and Lycos, 1987.

[5] Of those prone to such brevity of exposition, no one is likely to surpass Irwin who disposes of Cephalus' "behavioural" definition of justice by briskly observing that it is rejected "for the normal reasons" (1977: 178). In fairness, it should be mentioned that Irwin discusses behavioral definitions elsewhere (43–44, 295).

of that is small talk: mutual greetings, laments about Socrates' infrequent visits to the Piraeus, and ruminations about wealth and old age. Their genuinely philosophical exchange consists of only a few sentences from which Socrates coaxes a definition of justice and thereupon unleashes the celebrated madman counterexample with which he affects the speediest refutation in the Platonic corpus.

However, this reply overlooks the fact that the preliminary conversation is not mere polite chit-chat and completely irrelevant to the philosophical question about justice that Socrates abruptly asks at 331c1–9, but his very reason for asking it. What he really wants to know is not what Cephalus thinks about wealth and old age, but how he thinks they are connected to happiness. Only by attending closely to what he says will we be in a position to assess Socrates' refutation of Cephalus' views and Plato's portrayal of Cephalus himself – matters about which there is massive disagreement among commentators.

The historical Cephalus, the father of Polemarchus, Lysias,[6] Euthydemus,[7] and Brachyllus, was a wealthy Syracusan merchant and the owner of what was probably the largest business in Athens – a shield factory located in the Piraeus. According to Lysias (835c5–7), he had come to Athens in 470 at the request of Pericles and remained there for the next thirty years as a metic,[8] living with Polemarchus whose home[9] is the setting for the long discussion narrated by Socrates in the *Republic* – a discussion which the participants somehow manage to sandwich between the religious festival in honor of the Thracian goddess Bendis, from which Socrates and Glaucon were returning when they were accosted by

---

[6] Lysias was a famous orator and speech writer. According to Diogenes Laertius (2.40–41), he wrote a defense for Socrates to deliver at his trial which he declined on the ground that it was "more forensic than philosophical."

[7] Not the Euthydemus who appears in the Platonic dialogue of the same name.

[8] Metics (or resident aliens) made up a considerable part of the Athenian population. Although required to register in their demes and to pay taxes, they were non-citizens and could not own property. They could, however, serve as trierarchs, as members of the Athenian infantry or, if poorer, as oarsmen in the Athenian fleet. They were also free to worship their own gods. Their social status was ambiguous. In spite of their undisputed contributions to Athenian life, they were looked upon with disfavor bordering on contempt: partly because they were foreigners (and hence *barbaroi*) and partly because they were often manual laborers (and hence members of the despised *banausia*).

[9] Polemarchus was an apparent exception to the law forbidding metics to own property. According to Blass, 1887, 1: 343–45, his home was a favorite meeting place for Athenian intellectuals.

Polemarchus and his companions, and a torch race on horse-back which they have every intention of attending later that same evening.

When the party arrives, they find Cephalus, wearing a garland and just returned from offering a sacrifice. He is surrounded by a houseful of guests, most of whom remain silent during the ensuing discussion – Jowett[10] drolly dubs them "mute auditors." The scene is cordial. Cephalus seems genuinely appreciative of his sons – Polemarchus, a successful businessman with a keen interest in philosophy (*Phdr.* 257b3–4), and his younger brother Lysias, already embarked on a distinguished career as an orator. A professional man in his twilight years, Cephalus prides himself on the fact that he continues to cultivate wider interests, among them the pleasures of good conversation. All things considered, he seems to have bridged the generation gap quite well. Not every corporate executive could hobnob so unselfconsciously with the philosophy crowd or tolerate the likes of a Thrasymachus on the premises.

Cephalus' status as a wealthy non-citizen means that, from Plato's point of view, he starts out with two strikes against him. We know how important citizenship and immersion in the affairs of the polis were for Plato. We also know his attitude towards those who spend their lives in pursuit of wealth: the more men pursue wealth, the less they honor virtue (*R.* 550e4–8); such people have no place in the ideal city (*Laws* 729a2–b2, 831c4–e2, 870a2–d4). Although these later Platonic strictures about money and its potentially harmful effects cannot be retroactively applied to the early dialogues, Socrates often betrays a similar attitude. He never categorically condemns wealth as such or says that it is necessarily incompatible with virtue, but he often cautions his interlocutors against valuing money (or anything else) more highly than the well-being of their souls (*Ap.* 29d2–30a3, 41e3–7). These misgivings are never overtly expressed during the discussion with Cephalus – the two are, after all, old friends – but they are unmistakably implied.

Convinced that everyone present has much to learn from Cephalus, a man who has "travelled a road that we too will probably have to follow" (328e1–3), Socrates queries him about old age and how he is coping with it. He begins promisingly. Unlike most of his

---

[10] 1871, II: 5.

contemporaries, whose time is spent reminiscing about their lost youth, bemoaning their ebbing (or already ebbed) sexual capacities, and complaining about slights and indignities at the hands of their relatives, Cephalus is not troubled by such things. As he sees it, whether a person is happy or miserable does not depend on age, but on character (τρόπος). If one is temperate and content (κόσμιοι καὶ εὔκολοι), old age is only moderately burdensome; but if one is intemperate, youth and old age are equally difficult (329d2–6). For his part, he agrees with Sophocles who in his old age was happy to have escaped from "the savage and tyrannical master" of sexual desire and from bodily passions generally. As for dealing with one's relatives, the important thing is again character.

Filled with admiration and eager to hear more (329d7), Socrates introduces the potentially touchy subject of money. Not wishing to confront Cephalus head-on, he raises the point discreetly by alluding to the common resentment which "the Many" harbor towards the rich who, they think, buy their way through life. A hypocritical fraud would bristle at such an allegation and reject it out of hand. Cephalus does neither. "The Many" are not completely wrong, he candidly admits, but neither are they completely right. Their chief mistake is that they overestimate the importance of money in attaining happiness – a mistake which causes them to underestimate the importance of character. Although the good man (ὁ ἐπιεικής) would find old age more difficult if he were poor, money is not sufficient to insure happiness for the bad man (ὁ μὴ ἐπιεικής, 330a3–6).

Having observed that Cephalus is not overly concerned about money, Socrates asks whether he earned or inherited his wealth. In answering this question, obviously dear to his heart, Cephalus waxes autobiographical. Unlike his grandfather, who was obsessed with making money and amassed a great fortune, and his father, who died with much less than he had inherited, Cephalus is a mean between the two: although not obsessed with money, neither is he indifferent to it and the advantages it provides. In short, he is a moneymaker, but not a lover of money – a χρηματιστής, but not a φιλοχρήματος (330b1–2).

The fact remains, however, that he *is* wealthy; and Socrates would like to know what he thinks is the greatest benefit of wealth.

Since his answer has been interpreted in different – and even opposite – ways, to avoid tendentious interpretation, I will quote him at some length:

[W]hen someone thinks his end is near, he becomes frightened and concerned about things he didn't fear before. It's then that the stories we're told about Hades, about how people who've been unjust here must pay the penalty there – stories he used of make fun of – twist his soul this way and that for fear they're true ... [H]e is filled with foreboding and fear, and he examines himself to see whether he has been unjust to anyone. If he finds many injustices in his life, he awakes from sleep in terror, as children do, and lives in anticipation of bad things to come. But ... when someone lives a just and pious life (δικαίως καὶ ὁσίως τὸν βίον), *Sweet hope is in his heart, Nurse and companion to his age* ... It's in this connection that wealth is most valuable, I'd say, not for every man but for a decent and orderly one (οὔ τι παντὶ ανδρὶ ἀλλὰ τῷ ἐπιεικεῖ καὶ κοσμίῳ). Wealth can do a lot to save us from having to cheat or deceive someone against our will (ἄκοντά) and from having to depart for that other place in fear because we owe sacrifice to a god or money to a person. It has many other uses, but, benefit for benefit, I'd say that *this* is how it is most useful to a man of any understanding (νοῦν ἔχοντι, 330d4–331b7).

Some commentators find Plato's portrait of Cephalus sympathetic and think highly of him themselves. Shorey[11] describes him as the "venerable" Cephalus – "a prefiguring type of the happy old age of the just man." A. E. Taylor[12] judges him a "decent" and "honourable" man whose maxims exhibit a "sound and homely rectitude." Guthrie[13] calls him "an upright old gentleman" with a "moral credo." Friedländer[14] goes further, likening Cephalus' peace of mind to the "state of calm" enjoyed by the true philosopher whose life has been a preparation for death (*Ph.* 81a1–2). Nettleship[15] goes further still, extolling him as "a good man whose morality is summed up in the formula 'to have been true in word and deed, and to have paid one's debts to gods and men', which, if taken widely and deeply enough, says all that one need wish to say."

Other commentators are much less enthusiastic. Bloom[16] thinks Cephalus is a pseudo-pious irrelevance who must be "banished"

[11] 1937, I: ix.　[12] 1929: 266–67.　[13] 1975: 439.
[14] 1964, II: 53.　[15] 1929: 15.　[16] 1968: 312–14.

before serious discussion can begin. Mightily unimpressed by his
"outward" concern with justice, Bloom thinks this is a recent development and a sham; his youth had been "very erotic" and his
many "unjust activities" haunt him in his old age. Annas[17] is
equally hostile and thinks Plato's portrait contains enough "malicious touches" to show how little he thinks of "limited and complacent" people like Cephalus who take justice seriously only
when they "start thinking about hell-fire." More recently, Teloh[18]
has assured us that although Cephalus seems to be decent and
even devout, Socrates quickly reveals "the intellectual and moral
decay behind the facade" of this man whose old age is spent
"bribing ... the gods."[19] More recently still, McKim[20] has com-
pressed the entire foregoing tirade into a single trenchant phrase:
Cephalus is "corrupt but affable." If these commentators are
right, Cephalus is a moral fraud who is just only because of his
eschatological nightmares. The implication of his outlook on life is
off-puttingly crude: if the gods do not exist, then the poets' stories
are false and there is no reason to fear punishment in the hereafter
– in which case he would discard his garland, live as he pleased,
and sleep like a log.

The remarkable disparity between these assessments – ranging
from Nettleship's grand accolade to Teloh's dental imagery of
intellectual and moral "decay" – should send us scurrying back to
the texts. What do we find?

That Cephalus is an intellectually limited man few will deny,

---

[17] 1981: 19, 349.

[18] 1986: 85–86.

[19] Although "bribing the gods" is a possible abuse of sacrifice, the institution also had its
proper uses. Almost everyone feared punishment in the hereafter, but sacrifices were not
offered exclusively (or even chiefly) to escape it. Nor were the gods viewed as morally
perfect beings who demanded repentance (in the Judeo-Christian sense). Conducted in
accordance with a crowded calendar of religious festivals, sacrifices performed a variety
of functions: to remind the gods of past acts of piety on the part of the sacrificer, to offer
them libations as gratitude for past favors and even to attract their attention in hopes of
securing future favors (for the gods were notoriously inattentive to human affairs). Sacrifices are "due" to the gods: not because they are righteous and given to righteous judgments, but because they are gods (θεοί) – a status which included a broad (and not entirely
consistent) set of moral, non-moral, and immoral properties – including arbitrariness
and unpredictability. One sacrificed: not because one was sinful, but because one was
human; the ritual of sacrifice was a way of acknowledging one's limitations and thereby
avoiding *hubris*.

[20] 1988: 274, n. 33.

though I cannot help marveling at the petulance with which the point is made. What is it about him that elicits these ill-tempered outbursts? His detractors seem chiefly offended by two things: first, called upon to expound his "philosophy of life," he can only produce a handful of simpleminded rules – tell the truth, pay your debts, and so on – and adds that, in obeying them, money helps; second, his concern with justice is motivated solely by fear of punishment.

It seems to me that this is an unduly selective and highly distorted interpretation of what Cephalus actually says and that it ignores a good deal of what Plato has included in his portrait. My defense of Cephalus against his learned despisers is based on the conviction that traditional commentators have seen something of the greatest importance which their contemporary colleagues have, to varying degrees, missed.

Cephalus' use of the terms "decent" (ἐπιεικής), "orderly" (κόσμιος), and "content" (εὔκολος) – rather than "good" (ἀγαθός), "temperate" (σοφρόν), and "happy" (εὐδαίμων) in their strong Socratic senses – reveals that the virtue of which he speaks and on which he prides himself is, in many respects, quite different from Socratic virtue which is grounded in *epistēmē* and stands in a necessary connection to happiness. But it is not completely different. Like Socrates, Cephalus sees a connection between justice and happiness, by which he means primarily contentment and tranquillity of mind. Unlike Socrates, however, for whom the connection is logical and necessary (such that if one is just, it follows analytically that one is happy or, at least, happi*er*), Cephalus sees the connection as psychological and contingent (it just so happens that honest people enjoy tranquillity of mind and sleep better). But this view and the lower voltage terminology with which it is expressed is not sufficient to show that his concept of justice is "purely external," that his character is "shallow," and that his piety is a "sham." As a matter of fact, Socrates uses the term ἐπιεικής himself in referring to the decent and most reasonable people (οἱ ... ἐπιεικέστατοι) whose opinions Crito should take seriously (*Cr.* 44c7). Although one does not become ὁ ἐπιεικής by proclamation, it is important to notice that Plato portrays Cephalus as a man who perceives himself as belonging to this Socratically esteemed class. Socrates himself points out that Cephalus is very different from most people (329e1–2), and implies that his life represents a genuine achievement.[21]

But more can be said on Cephalus' behalf. Unlike most of his contemporaries, including his son Polemarchus, who think that justice consists in helping one's friends and harming one's enemies, Cephalus does not think that it is just to harm anyone (331a1–3). It has never been sufficiently emphasized that of all the interlocutors in the early dialogues there are only two who join Socrates in rejecting the *lex talionis*: one is Crito, and the other is Cephalus. In view of all this, there is no need to invoke Socratic irony or to deny that Plato's (admittedly qualified) admiration for him is anything less than genuine.

However, that is exactly what his detractors do deny. Accordingly, the first item of business is to rebut the charge that Cephalus' concern with justice is "purely external," a product of his old age, and traceable solely to fear of punishment.

Asked how he is coping with old age, Cephalus begins by making a distinction which is crucial for understanding him, but which his detractors largely ignore. The distinction takes the form of a contrast between the vast majority of Cephalus' contemporaries, who do not share his view of the primacy of character in attaining happiness, and Cephalus himself. Most old men, he observes, are given to nostalgia, complaining, and laments about their lost youth. He, however, is not. It is not simply that, unlike these others, he is happy that he is no longer plagued by youthful desires and passions and speaks of this newly acquired freedom as a kind of deliverance. He says this, but he says more than this; and his further remarks rebut the charge that he is just only because the "unjust activities" of his "erotic past" haunt him in his old age.

Cephalus says nothing of the kind. Looking back on his long and happy life, he does not just talk about his virtuous *actions*; he also talks about his virtuous *disposition* – indeed, of his lifelong wish, as a man of character, to live a just and pious life.[22] This ex-

---

[21] Reeve, 1988: 6–9 *passim*, goes much further that I am prepared to go: Cephalus is "an attractive figure, portrayed with delicacy and respect ... [Insofar as] he is to some degree moderate, just, pious, and wise without ... knowing what the virtues are, [h]e is a sort of living counterexample to Socrates' claim that virtue is that kind of knowledge ... It follows that Cephalus is an inappropriate subject for the elenchus. He is already of good character and disposed to virtue ... [H]is character is already as good as Socrates'."

[22] Inexplicably, Annas, 1981: 20, thinks that, for Cephalus, "[r]ight and wrong consist ... in the performance of certain actions ... [T]he *kind* of person you are does not matter."

plicit avowal of a lifelong disposition to be just casts a different light on his remarks about the utility of money in living the moral life. Wealth, he says, has many benefits; but the greatest is that it enables a man – not every man but a decent and orderly one – to discharge his moral obligations and thereby carry out his moral intentions. In saying this, Cephalus is not implying that his money has enabled him to buy his way through life. His point is, rather, that, unlike his grandfather and father, for whom wealth was an end in itself, for him it has been a means to a higher end – the end of being just. In short, money is neither necessary nor sufficient for happiness.[23] True, it helps; but only if one is already a good man (331a11–b1).

This explicit avowal of a lifelong disposition to be just also casts a different light on his remarks about punishment in the hereafter. Here, too, the contrast between Cephalus and his contemporaries is preserved. Just as most old men, but not Cephalus, lament the passing of the good old days, so also most old men, but not Cephalus, are haunted by their past misdeeds and toss and turn in their sleep for fear that the poets' stories about punishment in the hereafter might be true. Again, the contrast is between Cephalus, a man of character who does not fear death, and other men whose lack of character gives them good reason to fear it. Although glib chatter about the "uses" of money could, in the mouth of a different kind of person, betray an attitude of which "the Many" are justifiably resentful, the text provides no reasons for ascribing such crudity to Cephalus.

But nagging doubts about Cephalus die hard. Granted, someone might say, he does not spend his old age worrying about punishment in the hereafter. His life *has* been one of honesty and fair play. Still, in the final analysis, has he not been just from fear of punishment? And does this not reveal that, unlike most men, who sin first and worry later, Cephalus did not sin only because he did his worrying earlier?

However impressed some contemporary commentators might be by this argument, Socrates would be unimpressed by it. Although he occasionally expresses doubts about the morality and character

---

[23] A point overlooked by Méron, 1979: 113, who thinks that, for Cephalus, "la richesse est la condition de la justice" – "une proposition inquiétante." See also Cazeaux, 1989: xxiv: "Céphalos énoce un sentiment peu banal: il n'a pas de passion pour l'argent; mais l'argent lui rend la conscience tranquille."

of those who are just unwillingly and from fear of punishment, he does not invariably or even typically do so. In fact, he sometimes tries to instill this very fear in his interlocutors. He apparently believes that being just from fear of punishment, while not the highest form of moral motivation, is not necessarily indicative of some grave character flaw – something to be grumbled about and dismissed as mere prudence and feathering one's nest. The strategy of calling men to virtue by dwelling on the torments awaiting them in the hereafter may admit of abuse, but it apparently also has its proper and salutary uses. How else are we to understand the great eschatological myths – notably, that with which the *Gorgias* concludes (523a1–527d2)?

In this myth, punishment in the hereafter is depicted in such graphic and horrifying detail as to surpass the poets' stories in depriving the unjust man of a good night's sleep. Who can ever forget Socrates' picture of the unjust soul after death, stripped of its body and cowering in shame before the unerring judgment of Aeacus, Minos, and Rhadamanthus. Every unjust act has left its stain, and the soul, limping and crooked because of its falsity, disproportion, and ugliness, is sent to the prison house called Tartarus where it is hung up and afflicted with the greatest, the most intense, and the most painful suffering; for there is no other way that it can be purged of the effects of its injustice. Evil souls are of two kinds: curable and incurable. In the case of the former, the purpose of punishment is remedial. In the case of the latter, however, it requires a different justification. Incapable of improvement themselves, the incurables are punished in hopes of deterring other curables who, by contemplating their awful suffering, will be afraid (φοβούμενοι) and become better (*G.* 525b1–4). Clearly, Socrates has no scruples about using "fear of hell-fire" to get people to "take justice seriously."

Unlike the *Apology*, in which the prospect of punishment in the hereafter is qualified by skeptical doubts about whether there is a hereafter, and the *Crito*, in which the allusion to the hereafter is put into the mouth of the personified Laws of Athens, in the *Gorgias* Socrates recounts these eschatological horrors with unprecedented confidence and in his own person. Even if he does not think the myth is literally true, as many commentators believe, he clearly does think its hair-raising eschatological content is an appropriate vehicle for moral exhortation and he exploits it to the hilt.

These "vengeful"[24] myths have disturbed some students of Plato. If one is just unwillingly and from fear of punishment, what is such "justice" worth? Indeed, is it justice at all?

The point is well taken, and there is a sense in which Socrates would agree. The tacit but, according to him, false assumption on which the unjust man's life is based is that injustice is more profitable than justice – in a word, injustice pays. Hence were it not for the threat of punishment in the hereafter, he would unhesitatingly opt for the unjust life and have neither regrets nor fears for having done so. His only problem is this: *if* the gods exist – probably not but one can never be sure – they will punish him. Now if such a person, in his old age and in that state of mind, tried to escape punishment by "bribing the gods," Socrates would denounce him every bit as severely as Annas and her like-minded colleagues denounce Cephalus.

But this If-God-is-dead-everything-is-allowable mentality is not the whole story. There is also proper and salutary fear of punishment. This kind of fear is not fear of punishment *simpliciter* but fear of *deserved* punishment. The real issue is not fear of being punished for the life one has lived, and would continue to live were it not for one's eschatological nightmares, but fear which brings about amendment of life – moral renewal. The correlative of fear of punishment is love of the good, and the function of the eschatological myths is to awaken men's desire for that good as *their* good. Their aim is not (or is not merely) the purely psychological or emotional one of instilling terror, but the rational one of inculcating self-knowledge in hopes of bringing the unjust man to abhor himself; for in coming to abhor himself, he will come to love justice. And perceiving that the gods love it, too – since, like piety, justice is not just because it is loved by the gods but loved by the gods because it is just – he will no longer view them as morally capricious beings to be obeyed out of mere terrified flattery, but as morally good beings whose moral sanctions are internal to their commands and whose goodness they themselves exemplify. The morally suspect fear of aging immoralists who offer sacrifices hoping that the gods will look the other way should not be confounded with the morally salutary fear of men like Cephalus – or,

---

[24] The term is Ryle's, 1966: 219.

for that matter, Socrates himself – who wishes to present his soul as healthy as possible before the judges (*G.* 526d3–5).[25]

When one contemplates the unblushing allusions to happiness and the recurring appeals to rewards and punishments scattered throughout the early dialogues, one gets the distinct impression that Socrates does not find his interlocutors' desire for happiness too strong but too weak and directed to unworthy objects – like seaside dwellers who turn a deaf ear to the beckoning roar of the ocean and are content to splash about in the puddles it leaves along the shore. However, since no one errs voluntarily, the best way of getting them to be just is by persuading them that it is in their interest to be just, that is, by persuading them that it is not injustice but justice that leads to happiness – the "true wish" (βούλησις) of their souls (*G.* 466c9–e2). So understood, the eschatological myths are not externally imposed threats, but a form of spell-weaving. If the purpose of elenchus is to confront the interlocutor with his ignorance and to induce him to take up the quest for truth, the purpose of myths is to awaken his love for the truth he lacks but to which he aspires. His newly discovered self-knowledge must be enlisted in the service of his newly awakened desire. Nothing more tellingly reveals how completely Cephalus' detractors have overlooked this sublime aspect of Socratic thought than the fact that they are all (to varying degrees) disturbed by the "vulgarity" of the myth of the *Gorgias* (and by the eschatological myths generally) because their depictions of punishment and the fear it elicits "pull us right down to the level of Cephalus."[26]

It follows that, in assessing Cephalus, it is not enough to observe that he has been just from fear of punishment. We need to know what *kind* of fear and how it is connected to the life he has lived. Plato provides these all-important details by portraying him as a man of character with a lifelong disposition to be just – a self-description which reveals that Cephalus' overriding motivation has been lifelong contentment and tranquillity of mind, not just contentment and tranquillity of mind in his old age. Not only does he perceive, albeit from afar, something of the Socratic view of

---

[25] Commenting on Socrates' last request (*Ph.* 118a7–8) that Crito sacrifice a cock to Asclepius, Chambry, 1989: 9, n. 2. says: "Socrate mourant a les mêmes inquiétudes que Céphale."

[26] Annas, 1981: 349.

the connection between justice and happiness; to some extent, his life embodies it.

Having defended Cephalus textually against his critics, it remains to defend him philosophically against Socrates. Hand in hand with the picture of Cephalus as the morally corrupt briber of the gods goes the picture of Socrates as the morally earnest exposer of his indefensible view of justice. The received opinion among most traditional and contemporary commentators is that Cephalus has put forth a *definition* of justice.[27] And it collapses like a sand castle at the slightest Socratic nudge: "You say that justice consists in telling the truth and returning what you have borrowed? But surely it would not be just to tell the truth or to return weapons to a madman, would it? Of course not. So your definition fails." Exit Cephalus.

Now I have no wish to deny that Socrates is the undisputed master of the polemical technique of refutation by counterexample. Since in any acceptable Socratic definition the members of the classes denoted by the *definiens* and the *definiendum* must be coextensive,[28] counterexamples can be employed in a variety of ways: (i) by producing instances of the *definiendum* which are not covered by the *definiens*, such as, there are cases of courage other than remaining at one's post (*La.* 191c7–e2); (ii) by producing instances which are covered by the *definiens* but which are not cases of the *definiendum*, for example, courage is not wise endurance, since it is not the case that whoever endures in spending money wisely is courageous (*La.* 192e1–5); (iii) by producing cases of the *definiendum* which have the opposite property of that expressed by the *definiens*, e.g., some temperate actions are quick rather than quiet (*Ch.* 159c3–160d4); or (iv) by demonstrating that the *definiens* entails a moral judgment which no reasonable person would affirm.

Socrates' madman counterexample is often cited as an example of (iv). But it is not. Contrary to the assurances of many commen-

[27] See, e.g., Shorey, 1933: 208–9; Murphy, 1951: 2; Friedländer, 1964, II: 55; Crombie, 1962, I: 79; Cross and Woozley, 1964: 2; Gulley, 1968: 77–78; Guthrie, 1975: 439; and Lycos, 1987: 81–83.
[28] See McPherran, 1996: 39: "Socrates generally seems to be after (ideally) a definition of the form 'F is (=) D', where there is a relation of mutual entailment and extensional identity between the definiendum F and the definiens D, and where the definiens gives a complete *explanation* of why any individual action or thing x is F, an explanation that will put one in a position to recognize any F-instance x as being an F-instance."

tators, Cephalus never defines justice.[29] Indeed, at this early stage
of the discussion the question: What is justice? has not even been
raised. Cephalus' remarks are an answer to *a* question, but not to
that one. The formula, "Tell the truth and render to everyone
what is due" is not Cephalus' answer to the question: What is justice?; it is Socrates' tendentious interpretation of his answer to the
question: What is the greatest benefit of wealth? Having answered
that question, Cephalus discovers that his remarks have been construed – indeed, *mis*construed – as an answer to the very different,
completely general, and as yet unasked definitional question:
What is justice? and faulted for being an unsatisfactory answer. In
thus faulting Cephalus, Socrates ignores both the primary import
of his remarks and the question to which they were the intended
answer, coaxes from them an admittedly unsatisfactory definition
of justice which purports to state the necessary and sufficient conditions governing the application of the term "just," and then
"refutes" it with his madman counterexample – an action which,
though manifestly unjust, must be pronounced just if Cephalus'
"definition" is to stand. But although Socrates' counterexample
refutes *that* definition, it does not refute Cephalus who advanced *no*
definition. Indeed, in view of the striking contrast between the
casual and slow-paced nature of the foregoing conversation and
the formal and abrupt nature of Socrates' attack, it seems that
the unsuspecting Cephalus has been pounced on quite unfairly.
Naively supposing that he is participating in "the pleasures of
good conversation," he suddenly finds himself transformed into an
interlocutor upon whom, in Nozick's delicious phrase, Socrates
proceeds to "commit philosophy."[30]

I anticipate the following objection: Socrates does not coax a
definition of justice from Cephalus' remarks; he merely formulates
his remarks more succinctly and then deduces an inference to
which they logically commit him but from which he recoils, thereby refuting him "from his own beliefs."

But this rescue operation is a misdescription of Socrates' dialectical behavior – not only in this passage, but in the early dialogues generally. Bending over backwards to formulate his inter-

[29] This is recognized by J. Adam, 1938, I: 11; Bloom, 1968: 314; Méron, 1979: 111; and
Annas, 1981: 22–23.
[30] 1981: 5.

locutors' theses more succinctly and in the most charitable way is
not one of Socrates' most conspicuous characteristics; on the contrary, he often deliberately distorts their theses and then refutes a
strawman. So, too, here. Having "complimented" Cephalus for
speaking beautifully, he wonders whether, when speaking about
justice itself (τοῦτο δ' αὐτό, τὴν δικαιοσύνην), we should say so
unconditionally and without qualification (ἁπλῶς οὕτως, 331c1–3)
that it is always just to tell the truth and to render to everyone what
is due. The madman counterexample follows. Socrates introduces
it by saying he is confident that everyone would agree (πᾶς ἄν που
εἴποι, 331c5) that it would be unjust to return weapons to a madman – yet another attempt to refute his interlocutor by pointing
out that what he has just said is at variance with the opinions of
"the Many."[31] Cephalus concedes the point. Socrates thereupon
triumphantly concludes that "telling the truth and rendering to
everyone what is due" is not the definition (ὅρος) of "justice"
(331d2) – a remark which reveals that he does take Cephalus' remarks as a definition of justice: οὕτως refers to what Cephalus
had just said, construed as a ὅρος. To deny this is to defend Socrates at the cost of rendering the Greek unintelligible.

In response to Socrates' counterexample, Cephalus should have
said that he was not purporting to state the necessary and sufficient
conditions which govern the application of the term "just"; he was
merely trying to answer the question he had been asked. In fact,
he could have circumvented Socrates' counterexample very easily:
first, by distinguishing definitions of moral terms from moral rules;
and second, by distinguishing universal moral rules from general
ones, thereby allowing for exceptions to moral rules or building
them into the rules. Having done so, he could have pointed out
that Socrates' counterexample, far from refuting what he had said,
is otiose. Finally, he could have pointed out that although it is not
always just to tell the truth and to return what you have borrowed,
it *usually* is. And, as his response to the counterexample shows,
Cephalus can recognize exceptions as well as anyone.[32] In the

---

[31] For a different interpretation, see Hare, 1982: 42, according to whom this is not an empirical appeal to the opinions of "the Many," but a logical appeal to "the linguistic
facts," i.e., to "the linguistic usage of native speakers."

[32] Interestingly, at *R.* 433e2–10 "Socrates" seems to disallow exceptions himself. He asserts
that the rulers of the ideal city must see to it that no one has what belongs to others and
that no one is deprived of what is rightfully his own "because that is just." No worries
here about madmen on one's doorstep.

context in which it is employed, the madman counterexample proves only one thing – that justice cannot be defined as telling the truth and returning what you have borrowed. But Cephalus never said it could.

This raises awkward questions about the whole discussion. How, one wonders, has Socrates cared for Cephalus' soul? Of what ethical or meta-ethical blunders has he been convicted? Of what conceptual confusions has he been disabused? How will his encounter with Socrates enrich his conception of justice and improve his future dealings with gods and men?

I am not simply caviling about Socrates' logic. There is a deeper problem – a problem of interpretation. Socrates drops by, asks Cephalus a series of (what seem to be) genuine questions, applauds his answers, expresses admiration for him, and then abruptly pulls the rug from under him. After which Cephalus excuses himself and goes off to his sacrifice.

How should we read this bizarre tableau? One possibility is to read it straight. Socrates, moral gadfly, meets Cephalus, complacent businessman, and tries to improve his soul. But Cephalus resists. His alleged interest in "the pleasures of good conversation" wanes noticeably the minute he is asked to think hard about the way of life he has just advocated. His sudden loss of interest and speedy exit reveal that behind the mask of this ostensibly decent man lives a self-satisfied traditionalist who turns his back on a well-meaning critic who has momentarily forced him to see that the life of which he is so proud is, in fact, an empty sham.

This would be a plausible reading if sensitivity to textual nuance revealed, first, that Cephalus is a morally complacent man in need of having his illusions dispelled and, second, that Socrates confronts him with a cogent argument which should have dispelled them. Neither condition is satisfied. Cephalus is, in many respects, a good and admirable man; and Socrates' argument is based on (what seems to be) a deliberate misunderstanding. Unable to reply, Cephalus does the next best thing: he leaves. However, this is not one of those deplorable face-saving exits by yet another Socratic interlocutor in flight from self-knowledge with which the early dialogues allegedly abound. Far from being convicted of ignorance, Cephalus is completely untouched by Socrates' criticism and leaves without the slightest thought that his whole life has just been called into question.

Why not? Is he simply Annas' "complacent avoider of hell-fire" and McKim's "corrupt but affable" old man? I do not think so.

Dialectically silenced, Cephalus stands by his life. Although incapable of explaining how he has attained it, he has something which, however theoretically ungrounded, is an essential component happiness: he is at peace with his fellows and with himself. Although not rooted in *epistēmē* and intermixed with an exaggerated and probably false estimate of the importance of money in living the moral life, his fundamental decency and resultant contentment and tranquillity of mind are the hard-earned fruits of a lifetime, and Plato does not allow Socrates to deprive him of them. Cephalus' inability to defend his views does not call his life into question. It reveals that his practical ability to be just outstrips his theoretical ability to explain justice. Theoretical inability does not entail moral bankruptcy. Some people fail to live up to their moral principles, other people are better than their principles.

Socrates does not "banish" Cephalus as a superfluous encumbrance to the discussion. Perceiving that he is hopelessly out of his depth, Cephalus leaves voluntarily. Curiously, Socrates neither tries to prevail upon him to stay nor upbraids him with ironic taunts: "What? Leaving just when you were about to instruct me about justice and help me to live a better life?" And Cephalus' parting comment, "I must tend to the sacrifices," far from being one in a series of "malicious touches" on Plato's part, is in fact a gracious gesture which enables the old man to leave with his composure and dignity intact. The relentless and often morally censorious practitioner of the elenctic method is here made to behave in an uncharacteristically humane way.

Cephalus exits: not sheepishly and in disgrace, but good-naturedly and with a smile (γελάσας, 331d9). This can be taken in two ways. Following his detractors, we might say that he leaves as a complacent man – unable to say what justice is, unaware that the just life is difficult, but confident that he is just.[33] But why say that? Why not say that he leaves as a serious man bewildered by the frivolous turn the discussion has taken and in the dark about what on earth these philosophers are up to? Although we may not legitimately invest a fictional character with an historical past, we may legitimately invest him with an imaginative one – a past of

---

[33] See Annas, 1981: 21.

which he speaks with satisfaction and pride. Unaware that the just life is difficult? Here is a an old man looking back on a lifetime spent cultivating his character and living a life of honesty and fair play, at peace with himself and the world, untroubled by his physical ailments, and uncritical of his imperfect friends and relatives. And for his pains he is tripped up by out-of-the-blue rhetoric about a madman on his doorstep. Little wonder that he is amused and only too happy to bequeath the argument to Polemarchus. Perhaps the contentment and tranquillity of mind he enjoys arises from his conviction that the past seventy-odd years have been spent dealing with matters of greater moment than whether one should return weapons to madmen.

CHAPTER 10

Polemarchus

The second of three increasingly intractable interlocutors in *Republic* 1, Polemarchus[1] bursts into the discussion in the same brash and almost bullying way that he had invited Socrates and Glaucon to his home and would not take "No" for an answer. His only substantive contribution[2] occurs at *R.* 331d4–336a10 where, as the inheritor of the argument with Cephalus, he undertakes to defend his father's claim that justice consists in telling the truth and rendering to everyone what is due – a claim which Socrates had dismissed with the magisterial pronouncement that this is not the definition (ὅρος) of justice (331d2–3). "It certainly is," retorts Polemarchus, "if ... we're to trust Simonides" (331d4–5). Although it is not said of him, as will soon be said of Thrasymachus, that he had been trying for some time to break into the discussion and had to be restrained, his entrance is characterized by a similarly combative and even defiant tone. The name "Polemarchus" means "warlord," and at the outset it seems to suit its bearer very well. Within a few Stephanus pages, however, the warlord is as meek as a lamb being led to the dialectical slaughter.

Although alluded to at *Phdr.* 257b3–4 as a convert to philosophy, Polemarchus displays little philosophical aptitude in the *Republic* and is held in low esteem by most commentators. Annas[3] deplores his "complacency" too and faults him for holding views which have no "intellectual backing." Teloh[4] berates him for his "pliability" and "democratic tendency" to move whichever way

---

[1] After his death, the historical Cephalus' property was confiscated by the Thirty. In 404 the historical Polemarchus was imprisoned by Eratosthenes and a year later, without a trial or even a formal charge, executed by hemlock. (See Lysias *Against Eratosthenes*).

[2] He also appears briefly at *R.* 340a1–c2 and 449b1–6.

[3] 1981: 21.

[4] 1986: 88.

the wind blows. Nettleship[5] characterizes him as a member of the younger generation whose understanding of tradition is fragmentary and whose theory of justice is a "borrowed principle of which he is not the master." The somewhat more appreciative Lycos[6] thinks Polemarchus' understanding of justice goes deeper than Cephalus', but criticizes him for abandoning his father's view of justice as expressive of character.

It is often said that Polemarchus enters the discussion to defend his father's view as the correct definition (ὅρος) of justice. In support of this claim, it is urged that he is responding to – and denying – Socrates' contention that it is *not* the correct definition. But we need to proceed cautiously here. Polemarchus does not say that justice *is*, i.e., should be defined as, telling the truth and rendering to everyone what is due; he says that it is just (ὅτι ... δίκαιόν ἐστι, 331e3–4) to do these things. He is not defining "justice"; he is predicating the property "being just" of these actions.

Socrates feigns admiration for the "wise and divine" Simonides, but confesses that, although Polemarchus may understand this riddling utterance (ἠινίξατο, 332b9), he does not.[7] Surely Simonides does not mean that it is just to return weapons to a madman – even if they are due to him as their rightful owner. Polemarchus concurs (332a6). What, then, does he mean? Polemarchus explains that, by "what is due" (τὸ ὀφειλόμενον), Simonides means what is appropriate or fitting (τὸ προσῆκον, 332c2): what is due to friends is some good (ἀγαθὸν ... τι, 332a10) and what is due to enemies is some evil (κακόν τι, 332b8). In short, it is just to help one's friends and to harm one's enemies.

Polemarchus' view of justice is different from and inferior to his father's in several respects. As we have seen, Cephalus rejects the *lex talionis* and believes that a just man should harm no one. He also believes that being just involves more than performing certain actions. Just actions should be expressive of a just character and a disposition to be just, that is, justice is not simply a property of actions, it is also a property of persons. For Polemarchus, on the other hand, justice seems to have nothing to do with character; it

---

[5] 1929: 16.
[6] 1987: 32–33.
[7] In view of Socrates' recurring criticisms of poetry and poets, it is worth noticing that he nowhere explicitly challenges the moral authority of Simonides. The target of his objections is neither Simonides nor his dictum, but Polemarchus' interpretation of it.

is simply a property of actions the justice or injustice of which is determined by appeal to the Simonidean-Polemarchean principle "Render to everyone what is due."[8] In elucidating "what is due" as "helping one's friends and harming one's enemies," Polemarchus unabashedly endorses the *lex talionis* and thereby parts company with Cephalus who agrees that one ought to render to everyone what is due, but understands it in a way that precludes harming anyone.

Yet, however inferior to his father's, Polemarchus' understanding of justice enables him to operate on a higher level of generality which renders the Simonidean-Polemarchean principle immune to the madman counterexample which Socrates had employed with such apparent success against Cephalus. Given the moral rectitude of harming one's enemies, the question: Is it just to return weapons to a madman? cannot be answered *in general*. If the madman is your friend, the answer is "No"; but if he is your enemy, the answer is "Yes." It follows that Socrates was mistaken in claiming that everyone would agree that it would be unjust to return weapons to a madman (331c6–9). Although Polemarchus had agreed with this statement earlier, he should not have; it is not entailed by his actual position and is, in fact, incompatible with it. According to Polemarchus, there is an important conceptual distinction between *returning what you have borrowed* and *rendering what is due*. The first is a moral rule, whereas the second is a moral principle. If by returning weapons to a friend one harms him, one has returned what one has borrowed, but one has not rendered what is due; however, if by returning weapons to an enemy one harms him, one has done both. The criterion of whether one ought to return something is what is *really* due its rightful owner. Actual indebtedness must be distinguished from apparent (or *prima facie*) indebtedness.

Deprived of his madman counterexample, Socrates needs a new argument if he is to refute the Simonidean-Polemarchian definition of justice. In fact, he produces four.

Before examining them, however, a preliminary point needs to be emphasized. There is no scholarly consensus about what Plato is up to in the discussion between Socrates and Polemarchus. Traditional commentators treat Socrates' arguments as arguments

---

[8] See Lycos, 1987: 35: "The specific content of what is just to do in any given instance will be relative to the description under which the recipient is considered."

aimed at Polemarchus' view according to which justice is a skill or *technē* analogous to those possessed by the practitioners of the *technai* of carpentry, medicine, navigation, and so on, and, like them, capable of misuse. However, a growing number of contemporary commentators[9] think these arguments are aimed not so much at Polemarchus as at the *technē*-analogy itself which Plato had previously put into the mouth of Socrates, but now criticizes on the ground that there are important dissimilarities between justice and the *technai*. According to these commentators, Socrates' arguments are intended to show either that justice is not a *technē* at all or that it is a *technē* "unlike every other"[10] and "of a quite unusual sort"[11] in that it does not admit of misuse. A major difficulty with the traditional interpretation is that Polemarchus does not seem to think of justice as a skill – much less, as a skill analogous to those possessed by the practitioners of the various *technai*. A major difficulty with the more recent interpretation is that we are compelled on neither textual nor philosophical grounds to read the exchange between Socrates and Polemarchus as a criticism – much less, as a rejection – of the *technē*-analogy. I will return to this issue after examining the arguments Socrates advances against the Simonidean-Polemarchian definition of justice.

Argument One (332c5–333e2) tries to demonstrate that if justice is understood as a *technē*, it is useless because there is no service that the just man can provide which is not already provided by the practitioners of the other *technai*. Medicine produces health, cookery produces tasty food, navigation produces safe voyages. What does justice produce? Polemarchus hesitates before answering this question. Indeed, the question itself gives him pause. His "guarded"[12] reply (loosely translated by many)[13] is (the translation is mine):

If it is necessary to follow the previous examples (Εἰ ... δεῖ ἀκολουθεῖν ... τοῖς ἔμπροσθεν εἰρημένοις), Socrates, it benefits friends and harms enemies. (332d4–6)

---

[9] Among them, Cross and Woozley, 1964: 10–16; Bloom, 1968: 325; Irwin, 1977: 178–79, and (more cautiously) 1995: 68–70; Reeve, 1988: 8; and Kahn, 1996: 118.

[10] Irwin, 1995: 69.

[11] Kahn, 1996: 118.

[12] The term is Cross's and Woozley's, 1964: 11.

[13] "If ... we are to be guided at all by the analogy of the preceding instances" (Jowett); "If we are to follow these analogies" (Cornford); "If we are to follow the previous examples" (Shorey). Bloom comes much closer: "If the answer has to be consistent with what preceded."

Polemarchus hesitates because he is being asked to endorse a piece of analogical reasoning which strikes him as less than perspicacious. His misgivings – expressed in the protasis ("If it is necessary to follow the previous examples") – imply that he suspects that it may not be necessary; and even if it is, he does not understand why. His hesitation is justified. Why should he be required to accept without argument – and even without explanation – an analogy based on unstated assumptions and laden with only dimly-perceived implications?[14] But Socrates does not enlighten him; he ignores his misgivings and presses for his assent.

Of course, Polemarchus finally does "accept" the *technē*-analogy – or, rather, allows it to be "foisted on" him.[15] But his "acceptance" is reluctant, heavily qualified, and literally wrung from him by Socrates. It is, in fact, a paradigmatic example of the "iffy" – tentative and non-committal – kind of assent which, according to Vlastos, Socrates always disallows. Having "accepted" the analogy, he is quickly undone by its logic. But this does not show that he is operating with "a borrowed principle of which he is not the master." It merely shows that, like many other Socratic interlocutors, Polemarchus has been coerced into endorsing an analogy which he is disinclined to endorse and into affirming a thesis which had never entered his head, namely, that justice is a *technē* which produces a unique and antecedently determined end the attainment of which requires specialized expertise.[16] At no point in the discussion does Socrates urge Polemarchus to consider the matter carefully, to say only what he really believes, and to concur with the propositions propounded for his assent only if he sincerely assents to them; on the contrary, he takes little note of what Polemarchus really believes and even less note of his misgivings. Unfortunately, Polemarchus does not trust his logical instincts – a serious mistake; for once he "accepts" the *technē*-analogy, his difficulties are compounded. Although he tries to salvage what he can

---

[14] Cross and Woozley, 1964: 11, acknowledge that Socrates draws out the implications of the *technē*-analogy without examining whether it is sound and "entirely ignoring" Polemarchus' misgivings.

[15] The terminology is Annas's, 1981: 26.

[16] See Annas, 1981: 25: "[A] *technē* or skill is an organized body of knowledge of the ways to achieve a certain end." Cf. Irwin, 1977: "A craft is a rational procedure for producing a certain product" (77); hence "[t]he capacity to give an account distinguishes a real craftsman from someone who merely has a knack or technique which he cannot explain" (71). See also Penner, 1973a: 137, n. 5. Interestingly, Joseph, 1935a: 9–10, denies that this argument (or any other in *Republic* 1) is based on the *technē*-analogy.

and does not go down without a fight, the logic of the analogy inexorably takes its toll. The fact remains, however, that Socrates'
refutation of Polemarchus depends on his "accepting" the *technē*-
analogy whether he believes it or not, unaware of the implications
to which he is committing himself.

Polemarchus' "acceptance" of the *technē*-analogy also signals a
psychological turning point in the discussion. Deprived of the
freedom to protest and required to accept a (to his mind) dubious
analogy which had never entered his head, he must now make up
his view as he goes along. Prohibited from saying (and meaning)
what he had originally said (and meant), he must grope for some
unique (and possibly non-existent) end which justice produces and
for some equally unique (and also possibly non-existent) specialized expertise required to attain it. His subsequent answers,
strained and unconvincing, reveal that his initial enthusiasm as the
inheritor of the argument with Cephalus has waned and that his
heart is no longer in the discussion. Having just witnessed his
father silenced – unconvincingly, in his opinion – he now finds
himself forced to debate on uncongenial turf. But although refutation is just around the corner, it is inaccurate to say that Polemarchus is reduced to *aporia*; it is more accurate to say that he gives
up. Justice turns out not to be a *technē*. But Polemarchus never said
it was. So whomever Socrates has just refuted, it is not he.

Having been induced to assert that justice is a *technē* or skill
which enables one to help to one's friends and to harm one's
enemies, Polemarchus has unwittingly embarked on the road to
defeat. He proceeds further down that road when he tries to elucidate "his" thesis by explaining *how* justice enables a person to
achieve these ends, thereby providing content for the (according
to Socrates) still vacuous terms "help" and "harm." Whatever
Polemarchus may have thought (and meant) earlier, Socrates now
gets him to "agree" – albeit again very tentatively ("I believe so"
(Δοκεῖ μοι, 332d9) – that helping one's friends and harming one's
enemies is the *definition* of justice (δικαιοσύνην) and not simply, as
previously, actions which *are* just (δίκαιος).[17] He also gets him to
"agree" that justice is the *technē* which equips its possessor with the
expertise to do these things. Having elicited Polemarchus' "agree-

---

[17] This is overlooked by Irwin, 1995: 171, according to whom "Socrates does not say that
this is a definition of justice or of just action; he examines it simply as a purported property of just action."

ment" to these theses – and, in effect, put words into his mouth – Socrates proceeds to argue that justice, so understood, is useless.

As usual, the first step seems innocuous enough. Polemarchus need only endorse the apparent truism that the respective expertise of doctors and navigators enables them to help their friends and to harm their enemies in matters pertaining to health and sea-voyages. However, when confronted with the superficially similar but, in fact, very different question of by what action (ἐν τίνι πράξει) and for what work (πρὸσ τί ἔργον) the just man is best equipped to help his friends and to harm his enemies (332e3–4), Polemarchus is stumped and lamely replies that the just man is equipped to wage war against his enemies and to form military alliances with his allies. Socrates faults this (admittedly weak) response: not on the ground that the just man harms no one, but on the very different ground that it seems to imply that just as doctors and navigators are useless when no one is ill or wishes to sail, so also just men are useless in time of peace. Polemarchus insists that justice *is* useful in peacetime, for example, for drawing up contracts and forming partnerships; but Socrates relentlessly presses the *technē*-analogy. When it comes to laying bricks or playing the harp, skilled bricklayers and accomplished harpists are preferable to just men. By the process of elimination, he finally arrives at the conclusion that there seems to be no activity – or no important one – for which the just man can provide a service which is not already provided by the practitioners of the other *technai*. Polemarchus feebly suggests that just men are useful when people wish to deposit money for safekeeping – a perfectly innocent remark intended to underscore the importance of honesty in financial transactions, but which Socrates misinterprets to mean that just men are only useful when the money entrusted to their care is useless. "It looks that way" (Κινδυνεύει, 333d12), replies the by-now thoroughly befuddled Polemarchus.

Some commentators[18] are impressed by this argument while others[19] find it seriously deficient. How good is it?

---

[18] Annas, 1981: 27, thinks the argument is "fair enough" insofar as Socrates brings out that although Polemarchus thinks justice is a skill, he cannot identify any important end that it enables the just man to attain.

[19] Baccou, 1966, speaks of a "tour sophistique" in this passage (388, n. 13) and judges Socrates' argument "facile" (19). Diès, 1989: 13, n. 1, is more severe: "Socrate, ou plutôt Platon, s'amuse à conduire son jeune interlocuteur à une conclusion ridicule. Il abuse de la dialectique, comme les sophistes dont il réprouve ailleurs la méthode."

Annas thinks Polemarchus should have either affirmed that justice is a skill which enables the just man to achieve the all-important end of happiness or denied that it is a skill and rejected the *technē*-analogy. According to those who think Plato is criticizing the *technē*-analogy in *Republic* i, the latter is precisely what Socrates wants Polemarchus to see; on their view, the argument is a *reductio ad absurdum* of the thesis that justice is a *technē* and logically on all fours with a skill. If they are right, then of course Polemarchus need not specify the end which justice produces. It was, after all, not he but Socrates who introduced the idea that justice is a *technē* which produces some unique end. In any event, Polemarchus does not reject the *technē-analogy*.

The reason he does not, according to Annas,[20] is that he himself implicitly thinks of justice as a skill: the just man is skilled at helping his friends and harming his enemies. But the text provides no good reason for believing that this is true. In fact, it provides good reasons for believing that Polemarchus does not think of justice as a skill or *technē*: not because he thinks of it in some other way, but because he has not thought about it at all. As the discussion proceeds, it becomes painfully obvious that Polemarchus has no *theory* of justice. In saying that it is just to help one's friends and to harm one's enemies, he is not advancing a philosophical thesis; he is simply mouthing a basic principle of conventional Athenian morality and thereby espousing the *lex talionis*: if you are Polemarchus' friend, he will help you; if you are his enemy, he will not. Indeed, given the opportunity, he will harm you. As he sees it, justice is nothing more than a Simonidean sanctioned form of tit-for-tat. Polemarchus' claim that it is just to render to everyone what is due has nothing to do with having and exercising a skill. Nor does it commit him to believing that, like every skill, justice produces a unique end which can only be attained by those with the requisite expertise. In "foisting" the *technē*-analogy on Polemarchus, Socrates is not only making it impossible for him to say what he really believes; he is guaranteeing that he will say what he does *not* believe.

But whatever Polemarchus may or may not think, justice is clearly not a skill. Although helping (or harming) people often requires specific skills, being helpful (or harmful) is not one of them.

---

[20] 1981: 27.

"Being helpful" is not the name of a skill. Nor is it the name of an activity at which one can *be* skilled. Although we often help people by performing specific actions which are means to desired ends, the skills which enable us to perform these actions (and, thereby, to be helpful) need to be distinguished from the desire to achieve the ends to which they are the means. These skills also need to be distinguished from the ends themselves. I may become a superb pianist by practicing day and night from the desire to help others to appreciate the music of the great masters. I may also take perverse delight in practicing into the wee hours to harm my family by keeping them awake. But although it would be intelligible and accurate to say that I am skilled at playing the piano, it would be false and ludicrous to say that I am skilled at helping my audiences to appreciate the music of the great masters and at harming my family by depriving them of a good night's sleep. The fact that one achieves some end does not entail that one is skilled at achieving it.

But if Polemarchus does not think of justice as a skill or *technē* and if, as some commentators believe, Plato himself no longer accepted the *technē*-analogy when he wrote *Republic* i, why does he make Socrates introduce it? Why introduce an analogy you do not accept in order to refute a thesis your interlocutor does not believe? The answer cannot be that Socrates wants Polemarchus to see that justice is *not* a *technē*, for he never said it was. However, there is another possibility. Even if Plato no longer accepted the *technē*-analogy when he wrote *Republic* i, perhaps he makes Socrates induce Polemarchus to assert that justice is a *technē* because if he does, then, since it is not, he will not be able to specify the unique end at which it aims. If that is in fact the case, then Socrates is not trying to persuade Polemarchus that his inability to define justice is traceable to his acceptance of the (faulty) *technē*-analogy; on the contrary, he is trying to get him to accept an admittedly faulty analogy, thereby insuring that he will not be able to define justice. In short, in inducing Polemarchus to accept the *technē*-analogy, Socrates leads him down a blind alley.

Argument Two (333e3–334b6) is based on what is variously called "the paradox of misuse"[21] or "the principle of the ambivalence of the arts"[22]: Anyone who is skilled at X-ing is also skilled

---

[21] Irwin, 1977: 178.   [22] Penner, 1973a: 137.

at the opposite of X-ing. The boxer most skilled at landing punches is also most skilled at warding them off, the doctor most skilled at preventing disease is also most skilled at causing it, and so on (333e1–8). All expertise is neutral with respect to the ends for which it is employed. Hence every *technē* enables its practitioner to produce opposite effects depending on the purpose he wishes to achieve; in short, no *technē* precludes its own misuse. So if justice is a *technē*, it too can be employed to produce opposite effects, that is, it can be used for both just and unjust purposes. Two conclusions follow: first, if the just man is most skilled at guarding money, he must also be most skilled at stealing it and is, therefore, a kind of thief (334a5–9); second, justice itself is a kind of thievery (κλέπτης ... τις) which enables the just man to help his friends and to harm his enemies (334a10–b6).[23]

Asked if that is what he meant, Polemarchus replies with an oath that it most certainly is not, although he is no longer sure what he did mean. However, he is still confident that it is just to help one's friends and to harm one's enemies. Since Argument Two is closely connected with Argument Four, I will postpone my examination of it until later.

Argument Three (334c1–335b1) is based on the distinction between people who are worthy of being our friends and people who seem worthy but are not. Socrates wonders whether, by "friend" and "enemy," Polemarchus means the former or the latter. Assured that he means the former, Socrates points out that we sometimes err about these matters, believing people to be worthy of being our friends when they are not and *vice versa*, thereby mistaking the bad for the good and, more seriously, helping the bad (enemies who seem good) and harming the good (friends who seem bad). He thereupon concludes that it follows "from Polemarchus' reasoning" (κατὰ ... τὸν σὸν λόγον, 334d5) that it is just to help the bad (believing them to be good) and to harm the good (believing them to be bad), thereby harming those who have done us no wrong and benefiting those who have – the very opposite of what Simonides thinks just.

---

[23] Diès, 1989: 17, n. 1, writes: "Socrates abuse ici étrangement de l'analogie ... [m]ais l'interlocuteur de Socrates a vraiment peu de défense, et l'on comprend que sa complaisance indigne Thrasymaque." Méron, 1979: 129, on the other hand, comes to Socrates' defense: "Comme souvent, la faiblesse de l'entretien s'explique ici aisément par la faiblesse de l'interlocuteur."

At this point, Polemarchus does something that no Socratic interlocutor allegedly ever does. According to Kraut:

[I]t never happens in the early dialogues that an interlocutor retracts his earlier commitment to a premiss in standard elenctic debate.[24]

Vlastos is even more emphatic:

[Socrates] picks premises which he considers so eminently reasonable in themselves and so well-entrenched in his interlocutors' system of belief, that when he faces them with the fact that these premises entail the negation of their thesis he feels no serious risk that they will renege on the premises to save their thesis – as in fact, they never do.[25]

Polemarchus' response to Argument Three refutes that contention. Having agreed that we love those who seem good and that we hate those who seem bad, and having acknowledged that we sometimes err about both, Polemarchus refuses to endorse the conclusion that it is just to help the bad (believing them to be good) and to harm the good (believing them to be bad). To avoid drawing this conclusion, he proposes that they *retract* the propositions which generated it, namely, that our friends are those who seem good and our enemies are those who seem bad, and that they replace them with the propositions that our friends are those who seem, *and are*, good, and that our enemies are those who seem, *and are*, bad – thereby reneging on two previously agreed-upon premises.

It might be argued that Polemarchus is not reneging at all, but merely amending his original definitions of "friend" and "enemy" – a common phenomenon in the early dialogues. But this interpretation overlooks his reason for proposing the substitution. Unlike Charmides, Laches, Nicias, Euthyphro, and many other Socratic interlocutors, who *amend* their original definitions because they are too broad or too narrow, Polemarchus *abandons* his in order to avoid an unwelcome conclusion, thereby reneging on the previously agreed-upon premises which generated it.[26]

---

[24] 1983: 66.
[25] 1983b: 73.
[26] To my knowledge, this is the only passage in the early dialogues in which an interlocutor actually reneges on a previously agreed-upon premise. However, as we have seen (chapter 7, n. 22), the possibility is envisaged at *Ch.* 164c8–d3 where Critias assures Socrates that if his previous admissions entail that a person can be temperate without knowing it, he will withdraw them.

Polemarchus' new definitions of "friend" and "enemy" radically change his position. Unlike his original definitions, according to which it is just to help one's friends and to harm one's enemies *because they are friends and enemies,* his new ones require him to say that it is just to help one's friends and to harm one's enemies *because they are good and bad.* That is to say, it is just to help one's friends and to harm one's enemies not *qua* friends and enemies, but *qua* good and bad men. In short, the new definitions make virtue and vice necessary (and, perhaps, sufficient) conditions for someone's being a friend or an enemy.[27] Although Socrates does not explicitly say so, it follows that to say that it is just to help one's friends and to harm one's enemies is tantamount to saying that it is just to help those who are just and to harm those who are unjust. Yet, however different Polemarchus' new definitions of "friend" and "enemy" – and the resulting obligations towards both – his new view of justice retains what, for Socrates, was the most objectionable ingredient in his original one, namely, the contention that harming others is a part of justice and, therefore, one of the avowed intentions of the just man. It is precisely these objectionable theses which next come under attack.

Argument Four (335b2–335e6) is preceded by a question: Should a just man harm anyone? Polemarchus replies that he should indeed: he should harm those who are both bad and enemies. Socrates argues against this thesis as follows:

(i)   When horses or dogs are harmed, they are deprived of their uniquely equine and canine virtues and, therefore, become less excellent specimens of their kinds.

(ii) In the same way, when men are harmed, they are deprived of their uniquely human virtue, which is justice, and, therefore, become less excellent specimens of their kind.

(iii) To be deprived of justice is to be made more unjust.

(iv) The musician cannot make men unmusical by the art of music, and the horseman cannot make men unfit riders by the art of horsemanship.

(v)   In the same way, the just man cannot make men unjust by the art of justice; nor, since good and bad are opposites, can the just man, being good, make men bad, i.e., unjust.

---

[27] Cross and Woozley, 1964: 19, rightly point out that, in making this move Plato "has tried to tie together the notions of liking and approving far more closely than they in fact are tied."

(vi) Therefore, it cannot be the function (ἔργον) of the just man to harm anyone – whether friend or enemy. It is, rather, the function of his opposite, the unjust man.

So, in saying that justice consists in rendering to everyone what is due, Simonides could not have meant that it is just to help one's friends and to harm one's enemies. Polemarchus concurs. Surprisingly, instead of concluding that the Simonidean definition of justice is false, Socrates denies that Simonides held this view. Even more surprisingly, Polemarchus again concurs and vows to join Socrates in doing battle against anyone foolish enough to ascribe so absurd an opinion to Simonides (335e7–10).[28]

Although Socrates is right in denying that harming anyone is a part of justice and, therefore, one of the avowed intentions of the just man, in the process of refuting these theses, he changes the meaning of the term "harm" (βλάπτειν).[29] Unlike Polemarchus, for whom harming one's enemies means vanquishing or destroying them, Socrates means making them worse with respect to their uniquely human excellence (ἀρετή), that is, justice, thereby making them more unjust and, therefore, worse specimens of their kind. It is this subtle but undetected shift of meaning which enables him to refute the thesis that the just man should harm his enemies.[30] However, in refuting this thesis, he has not refuted Polemarchus who meant something different by "harm" and, therefore, never asserted the thesis just refuted.[31]

It is futile to defend Socrates by pointing out that his use of the term "virtue" is systematically ambiguous or by noting that he makes no sharp distinction between moral and non-moral goods and can, therefore, argue that people who are harmed are made worse without having to specify whether he is employing "worse"

---

[28] Irwin, 1995: 173–74, thinks this "charitable attitude" towards Simonides is not ironic but seriously intended on the ground that the later books of the *Republic* make extensive use of the principle of rendering what is due and, therefore, constitute a vindication of the Simonidean view, properly understood.

[29] The same criticism is made by many other commentators – among them, Gomperz, 1905, III, 55–56; and Cross and Woozley, 1964: 20–21. It is vigorously denied by Joseph, 1935a: 13–14.

[30] See Diès, 1989: 17, n. 1: "La conclusion est belle, mais elle repose, comme la discussion avec Polémarque, sur un raisonnement sophistique."

[31] Reeve, 1988: 8, thinks Plato is aware of this blunder: "Thus Socrates' refutation of Polemarchus is flagged by Plato as trading on a transparent misinterpretation, which Polemarchus is neither sharp enough nor well trained enough to detect." Lycos, 1987: 101–3, disagrees.

in a moral or non-moral sense.[32] The reason why it is futile is because it is the term "harm" that is doing all the work in his argument. It is no part of Polemarchus' view that to harm someone is
to make him less just and, therefore, a worse specimen of his kind.
Polemarchus never says this, and the text provides no reason for
thinking he believes it. This is yet another thesis which is "foisted"
on him by Socrates. I conclude that Argument Four fails. Socrates
has still not refuted the definition of justice as helping one's
friends and harming one's enemies.[33]

Having examined Arguments One, Three, and Four, I turn
finally to Two. It will be recalled that this argument is based on
what is variously called "the paradox of misuse" and "the principle of the ambivalence of the arts": Anyone who is skilled at
X-ing is also skilled at the opposite of X-ing. Although Socrates
wields this principle as if it were a self-evident truth, it is, in fact,
open to several objections.

First, as a matter of empirical fact, when applied to particular
cases, the principle is patently false. It is not the case that anyone
who is skilled at X-ing is also skilled at the opposite of X-ing. The
boxer most skilled at offensive tactics is not necessarily most skilled
at defensive ones. As more than one ephemeral title holder has
ruefully discovered, being a devastating puncher is perfectly compatible with having a glass jaw. Similarly, the competent and eternally vigilant security guard is usually an inept thief. The counterexamples could be multiplied *ad nauseam*.

Second, even if the principle were true, it would not refute the
Simonidean-Polemarchean definition of justice. If there are exceptions to the moral rule "Return what you have borrowed," as
Socrates argued against Cephalus, are there not also exceptions to
the moral rule "Do not steal"? And if there are, then even if it were
true that those most skilled at guarding money are most skilled at
stealing it, it would not follow that, in stealing it, they are acting
unjustly – *unless stealing is always unjust*. However, since, unlike his

---

[32] Annas, 1981: 31–33, defends Socrates on precisely this ground and, before her, Cross and
Woozley, 1964: 20–21.

[33] In saying this, I am not implying that the just man *should* harm his enemies. One can disagree with a view without accepting every argument against it, however bad or inconclusive. Thus when Shorey declares that the *lex talionis* was a virtually unquestioned
principle of traditional Athenian morality which Plato was the first to "transcend" (1937,
I: 25, n. d), he is not so much describing what Plato did as endorsing it. One can applaud
Plato for "transcending" the principle, but reject his reasons for doing so.

allegedly benighted interlocutors, Socrates does not hold such "simpleminded" rules which have no "intellectual backing," it would be ill-advised to burden him with so unpromising a thesis against which even a modestly endowed dialectician could produce endless counterexamples. Indeed, if one of his interlocutors were to assert that justice consists in refraining from stealing, thereby implying that stealing is always unjust, I am confident that he would live to regret it. Accordingly, in suggesting in shocked tones that, "according to Polemarchus," the just man is "a kind of thief," thereby implying that stealing is always wrong, Socrates is guilty of the same error of which he accused Cephalus – the error of defining justice in terms of a simple and universally applicable moral rule (or set of rules) when, in fact, there are exceptions to the rule "Do not steal," just as there are exceptions to the rules "Tell the truth" and "Return what you have borrowed."

Third, according to "the principle of the ambivalence of the arts," the doctor most skilled at making his patients better is also, and for that very reason, most skilled at making them worse. As we have seen, this principle is based on the assumption that insofar as no *technē* precludes its own misuse, every *technē* is neutral with respect to the end(s) for which it can be employed. It follows that there is only a contingent connection between possessing a *technē* and using it properly; indeed, it is precisely this contingency which makes the *mis*use of a *technē* possible. It is also precisely this contingency which invests Argument Two with whatever cogency it seems to have. But the cogency is illusory.[34] If there is only a contingent connection between possessing a *technē* and using it properly, then Argument Four is unsound for a further reason. In addition to equivocating on the term "harm," it employs a premise which is false on Socrates' own ground, namely, that the musician and the horsemen cannot make men unmusical or unfit riders by the *technai* of music (τῇ μουσικῇ) or horsemanship (τῇ ἱππικῇ, 335c9–12).

Arguments Two and Four are, in fact, inconsistent. According to Argument Two, since no *technē* precludes its own misuse, every *technē* is neutral with respect to the end(s) for which it can be em-

---

[34] For a different view, see Cross and Woozley, 1964: 16, who think the argument is "entirely successful." They are right *if*, as they suppose, the argument is intended as a *reductio ad absurdum* of the thesis that justice is a *technē*. But are they right? If they are, why does Socrates himself base Argument Four on the assumption that justice *is* a *technē*?

ployed. It is precisely this teleological neutrality which insures that the malevolent doctor can make his patients unhealthy "by the art of medicine." According to Argument Four, on the other hand, this teleological neutrality has vanished: the musician and the horseman cannot make men unmusical and unfit riders "by their arts." But why not? This could only be true if the connection between having a *technē* and using it properly were not contingent but necessary, thereby precluding the possibility of misuse. But that is exactly what Argument Two denies. Something is very wrong here. Either the practitioner can misuse his *technē* or he cannot. If the malevolent doctor can misuse his *technē* to make people unhealthy, what prevents a malevolent musician from misusing his to make them unmusical? And if the musician cannot misuse his *technē*, neither can the doctor. Socrates cannot have it both ways.

Socrates' inconsistency is traceable to an equivocation on the term *technē*. That this is so may be seen by asking the following question: Does the malevolent surgeon who expertly amputates the perfectly healthy leg of his enemy in order to maim him do so "by his art"? Surely he does. A non-surgeon might inadvertently cause him to bleed to death, thereby failing to achieve the desired end of making him miserable for the rest of his life. I will call this the descriptive sense of practicing a *technē* (hereafter TD). This descriptive sense, which does not preclude the misuse of a *technē* and is employed by Socrates in Argument Two, needs to be distinguished from the very different sense of practicing a *technē* which does preclude misuse and is employed by Socrates in Argument Four. I will call this the normative sense of practicing a *technē* (hereafter TN). Unlike TD, TN is inherently value-laden and value-oriented. It is for this reason that, unlike the musician and the horseman, who cannot make people unmusical and unfit riders "by their arts," the surgeon can make people unhealthy "by his art." Arguments Two and Four trade on this equivocation – an equivocation which Polemarchus does not detect.

Instead of allowing himself to be undone by these alternately fallacious, unsound, and internally inconsistent arguments, Polemarchus should have rebutted them. Several replies are open to him. First, and most radically, he could have rejected the *technē*-analogy by denying that justice is a *technē*. This would have demolished Argument One; for if justice is not a *technē*, it is no longer necessary to specify the end it produces. Having rejected the *technē*-analogy, he could have demanded that Socrates *argue* for its appositeness instead of coercing him into accepting it and announced that he will postpone considering Arguments Two, Three, and Four until the case for the appositeness of the analogy has been made.

Second, having detected Socrates' equivocation on the term *technē* and his inconsistent claims about the possibility of misuse, he could have employed the term *technē* univocally by opting for either TD or TN. Had he opted for TN, he could have undercut "the principle of the ambivalence of the arts" by denying that a *technē* can be misused, thereby rebutting Argument Two and exposing Socrates' equivocation and inconsistency. Had he opted for TD, he could have formulated a modified and consistent version of "the principle of the ambivalence of the arts," thereby rebutting Argument Four and again exposing Socrates' equivocation and inconsistency. Finally, having rebutted Arguments One and Two, he could have rebutted Argument Three by defining "friend" as someone who is *really* a friend (as opposed to merely *seeming* to be) and by acknowledging that although it is possible to make mistakes about people, he is willing to live with his fallibility as well as with his friends' periodic moral lapses. Whatever the weaknesses of the resulting view, none of Socrates' arguments touch it.[35]

I said earlier that whereas traditional commentators treat Socrates' arguments as arguments aimed at Polemarchus' view according to which justice is a skill or *technē* analogous to those possessed by the practitioners of the *technai* of carpentry, medicine, navigation, and so on, and, like them, capable of misuse, a growing number of contemporary commentators think these arguments are aimed not so much at Polemarchus as at the *technē*-analogy itself which Plato had previously put into the mouth of Socrates, but now criticizes on the ground that there are important dissimilarities between justice and the *technai*. According to these commentators, Socrates' arguments are intended to show either that justice is not a *technē* at all or that it is a *technē* "unlike every other" and "of a quite unusual sort" in that it does not admit of misuse. I now want to add that, for my purposes, it does not matter which

---

[35] Nicholas White, 1979: 63–64, acknowledges that Socrates' arguments against Polemarchus are often "too briskly framed to be cogent," but he excuses him on the ground that their purpose is "to point to problems latent in treating justice in certain ordinary ways."

of these views is correct. Whatever Plato may have thought about the *techne*-analogy when he wrote *Republic* 1, the fact is that throughout the discussion, it is not Polemarchus but Socrates who has an inconsistent belief-set, arguing both that justice is and is not a *technē*, and that a *technē* does and does not preclude its own misuse.

During his lifetime, Socrates was often identified with the sophists. Unlike proponents of the standard picture, who vigorously protest this allegedly mistaken identification, Werner Jaeger offers a less apologetically motivated assessment:

True philosophy always endeavoured to keep itself free from eristic, although the methods of Plato's Socrates often seem to have much in common with it ... [T]here are in Socrates' conversations many triumphs of argument, which remind us of the catch-arguments so beloved by the "eristics". We must not underestimate the pure love of verbal competition in his dialectic. Plato has given a lifelike representation of it, and we can see why rivals or contemporaries (like Isocrates) who did not belong to the Socratic school could simply call the Socratics professional arguers.[36]

The argument with Polemarchus helps to explain why.

---

[36] 1943–45, III: 56; II: 64.

CHAPTER 11

Thrasymachus

The successor of Polemarchus and one of the most unsympa-
thetically depicted interlocutors in the early dialogues, Thrasymachus of Chalcedon[1] makes his stormy appearance at *R.* 336b1.
His name, which means "bold fighter," conveys only the slightest
hint of his character which has been variously described as
shallow, stupid, abrasive, nasty, insolent, abusive, repulsive, pug-
nacious, violent, and even savage.[2] An admittedly irascible man
lacking even the most rudimentary civility, he has elicited universal disapproval and is, without a doubt, top contender for the title
of Socrates' Most Obnoxious Interlocutor – with Callicles a close
runner-up. Initially confident and condescending, he is methodically hammered into submission by an unusually combative Soc-

---

[1] Little is known of the historical Thrasymachus. Even his dates are conjectural. Juvenal's
cryptic remark – "Witness the ends of Thrasymachus and Secundus Carrinatis" (*Satires*
7.203–5) is glossed by the scholiast as an oblique allusion to Thrasymachus of Chalcedon
who allegedly hung himself – an uncorroborated assertion which is not taken seriously by
most scholars and, according to John Delaware Lewis, 1882, 1: 228, was "probably invented to explain the passage." Cf. Friedlaender, 1895: 394; Untersteiner, 1954: 311;
Green, 1967: 174, n. 15; Ferguson, 1979: 228; and Sprague, 1972: 88, n. 3. A famous rhetorician and teacher of rhetoric, he was highly regarded by classical antiquity. Aristotle
credits him with being instrumental in bringing rhetoric to its present perfection (*S.E.*
183b32–35). Cicero (*Brutus* 30) and Dionysius of Halicarnassus (*Isaeus* 20, *Demosthenes* 1–2)
shower him with equally high praise. Plato is less enthusiastic. Although willing to concede that he is a powerful speaker (*Phdr.* 266c1–5) and adept at manipulating the emotions of his audience (267c6–d1), he denies that he is a "true" rhetorician because the
conviction he induces in his hearers is not based on knowledge (269e4–270b9). His very
ability makes him an object of Socratic ridicule: like an attendant at a public bath house
who drenches his patrons with water, Thrasymachus drenches his audiences with words
(*R.* 344d1–3).

[2] Detailed documentation would be tedious. Whether Plato's portrayal is accurate has been
much debated (see, e.g., Gomperz, 1905, III: 58–59; Maguire, 1971: 142–63; Guthrie,
1971a: 295–97; Kerferd, 1981: 120–23; Rankin, 1983: 60–61; and de Romilly, 1992: 118).
Aristotle also attests to Thrasymachus' fiery temper (*Rh.* 1400b18–20), but it is unclear
whether he is referring to the historical figure or to Plato's character.

rates, whose dialectical prowess he had foolishly minimized, and mercilessly subjected to progressively withering sarcasm compared with which the deflating mockery of Ion, Hippias, and Euthyphro seems playful and even benign.

Since Thrasymachus charged a fee for his services – at one point he refuses to debate with Socrates unless he is paid (337d6–7) – some commentators[3] have concluded that he was a sophist. This claim is disputed by others[4] on the ground that Plato usually goes out of his way to identify sophists and never numbers Thrasymachus among them. But even if he was not, that would hardly render him immune to Plato's censure which extended equally to the rhetoricians who were so similar to the sophists that they were practically indistinguishable from them (*G.* 465c3–7, 520a6–8). Guthrie's contention that Plato "disliked" Thrasymachus[5] seems amply borne out by the text and even something of an understatement. It is more than rectified by Annas's hearty assurance that Plato "detested" Thrasymachus and "intends us to dislike and despise him."[6]

But whatever Plato may have thought of Thrasymachus personally, he clearly recognized that his views had gained considerable currency and that they had to be taken seriously. That the situation had all but gotten out of hand in some quarters is implied at *Cleitophon* 410c6–8 – a dialogue generally regarded as spurious[7] – where a disenchanted Cleitophon[8] threatens to forsake Socrates in favor of Thrasymachus who, in his opinion, is not only better informed about justice but also has positive convictions which he is willing to defend.[9]

Plato introduces Thrasymachus in a way that is calculated to

---

[3] See, e.g., Nettleship, 1929: 23–26; J. Adam, 1938, I: 41, n. 344d–347e; Cross and Woozley, 1964: 23; Guthrie, 1971a: 295; Kerferd, 1981: 51–52; Rankin, 1983: 58–63; and de Romilly, 1992: 1–2, 180–81.

[4] See, e.g., Sidgwick, 1874: 79; Irwin, 1977: 291, n. 31; and Lycos, 1987: 41.

[5] 1971a: 297.

[6] 1981: 35.

[7] "[F]or no very good reasons," according to Annas, 1981: 17.

[8] The historical Cleitophon was an Athenian politician who was actively involved in the attempt to restore a limited democracy after the Peloponnesian War. His fictional counterpart makes a brief appearance during the exchange between Socrates and Thrasymachus.

[9] Although Cleitophon's complaints are spelled out at some length and with considerable force in the *Cleitophon*, they elicit no reply from Socrates – a deficiency remedied with a vengeance by the "Socrates" of *Republic* II–X. For suggestive analyses of the *Cleitophon* and its relevance to the *Republic*, see Grote, 1867, III: 19–26; and Souilhé, 1981: 163–81.

make us dislike him before he says a word. Socrates' narration abounds with hostile remarks and disapproving asides about his unlikable character traits and socially barbaric conduct. We are told that Thrasymachus had been trying for some time to break into the discussion between Socrates and Polemarchus and had to be restrained. Finally, he can control himself no longer. Out of patience with their nonsense (φλυαρία) and the insipid way in which they have been truckling to one another, he pounces on them like a wild beast as if to tear them to pieces (336b1–6).

It would be idle to deny that Thrasymachus is a volatile man. But bad manners do not make one a bad philosopher. As a matter of fact, the scholarly response to Thrasymachus exhibits a glaring *prima facie* inconsistency. On the one hand, many commentators are quite critical of the arguments that Socrates employs against Polemarchus and find them (to varying degrees) unconvincing; on the other hand, many of these same commentators are severely critical of Thrasymachus for being put off by these very arguments. This is curious. If Socrates' arguments are as weak as these commentators say they are[10] and if Thrasymachus has spotted some of their weaknesses, it seems to me that his objections should not be chalked up to his ill-temperedness, but taken seriously. Accordingly, instead of dismissing him as a hothead, it is worth taking the trouble to find out what he is so angry about. If we do, several philosophically interesting points emerge.

First, he is irritated by the fact that Socrates continually asks questions which he refuses to answer, preferring instead to gratify his intellectual vanity by refuting whatever his interlocutor says. This, according to Thrasymachus, is mere one-upmanship. If Socrates genuinely wants to find out what justice is, he should stop asking other people and state his own opinion. This is a common criticism of Socrates to which he typically responds by disavowing all knowledge. So, too, here. Confronted with Thrasymachus' criticism, he explains that his failure to answer his own questions is not traceable to lack of seriousness, but to lack of ability. This hallowed reply, accepted at face value by generations of commentators, leaves Thrasymachus cold. He has a different explanation. Socrates' unwillingness to advance an opinion is not trace-

---

[10] Annas, 1981, describes several of them as "dubious" (31), "irritating" (32), and based on "rather odd" analogies (33).

able to ignorance; it is simply a clever dialectical trick and a form of dissembling (εἰρωνεύσοιο, 337a6). But Thrasymachus has seen through Socrates' little game and refuses to play it.

Second, Thrasymachus objects to the *kinds* of claims that Socrates and Polemarchus have been examining. His objection has been characterized in a variety of ways – as a protest against "stale and barren platitudes,"[11] "definition by substitution of synonyms,"[12] and "one-word equivalent[s]."[13] But Thrasymachus is much clearer than his would-be interpreters. He does not lodge his objection in technical jargon, but with concrete examples. He does not want to be told that justice is the obligatory (τὸ δέον) or the beneficial (τὸ ὠφέλιμον) or the profitable (τὸ λυσιτελοῦν) or the advantageous (τὸ συμφέρον, 336c6–d3). He has no use for these vagaries. In a word, he wants Socrates to stop wasting time on secondary questions of what justice is *like* and address himself clearly and exactly (σαφῶς ... καὶ ἀκριβῶς) to the more fundamental question of what justice *is* (τί ... εἶναι τὸ δίκαιον, 336c6). This criticism should not be dismissed as a sorehead's quibble. For it is identical with criticism that Socrates makes of himself at the end of Book I where he confesses that he has not dined well at the banquet provided by Thrasymachus, gluttonously sampling every dish instead of properly savoring what went before (354a13–b3) – an illuminating metaphor which amounts to an admission that he has been investigating the properties of justice without having addressed himself to the primary question of what justice is (τὸ δίκαιον ὅτι ποτ' ἐστίν, 354b4–5). Thrasymachus' demand for greater clarity and precision is not an "ironic" touch on Plato's part calculated to expose his intellectual pretentiousness; it is a serious demand which underscores the fact that the definitional question is prior to every other – a demand to which Plato is always sensitive and to which he is particularly sensitive in the middle dialogues. It is, in fact, arguable that in this passage Plato is employing Thrasymachus as a mouthpiece for criticizing Socrates and for advancing Platonic doctrine.

There is a further point. Unlike every other interlocutor in the early dialogues except Charmides, Thrasymachus does not initially confuse definition with enumeration of examples. On the

---

[11] J. Adam, 1938, I: 24.   [12] Shorey, 1937, I: 39, n. d.   [13] Sparshott, 1966: 456.

contrary, he is credited with understanding both *that* definitions are important and *why*.[14] He is also credited with understanding that a satisfactory definition must state the character common to and the same (ταὐτόν) in every instantiation of justice (πανταχοῦ εἶναι τὸ αὐτὸ δίκαιον, 339a1–3).[15] Although the logical apparatus is not at his (or Plato's) disposal, Thrasymachus is, in effect, distinguishing between two senses of "is": the "is" of predication (as in "Justice is profitable") and the "is" of identity (as in "Justice is X" where "X" is replaceable by the "essential property" or "defining characteristic" – the *eidos* of justice which is common to all just actions and "by which" they are just). In short, Thrasymachus wants (and subsequently tries to provide) a definition of justice in which the *definiens* and the *definiendum* are identical and inter-entailing – a definitional statement expressive of identity or "essence." Cephalus and Polemarchus had neither produced this kind of definition nor given the slightest indication that they grasped the logical point at issue. Thrasymachus does – a fact which throws a different light on his admittedly aggressive conduct and seemingly petulant complaints.

Socrates' reply to the charge of dissembling is instructive and, in view of his usual explanation, not what we would have expected. Having just traced his failure to answer his own questions to lack of ability, he now gives a different explanation:

> [Y]ou're a clever fellow, Thrasymachus. You knew very well that if you ask someone how much twelve is, and ... warn him by saying "Don't tell me ... that twelve is twice six, or three times four, or six times two, or four times three, for I won't accept such nonsense," then you'll see clearly ... that no one could answer a question framed like that. (337a8–b5)

He thereupon suggests that, in forbidding him to give these kinds of answers, Thrasymachus is requiring him to say something other than the truth. That, of course, is patently false. In forbidding Socrates to make predicative statements about justice, Thrasymachus is not asking him to suppress truth; he is specifying the

---

[14] This is denied by Sparshott, 1966: 422–23, according to whom Thrasymachus is not defining justice, but simply reevaluating the traditional concept and trying to provide a better answer than Cephalus and Polemarchus.

[15] See Shorey, 1937, I: 49, n. c.

kind of truth he wants.[16] He rightly disputes Socrates' mathematical example on the ground that "$12 = 4 \times 3$" is not logically on all fours with "Justice is beneficial" – a criticism Socrates immediately concedes (337c3–6).

Having faulted Socrates for refusing to answer his own questions or for giving synonymous answers to them, Thrasymachus offers to provide a better answer which does not predicate some non-defining property of justice, for example, being beneficial, but which elucidates its "essential nature" and thereby explains what justice is.

Although most commentators think that, like his disavowals of knowledge generally, Socrates' professed ignorance of the nature of justice is not feigned but real, it is understandable that Thrasymachus thinks he is dissembling. For if Socrates really does know nothing about justice, how did he ever manage to refute the Simonidean-Polemarchean definition of justice as helping one's friends and harming one's enemies? In the course of refuting it, he had advanced the following claims: (i) to harm someone is to make him a less excellent specimen of his kind; (ii) to make someone a less excellent specimen of his kind is to deprive him of his uniquely human excellence; (iii) the uniquely human excellence is justice; (iv) to harm someone is to make him less just; (v) just men are good; (vi) it cannot be the function of a good, i.e., just, man to make anyone unjust; and, therefore, (vii) a just man should harm no one. On the strength of these claims, he had concluded that the Simonidean-Polemarchean definition of justice "is not true" (οὐ ... ἀληθῆ, 335e4) and announced his readiness to do battle against all who think otherwise. Anyone who, like Thrasymachus, had been following this argument and had taken note of the truth-claims on which it depends could be pardoned for thinking that its proponent knows something about justice. He could also be pardoned for becoming impatient upon finding him refusing to answer any questions about justice on the ground that he knows nothing about it. In fact, Socrates' behavior so far has been any-

---

[16] This is overlooked by Cross and Woozley, 1964: 24, according to whom Socrates "not unreasonably" points out that it is unfair to demand an answer to a question and then preclude certain kinds of answers in advance. This is a curious objection. If they are right, Socrates is as "unfair" as Thrasymachus. Insofar as he disallows every appeal to examples and concrete cases as an answer to his "What-is-*F*"? question, he does the same thing throughout the early dialogues.

thing but straightforward; and Thrasymachus is quite justified in thinking that he is being disingenuous. However rude and abrasive, he has a legitimate complaint. Accordingly, let us not judge him too harshly before the discussion has even begun.

Thrasymachus thereupon defines justice as the advantage of the stronger (τὸ τοῦ κρείττονος συμφέρον, 338c2).[17] Behaving more like a practical joker than like an improver of souls, Socrates requests a "clarification": does Thrasymachus mean that athletes who consume vast quantities of beef, which makes them stronger than ordinary people, are also (and for that reason) more just? (338c5–d2)[18] Thrasymachus is understandably annoyed by this preposterous interpretation of his definition – a feeble attempt at Socratic humor. His indignant reply – exactly on target – is that Socrates has deliberately interpreted his statement in the most damaging sense (κακουργήσαις μάλιστα τὸν λόγον, 338d3–4). Does he not realize that whether a city is governed by a democracy, an oligarchy, or a tyranny, its rulers always enact laws with a view to their own advantage? It is precisely that which is the same (ταὐτόν) in all instances of justice – a claim which, as Socrates knows perfectly well, has nothing to do with the consumption of beef.

Instead of commending Thrasymachus for trying to state what is common to all instances of justice, Socrates faults him for producing the very type of predicative statement that he had previously disallowed. The charge is unfounded.[19] In saying that justice is the advantage of the stronger, Thrasymachus is not predicating a non-defining property of justice, thereby implying that it must be defined in terms of some other "essential" or defining characteristic which is logically independent of and logically prior to it; he is *defining* "justice" as the advantage of the stronger. The "is" is not the "is" of predication, but the "is" of identity: "being to the advantage of the stronger" is the defining characteristic – the "essential nature" – of justice. Although the proposition "Justice

---

[17] For recent discussions of how this thesis is to be understood and whether it is consistent with other theses advanced by Thrasymachus, see Kerferd, 1947; Hourani, 1962; Cross and Woozley, 1964: 29–41; Sparshott, 1966; Henderson, 1970; Maguire, 1971; Nicholson, 1974; Annas, 1981: 34–57; Lycos, 1987: 40–53; Reeve, 1988: 9–22; and Irwin, 1995: 174–79.

[18] Shorey, 1937, I: 47, n. f, glosses this passage by saying that although "hasty readers" may accuse Socrates of sophistry, his "perverse" interpretation of Thrasymachus' definition is offered "jocosely." J. Adam, 1938, I: n. 338d23, thinks "[t]he sophistry is undisguised."

[19] Most commentators disagree. See especially White, 1979: 67, and Annas, 1981: 38.

is the advantage of the stronger" is grammatically identical to the proposition "Justice is beneficial" – the kind of proposition for which Thrasymachus had previously faulted Socrates – its logical status is quite different.

Having "thanked" Thrasymachus for "enlightening" him about the nature of justice, Socrates concedes that he also thinks justice is a kind of advantage (συμφέρον ... τι, 339b3) – albeit not of the stronger. But instead of explaining what he means by "advantage" and how his view differs from Thrasymachus', he sets out to show that the position Thrasymachus has just articulated is internally incoherent. His argument – 339b7–d3 – is as follows:

(i) Obedience to rulers is just.
(ii) But rulers are fallible and prone to error, rightly enacting some laws, but wrongly enacting others.
(iii) A rightly enacted law is one which is to the rulers' advantage, whereas a wrongly enacted law is one which is not.
(iv) Since obedience to rulers is just, it follows that it is just to obey *all* laws – including those which are not to the rulers' advantage.

In one of his rare post-defeat appearances, Polemarchus agrees with an oath that nothing could be plainer; Thrasymachus has asserted both that it is just to obey all laws and that rulers sometimes enact laws which are not to their advantage – in which case justice would be no more (οὐδὲν μᾶλλον) to the advantage of the stronger than injustice (340b3–5).

At this point, Cleitophon intervenes to offer Thrasymachus a way out: by "the advantage of the stronger," he did not mean what is *actually* to the rulers' advantage, but what they *believe* is to their advantage. Polemarchus rightly points out that that is not what Thrasymachus said. Socrates agrees, but adds that if that is what he meant, his claim should be taken in the sense in which he intended it – a charitable and genuinely helpful response which, unlike the beef counterexample, gives Thrasymachus the opportunity to clarify (and possibly to strengthen) his position. But Thrasymachus rejects Cleitophon's solution.[20] That is *not* what he

---

[20] Rightly, according to Kerferd, 1947: 20–21; Sparshott, 1966: 424; Hendersen, 1970: 224; and Nicholson, 1974: 224–25; but wrongly, according to J. Adam, 1938, I: 31–32; Shorey, 1933: 211–12; Joseph, 1935b: 17–18; Cross and Woozley, 1964: 46; Bloom, 1968: 329; Guthrie, 1971a: 95–97; Maguire, 1971: 145; and Annas, 1981: 42.

meant. He does not apply the term "strong" to a ruler who errs in enacting laws any more than he applies the term "doctor" to a practitioner of medicine who errs in treating his patients. A ruler who enacts laws which are not to his advantage is not a mistaken ruler; he is not a ruler at all.[21] In accusing him of believing that it is just to obey *all* laws – including those which are not to the rulers' advantage – Socrates is behaving like a false witness (συκοφάντης), that is, like an informer or a pettifogger[22] who twists the plain meaning of his opponent's statements (340d1).

To prevent his position from being parodied beyond recognition, Thrasymachus expounds it at some length. It is true that we often say things like "The doctor erred in treating his patient" rather than resorting to clumsy circumlocutions like "The medical school graduate's expertise momentarily failed him." But this is merely a loose way of speaking. Strictly speaking, a doctor who errs in treating his patient is, at that moment, not a doctor; that is, he is not a doctor insofar as he errs (κατ' αὐτὸ τοῦτο ὃ ἐξαμαρτάνει, 340d3).[23] The same is true of accountants who make mathematical errors, grammarians who make grammatical mistakes, and so on. No practitioner of a *technē* ever errs *qua* practitioner.[24] Accordingly, insofar as a ruler errs by enacting laws which

---

[21] See Diès, 1989: 25, n. 1: "Cette théorie est juste, si l'on s'en tient à l'idéal; mais dans la pratique, elle est sans portée ... La force de la théorie de Thrasymaque était dans sa correspondance avec les faits, et c'est aux faits qu'il reviendra (343a), quand Socrate l'aura réfuté."

[22] See chapter 3, n. 10.

[23] It is sometimes said that, in making this move, Thrasymachus retreats into an absurd position which requires him to say that just as rulers who err in making laws are, at that moment, not rulers, so also doctors who err in treating their patients are, at that moment, not doctors. That his position is not as absurd as it is often made out to be is effectively argued by Reeve, 1988: 276, n. 6: "The Thrasymachus lurking in all of us emerges when we say such things as 'Call yourself a doctor? Butcher would be more like it' ... This view may be mistaken, but it is certainly not silly."

[24] Henderson, 1970: 224, claims that Thrasymachus never says that doctors or accountants who make mistakes are not really doctors or accountants; he merely says that our grounds for calling someone a doctor or an accountant are not that he makes, or is capable of making, mistakes in the practice of his profession, and that the same holds for rulers. But Henderson has misread the passage. That is exactly what Thrasymachus says: "When someone makes an error in the treatment of patients, do you call him a doctor in regard to that very error? Or when someone makes an error in accounting, do you call him an accountant in regard to that very error in calculation? ... [W]e express ourselves in words that, taken literally, do say that a doctor is in error, or an accountant, or a grammarian. But each of these, insofar as he is what we call him, never errs, so that, according to the precise account (and you are a stickler for precise accounts), no craftsman ever errs. It's when his knowledge fails him that he makes an error, and in regard to that error he is no craftsman" (340d1–e4).

are not in his interest, he is not a ruler. Since mistaken rulers are not rulers-in-the-strict-sense, the laws they enact are not laws-in-the-strict-sense either and, therefore, need not be obeyed.[25] This distinction between loose and precise ways of speaking enables Thrasymachus to rebut Socrates' argument without availing himself of Cleitophon's solution.[26]

Before resuming the discussion, Socrates woundedly asks whether Thrasymachus really thinks he is a pettifogger who twists his opponent's meaning in order to win the argument. Thrasymachus retorts that he does not just *think* so, he *knows* so; he adds that these tricks will not work against him, and without trickery Socrates will never defeat him in argument. Socrates piously confides that he would never dream of doing such a thing. However, to prevent similar "misunderstandings", he asks Thrasymachus to indicate how he will be employing the term "ruler" in the future. Will he be employing it loosely, as before, or in the strict sense just specified? With the air of one called upon to explain the obvious, Thrasymachus replies that he will henceforth be employing the term in the strict sense. He uncordially adds that Socrates should feel free to twist and distort (κακούργει καὶ συκοφάντει) his subsequent assertions, too (341b9).

"Enough of this" (Ἄδην ... τῶν τοιούτων, 341c4), snaps Socrates, apparently having had his fill of abuse – albeit without having rebutted the charges that prompted it.[27] This tendency to silence criticism without penetrating to its root and thereby removing its cause is characteristic of Socrates. It is an unfortunate tendency in a would-be inculcator of self-knowledge. How much better to recognize that hostile criticism based on the perception that one's opponent is not playing fair is symptomatic of deep psychological resistance which cannot be uprooted by mere argumentation, however cogent, and which is every bit as worthy of

---

[25] Hourani, 1962: 110, is mistaken in claiming that Thrasymachus holds some version of "conventionalism" (or "legalism"), according to which a law is just and should be obeyed simply by virtue of its being a law.

[26] Reeve, 1988: 13, thinks that, in making Thrasymachus reject Cleitophon's solution and adopt the Socratic principle that no practitioner ever errs qua practitioner, Plato transforms him into "a Socratic figure, albeit an inverted one." For a different assessment, see Cross and Woozley, 1964: 47, according to whom Thrasymachus' distinction "is simply a quibble."

[27] Cf. *Eu.* 11e1–2 where, in response to Euthyphro's complaint that Socrates continually makes the argument go around in circles (11b6–8), he also retorts: "[E]nough of this" (καὶ τούτων μὲν ἄδην, 11e1–2).

investigation as the precise meanings of "stronger" and "ruler." These recurring Socratic refusals to confront (or even to acknowledge) just criticism should not be ignored or explained away in the name of "irony" or alleged nobility of purpose. They reveal Socrates' indomitable urge to control the discussion, to force his interlocutors to think in his terms, and to argue on his carefully chosen turf. They also reveal his unwillingness to engage them at a level of experience deep enough to insure a genuinely "joint" inquiry and thereby affect the inner change which is his ostensible reason for entering into discussion with them.

Having silenced criticism and, by implication, issued a ban on future complaints, Socrates asks whether Thrasymachus' doctor-in-the-strict-sense is a wage-earner (ξρηματιστής) or a healer of the sick (341c4–7). "The latter," replies Thrasymachus. What about a ship's captain: is he a ruler of sailors or a sailor, that is, a mere sailor? asks Socrates, elaborately bending over backwards to avoid "misunderstanding" his interlocutor again and facetiously adding that it is hardly necessary to belabor the point by explaining that although a captain is a sailor insofar as he sails his ship, he is not a mere sailor insofar as he is the captain of the ship which, as a sailor, he sails. Furthermore, since the doctor and the captain provide advantages, namely, health and safe voyages, and since the *technai* of medicine and navigation exist to promote them, it would seem that a *technē* has no advantage over and above the end for the sake of which it exists. For example, medicine does not seek its own advantage but that of the body, i.e., physical health; and the same is true of every other *technē*. Having elicited Thrasymachus' very reluctant agreement – he conceded all these points with great difficulty (342c10) – Socrates next argues that just as no doctor-in-the-strict-sense seeks his own advantage but that of his patient, so also no ruler-in-the-strict-sense seeks his own advantage but that of his subjects (342e6–11).

At this point, Socrates congratulates himself by noting that it was clear to everyone that Thrasymachus' definition of justice had been completely reversed – to everyone but Thrasymachus, that is. Still convinced that he is both right and intellectually superior to his opponent but finding it increasingly difficult to convince anyone else, the "bold fighter" loses his temper. Again resorting to verbal abuse, he sneeringly asks whether Socrates has a nurse and, if so, why she allows him to run about "with a snotty nose" – a remark which constitutes a new low in his dialectical performance. Unlike his previous criticisms which, however ill-tempered and abrasive, were prompted by legitimate complaints, this one is simply nasty. A running nose was a metaphor for stupidity bordering on insanity. Lucian equates the two – "half crazed and full of drivel" (ἡμιμανεῖς καὶ κορυζῶντας, *Lexiphanes* 18) – and puts into the mouth of a character named "Socrates" the thesis that "pre-judgment" (τὸ πρὸ δίκης), that is, deciding in advance that one is right, "is terribly unprofessional [and] characteristic of hot-headed (οργίλων) fellows who hold that might is right" (*The Dead Come to Life* 10) – an obvious allusion to Thrasymachus. According to Thrasymachus, Socrates' "stupidity" consists in naively believing that shepherds care about their sheep when, in fact, all they care about is fattening them up so that they yield higher profits. In short, it is to the shepherds' advantage to care about their sheep. Rulers care about their subjects in the same way, enacting laws which are ultimately to their – the rulers' – advantage. He thereupon formulates this thesis on the level of complete generality: justice always promotes another person's good (ἀλλότριον ἀγαθόν, 343c3)[28] whereas injustice always promotes one's own good. That is why the unjust man enjoys all the advantages and always comes out ahead – not only in politics, but also in business and everywhere else. In a word, injustice pays. Having advanced this completely general thesis, he adds an important disclaimer: this is not true of all unjust men, only of those capable of *pleonexia*, that is of overreaching on a grand scale (τὸν μεγάλα δυνάμενον πλεονεκτεῖν, 344a1). The best example is the tyrant who by trickery and force usurps what belongs to others. The ordinary unjust man lacks this power and cannot proceed so brazenly; incapable of engaging in blatantly unjust conduct, he must proceed more cautiously so as to seem just. It is not fear of committing wrongdoing but of suffering it – which is far worse – that prompts men to praise justice and to revile injustice. Since injustice on a sufficiently grand scale is better and more profitable than justice, it follows that justice, properly understood, is what promotes the advantage of the sufficiently strong man.[29]

---

[28] Cross and Woozley, 1964: 41, think this assertion is inconsistent with Thrasymachus' previous definition of justice as the advantage of the stronger. Nicholson, 1974: 212–17, disagrees.

[29] According to Annas, 1981: 37, 44–45, this is Thrasymachus' real position – which is not "conventionalism" (or "legalism") but "immoralism."

Having made this long speech, which Socrates likens to a word bath, Thrasymachus prepares to leave. However, he is prevailed upon to stay by everyone present, and by no one more outspokenly than Socrates who reproaches him for his apparent lack of interest in the most important of all philosophical questions – how should we live? – and for his lack of concern for the well-being of those present who are still ignorant of what he claims to know but is unwilling to teach them. He adds that he himself is still not persuaded that injustice is more profitable than justice and that he would like to hear Thrasymachus out. Apparently unaccustomed to finding dissenters in his midst, Thrasymachus wonders what else he can do to persuade Socrates. Must he ram the argument into his soul (345b4–6)? Socrates sagely assures him that that will not be necessary; it will be sufficient if he stands by what he has said or, if he finds it necessary to shift ground, to do so openly and without trying to conceal it.

Has Thrasymachus shifted ground? Socrates thinks so. His reason is as follows. Having announced that he would henceforth be speaking about the practitioner-in-the-strict-sense, for example, about the doctor *qua* doctor and insofar as his knowledge does not fail him, Thrasymachus has not employed a correspondingly strict sense in speaking about the shepherd. If he had, he could not have claimed that it is to the shepherd's advantage to care for his sheep. For just as the doctor-in-the-strict-sense never promotes his own advantage but that of his patients, so also the shepherd-in-the-strict-sense never promotes his own advantage but that of his sheep. The same is true of every other practitioner of a *technē* – including rulers-in-the-strict-sense. That is why rulers demand pay for holding office – a fact which reveals that it is not they but their subjects who benefit from being ruled. Do we not say that each *technē* differs from every other because of its unique function (δύναμιν, 346a3)? Before allowing his interlocutor to answer, Socrates invokes the sincere assent requirement.[30] Thrasymachus is solemnly informed that he must not answer contrary to his real opinion (παρὰ δόξαν) so that the discussion can achieve some result (346a3–4).

Thrasymachus agrees that every *technē* has a unique function. He also agrees that it is this function which enables every *technē* to

---

[30] For the first time in Book i. There was no mention of it during the discussions with Cephalus and Polemarchus.

provide a unique benefit: medicine provides health, navigation provides safe sea voyages, and so on. But if the unique function of every *technē* is defined by the end (or benefit) at which it aims, then every practitioner-in-the-strict-sense, i.e., every "true" practitioner, aims at that end in hopes of producing that benefit. Furthermore, just as the *technē* of the doctor, which aims at health, should not be confounded with that of the wage-earner (μισθωτικὴ τέχνη), which aims at collecting a salary – a point Thrasymachus had previously conceded (341c8) – so also the *technē* of the wage-earner should not be confounded with that of the shepherd, which aims at caring for his sheep. It follows that the shepherd-in-the-strict-sense, that is, the "true" shepherd – *does* care about his sheep. If he cared only about collecting his salary, he would not be a shepherd but a wage-earner.

As always, Socrates argues with great confidence. But his argument is open to several objections.

First, there is no such thing as a *technē* of wage-earning – and, therefore, *a fortiori* – no such thing as a wage-earner.[31] Of course, people do earn wages; and anyone who earns wages is a wage-earner. But not in Socrates' sense. He is, in fact, rather fuzzy about the precise nature of this alleged *technē*, describing it as an art which "accompanies" (ἑπομένη) a *bona fide* art like medicine (346d4) in such a way that a doctor heals the sick by the *technē* of medicine but earns his wages by the allegedly distinct but somewhat shadowy *technē* of wage-earning. The distinction is a bogus one. Wage-earners are people who are paid for services rendered, but earning wages is not one of them. No sane employer has ever advertised an opening for the position of wage-earner. Nor has any sane prospective employee ever applied for such a position. A person cannot be a wage-earner *simpliciter*. It is true that doctors and shepherds earn wages for practicing medicine and caring for sheep. But this does not show that wage-earning is a *technē* distinct from the *technai* of medicine and shepherding; it merely shows that people earn wages for doing legitimate work. Nor does it show that a doctor – and, by implication, every practitioner of a *technē* – possesses two arts: one which enables him to heal his patients and another which enables him to earn wages.

Second, Socrates is mistaken in thinking that shepherds care –

---

[31] Both points are powerfully argued by Garland, 1976: 11–13.

in any ordinary sense of "care" – about their sheep. Any plausibility this claim may have depends on sentimental images of idyllic pastoral scenes featuring peacefully grazing furry creatures presided over by a solitary rustic figure clothed in flowing garments and wearing a kindly expression. Thrasymachus gives no credence to these romantic stereotypes. He is right. People raise sheep so that the world can have lamb-chops and wool, not so that shepherds can have objects on which to lavish their affection. One might as well claim that mallet-wielding employees of slaughterhouses and factory farms entertain benevolent sentiments towards the steers whose skulls they routinely smash.[32]

Finally, Socrates' argument can be faulted on logical grounds. It will be recalled that Socrates had previously argued that every *technē* exists to promote the interest of someone or something *other than* the *technē* or its practitioner (342b1–7). The wage-earner argument contradicts this claim. Insofar as the wage-earner collects a salary for practicing his alleged *technē, he* is its sole beneficiary – from which it follows that the *technē* of wage-earning exists solely for *his* sake and not for the sake of anyone else. I conclude that the wage-earner argument – perhaps the weakest in the early dialogues – establishes nothing.[33]

On the strength of this argument, Socrates concludes that just as shepherds-in-the-strict-sense, that is, "true" shepherds, care about their sheep, so also rulers-in-the-strict-sense, that is, "true" rulers, care about their subjects. He adds that it is precisely because they rule in their subjects' interest rather than in their own that they are paid wages – either in the form of money or honor – and are assessed a penalty if they refuse (347a3–6).

---

[32] Irwin, 1995: 176–77, rightly points out that Thrasymachus' claim that shepherds are more interested in profits than in sheep does not undercut the proper end at which the *technē* of the shepherd aims; it merely underscores the possibility of abusing that *technē*. However, Socrates does not avail himself of this argument and rests his case on the *technē* of the wage-earner.

[33] Many commentators agree. Annas, 1981: 49, finds Socrates' wage-earner argument "very artificial" and thinks his claim that every *technē* is practiced for the sake of some "proper" object is "absurdly optimistic." So, too, Bloom, 1968: 334, according to whom the *technē* of wage-earning is a Socratic "fabrication" and the basis for one of several "dishonest arguments." On the other hand, J. Adam, 1938, I: 41, thinks the argument contains an analysis which is "new and valuable in itself." So, too, Joseph, 1935b: 25–26, according to whom the Socratic art of the wage-earner, although seemingly far-fetched, is in fact "profoundly important" and an anticipation of (what Aristotle calls) "the architectonic art" of ordering one's life so as to achieve happiness.

"What do you mean?" asks Glaucon. I am glad he asked because I did not understand what penalty Socrates was talking about either. Socrates explains that Glaucon's question reveals that he does not understand why the best men are unwilling to accept pay for ruling. Openly to demand money for one's services reveals that one is covetous of wealth – which is a basis for reproach. Nor are the best men covetous of honor. Hence, unwilling to rule either for money or honor, they must be given some other incentive, namely, the desire to avoid being assessed the "penalty" of being ruled by men less good and less capable than themselves. In short, the best men consent to rule as a necessary evil – yet another proof that "true" rulers do not rule in their own interest. Having answered Glaucon's question, Socrates reminds everyone that the weightiest question of all still remains unanswered: Is Thrasymachus right in thinking that the unjust life is better and more profitable than the just? Like Socrates, Glaucon is not persuaded of this and asks Socrates to refute this claim. Characteristically rejecting the method of long speeches (μακρολογία), which requires an impartial judge to weigh the *pros* and *cons* adduced by both sides, Socrates proposes the method of question-and-answer, which enables the participants to be their own judges (348a7–b4). Glaucon agrees. As for Thrasymachus, the very person to be questioned, he is not consulted.

Thrasymachus has said that injustice is better and more profitable than justice. Although he does not think that injustice is a virtue and justice a vice, he does think that justice is a very noble form of simplicity (πάνυ γενναίαν εὐήθειαν, 348c12); furthermore, unlike those who think injustice is evil and shameful, he thinks it is good counsel (εὐβουλίαν, 348d2) and even a kind of wisdom. He acknowledges that the unjust man is not unqualifiedly wise and good and thinks that he merits this description only insofar as he succeeds in being completely unjust, thereby overreaching everyone by means of unlimited *pleonexia*. Socrates' next argument is designed to show that no one is wise and good whose uppermost motive is to overreach everyone else.

Before launching it, he again exhorts Thrasymachus to say what he really believes (ἅπερ διανοῇ) and to concur with propositions propounded by Socrates only if he thinks they are true (τὰ δοκοῦντα περὶ τῆς ἀληθείας, 349a4–8). This invocation of the sincere assent requirement is followed by an exchange which, to my knowledge, is unprecedented and without parallel in the early dialogues. Thrasymachus pointedly asks what difference it makes whether he says what he really believes and wonders why Socrates does not just test the argument (τὸν λόγον, 349a9–10). We expect Socrates to say that it makes all the difference in the world because the Socratic elenchus has an "existential dimension" which enables him to examine his interlocutors' lives as well as their theses. But he says nothing of the kind. Instead, he says that it makes no difference (οὐδέν, 349b1). Sincere assent is not important after all, and Socrates is perfectly willing to proceed whether Thrasymachus says what he really believes or not.[34]

More questions follow. Does Thrasymachus think that one just man would ever wish to overreach and to outdo another just man? He does not: he adds that, indeed, that is exactly what makes the just man a simpleton (εὐήθης, 349b5). Furthermore, if he did wish to do so, he would fail. On the other hand, the unjust man wishes to overreach and to outdo both just and unjust men; and he is able to do it. That is why he is like the wise and the good (φρόνιμός τε καὶ ἀγαθός), whereas the just man is like neither; on the contrary, he is like the ignorant and the bad. So each is like those he is like (τοιοῦτος ἄρα ἐστίν ἑκάτερος αὐτῶν οἷσπερ ἔοικεν, 349d10–11), Socrates adds – pleonastically, in Thrasymachus' opinion.

An analogical argument follows – 349d13–350c12 – the purpose of which to demonstrate that the opposite is the case:

(i)   Some are musical whereas others are unmusical.
(ii)   The former are wise whereas the latter are foolish.
(iii) The musician is good in the things about which he is wise and bad in the things about which he is foolish.[35] And the same is true of the doctor.
(iv)   No musician wishes to overreach and to outdo other musicians in tuning a lyre, but he does wish to overreach and to outdo non-musicians. Similarly, no doctor wishes to overreach and to outdo other doctors in prescribing medicine, but he does wish to overreach and to outdo non-doctors.
(v)   Formulated in full generality, for every kind of knowledge,

---

[34] Vlastos, 1983: 35, n. 24, accounts for Socrates' "apparent willingness" to waive the sincere assent requirement at 340c1–2 by saying that it is "ironical," as is clear from the fact that he reiterates it at 350e5, "though here again he resigns himself, as a *pis aller*, to Thrasymachus' saying he will ignore it."

[35] See *La.* 194d1–3.

no one who knows wishes to overreach and to outdo others who know the same things.

(vi) Those who do not know, on the other hand, being foolish and ignorant, do wish to overreach and to outdo both those who know and those who do not.

(vii) Anyone who knows is wise and good.

(viii) Anyone who is wise and good will not wish to overreach and to outdo those like him but only those unlike him.

(ix) But anyone who is bad and ignorant will wish to overreach and to outdo both those like him and those unlike him.

(x) Since the unjust man wishes to overreach and to outdo both those like and unlike him, and since the just man wishes to overreach and to outdo only those unlike him, it follows that, since each is like those he is like, the just man is like the wise and the good, and the unjust man is like the ignorant and the bad.

(xi) Hence the just man is wise and good, and the unjust man is ignorant and bad.

In short, contrary to what Thrasymachus has claimed, justice is virtue and wisdom whereas injustice is vice and ignorance. Having concluded his argument, Socrates gleefully reports that Thrasymachus made all these admissions with great reluctance, sweating profusely, and even blushing.

How good is Socrates' argument? Joseph[36] judges it "absolutely convincing" whereas Cross and Woozley[37] find it "almost embarrassingly bad." I think they are right.

Insofar as it depends on the claim that musicians, doctors, and (by analogy) just men are able to overreach and to outdo non-musicians, non-doctors, and (by analogy) other unjust men because of their expertise, the argument presupposes that, like music and medicine, justice is a *technē* – the very thesis which, according to many commentators, was refuted during the foregoing discussion with Polemarchus. Cross and Woozley[38] think Plato is aware of the inconsistency and is trying to see whether Thrasymachus can detect it. This suggestion must be rejected: first, it is nothing more than an *ad hoc* rescue operation designed to defend Socrates against the charge of (apparently deliberate) inconsistency; sec-

---

[36] 1935: 31.   [37] 1964: 52.   [38] *Ibid.*: 53.

ond, it falsely implies that Thrasymachus is an actually existing person for whose response Plato must wait rather than a dramatic character for whom he is writing the script.

Having charged Socrates with (apparently deliberate) inconsistency, Cross and Woozley seem to have second thoughts and cautiously add that it is "not entirely clear" that he is inconsistent. Their reason for saying this is that the term *technē*, which plays such a key role in the argument with Polemarchus, according to which justice is a skill or *technē*, does not occur in the argument with Thrasymachus. Hence "the most we can say" is that Socrates' argument "*implies* that justice is a skill or *technē*."

But surely the rejoinder is obvious. First, insofar as the argument implies this, it is equally inconsistent and for the same reason. Second, the argument trades on an equivocation. Having argued that musicians and doctors overreach and outdo non-musicians and non-doctors by being *better at* music and medicine, Socrates concludes that the unjust man overreaches and outdoes both just and other unjust men by *getting the better of* them – a very different thing.[39] Finally, why should we accept Socrates' contention that the fact that the unjust man does not possess the *technē* of justice – if, indeed, it is a *technē* – entails that he is less able to achieve his end(s) than the just man? Instead of sweating and blushing because of this argument, Thrasymachus should have taken a closer look at it.

Having apparently established that justice is virtue and wisdom and that injustice is vice and ignorance, Socrates reminds Thrasymachus that they had also previously agreed that injustice is a strong and powerful thing. Thrasymachus remembers, but for the time being he is more interested in expressing his disagreement with the foregoing argument and would like to reply to it. However, in view of Socrates' ban on long speeches, he suspects he will be prohibited from doing so. He is right. Forbidden to speak, he agrees to be interrogated further. He adds that he will answer "Yes" and "No" in accordance with Socrates' wishes. "Don't do that, contrary to your opinion" (παρά γε τὴν σαυτοῦ δόξαν, 350e5), admonishes Socrates, abruptly reinstating the previously suspended sincere assent requirement. "I'll answer so as to please you (σοί ... ἀρέσκειν, 350e6) ... What else do you want?" asks

---

[39] This criticism is also made by Cross and Woozley, *ibid.*: 52.

Thrasymachus.[40] "Nothing, by god" (Οὐδέν μὰ Δία), replies Socrates. "[I]f that's what you're going to do, go ahead and do it"
(350e8–9), thereby again waiving the sincere assent requirement as
abruptly as he had just reinstated it. This passage is yet another
indication of how unimportant the requirement really is. Although
Thrasymachus agrees to play along, he makes it very clear that the
answers he is about to give are not his real opinions. Again Socrates seems not to mind.

As we have seen, what Thrasymachus really believes is that injustice is stronger and more profitable than justice. But if, as Socrates has argued, justice is virtue and wisdom and injustice is vice
and ignorance, it can easily be shown that it is justice which is
stronger and more profitable. Socrates' argument – 351b1–352c8 –
is as follows (with Thrasymachus assenting to each step, albeit
insincerely):

(i) An unjust city can unjustly enslave other cities and hold them
in subjection.

Before proceeding further, Socrates asks whether an unjust city
which enslaves other cities does so by means of justice or injustice.
Thrasymachus non-committally replies that if justice is wisdom, *as
Socrates has just said* (ὡς σὺ ἄρτι ἔλεγες, 351c1), then it would follow
that an unjust city enslaves other cities by means of justice. We
expect Socrates to rebuke Thrasymachus on the ground that he
himself has said nothing, that he was just asking questions, and
that all the foregoing claims were Thrasymachus'. But he does
not. Abandoning his usual policy of disclaiming all responsibility
for the theses under discussion, he ignores the remark and "compliments" Thrasymachus for his "excellent" answers. When Thrasymachus explains that he answered as he did, not out of conviction but simply to please Socrates (Σοὶ ... χαρίζομαι, 351c6),
Socrates again ignores the remark and asks Thrasymachus to
please him some more (351c7). Throughout the entire passage,
Socrates is not even pretending to be eliciting Thrasymachus' sincere assent. He knows it. And so does Thrasymachus. The argument continues as follows:

(ii) An unjust city whose citizens are unjust could accomplish no
common action if its citizens wronged one another.

---

[40] Thrasymachus' withholding of sincere assent is noticed by Guthrie, 1971a: 90–91; Nicholson, 1974: 222; and Nails, 1995: 94–95.

(iii) Since injustice engenders hatred, the citizens of an unjust city could not avoid wronging one another.

(iv) Since injustice renders unjust men incapable of cooperative collective action, the unjust man is necessarily at odds with himself and the enemy of the just man.

(v) Moreover, since the gods are just, the unjust man will also be hateful to them whereas the just man will be loved by them.

(vi) But if the just are wise and better and, therefore, more capable of cooperative collective action than the unjust, it follows either that the unjust cannot engage in such action at all or, insofar as they do, they are not completely unjust.

(vii) Therefore, whatever unjust men accomplish, they accomplish by means of justice.

Socrates' final argument follows immediately. It is designed to show that the just man is happier than the unjust. The argument – 352d8–354a9 – is as follows:

(i) A horse has a unique function (ἔργον).

(ii) The function of a thing is that for which it is the best or only instrument, for example, we see with our eyes, hear with our ears, prune with a pruning knife, and so on.

(iii) Every function has a corresponding excellence (ἀρετή) which consists in the proper performance of the function: the good eye sees well, the good pruning knife cuts well, and so on.

(iv) Nothing can achieve its proper excellence if its function is vitiated by a defect.

(v) The soul has a unique function, namely, to deliberate and to rule.

(vi) However, like everything which has a function, the soul cannot achieve its proper excellence if it is deprived of its function.

(vii) The excellence of the soul is justice, and its defect is injustice.

(viii) He who lives well is happy, and he who lives badly is unhappy.

(ix) Hence it is the just man who is happy and the unjust man who is miserable.

(x) It is not profitable to be miserable, but it is profitable to be happy.

(xi) Therefore, injustice is not more profitable than justice.

"Let that be your banquet," grumbles Thrasymachus. Rubbing it in, Socrates retorts that it was Thrasymachus who provided it.

Many criticisms have been levelled at this argument: (i) that it employs the terms "function" and "excellence" carelessly; (ii) that insofar as it depends on the claim that the just soul lives well, it identifies the just man with his soul; (iii) that it trades on an ambiguity in "living well"; (iv) that Thrasymachus has been given no reason for believing that the soul has a function – much less, that its function is to deliberate and to rule, and that the excellence of the soul is justice; and (v) that although Socrates may have shown that justice is a necessary condition for happiness, he has not shown that it is a sufficient condition.

Although some of these criticisms are stronger than others, it would be pointless to rehearse them in detail. However, even if they are all wide of the mark, the fact remains that Socrates has not refuted Thrasymachus' claim that the unjust life is better, happier, and more profitable than the just. His last two arguments are, in fact, a charade. Both ultimately fail: not because of some irreparable logical defect, but because Thrasymachus does not believe, that is, sincerely assent to, the premises from which the conclusions follow. And Socrates knows it. Although he momentarily behaves as if he has scored a great dialectical victory, he knows better. For after briefly savoring his "victory" and gloating over Thrasymachus' discomfiture, he offers a much more sober and accurate estimate of the foregoing arguments: they are worthless and have established nothing. This is not just because Thrasymachus has withheld his sincere assent to the premises on which they depend, but also (and more radically) because it is impossible to prove that the just life is more profitable than the unjust or that the just man is happier than the unjust *until one has determined what justice is* – something Socrates has not even attempted to do (354c1–3) and the very methodological objection that Thrasymachus had launched at the outset of the discussion.

By the end of Book I, Thrasymachus has so completely distanced himself from the theses under attack that he will "assent" to anything Socrates says, however damaging to "his" position. He has, in fact, lost all interest in the discussion, and refutation – or what purports to be refutation – no longer has any effect in him. He is no longer an active participant, but a mere Yes-Man – and with Socrates' full approval. Socrates does not waive the sincere assent requirement "ironically" and as a "*pis aller*"; he waives it because he does not care whether Thrasymachus sincerely assents or not. When Thrasymachus asks what difference it makes whether he says what he really believes, Socrates tells him that it makes no difference. When he asks whether Socrates wants anything more than perfunctory assent, Socrates says that he does not and authorizes Thrasymachus to answer however he pleases. And when Thrasymachus taunts Socrates by cynically reiterating that he is not saying what he really believes but merely trying to please him, Socrates does not protest on the ground that anyone who does this renders himself an unfit dialectical partner (*G.* 495a8–9); he tells him that he is doing very well (Εὖ ... σὺ ποιῶν, 351c7) and asks him to please him some more. This is not "irony," it is eristic – arguing for the sake of victory and indifferent to what effect, if any, one's arguments are having on one's interlocutor. Little wonder that Thrasymachus loses all interest in the argument.

In saying this, I am not wholly excusing him. Initially confident, condescending, and boasting that Socrates' dialectical tricks will not work against him, Thrasymachus gradually discovers that bravado is not enough and, having discovered it, drops out of the discussion. The blame is partly his. But only partly. Socrates is also deeply implicated – not just for employing dubious arguments and even more dubious dialectical tactics, but also for his willingness – indeed, eagerness – to do exactly what, according to Vlastos, he categorically refuses to do, namely, refute "a proposition detached from a person willing to predicate his life on it."[41] If we refuse to take Socrates' periodic avowals of concern for the souls of his interlocutors at face value and attend to his actual dialectical behavior, the required verdict is clear: Socrates cares no more about Thrasymachus' soul than shepherds care about their sheep.

Socrates' lack of concern for Thrasymachus' soul is compounded by the fact that throughout the discussion he repeatedly claims to have established the truth of a series of very important predicative statements about justice – for example, that it is virtue and wisdom, that it is beneficial, that it is more profitable than injustice, and that it is productive of happiness – without having answered the prior definitional question of what justice *is* – a self-confessed blunder which not only vitiates the argument with Thrasymachus, but undercuts the argument of Book I as a whole. However, the blunder has particular relevance to Thrasymachus.

---

[41] 1983: 38.

How can one honestly claim to be caring for the soul of one's interlocutor by trying to refute him on the basis of a series of predicative statements about an as-yet undefined virtue to which he does not sincerely assent and which, *even if he did sincerely assent,* cannot be known to be true until the prior but as-yet unasked definitional question has been answered?

The argument with Thrasymachus provides an unusually clear portrait of Socrates the controversialist, much more interested in winning the argument than in discovering moral truth. Little wonder that he is unhappy with his performance by the end of Book 1. Only by taking with a grain of salt his "official" statement of his lofty goals and his exaggerated account of his encounters with his interlocutors, as set forth in the *Apology,* and by taking careful note of his actual behavior in the early dialogues can we resist the beckoning seductiveness of the standard picture and realize that there are disturbing wrinkles in the face we thought we knew so well.

CHAPTER 12

Hippocrates

Of all the early dialogues, the *Protagoras* most vividly portrays the typical, well-to-do Athenian youth's desire for an education that would enable him to make his mark in the political arena and his belief that the most likely source of such an education was the sophists. Although non-Greek,[1] these itinerant teachers were familiar figures in Athens and throughout the Greek world. Their wide-ranging theoretical knowledge and practical know-how bordered on omnicompetence, and it was available to anyone who could afford it. Their most coveted possession was rhetoric – an indispensable skill for aspiring politicians as well as private citizens. Athens was a highly litigious society, and people were always dragging each other into court. Lacking both public prosecutors and public defenders, they were required to initiate their own litigation and to defend themselves against the litigation of others; in both undertakings, the chances of success were greatly enhanced by the ability to speak persuasively. Rhetoric was the art of persuasion, and the sophists taught it.

The dialogue falls into two parts of conspicuously unequal length. The second – and much longer part (*Pr.* 314c3–362a4) – depicts a gruelling encounter between Socrates and Protagoras. The first – 310a8–314c2 – depicts a comparatively brief conversation between Socrates and Hippocrates,[2] son of Apollodorus and would-be pupil of Protagoras. Although often treated as a mere preliminary, it raises many questions which are central to Socratic philosophy and repay careful study. The dramatic date of the dialogue, narrated by Socrates, is *circa* 433.

---

[1] See chapter 5, n. 4.

[2] The Hippocrates of the *Protagoras* should not be confounded with Hippocrates of Cos – physician, founder of a school of medicine, and author of numerous medical treatises.

His narration begins with an account of how he had been awakened before dawn that very morning by Hippocrates, pounding on
his door and bursting with the news that Protagoras is in town. His
excitement is shared by all the young intellectuals, who are flocking
to the famous sophist *en masse*, and by the entire citizenry, which
has been swept off its feet by his unsurpassed wisdom, rhetorical
prowess, and personal charisma. Socrates sardonically quips that
Protagoras will be happy to make Hippocrates wise – provided
that he can afford his fee. Missing the irony, Hippocrates breath-
lessly explains that money is no obstacle; he is prepared to spend
everything he has and, if need be, to go into debt. Which brings
him to the point of his visit: would Socrates introduce him to Protagoras and put in a good word on his behalf?

Of course, anyone bold (or foolish) enough to admit that he is
enamored of a sophist should be braced for criticism. And commentators have found much to criticize. A. E. Taylor[3] observes that
the dialogue contains many satirical touches which are directed not
so much at Protagoras himself as at the "excessive adulation" of
his admirers. As for Hippocrates, he is variously described as "unreflective,"[4] "excitable,"[5] "overenthusiastic,"[6] and "impetuous"[7]
– a young man with no first-hand knowledge of Protagoras who is
"only repeating the general consensus" about him.[8] Those seeking
further ammunition against Hippocrates might gravely observe
that his behavior marks him as his father's son; at *Sym.* 173a1–3
Apollodorus reports that before meeting Socrates he, too, could be
seen dashing aimlessly about the city, convinced that he was living
a full and interesting life. Hippocrates' detractors might also ruefully note that his excitement at the prospect of sitting at the feet
of Protagoras reveals that it was not only politically ambitious
men like Pericles who failed to educate their sons, allowing them
to graze like sacred oxen (319e3–320a3), but that the same was
true of fathers like Apollodorus, a member of the Socratic inner
circle.

But why be so hard on Hippocrates? It is true that he has no
first-hand knowledge of Protagoras and is simply repeating the
general consensus about him. But on what else could he have
based his opinion? A mere child the last time Protagoras visited

---

[3] 1929: 239.   [4] Arieti, 1991: 118–19.   [5] Coby, 1987: 25.
[6] Friedländer, 1964, II: 6.   [7] Shorey, 1933: 119.   [8] Stokes, 1986: 185.

Athens, he has never heard him speak or even caught a glimpse of him (310e3–5). Furthermore, why berate him as "excitable" and "overenthusiastic"? Outside the context of the early dialogues, such a young man would be commended for his interest in the intellectual and cultural affairs of the city. Flocking to a celebrity – intellectual or otherwise – is not in itself grounds for censure, as is abundantly clear from the fact that the same commentators who criticize the youth for flocking to Protagoras would be the first to applaud them if they flocked to Socrates. It is not the activity of "flocking" as such, but the estimate of the person "flocked" to, which accounts for these negative assessments.[9]

Hippocrates' irrepressible ebullience stands in marked contrast to Socrates' spectacular reserve. Coolly observing that it is too early to call at the home of Callias[10] where Protagoras is staying, Socrates passes the time by drawing Hippocrates into discussion. He poses two questions: first, in going to Protagoras, in what capacity will he be consulting him?; second, with a view to becoming what? (311b4–5).

In view of the high value that Hippocrates attaches to rhetorical ability, we expect him to say that he will be consulting Protagoras in his capacity as a teacher of rhetoric in hopes of becoming a better speaker. But before he can say a word, Socrates follows up with a series of further questions whose self-evident answers are obviously intended to serve as models for the kind of answers he wants to his original ones. In what capacity would Hippocrates consult Hippocrates of Cos? Answer: in his capacity as a doctor. Why? Answer: to become a doctor. In what capacity would he consult Polyclitus and Phidias? Answer: in their capacity as sculptors. Why? Answer: to become a sculptor. In short, Socrates' questions are framed in such a way as to ensure that he gets the answers he wants and thereby induce Hippocrates to affirm a (in many ways highly counterintuitive) thesis which will play a crucial role in the sequel, namely, that one consults a practitioner of a *technē* to become a practitioner of that *technē* oneself.

---

[9] Poulakos, 1995: 79–80, also warns against "a certain double standard that often escapes notice ... If youths are immature and impressionable, they are so both when listening to sophists and when talking with Socrates."

[10] A wealthy Athenian, Callias was enamored of the sophists (*Th.* 164e7–165a3) and regularly opened his home to them. He allegedly spent more money on sophists' fees than everyone else combined (*Ap.* 20a2–6; *Crat.* 391b9–c4).

Initially, this seems like a dubious line of questioning. People do not ordinarily consult doctors to become doctors, but to get well; they are not in quest of medical instruction, but of medical treatment. Nor do art collectors ordinarily consult sculptors to become sculptors, but to purchase specimens of their work; they are not in quest of aesthetic instruction, but of aesthetic objects. But this first impression is mistaken. As always, Socrates knows exactly what he is doing. His line of questioning must be understood in light of the larger context in which his questions are raised. Socrates does not want Hippocrates to say that he will be consulting Protagoras in his capacity as a teacher of rhetoric in hopes of becoming a better speaker. He wants a very different answer. That this is so is clear from his questions about why people consult doctors and sculptors. And it is clearer still from his next question – a leading question calculated to insure that Hippocrates will produce the desired response: What is the name that is commonly attached to Protagoras? Answer: sophist. Very well then. If Hippocrates would consult Hippocrates of Cos, who is a doctor, to become a doctor; and if he would consult Polyclitus, who is a sculptor, to become a sculptor; why would he consult Protagoras, who is a sophist? Hippocrates warily replies, "If this is at all like the previous cases, then, obviously to become a sophist" (312a3–4) – an answer which causes him to blush. Socrates thereupon exploits his embarrassment to extract the further admission that he would be ashamed to present himself to his fellow citizens as a sophist.

So far, Socrates' dialectical tactics leave much to be desired. Although the discussion is ostensibly carried out under the joint auspices of conceptual clarification and moral enlightenment – to make Hippocrates think twice before entrusting his soul to a sophist – in fact, nothing has been clarified and a great deal has been obscured. Instead of helping Hippocrates to clarify his educational goals, Socrates has burdened him with his own conceptual scheme and invested him with a course of action and a set of intentions very different from his announced ones. Hippocrates' original and perfectly harmless intention of consulting Protagoras in his capacity as a teacher of rhetoric to become a better speaker has been replaced by the Socratically reformulated and risk-laden intention of consulting him in his capacity as a sophist to become a sophist.

Although Hippocrates thinks he is logically committed to accepting this unsettling inference, he is not. He countenances Socrates' travesty of his original intention only because he has allowed himself to be unduly influenced by his coaching. Having just minutes ago expressed great admiration for Protagoras' rhetorical ability and having been asked why he wants to consult him, he would have said exactly what we expected him to say – "To become a better speaker" – had Socrates permitted him to give his actual reason. It would never have occurred to him to say, "To become a sophist." But Socrates does not permit him to give his actual reason; indeed, he coached him in order to prevent him from doing so. This strategy enables him to secure the answer he wants and, in securing it, to embarrass Hippocrates.

Why does Hippocrates blush? Many commentators[11] attribute his embarrassment to his belief, allegedly shared by the Athenian citizenry, that there is something vaguely disreputable about the sophists and, therefore, something equally disreputable about wanting to become one. But this explanation is unconvincing. Whatever the Athenians may have thought of the sophists generally, the opening pages of the dialogue make it very clear that they held Protagoras in the highest esteem. Why should Hippocrates be embarrassed to sit at the feet of the very man whose praises are being sung by the whole city?

Hippocrates' embarrassment is not only puzzling, it is also unnecessary. His initial reluctance to endorse Socrates' analogical argument ("If this is at all like the previous cases, then, obviously . . .") was well founded, and he should have trusted his logical instincts: the case of the sophist is not like the previous ones.

I said earlier that people do not ordinarily consult doctors to become doctors, but to get well. The obvious reply is that although this is true of medical patients, it is not true of medical students who consult doctors for precisely that reason. The professional expertise of the doctor, which is ordinarily valued as a means to the desired end of health is, from the point of view of the prospective practitioner of medicine, valued as an end in itself and the very thing he wants to learn. The point is well taken, but the analogy is not thereby rehabilitated. Although it is plausible to say that medical students consult doctors to become doctors, it is implausible in the extreme to say that people consult sophists to become

---

[11] See, e.g., Vlastos, 1956: vii; Teloh, 1986: 167; A. E. Taylor, 1929: 238; C. C. W. Taylor, 1976: 66; and Hubbard and Karnofsky, 1982: 71.

sophists. The implausibility is traceable to the disparity between their respective kinds of expertise. The doctor's consists in a specific, clearly defined, and comparatively narrow range of skills. *Qua* doctor, his competence to teach is limited to those skills. The sophist's, on the other hand, is general, wide-ranging, and multi-faceted. One need only recall the versatility of Hippias – undisputed even by Socrates – whose expertise included rhetoric, mathematics, astronomy, history, geography, literature, mnemonics, music theory, and many other subjects. But of all the things he may have taught his pupils, there is no reason to believe that he taught them to be sophists.

Having embarrassed Hippocrates, Socrates immediately lets him off the hook. Perhaps he wants to study with Protagoras not to become a sophist, but to acquire a general education which befits a gentleman (312a7–b6). Hippocrates eagerly grasps at this welcome straw, obviously unaware of the fact that a general education is precisely what Protagoras does *not* claim to offer. Unlike the other sophists, who force their pupils to study arithmetic, astronomy, geometry, music, and many other subjects in which they have no interest, he teaches his only what they want to know – in particular, good judgment in their own affairs and the affairs of the city (318d5–319a2).

At this point, Socrates abruptly turns from pedagogical considerations to moral ones: Is Hippocrates aware of the risk he is about to incur in entrusting his soul to a sophist without knowing what a sophist is and whether the effects of his teaching will be good (ἀγαθῷ) or evil (κακῷ, 312b7–c4)? Hippocrates begs to differ: he thinks he *does* know what a sophist is. As the name implies, a sophist is a wise man; and wise men have "an understanding of wise things" (τῶν σοφῶν ἐπιστήμονα, 312c5–6). Socrates dismisses this answer on the ground that the same could be said about the practitioner of any *technē*. Perhaps thinking of Gorgias, who did not profess to be a teacher of virtue (*M.* 95c1–4), Hippocrates suggests that perhaps the sophist's educational task is not to impart wisdom to his pupils but to make them clever speakers. "Clever speakers *about what*?" asks Socrates. "About the subjects of which they have understanding," replies Hippocrates, spinning his wheels tautologically. "And what subjects are they?" asks Socrates. Alas, Hippocrates does not know. Socrates thereupon administers an uncharacteristically petty rebuke tinged with a dash of pique. Instead of coming to Socrates to ask *whether* he should consult Protagoras, Hippocrates has already made up his mind about that and has come to Socrates only because he needs an introduction. The chastened interlocutor agrees that Socrates is right.

But Hippocrates has given up too quickly. We do not ordinarily assess the competence of a teacher of public speaking by demanding to know the specific subject matter about which he enables his pupils to speak more cleverly. It is not Hippocrates' inability to answer Socrates' question that is problematic, it is the question itself. At the risk of belaboring the obvious, the only possible answer is that a teacher of public speaking teaches his pupils to speak cleverly about whatever subjects they wish. This is not a slippery evasion of a searching question. It is a truism. *Qua* teacher of rhetoric, the sophist imparts no specific subject matter; he simply imparts the techniques of persuasion. There is something bizarre, and even comical, about confronting a teacher of rhetoric with the question, "It is all very well for you to claim that you will teach me to speak more cleverly, but *about what?*" One might just as well ask an Olympic trainer, "It is all very well for you to claim that you will teach me to run faster, but *to where?*" As the master rhetorician Gorgias declares:

[T]here isn't anything that the [rhetorician] couldn't speak more persuasively about to a gathering than could any other craftsman whatever. (*G.* 456c4–6)

He adds that the reason for this is not because the rhetorician knows more about specific subject matter than the practitioners of the relevant *technai*, but because he possesses the power of persuasive speech. In short, a competent teacher of rhetoric is qualified to teach: not because he is the master of specific subject matter, but because he is master of the art of speaking – an art which is content-independent and content-neutral. Aristotle held the same view. Rhetoric is useful:

because . . . in dealing with certain persons, even if we possessed the most accurate scientific knowledge, we should not find it easy to persuade them by the employment of such knowledge. (*Rh.* 1355a12)

It follows that what Socrates thinks is rhetoric's greatest weakness Aristotle thinks is its greatest strength: the usefulness of rhetoric consists precisely in the fact that it does not deal with specific subject matter, but is of general application. He, in fact, defines "rhetoric" as "the faculty of discovering the possible means of persuasion in reference to any subject whatever" (*Ibid.*).

It is, of course, true, as Socrates never tires of pointing out, that all speech is necessarily *about something*. But it does not follow that to teach someone to speak more persuasively is necessarily to teach him to speak more persuasively *about something*, that is, about some specific subject matter of which the teacher must himself be the master. It is perfectly reasonable to expect a teacher of public speaking to improve a piano tuner's forthcoming speech about piano tuning by telling him to stop mumbling, to make more eye contact with his audience, to use more gestures, and so on. But it would be completely unreasonable to expect him to provide the tuner with technical information about piano actions, optimum string tension, and the harmonic series. It is also true, as Socrates observes in passing, that an overly garrulous lyre teacher might occasionally digress and teach his pupils to speak cleverly about playing the lyre. But his primary aim, *qua* lyre teacher, is to teach them to play the lyre, not to talk about playing it.[12] And the same is true of practitioners of the *technai* generally.

None of these objections occur to Hippocrates. Having wrongly conceded the legitimacy of Socrates' question: *About what* does the sophist teach his pupils to speak cleverly? he is maneuvered into confessing that he does now know – from which it seems to follow that although he thought he knew what a sophist is, it is now clear that he does not.

J. Adam[13] thinks that, in reducing Hippocrates to *aporia*, Socrates has demonstrated that he is "in the worst of all states" and "proceeds to convict him of ignorance." So, too, Grote, whose more detailed assessment is worth quoting at some length:

[T]he preliminary conversation ... with Hippocrates ... brings to light that false persuasion of knowledge, under which men unconsciously act ... Common fame and celebrity suffice to determine the most vehement aspirations towards a lecturer, in one who has never stopped to reflect or enquire what the lecturer does. The pressure applied by Sokrates in his

---

[12] Stokes's contention, 1986: 188, that Socrates' suggestion has "a certain plausibility" in that we often require music students to expound on the musical principles they have learned strikes me as a piece of special pleading.

[13] 1893: 85.

successive questions, to get beyond vague generalities to definite particulars – the insufficiency, thereby exposed, of the conceptions with which men usually rest satisfied – exhibit the working of his Elenchus in one of its most instructive ways.[14]

With all due respect to Adam and Grote – and essentially the same assessment is given by every other commentator I have consulted[15] – I think they are wrong. There is a sense in which Hippocrates knows perfectly well what a sophist is and whether the effects of his teaching will be good or evil. He knew this before his encounter with Socrates, and he knows it still.

According to Socrates, however, this commonsensical understanding is not enough; one must "know what a sophist is" in a deeper sense: not because Socrates invokes more rigorous criteria in the case of the sophists than in the case of the practitioners of the other *technai*, but because he suspects that, unlike doctors, carpenters, and cobblers, who unquestionably do possess knowledge of medicine, carpentry, and cobbling which they can impart, the sophists do not possess knowledge of virtue which they can impart. So whatever they do impart will almost certainly be harmful. That is precisely why the unsuspecting Hippocrates needs to be warned.

What Socrates has overlooked is this. Just as Hippocrates knows perfectly well – in the ordinary sense of "knows" – what a sophist is, so also he knows perfectly well – in the ordinary sense of "knows" – that learning to speak more effectively is good and that, insofar as Protagoras teaches his pupils to do this, the effects of his teaching will be good. And just as his inability to explain what a sophist is in the Socratic sense does not entail that he does not know what a sophist is in the ordinary sense, so also his inability to explain whether the effects of his teaching will be good in the Socratic sense does not entail that he does not know whether they will be good in the ordinary sense.

Surprisingly, Socrates now comes to Hippocrates' aid by telling him what a sophist is: a sophist is "a kind of merchant who peddles provisions upon which the soul is nourished" (313c4–6). In saying this, he does not mean that the sophist's "provisions" really nourish the soul, but only that this is what the sophist claims. It is precisely

---

[14] 1867, II: 33–34.
[15] Schofield, 1992: 125, describes the encounter between Socrates and Hippocrates as a "paradigmatic Socratic conversation, sadly neglected by scholarship."

for this reason that Hippocrates must be careful. The well-known and much-quoted Socratic warning follows: Just as grocers do not know what is beneficial and harmful to the body but praise all their wares indiscriminately, so also sophists do not know what is beneficial and harmful to the soul and do the same thing. And just as shoppers need to be cautious before buying groceries and ingesting them into their bodies, so also Hippocrates needs to be cautious before "buying knowledge" from Protagoras and ingesting it into his soul. Unlike groceries, knowledge cannot be carried away in a parcel and inspected later; it is immediately assimilated into the soul and the buyer is harmed or benefited accordingly (313c7–314b6).[16]

But the warning goes unheeded. Having concluded their discussion, the pair set out for the home of Callias. Except for two brief allusions (316b1–c2 and 328d6–9), Hippocrates is heard from no more.

Before leaving him, however, two points should be noted. First, unless we are prepared to endorse a whole cluster of Socratic assumptions – some of them highly counterintuitive and others demonstrably false – Hippocrates' resistance is defensible. Consorting with a sophist is a morally risk-laden venture only if we define "sophist" in Socratic terms. There is nothing risky about enrolling in a course in public speaking in hopes of becoming a better speaker. Second, since this is why Hippocrates wants to consult Protagoras, Socrates' warning is really quite beside the point. Hippocrates has no intention of "buying knowledge" from Protagoras. It is true that Protagoras claims to impart knowledge about how to manage one's personal affairs and the affairs of the city.

---

[16] In this passage, there is no mention of *investigating* Protagoras' views to determine whether they are true or false. The operative assumption seems to be that merely *exposing* oneself to a sophist's "wares" is dangerous. This sounds more like the "Socrates" of *Republic* II and III with his doctrine of the soul as a tender plant which is deeply and permanently affected by the persons and things to which it is exposed which, like music, "pour into his soul through the funnel of his ears" (*R.* 411a5–6) than like the Socrates of the early dialogues who stands ready to examine *any* opinion, the truth-value of which cannot be known in advance and who never gives the slightest hint that merely listening to false or dubious doctrine is a risk-laden venture. Such passages lend credence to the claim – made by some commentators (notably Kahn, 1981, and Mazel, 1987: 37) – that the so-called "Socratic" dialogues, far from being faithful and philosophically neutral representations of the historical Socrates written by the philosophically immature Plato are, in fact, idealizations of him with Plato interjecting his own opinions without apology and without indication whenever the perceived need arises.

But we should assess Hippocrates in terms of his own announced educational goals rather than in terms of the educational goals advocated by Socrates or the less self-consciously moral but equally expansive ones proposed by Protagoras.

Socrates does not persuade Hippocrates to reconsider what he is about to do. There is nothing in the text to support Guthrie's contention that the foregoing discussion puts Hippocrates "on his guard" and enables him to approach Protagoras "in a mood very different from that of the flatterers who throng the house where he is staying."[17] That is not exegesis, it is wishful thinking. Hippocrates undergoes no discernible change as the result of his conversation with Socrates. Like countless teenagers before and since, he endures the Socratic sermon with enforced stoicism, putting on a serious face and nodding gravely while at the same time consoling himself with the reassuring thought that it will soon be over and he will then be free to do exactly what he had originally planned, namely, pay Protagoras a visit and thereby expose himself to the very "dangers" against which he has just been warned. And that is exactly what he does.

Hippocrates is yet another Socratic interlocutor who is untouched by Socrates' criticism. Having been advised of his allegedly deficient understanding and his allegedly foolhardy goals, he continues to act on the same beliefs and with the same motivation. Like most Socratic interlocutors, he is reduced to silence; but, beyond that, nothing of any importance seems to have occurred. Socrates knows this perfectly well. Why else would he introduce Hippocrates as a young man who wants to make a name for himself in the city – something that Hippocrates never said – and who thinks that the best way of doing so would be by studying with Protagoras (316b8–c2)? That is not the description of someone who has recently been alerted to the dangers of consorting with sophists and who, as a result, has become eternally vigilant about the care of his soul. Indeed, in view of the fact that Hippocrates is not heard from again, one wonders how interested in him Socrates really is.

H. D. F. Kitto is sensitive to this point. Commenting on Plato's "obvious error" of forgetting about Hippocrates, he remarks:

---

[17] 1975: 216. So also Coby, 1987: 33, according to whom Hippocrates is now "in far less of a hurry" to meet Protagoras.

Plato relies on his reader to read with that degree of imaginative cooperation that makes direct statement unnecessary and the result more effective.[18]

That is a possible explanation. But it is not the only one. Whatever interest Socrates may initially have had in privately dissuading Hippocrates from consulting Protagoras, it pales into insignificance in the face of the much more interesting prospect of publicly trouncing Protagoras. That this is a possibility worth considering will become clear in the next chapter.

---

[18] 1966: 248–49. See also Schofield, 1992: 127.

CHAPTER 13

Protagoras

Although the Platonic corpus contains many allusions to the sophists, the *Gorgias*, the *Hippias Minor*, and the *Protagoras* are the only early dialogues in which a sophist appears in the role of a Socratic interlocutor. And although Socrates is universally skeptical about the sophists' claim to be teachers of virtue, the *Protagoras* is the only early dialogue in which that claim is seriously examined. The fact that it is put into the mouth of Protagoras[1] is often cited as evidence of the high esteem in which Plato held him. Socrates' allegedly respectful treatment of him throughout the dialogue is often adduced as further evidence. Neither contention can withstand scrutiny. In billing himself as a teacher of virtue, Protagoras was promoting himself as a moral expert and implying that virtue can be taught. Socrates disputed both claims. Intellectual pretension and false doctrine are not grounds for esteem and respect.

It is true that Protagoras is treated with less overt contempt than the other sophists. Unlike Hippias, he is not the object of stinging irony bordering on open ridicule; unlike Gorgias, he is not accused of being a "seemer" whose linguistic facility enables him to pass himself off as an expert; unlike Prodicus, he is not disparaged for his preoccupation with trivial semantic distinctions; and, unlike the sophists generally, he is not accused of arguing for

---

[1] The historical Protagoras of Abdera (490–422) was the most celebrated sophist of classical antiquity. A dazzling rhetorician and sought-after teacher, he was also the author of numerous treatises on a variety of subjects. According to Diogenes Laertius (9.51), he was the first to maintain that there are two sides to every question; he was also the first to argue in this fashion. His religious agnosticism allegedly prompted the Athenians to banish him from the city and to collect and burn all existing copies of his book, *On the Gods*, in which this heresy was promulgated (9.51–2) – a claim nowhere corroborated by Plato and, in fact, incompatible with his scattered remarks about Protagoras. His career spanned more than forty years, and his reputation persisted long after his death – a fact attested to by Socrates (*M.* 91e6–92a6) and reinforced by middle-period Plato who still thought it important to examine (and to refute) his *Homo Mensura* doctrine in the *Theaetetus*.

victory and of employing those eristic tactics with which sophistry was (and still is) synonymous. But if Protagoras elicited Plato's respect, it is not evident from this dialogue. A stunning example of Plato's dramatic art, the *Protagoras* depicts an exhausting, knock-down dialectical encounter in which the great sophist suffers a humiliating public defeat at the hands of a superficially deferential but uncommonly predatory Socrates. No other interlocutor is so premeditatively targeted and so relentlessly stalked. Not even Callicles is subjected to the methodical, no-stone-unturned scrutiny with which Protagoras is mercilessly demolished. It is as if the very fact that he is less obviously objectionable than the run-of-the-mill sophist makes him all the more dangerous and deserving of refutation.

Having cautioned Hippocrates against uncritically imbibing the "wares" of a sophist without knowing what a sophist is and how his soul will be affected by them, Socrates accompanies him to the home of Callias. As if to italicize his monumental lack of excitement, he casually reports that they did not try to gain immediate entry because they were discussing "some point" (τινος λόγου, *Pr.* 314c4) which they did not want to leave hanging – a deflating aside which quietly demotes the hitherto irresistible Protagoras to the status of someone that Hippocrates can wait to meet. When they do try to gain entry, the door is slammed in their faces by Callias' doorkeeper who mistakes them for sophists. Although his fear is instantly put to rest by Socrates' assurance that they are not, one may perhaps be pardoned for wondering whether the doorkeeper might have had second thoughts had he witnessed the conversation that follows.

Once inside, they find themselves in the presence of Protagoras, walking about the portico and expounding on a variety of topics. He is followed by several groups of auditors made up of familiar Athenian figures like Charmides, Critias, Alcibiades, and the sons of Pericles, as well as by other anonymous persons who are identified only as strangers who accompany Protagoras wherever he goes. Never far behind but obsequiously stepping aside whenever he changes direction so as to afford him complete freedom of movement, these zealous constituencies somehow manage to avoid stumbling over each other in Protagoras' wake while simultaneously straining to catch his every word. Protagoras' all-too-human side is evident from the studied casualness with which he accepts the self-effacing genuflections of his awe-struck entourage. Also present is Hippias of Elis, prominently perched on an elevated chair and surrounded by a group of auditors of his own to whom he is learnedly discoursing about astronomy. Not far away is Prodicus who, although still in bed, sleepy-eyed, and wrapped in multiple blankets and rugs, is addressing yet another group – but with minimal success owing to the fact that his deep and resonant voice echoes so loudly through the room that it drowns out his actual words.

In the *Protagoras*, Plato's tendency to portray the respected politicians and educators of his day as comic figures is given its head. Many of the big names have gathered at Callias' home, and before the dialogue is over all have made fools of themselves. Generations of commentators have luxuriated in Plato's brilliant and humorous scene-painting.[2] Brilliant and humorous it is, but what kind of humor is it? Peter De Vries[3] once distinguished the humorist from the satirist on the ground that whereas the latter shoots to kill, the former brings his prey back alive and releases him for another chance. Socratic humor strives for an effect midway between the two. Socrates may not shoot to kill, but he does shoot to maim. His humor is always at someone else's expense – usually demeaning, often unkind, and occasionally cruel.[4] Unlike the self-implicating humor of the humorist who laughs at others while laughing at himself, Socratic humor is self-insulating and aimed exclusively at its object. Socrates laughs at others, but he cannot laugh at himself. His ostensibly self-deprecating remarks are always thinly veiled criticisms of his interlocutor: "You must keep your answers short because I have a very poor memory" means "Unlike you, I value clarity and economy of utterance and will tolerate nothing else"; "I am devoid of wisdom and eager to become your disciple" means "Your arrogance is more than I can bear, and I will not rest until I have exposed you as a pretentious fool." Even his interpretation of the Delphic oracle's "riddling" utterance is self-serving. Who but Socrates could have transformed the intellectual vice of moral ignorance into the intellectual virtue

---

[2] See Trédé and Demont, 1993: 23–24: "[L]e lecteur, lui, n'applaudit que l'art du pastiche, de la caricature même, dont témoigne Socrate (ou Platon)"; and, more recently, Allen, 1996: 167: "The *Protagoras* is a very funny dialogue."

[3] Newquist, 1964: 149.

[4] Even Vlastos agrees (see 1956: xxiv).

of "a kind of wisdom" possessed by him alone? Some men boast by flaunting their knowledge. Socrates boasts by assuring everyone that he has none.

Socrates' superior air, often bordering on contempt, betrays his real attitude towards the people by whom he is surrounded and raises serious doubts about his announced concern for the souls of his fellows. If he really cared about their souls, would not the mockery to which he subjects them be tempered by the (to him) sobering fact that these impressionable folk are doing exactly what he had just cautioned Hippocrates not to do – uncritically imbibing the "wares" of a sophist? Would not this fact have prevented him (and legions of commentators)[5] from perceiving the situation as *merely* funny? Here are the flesh-and-blood incarnations of the various character types which are classified more systematically in the *Phaedrus* and the *Republic* – the sophist, the rhetorician, the enthusiast, the charlatan, and so on. In these dialogues, we learn a good deal about who is (and who is not) to be numbered among the tiny remnant worthy of consorting with philosophy; in the *Protagoras*, we meet them face to face. But instead of being asked to worry about them and to fear for their souls, we are merely asked to laugh at them. It is one of the many ironies of Socratic scholarship that the same commentators who are offended by Aristophanes' portrait of Socrates in the *Clouds* and dismiss it as an inaccurate, unfair, and even malicious caricature lay aside these scruples when Plato subjects other historical figures to the same treatment.

It is amid – and, doubtless, because of – the bedlam by which they are surrounded that Protagoras regally asks whether Socrates and Hippocrates would prefer a private audience. Socrates replies that it makes no difference to him and proposes that he explain their purpose for being there and let Protagoras decide. The young Hippocrates is eager to make a name for himself in the city and has been wondering whether he would be well advised to study with Protagoras. In view of this purpose, would he prefer a private or a public discussion?

Protagoras responds to this simple question at considerable

---

[5] Arieti, 1991: 119, is representative: "It is not only the sophists who are being mocked here ... but also their ... disciples ... who hang on their every word like hungry gaping-mouthed dogs. As Plato's audience, won't we smilingly shake our heads at the folly of this unthinking enthusiasm?"

length and with an openness and directness which "seems to lay his innermost self before us."[6] Prefacing his reply with an expression of profuse gratitude for Socrates' thoughtfulness, he explains that foreigners like himself who visit Athens and other great cities claiming to be better equipped to instruct the youth than local teachers are apt to arouse resentment and hostility. In fact, many of his predecessors had concealed the fact that they were sophists in hopes of rendering their presence more palatable to envious colleagues and the general public.[7] However, he has always eschewed this secretive policy and candidly admitted that he is a sophist. *And therefore*, he concludes, as if every word of this elaborate preface had been absolutely essential for understanding what he is about to say, he would prefer a public discussion. As for Hippocrates, he would indeed be well advised to become his pupil; for if he does, he will go home a better man; and he will continue to get better with every passing day.

Better *at what?* asks Socrates, resuming the same line of questioning he had pursued with Hippocrates. Protagoras congratulates Socrates for having asked exactly the right question. However, instead of answering it, he proceeds to explain why it is the right question. Unlike most sophists, who mistreat their pupils by forcing them to learn things which are of no interest to them, he teaches his only what they want to know; in particular, how to become good citizens – the political art (τὴν πολιτικὴν τέχνην, 319a4).

Socrates agrees that it would certainly be a fine thing to teach this to the youth, but he wonders whether it is teachable. His reasoning is as follows. Before erecting a building, fortifying a harbor, or embarking on anything else that requires expertise, people always consult skilled craftsmen. However, when deliberating about matters of public policy, they solicit the opinion of anyone and everyone – a fact which suggests that they do not think these things require special expertise. Even wise and good men like Pericles, who spared no expense on their sons' education, did not teach them to be virtuous. Having heard Protagoras' speech, however, he finds himself vacillating. Can Protagoras dispel his doubts by demonstrating that virtue can be taught?

---

[6] The admirable phrase is Goldberg's, 1983: 13.

[7] Protagoras' claim to be the practitioner of an ancient art (316d3–4) counts against C. C. W. Taylor's contention, 1976: 61, that he was the first professional sophist.

Protagoras is happy to oblige. Opting for a demonstration in the form of a myth (μῦθον)[8] rather than an argument (λόγον), he recounts how the gods created mortal creatures and appointed Epimetheus and Prometheus to equip them with the requisite skills, and how the improvident Epimetheus had provided so extravagantly for the animal kingdom that he exhausted his supply before he had provided for mankind. To save the day, Prometheus had stolen fire and technical knowledge from Hephaestus and Athena and given them to mankind, thereby partly remedying Epimetheus' lack of forethought – but only partly, for this knowledge did not include political wisdom. Fearing the destruction of the human race, Zeus had instructed Hermes to endow it with a sense of justice and temperance in such a way that all would have an equal share. That is why people consult experts about technical matters, but solicit the opinions of anyone and everyone about political ones. As for Socrates' more general complaint that even wise and good men like Pericles taught their sons everything but virtue, it is false. Every father teaches his sons what is just, noble, and pious. Every nurse and teacher does the same thing, exposing the young to poetry that depicts good men and punishing them when they go wrong. Sons of good fathers turn out badly with respect to virtue for the same reason that they turn out badly with respect to anything else. In short, to ask: Who teaches virtue? is like asking: Who teaches Greek? The answer is: Everyone. And just as we should be grateful to anyone who can teach us a skill, so also we should be grateful to anyone who can teach us to be virtuous. In fact, Protagoras considers himself preeminently qualified to do precisely that.[9]

---

[8] The fact that Protagoras presents his case in the form of a myth in no way diminishes its importance. Here and elsewhere, Plato's use of myth suggests that he thinks that, insofar as its pictorial vividness renders its content more accessible to the imagination and the emotions of the reader, it is often a more effective instrument of persuasion than discursive argument. Unlike rational argumentation, which tries to elicit assent that can be withheld because of psychological resistance of one kind or another, myth tries to elicit a response from that "part" of the self to which that resistance is traceable. See Croiset, 1984: 10, according to whom Plato employs myth "non pour démontrer rigoureusement, mais pour compléter la démonstration dialectique par une sorte d'intuition poétique capable de s'envoler jusque dans régions où la science proprement dite ne peut atteindre."

[9] There are striking parallels between the theory of early education that Plato puts into the mouth of Protagoras in the *Protagoras* and the theory that he puts into the mouth of "Socrates" in *Republic* II–III. The former may, in fact, be an anticipation of the latter. In both, the task of moral education is carried out not by theoretical instruction but

That Plato considered Protagoras a cut above the run-of-the mill sophist seems clear from the remarks he puts into his mouth about the (for Socrates) always touchy subject of charging a fee for services rendered. Protagoras conscientiously explains that he has no fixed fee. If a pupil thinks he has been overcharged, Protagoras will accept whatever fee the pupil thinks fair – provided that he swears in a temple that this is his honest opinion and deposits that amount (328b1–c2).[10]

It is a grand speech in both manner and content. If Socrates sometimes formulates his interlocutors' views in ways that make them seem highly implausible, he is also capable of formulating them with great persuasiveness. Protagoras' speech is a case in point. Not only does it deny the Socratic thesis that virtue cannot be taught; insofar as it presupposes that human beings are equally endowed with a sense of justice, it also contains an implicit defense of the very democracy that Plato repudiated.

Socrates is "astonished" by Protagoras' speech and confesses that whereas he previously thought that virtue cannot be taught, he is now inclined to think that it can. However, there is one small point about which he would like a bit more precision.[11] In saying that the gods infused mankind with a sense of justice, Protagoras seemed to be implying that virtue is a single whole of which justice, temperance, piety, and so on are "parts" (μόρια, 329c2–d1). Is that his view? Or does he think "justice," "temperance," "piety," etc. are simply different names for the same thing? Assured that he means the former, Socrates presses for still greater precision. Does Protagoras think that justice, temperance, piety, and so on are "parts" of virtue in the sense that the mouth, the nose, and the

---

by emotional habituation – carefully supervised exposure to persons and objects worthy of imitation and reinforced by remedial punishment the purpose of which is not simply to insure virtuous conduct, but also to inculcate virtuous dispositions and virtuous character. Like Protagoras, middle-period Plato thinks that true virtue is not virtue intellectually communicated and grasped, but virtue emotionally inculcated and absorbed. True teachers of virtue do not simply teach their pupils *that* certain actions are just, noble, and pious; they also teach them to *be* just, noble, and pious. However strongly Plato may have repudiated the values inculcated by Protagoras, he fully agreed with the method by which they were inculcated.

10 As Grote, 1888, VIII: 362, trenchantly remarks, "Such is not the way in which the corruptors of mankind go to work."

11 This response has elicited contradictory responses. Goldberg, 1983: 96, thinks Socrates' allusion to the "one small point" is an "implied deflation of Protagoras' grandiosity." Stone, 1988: 45, describes it as a refusal to take Protagoras' case for democracy seriously and an evasion of the issue which enables Socrates to take off "into a semantic fog."

eyes are parts of the face? Or in the sense that a lump of gold is composed of parts? Again, he means the former. One final question: Does he think that the virtues are separable in such a way that a person can have one without having the others? Or if a person has one, must he have them all? Protagoras replies that he thinks the virtues are separable on the ground that there are many people who are courageous but not just and just but not wise.

At this point, Socrates abandons his usual strategy in favor of a very different one. Instead of asking questions and eliciting Protagoras' answers, he asks a question, answers it himself, and asks whether Protagoras agrees: Is justice *something* (πρᾶγμά τί ἐστιν, 330c1), that is, an actually existing thing? Socrates thinks so. Protagoras does too.

Socrates thereupon opts for yet another strategy. Instead of asking questions, answering them himself, and asking whether Protagoras agrees, he envisages Protagoras and himself being jointly interrogated by a third party who wonders whether they think that justice is just or unjust. Socrates thinks that justice is just and "the sort of thing that is just" (τοιοῦτον ἡ δικαιοσύνη οἷον δίκαιον εἶναι, 330c7–8). Again, Protagoras does too. But what if the questioner also asked whether they think that piety is an actually existing thing, that it is pious, and that it is "the sort of thing that is pious" (τοιοῦτον πεφυκέναι οἷον ... εἶναι ... ὅσιον, 330d5–6)? Socrates does. Would Protagoras again agree? Before allowing him to answer, Socrates confesses that he himself would be annoyed by the question: Is piety pious? For how could anything be pious if piety is not?[12]

Taken at face value, this "confession" is puzzling and patently insincere. Socrates asks such questions all the time, and it would be absurd to suggest that he is annoyed by his own questions. Taken contextually, however, the "confession" is perfectly intelligible. It also explains why Socrates temporarily opts for the strategy of the third-party questioner. Suspecting that Protagoras is getting tired of these seemingly self-answering questions but needing his assent in order to refute him, Socrates puts the potentially troublesome queries into the mouth of a hypothetical and thoroughly tiresome third party whom they can jointly deplore, there-

---

[12] On the difference between "ordinary predication," as in "The Pope is pious," and so-called "Pauline predication," as in "Piety is pious," see Vlastos, 1981b: 252–59.

by declining responsibility for the questions while at the same time insuring that he obtains the required answers.

Returning to the discussion, if the questioner were to point out that Socrates and Protagoras seem to be implying that the virtues are completely different from each other, Socrates would reply that it was not he but Protagoras who said this, and that he himself was just asking questions. Finally, what if the questioner were to conclude that since piety is neither just nor "the sort of thing that is just" and since justice is neither pious nor "the sort of thing that is pious," it follows that piety is unjust and that justice is impious? Still advancing theses of his own, Socrates says that, in that case, he would reply that justice *is* pious and that piety *is* just; indeed, justice is the same thing (ταὐτόν) as piety or very similar (ὁμοιότατον), and it is certainly "the same sort of thing" (331b3–6). Would Protagoras agree? He would not.

Before considering his reasons, it is worth noticing that the third-party questioner has argued fallaciously.[13] From the fact that piety is not just and that justice is not pious, it does not follow that piety is unjust and that justice is impious. A thing can lack a property without having the opposite property: "X is *not* just" does not entail "X is *un*just." The third-party questioner has confounded contraries with contradictories.[14]

Protagoras does not spot the fallacy. But neither does he endorse the inference. However, he is willing to concede that justice is pious and that piety is just for the sake of argument – a response which elicits a sharp rebuke from Socrates:

Don't do that to me! It's not this "if you want" or "if you agree" business I want to test. It's you and me I want to put on the line, and I think

---

[13] Not everyone agrees. For an incisive discussion of the passage and its possible interpretations, see Hubbard and Karnofsky, 1982: 105–14.

[14] See Châtelet, 1980: 326, n. 51: "Il est légitime, si A n'est pas ce qu'est B, de *nier, sans plus*, que A ait la qualité qui fait de B telle chose déterminée. Mais ce n'est pas une raison de *affirmer* déterminément que A et B ont telles *qualités privatives*, C et D. Au scandale moral s'ajoute alors le scandale logique, qui consiste à confondre la négation indéterminée et vague qu'est, à l'égard d'un terme, le terme *contradictoire*, avec la négation déterminée et précise qu'est le terme *contraire*." Cf. Guthrie, 1975: 222. Grote, 1867, II: 51, thinks Socrates' reasoning in this passage is so flawed that if Plato had put it into the mouth of Protagoras, commentators would have denounced him for his sophistry. Allen, 1996: 106, acknowledges Socrates often argues "much like a sophist himself," but he defends him on the ground that although dialectic often resembles eristic, "the inner reality is different." Does this mean that fallacious arguments should be tolerated if they spring from good intentions? If not, what does it mean?

the argument (λογόν) will be tested best if we take the "if" out. (331c4–d1)

In short, Protagoras must say what he really believes.

Protagoras concedes that justice bears some resemblance (προσέοικέν τι) to piety; after all, everything resembles everything else in *some* respect (331d1–3). At the same time, he thinks that it is misleading to say that two things are the same (or almost the same) just because they have some small characteristic in common – a response which troubles Socrates because it implies that justice and piety only resemble each other in some small way. Protagoras explains that that is not what he meant. But neither does he think that one can say without qualification that justice is pious and that piety is just. Perceiving that Protagoras will not assert the identity (or virtual identity) of justice and piety, Socrates drops the point and introduces a different line of argumentation designed to demonstrate the identity of wisdom and temperance. The argument – 332a4–333b4 – is as follows:

(i) There is something called folly (ἀφροσύνην), and it is the opposite of wisdom (σοφία).

(ii) Those who behave rightly are temperate, and they are temperate "by temperance"; whereas those who do not behave rightly behave foolishly, and they are foolish "by folly."

(iii) Behaving foolishly is the opposite of behaving temperately.

(iv) Whatever is done "by strength" is done strongly, and whatever is done "by weakness" is done weakly; formulated in full generality, whatever is done in a particular way is done by the faculty appropriate to it and whatever is done in the opposite way is done by the opposite faculty.

(v) There is such a thing as the beautiful whose opposite is the ugly, and there is such a thing as the good whose opposite is the bad.

(vi) Everything has one and only one opposite.

(vii) Whatever is done in an opposite way is done "by opposites."

(viii) Whatever is done foolishly is done in the opposite way of whatever is done temperately.

(ix) Whatever is done temperately is done "by temperance," and whatever is done foolishly is done "by folly."

(x) Folly is the opposite of temperance.

(xi) Since folly is the opposite of wisdom, and since everything has one and only one opposite, it follows that temperance and wisdom are the same, since folly is the opposite of both.

Socrates does not explain what he means by "opposites," but commentators have come forward with numerous suggestions. Goldberg[15] thinks he means "mutually exclusive" properties or "precise opposites." Weingartner[16] thinks he means contradictories: to say that F and G are opposites is to say that "if anything is F, it is not G *and* if it is G, it is not F *and* (assuming F and G can be meaningfully predicated of it) if it is not F, it is G and if it is not G, it is F." Vlastos[17] thinks he means (what in set theory is called) complements: for any two classes A and not-A, A and not-A are "mutually exclusive and jointly exhaustive of their universe of discourse." C. C. W. Taylor[18] thinks he means "polar opposites," that is, qualities at opposite ends of a continuum. Since Socrates' argument crucially depends on the thesis – Guthrie calls it the "dogma"[19] – that every property has one and only one opposite, it is important to determine whether this thesis is true.

The thesis has a surface plausibility. Asked for the opposites of "fat," "tall," and "happy," any toddler could produce them. However, this initial plausibility begins to erode once we notice that ordinary language is not nearly so exact, neat, and accommodating as the continuum hypothesis suggests. The opposites of "fat," "tall," and "happy" are "thin," "short," and "sad." But what are the opposites of "damp," "sandy," "average," "blustery," "tepid," "morose," "vexatious," "churlish," and "desultory"? I am not denying that a native speaker with sufficient linguistic ingenuity and lots of time could come up with opposites-of-sorts for these terms and many others like them. But I am denying that any obvious and intuitively correct candidates come instantly to mind. Once we liberate ourselves from sharp dichotomies like "fat"/"thin," "tall"/"short," "happy"/"sad," "hot"/"cold," "wet"/"dry" – dichotomies of which Socrates is far too fond – we are seized by the fact that natural languages abound with terms which have no exact opposite – in any ordinary sense of "opposite" – much less one and only one opposite.

Even the seemingly obvious and intuitively correct cases are not

---

[15] 1983: 118–19. [16] 1973: 83–84. [17] 1981b: 244.
[18] 1976: 127–28. [19] 1975: 226.

nearly so straightforward as they seem. It is not true that "fat" is *the* opposite of "thin." The most that can be said is that it is *an* opposite of "thin." But so, in some sense, are "plump," "portly," "chubby," "corpulent," "stout," "full-figured," "rotund," and "obese." Conversely, "thin" is *an* opposite of "fat." But so, in some sense, are "slender," "slim," "under-fed," "gaunt," "scrawny," "emaciated," "wraithlike," and "skeletal." People are not just fat or thin any more than they are just tall or short or wise or foolish. Few languages suffer from such extreme adjectival impoverishment. But in what sense are these terms opposites? According to the continuum hypothesis, "fat" and "thin" are "polar opposites" which constitute the terminal points of a continuum. Adjectives like "portly," "chubby," and "obese," on the one hand, and "slender," "emaciated," and "skeletal," on the other, are either synonyms and, therefore, interchangeable – which they plainly are not – or they are non-synonyms that fall somewhere between "thin" and "fat" on the continuum, their precise position being determined by the degree of fatness or thinness each connotes – a degree which cannot exceed that of the terminal points themselves. Both alternatives are false.

Clearly, these terms are not synonyms. "Portly" and "obese" do not mean the same thing. Neither do "slender" and "emaciated." Furthermore, "obese" and "emaciated" connote greater, not lesser, degrees of fatness and thinness than "fat" and "thin" and, therefore, do exceed the alleged terminal points of the continuum. That this is so is borne out by several considerations. First, like all adjectives, "fat" and "thin" have comparative and superlative degrees. But if both "fatter" and "fattest" and "thinner" and "thinnest" connote greater degrees of fatness and thinness, then "fat" and "thin" cannot be "polar opposites" which constitute the terminal points of the continuum. Second, adjectives are not all equally descriptive. They can, in fact, be ranked in a linguistic hierarchy of specificity, ranging from very general ones like "fat" to more informative ones like "rotund," "portly," "chubby," and "obese." Third, adjectives like "rotund," "portly," "chubby," on the one hand, and "slim," "emaciated," and "skeletal," on the other, need not connote *degrees* of fatness or thinness at all. Nor need their descriptive adjectival content be purely quantitative. "Obese" and "skeletal" are not so much degrees as *kinds* of fatness and thinness. To learn that someone is obese or skeletal is to acquire qualitative information about him. The linguistic function of these adjectives is not so much to describe people as fat or thin as to invest the terms "fat" and "thin" with richer content by answering the question: fat or thin in what way? Moreover, many of these adjectives are applied or withheld on the basis of properties other than mere considerations of weight. "Chubby" is a more affectionate term than "obese" and is more likely to be applied to a person of whom one is fond. The statement, "You're getting rather chubby" has a considerably different impact on one's hearer than the statement, "You're getting rather obese." (Compare: "You're looking slim these days" and "You're looking skeletal these days.") Since each of the adjectives on the foregoing list (which could be expanded indefinitely) has a different shade of meaning, it would be as futile to try to search for its precise opposite as it would be to argue that they all mean the same thing on the ground that they are all opposites of thin.

What is true of "fat"/"thin" and "wise"/"foolish" is equally true of "temperate"/"intemperate." People are not just temperate or intemperate any more than they are just fat or thin or tall or short. Unlike "foolish," which is a highly general and comparatively vague term, "intemperate" is more specific and informative. Its linguistic function is to answer the question: foolish in what way? But although "foolish" is often rightly predicable of intemperate conduct, it is not the *opposite* of temperance. It is surprising that Protagoras should have conceded that it is. It is even more surprising that Socrates should have advanced such a claim in the first place. We would have expected him to say that the opposite of "temperance" is "intemperance," that is, lack of self-control or excess in any of its forms. To say that intemperance is foolish is to say that it is ill-advised and (usually) a cause for regret. But the same could be said of unjust or impious conduct – and of immoral conduct generally. So if "folly" is the opposite of "temperance," it could equally be said to be the opposite of "justice," "piety," and every other virtue. That, of course, would be extremely convenient. For if "folly" is the opposite of *every* virtue, then Socrates could have demonstrated "the unity of the virtues" with a single argument, and the *Protagoras* would have been a much shorter dialogue. But not even Socrates is bold enough to advance so counterintuitive a claim. Clearly, "folly" is not the opposite of every virtue. But neither is it the opposite of "temperance." Hence Socrates has not demonstrated that wisdom and temperance are the same.[20]

Protagoras fails to see what is wrong with Socrates' argument and reluctantly concedes that wisdom and temperance are the same. Socrates jubilantly chalks this up as his second dialectical victory on the ground that they had previously concluded that justice and piety are the same – or almost the same (333b6). Again he is wrong. Protagoras had agreed to no such thing; on the contrary, he had explicitly denied it (331d1–332a1). However, he does not protest the point now – an omission which allows Socrates to proceed to the next stage of the discussion and to argue that temperance and justice are also the same.

At this point, three significant changes in elenctic procedure occur. First, having asked Protagoras whether he thinks that those who act unjustly act temperately and having discovered that Protagoras would be ashamed to endorse this thesis in spite of the fact that it is widely believed, Socrates lets his interlocutor off the hook; second, he proposes that they jointly investigate this thesis with Protagoras answering on behalf of its proponents; third, he instructs Protagoras to answer on behalf of the proponents of the thesis "whether it is [his] own position or not" (333c5–9). That is to say, having emphatically invoked the sincere assent requirement at 331c4–d1, Socrates now waives it[21] on the ground that he is chiefly interested in testing the argument (τὸν ... λόγον) and only secondarily interested in testing his interlocutor and himself (333c7–9) – a significant remark which reveals that the Socratic elenchus is not always *ad hominem*, that the testing of a thesis *can* take place without the simultaneous testing of its proponent, and that the connection between testing theses and testing lives is a contingent one. This is peculiar. If it does not matter whether Protagoras says what he really believes, why did Socrates say earlier that it did? And if it mattered then, why does it not matter now?

In any event, Protagoras agrees to answer on behalf of the proponents of the thesis. He begins inauspiciously by conceding that it is possible to be temperate but unjust; he adds that the unjust man is sensible (σωφρονεῖν), that is that he shows good judgment

---

[20] For a more favorable assessment of Socrates' argument, see Savan, 1965: 22–25.
[21] This is noticed by Nails, 1993: 287.

(εὖ φρονεῖν) in acting unjustly – provided that he fares well. He also concedes that some things are good (ἀγαθά) and that all good things are beneficial (ὠφέλιμα); however, he thinks that good things remain good even if they are not beneficial to human beings – provided that they are beneficial in some other way, for example, to animals or plants. In short, the good is a diverse and many-faceted thing (ποικίλον ... καὶ παντοδαπόν, 333d3–334b7).

Although this is judged an excellent answer by the assembled guests, Socrates' response is less enthusiastic. Since his "poor memory" prevents him from following long speeches, he wonders whether Protagoras would be good enough to give shorter answers – a request which strikes Protagoras as a piece of effrontery. How much shorter? Shorter than they should be? Surely not. And who is to decide?

A monumental quibble is in the making which Socrates tries to avoid by administering a heavy dose of flattery. Rumor has it that although Protagoras can discourse with admirable exhaustiveness, he can also discourse with equally admirable brevity. Socrates would like a display of the latter. Protagoras refuses to take the bait. He never accommodates himself to the demands of others. But Socrates has another card up his sleeve. Perceiving that his interlocutor is unwilling to abide by the brevity requirement, he feigns a pressing engagement and prepares to leave (335c3–6). Horrified by this unexpected turn of events, Callias implores him to stay. After a bit of coaxing, he agrees on the condition that Protagoras must refrain from making speeches and promise to keep his answers short.

Protagoras still thinks he should be allowed to speak at whatever length he deems necessary. Callias agrees. Alcibiades casts his vote with Socrates, but Critias rejects the idea of taking sides and simply wants the discussion to continue in a friendly manner. Hippias enterprisingly proposes that an umpire be appointed to affect a middle course between extreme brevity and unrestrained verbosity, but Socrates rejects this suggestion on the ground that an umpire who was inferior to Protagoras and himself would be useless whereas an umpire who was superior to them would be impossible to find because no one is wiser than Protagoras. Still preserving the myth that he lacks the ability to make long speeches and that, even if he did not, he would rather take part in a discussion than listen to a speech, he proposes that Protagoras and he temporarily exchange roles: let Protagoras ask questions and let Socrates demonstrate how a concise answerer should reply – after which Protagoras can again resume the role of answerer. Although increasingly unwilling to continue, Protagoras reluctantly agrees.

A bizarre and much discussed interlude follows (338e6–347a5) during which Socrates goes off on an extended and increasingly zany excursion into literary criticism.[22] The subject is a poem by Simonides which Socrates thinks beautiful (καλῶς) and well crafted (πεποιῆσθαι), but which Protagoras judges self-contradictory on the ground that the poet contradicts himself: in one passage Simonides says that it is hard (χαλεπόν) for a man to become truly good (ἄνδρ᾽ ἀγαθὸν μὲν ἀλαθέως γενέσθαι χαλεπόν, 339b1), but in another passage he criticizes Pittacus[23] for saying that it is hard to be good (χαλεπὸν ... ἐσθλὸν ἔμμεναι, 339c4–5). Socrates claims not to see the contradiction, although he admits – in his narration but not publicly in the presence of the assembled guests – that he feared Protagoras might be right (339c8–9). Having just violated his own sincere assent requirement, the unrivalled master of detecting inconsistencies disingenuously asks Protagoras to explain why he thinks the statements are inconsistent. The somewhat nonplussed Protagoras points out that Simonides cannot simultaneously assert *p* himself and then pronounce *p* false when Pittacus asserts it, thereby affirming and denying the same proposition – a logical point which elicits thunderous applause from everyone present.

Everyone, that is, except Socrates. Still feigning mystification and, by his own admission, stalling for time (ἵνα μοι χρόνος ἐγγένηται, 339e4) to consider what the poet meant – or, less euphemistically, to figure out how to persuade his auditors that what he himself suspects is a contradiction is, in fact, not one – he hits upon a solution. Appealing to Prodicus, whose linguistic opinions are not taken lightly by those present, he asks whether being (τὸ εἶναι) and becoming (τὸ γενέσθαι) are the same or dif-

---

[22] Commentators disagree about whether this passage is intended as serious exegesis or as comic relief and a parody of the sophists. See, e.g. J. and A. M. Adam, 1893: xxvii; A. E. Taylor, 1929: 251; Friedländer, 1964, ii: 24; Weingartner, 1973: 95; Guthrie, 1975: 227; C. C. W. Taylor, 1976: 146; Stokes, 1986: 321–23; Coby, 1987: 128–30; Vlastos, 1991: 135–38; Schofield, 1992: 128; Trédé and Demont, 1993: 39–40; and Allen, 1996: 115.

[23] Pittacus (*circa* 650–570) was ruler of Mytilene on the island of Lesbos and was numbered among the Seven Sages.

ferent (340b3–5). Prodicus thinks they are different. Armed with the "authoritative" opinion of one sophist, Socrates sets out to refute another sophist by discrediting a thesis which, in his heart of hearts, he suspects is true. By appeal to the distinction just authorized by Prodicus, he implausibly – and, as he later admits, dishonestly – claims that in the first passage Simonides is stating his own opinion (that it is hard to *become* good) whereas in the second passage, he is criticizing Pittacus – not, as Protagoras mistakenly believes, for saying the same thing, but for saying something different, namely, that it is hard to *be* good. Since being and becoming are different, Simonides is not contradicting himself.

Prodicus accepts Socrates' exegesis, but Protagoras thinks his solution is more erroneous than the error it was designed to correct. Simonides would be monumentally ignorant if he thinks it is easy to be good when, in fact, it is universally acknowledged to be the hardest thing in the world. Socrates responds by pointing out that although Protagoras' wide experience has made him the master of many things, the exegesis of poetic texts is not one of them. Prodicus and he, a disciple of Prodicus, are much better at it. In addition to overlooking the distinction between being and becoming, Protagoras has failed to notice the ambiguity of "χαλεπόν" – a term which often means "hard," but which can also mean "bad," as it does in this passage. Any competent exegete could see that Simonides is not criticizing Pittacus for saying that it is hard to be good, but for saying that it is bad to be good (341c3–5). Prodicus concurs.

The not-easily-impressed and – in view of the exegetical travesty to which he has just been subjected – remarkably long-suffering Protagoras assures Socrates that he knows very well (εὖ οἶδ') that that is not what Simonides meant. What he meant was what we ordinarily mean – that being good is not easy and requires much effort (341d2–5). Astonishingly, Socrates concurs and admits that he had actually agreed all along. Laughing hollowly, he blames the whole fiasco on Prodicus, ascribing the foregoing interpretation to him and absolving them both of all responsibility on the ground that they were only joking.[24] He thereupon explains that

---

[24] At G. 500b5–c1 Callicles is rebuked for joking during (what purports to be) serious philosophical debate – another procedural stipulation from which Socrates is apparently exempt.

Simonides actually wrote this poem to criticize Pittacus. His explanation takes the form of a speech – the details of which need not detain us – which is much longer by far than any made by Protagoras whose intolerable offenses against brevity had all but compelled Socrates to walk out in protest and who had agreed to stay only on condition that Protagoras would keep his answers short. How nice it would have been if Protagoras had responded by saying that his "poor memory" prevents him from following long speeches and by threatening to leave unless Socrates promises to keep his remarks short.[25]

Hippias judges Socrates' speech fine and offers to favor the group with an equally fine one of his own. Predictably, his offer is refused; only Socrates is allowed to make speeches. Before resuming the role of questioner, Socrates expresses the pious hope that they will henceforth abandon the frivolous and time-wasting activity of poetic exegesis – an appropriate activity for uneducated and commonplace people devoid of conversational resources who frequent "the second-rate drinking parties of the agora crowd," but singularly inappropriate for educated truth-seekers like themselves who have no need of plebeian forms of entertainment (347b8–348a6).

This scathing indictment is rather belated. It is also a self-indictment. If poetic exegesis is a frivolous activity unworthy of serious truth-seekers, why has Socrates himself been indulging in it with such gusto for the last nine Stephanus pages? Holding this view, he should have avoided the foregoing exercise in futility by announcing his objection at the outset. Having delivered himself of these astonishingly disdainful sentiments, the greatest speech-maker of them all once again expresses his distaste for speech-making and his preference for joint inquiry – especially with someone like Protagoras who, in addition to being noble and good himself, is able to make others noble and good and who does not conceal the fact that he is a sophist, but openly proclaims it to the whole world which he is ready to instruct – provided, of course, that he is adequately compensated.

Having noticed that Protagoras seemed disinclined to continue,

---

[25] For a rather severe critique of Socrates' dialectical behavior throughout the entire passage, see Vlastos, 1991: 135–39. However, having castigated him for all sorts of dialectical aberrations, Vlastos excuses him on the ground that he is not "arguing seriously."

Socrates tries to rekindle his interest by explaining his reason for engaging him in debate:

I don't want you to think that my motive in talking with you is anything else than to take a good hard look at things that continually perplex me. (348c5–7)

Proponents of the standard picture are attracted to such passages like bees to jam. This remark is yet another alleged proof of Socrates' seriousness; and, like many similar ones scattered throughout the early dialogues, it does give that impression when wrenched from its context. Seen in context, however, it is simply one of the official bulletins he periodically issues to remind everyone that philosophy is serious business and that no one is more serious than he. Anyone given to saying such things must reckon with the fact that his credibility will begin to erode once people start noticing that this announced seriousness is absent from long stretches of the dialogue during which his dialectical behavior borders on the outrageous. No one who has followed the foregoing discussion will believe for a minute that Socrates' sole motive has been to investigate things "that continually perplex [him]." On the contrary, the "perplexities" so far "investigated" are largely contrived, polemically motivated, and (in the case of the Simonides' poem) patently dishonest. Nor is "irony" the best description of Socrates' characterization of Protagoras as a "noble and good" man who is able to make others noble and good. "Withering sarcasm" would be better. "Casting a tempting dialectical lure under Protagoras' lily-pad in hopes of a strike which will allow him to be scooped into the Socratic net and landed" would be better still. What we have witnessed in the foregoing pages is not a serious philosopher caring for the soul of his interlocutor, but a mischievous prankster toying with his victim.[26]

Protagoras is still reluctant to continue. Although he has been much criticized for this, his reluctance is understandable. In fact, any other reaction would have been astonishing. Nevertheless, he is shamed into doing so by the relentless solicitations of Socrates and the collective pleas of everyone present. Perceiving that his reputation is on the line, he summons his last ounce of enthusiasm

---

[26] In view of all this, I find Schofield's remark, 1992: 130, that the Socratic elenchus "falls short of the disinterested ideal of cooperative inquiry" in the *Protagoras* a decided understatement.

and half-heartedly consents, like a dutiful father weary of romping in the snow with his children, but vigorously clapping his frost-bitten hands in a futile attempt to convey the impression that he is having more fun than he really is.

Socrates picks up the thread of the argument by reminding Protagoras that he had originally asserted that wisdom, temperance, courage, justice, and piety are distinct "parts" of virtue; and he wonders whether he still holds this view. Uncharacteristically charitable, he explains that Protagoras is not bound by what he said earlier; if he has changed his mind, he is free to make whatever modifications he wishes. He gratuitously adds that he would not be surprised if Protagoras does not hold this view at all and is merely testing him. Ignoring this pointless and potentially inflammatory remark, Protagoras explains that this is indeed his view; however, he would like to modify it slightly by making a distinction: unlike wisdom, temperance, justice, and piety, which resemble each other quite closely and are intimately connected, courage is very different (πολὺ διαφέρον) in that there are many people who are ignorant, intemperate, unjust, and impious, and yet very courageous.

Socrates disputes this contention and advances an argument designed to show that courage and wisdom are the same. The argument – 349e2–350c5 – is as follows:

(i) The courageous (τοὺς ἀνδρείους) are bold (θαρραλέους) and prepared to do what others fear.
(ii) Virtue is admirable (καλόν) without qualification, i.e., the term "admirable" applies to virtue as a whole as well as to the individual virtues of which it is composed.
(iii) Those who have the requisite knowledge and/or skill are always bolder than those who do not, e.g., skilled divers plunge more fearlessly into wells than non-divers, trained cavalry-riders fight more fearlessly than people ignorant of horsemanship, and so on; furthermore, those who acquire the requisite knowledge and/or skill are always bolder after they acquire it than they were before.

What about people who are bold without the requisite knowledge and/or skill? Does Protagoras think this kind of boldness is courage? He does not. If it were, courage would not be admirable (καλόν) but shameful (αἰσχρόν); for such people are mad (μαιν-όμενοι, 350b5–6).

In view of the fact that Socrates refutes Laches' definition of courage as wise endurance by producing a series of counter-examples designed to show that a person can be courageous even though he is not wise – indeed, even though he is foolish – we expect him to reject Protagoras' contention that boldness without wisdom is madness. But he does not; he agrees with it. Since virtue is admirable without qualification and since courage is *a* virtue, it follows that it is admirable. And since boldness without the requisite knowledge and/or skill is madness, which is shameful, and since being shameful is the opposite of being admirable, it also follows that this kind of boldness is not courage. In short, the proposition "Those who are bold without the requisite knowledge and/or skill are courageous" is pronounced true in the *Laches*, but false in the *Protagoras*.[27]

Here a disclaimer is in order. I am not accusing Socrates of self-contradiction, i.e., of claiming that the very same proposition is true in one dialogue and false in another. Neither am I faulting him for changing his mind. But I am faulting him for something else. If the proposition "Those who are bold without the requisite knowledge and/or skill are courageous" *is* false, then it cannot legitimately be employed as a premise in this (or any other) argument. But Socrates does employ it in the last step of his argument against Protagoras' claim that it is possible for a person to be ignorant, intemperate, unjust, and impious, and yet very courageous.[28] Having primed Protagoras for the dialectical kill by eliciting his assent to:

(v) The courageous (τοὺς ἀνδρείους) are the bold (τοὺς θαρρα-λέους),

he concludes:

(vi) Since those who are bold without the requisite knowledge are not courageous but mad, and since those who are most wise are most bold (οἱ σοφώτατοι οὗτοι καὶ θαρραλεώτατοί εἰσιν),

---

[27] It is precisely for this reason that some commentators think the arguments of the *Laches* represent an advance in Plato's "intellectualist" understanding of courage, as set forth in the *Protagoras*, and that it must, therefore, have been written later. See chapter 6, n. 25. (Which dialogue was actually written earlier and which later is an issue involving chronology and, therefore, beyond the scope of this book.)

[28] According to many commentators, Socrates does not ask Protagoras to assert this false thesis. Vlastos, 1956: xxxiii, goes further: since Socrates thinks this thesis is false, he would have been "an utter fool" had he elicited Protagoras' assent to it and then employed it against him. So, too, Weingartner, 1973: 106. As we will see, that is precisely what Socrates does.

then *since those who are most bold are most courageous* (θαρραλεώτατοί δὲ ὄντες ἀνδρειότατοι), it follows that their knowledge is courage, i.e., courage and wisdom are the same.

At this point, Protagoras strenuously protests:

You are doing a poor job of remembering what I said when I answered
your questions. When I was asked if the courageous are [bold], I agreed.
I was not asked if the [bold] are courageous. If you had asked me that, I
would have said, "Not all of them. You have nowhere shown that my
assent to the proposition that the courageous are [bold] was in error."
(350c6–d1)

In short, "The courageous are bold" does not entail "The bold
are courageous." Socrates is guilty of illicit conversion.[29] It is a
pity that Socrates ignores this desperately needed logic lesson because Protagoras is right on every count.

R. E. Allen disagrees:

Faced with a conclusion that follows validly from premises he has himself
admitted, Protagoras attacks the truth of the conclusion instead of reexamining the agreements which imply it.[30]

But this is a misdiagnosis of the logical situation. Far from "attack[ing] the truth of the conclusion instead of reexamining the
agreements which imply it," Protagoras repudiates the alleged
agreements. He does so by pointing out that he did not affirm that
the bold are courageous.

However, he did affirm a proposition which seems to be its converse, namely, (v) The courageous are the bold. That was a mistake and a costly one. The fact is, however, that in affirming this
proposition, Protagoras thought he was merely *re*affirming (i) The
courageous are bold. In fact, Socrates encouraged him to think
this by "reminding" him of what he had allegedly said earlier:

---

[29] See Châtelet, 1980: 329, n. 87. Protagoras goes on to say that Socrates might just as well
argue that wisdom and strength are the same on the ground that the strong are powerful
and those who know how to wrestle are more powerful than those who do not. Many
commentators think this analogical argument is faulty (see, e.g., Guthrie, 1975: 230; C.
C. W. Taylor, 1976: 156–57; and Allen, 1996: 121–22). But even if it is, the cogency of
Protagoras' original criticism is unaffected.

[30] 1996: 121–22. According to Allen, insofar as Protagoras thinks Socrates' argument depends on the truth of "All the bold are courageous" – a premise Socrates thinks is false –
he "has flatly misunderstood the argument" (121, n. 43). For other interpretations of the
argument, see Vlastos, 1956: xxxiii–iv; Weingartner, 1973: 104–7; Guthrie: 1975: 227–31;
C. C. W. Taylor, 1976: 150–61; Goldberg, 1983: 232–33; and Stokes, 1986: 328–49.

"[W]hat do you mean by the courageous (τοὺς ἀυδρείους)? Did you not say that they are the bold (τοὺς θαρραλέους)?" (350b6–7). Although Protagoras agrees that he did say this (350b7), he is wrong; he did not say this at all. In fact, he has been tricked. What he should have said is: "No. I did not say that the courageous are *the* bold (τοὺς θαρραλέους); I said that they *are* bold (θαρραλέους). I was predicating 'boldness' of the courageous; I was not asserting that the classes of the bold and the courageous are coextensive."[31] The minute Socrates draws his conclusion, Protagoras realizes his mistake and immediately sets the record straight by eliminating the surreptitiously introduced definite article.[32] This is not the unscrupulous, face-saving maneuver of a slippery sophist unwilling to acknowledge that he has been legitimately refuted; it the just criticism of a would-be responsible debater who suddenly realizes he has been maneuvered into asserting a thesis which he does not believe, mistakenly thinking that he was merely being asked to reaffirm a very different thesis which he does believe.

Some may defend Socrates on the ground that he does not assert that the most bold are the most courageous, but rather that the most bold are the most courageous if and only if their boldness is the result of wisdom. But this interpretation must be rejected. Socrates and Protagoras have already agreed that one can be bold without being wise. So wisdom is not a necessary condition for boldness, although, according to Socrates, it *is* a necessary condition for courage. (It cannot be a sufficient condition for courage; for if it were, then a person could be courageous without having all the other virtues – provided that he had wisdom – a view Socrates rejects.)[33] So the only ground we have been given for asserting that those who are most wise are also most bold, *and therefore most courageous*, is the proposition "The most bold are the most courageous" – a proposition which, as we have seen, both Socrates and Protagoras think is false.[34] In short, Socrates does

---

[31] Stokes, 1986: 331, is mistaken in claiming that although Protagoras has not said that all bold people are courageous "in so many words," he has said it "in the sense that such is the impression his words convey."

[32] See J. and A. M. Adam, 1893: 172; and Guthrie, 1975: 229.

[33] Weingartner, 1973: 106, is mistaken in claiming that Socrates thinks wisdom is a sufficient condition for courage.

[34] This passage is sufficient to cast doubt on Vlastos's denial (1981b: 223, n. 3) that Socrates "would ever (knowingly, and in a serious vein) assert categorically a false premise or endorse a fallacious argument."

not argue that the most bold *whose boldness is traceable to wisdom* are the most courageous; he argues that the most bold are the most courageous.[35]

At this point, Socrates abruptly changes the subject. Abandoning the question of the relation between virtue and its "parts," he raises the very different (and seemingly unconnected) question of how to achieve happiness. Protagoras agrees (i) that there is a difference between living well and living badly, (ii) that whoever lives painfully does not live well, and (iii) that whoever lives pleasantly does. He also agrees that to live pleasantly is good and that to live unpleasantly is bad – *provided that* the person who lives pleasantly takes pleasue in admirable things (351b7–c2). This is a very important qualification, and it underscores an equally important disagreement between Socrates and Protagoras. Unlike Socrates, who holds (or seems to hold)[36] that things are good insofar as they are pleasant (καθ' ὃ ἡδέα ἐστίν) and bad insofar as they are unpleasant (καθ' ὅσον ἀνιαρα, 351c4–6), Protagoras cannot unqualifiedly (ἁπλῶς οὕτως) endorse unrestricted hedonism and its implicit identification of the good and the pleasant. Like "the Many," he believes that some pleasures are not good, that some pains are not bad, and that some pleasures and pains are neither good nor bad but morally neutral (οὐδέτερα, 351d6). Although he believes that pleasant things partake of or produce (μετέχοντα ἢ ποιοῦντα) pleasure (351e1), he does not believe that things are good insofar as they are pleasant. Accordingly, the next thesis to be investigated is whether the pleasant and the good are the same.

Socrates begins by asking whether Protagoras agrees with "the Many" that knowledge (ἐπιστήμη) can be overcome by passion, pleasure, pain, love, and fear – in short, that it can be "dragged around by all these things as if it were a slave" (352b8–c2). Or, like Socrates, does he think that knowledge is a fine and powerful thing which enables its possessor to rule himself in such a way that a person who knows what is good will never be overcome by pleasure or anything else (ὑπὸ μηδενός) and, therefore, never act contrary to what knowledge commands (352b2–c7)? To Socrates'

---

[35] Hubbard and Karnofsky, 1982: 135–36, get it right: "The wise are *tharraleoi*. The *tharraleoi* are *andreioi*. [Therefore] [s]*ophia* is (the same as) *andreia*."

[36] Whether Socrates actually embraces unrestricted hedonism in this passage is a much-debated question which lies beyond the scope of this book. For a probing discussion of the issues, see Zehl, 1980.

delight, Protagoras opts for the latter. Socrates thereupon invites him to take part in a joint investigation designed to demonstrate that "the Many" are mistaken in believing that a person can know what is good and not do it, and that what they call "being overcome by pleasure" is an incoherent explanation of the alleged phenomenon of acting contrary to knowledge. He adds that although the opinions of "the Many" are erroneous, their errors are instructive; by examining them, Protagoras and he will arrive at a better understanding of courage and how it is connected to the other virtues (353b1–5).[37]

According to "the Many," it is possible to know that an action is base and yet do it; such people are overcome by the prospect of the pleasure afforded by the base action. Before arguing against this view, Socrates raises two questions. First, do "the Many" mean that the baseness of base actions consists in the fact that they are pleasurable or in the fact that, although momentarily pleasurable, they are ultimately productive of pain? Socrates and Protagoras agree that they mean the latter. However, they also believe that some painful things are good, for example, undergoing necessary surgery. This leads to the second question: Do they mean that the goodness of painful things consists in the fact that they are painful or in the fact that, although momentarily painful, they are ultimately productive of pleasure? Socrates and Protagoras again agree that they mean the latter. According to "the Many," people pursue pleasure as being good (ὡς ἀγαθὸν ὄν) and avoid pain as being bad (ὡς κακόν); and it is only with reference to something other than the pleasure or pain to which they lead that pleasure is called bad and pain good (354c4–5).

The dispute between Socrates and Protagoras, on the one hand, and "the Many," on the other, turns on this point. If the foregoing analysis is correct, it is absurd to say that people do what is bad, knowing it to be bad, because they are overcome by pleasure. The absurdity may be seen in the following way. Since things are good or bad insofar as they are pleasant or painful, it follows that we are not talking about four things – the good, the bad, the pleasant, and the painful – but about two things each of which can

---

[37] C. C. W. Taylor, 1976: 161, is mistaken in claiming that the text provides no connection between the foregoing discussion of the connection between courage and the other virtues and the ensuing discussion of hedonism.

be called by two names: "the good" or "the pleasant" and "the bad" or "the painful."[38] Given this equivalence of "the good" and "the pleasant" and "the bad" and "the painful," to say that people do what is bad, knowing it to be bad, because they are overcome by pleasure is to say that they do what is bad, knowing it to be bad, because they are overcome by good. To avoid this absurdity, "the Many" will ask whether those who do what is bad, knowing it to be bad, are overcome by good because the good is worth the ensuing evil or because it is not worth it. The answer, of course, is the latter. If the good were worth the ensuing evil, then, in being overcome, they would not have acted wrongly. However, "the Many" will reply that this is true only if the one is either greater and the other smaller or if the one is more and the other less, that is, only if those who are overcome attain a greater evil rather than a greater good. Socrates agrees that on this point "the Many" are right.

So far we have only been employing the first pair of terms, "the good" and "the bad." However, if we employ the second pair, "the pleasant" and "the painful," this reply is no longer possible. Instead of saying that people do what is bad, knowing it to be bad, let us say that they do what is painful, knowing it to be painful, because they are overcome by a pleasure which is not worth the ensuing pain. This unworthiness is either an excess or a defect, that is, the one is either greater and the other smaller or *vice versa*. If "the Many" say that the immediate pleasure is different from the subsequent pleasure, Socrates would agree; however, they are overlooking the fact that the difference is a difference *in pleasure or pain*. Weighed against each other, greater and more numerous pleasures are always preferable to lesser and fewer ones, just as lesser and fewer pains are always preferable to greater and more numerous ones. Hence if actions are weighed in the scale of pleasure and pain, everyone would always prefer the former to the latter. To this, Socrates concludes, "the Many" have no reply (356c2–3).

Human happiness depends on this art of measurement (ἡ μετρητικὴ τέχνη, 356d4). In claiming that knowledge is a fine and

---

[38] I follow C. C. W. Taylor, 1976: 179, according to whom the identity underlying the interchangeability of "the good" and "the pleasant" and "the bad" and "the painful" is not an identity of sense but an identity of reference, i.e., "good" and "pleasant" do not have the same meaning, but they are nevertheless extensionally equivalent.

powerful thing which cannot be dragged around by the passions like a slave, Socrates meant knowledge of this art. Those who do what is bad do so not because they are overcome by pleasure but because, lacking this art, they lack the knowledge necessary (and, presumably, sufficient) for making the right choices. In short, wrongdoing is the result of ignorance (ἀμαθίᾳ, 357e2). It follows that what "the Many" call "being overcome by pleasure" should actually be called "being overcome by ignorance." Since the pleasant is the good and the painful is the bad, and since no one prefers pain to pleasure, it follows that no one ever voluntarily does what he thinks bad (358d1–2). Just as it is not in human nature to prefer pain to pleasure, so also it is not in human nature to prefer evil to good. And when compelled to choose between two evils, no one will choose the greater if is it open to him to choose the lesser (358d2–4).

Although Socrates proceeds with great confidence, his argument is fallacious.[39] It is not the case that if A and B are the same, whatever is true of A is also necessarily true of B. In describing human actions, we need to take intentional contexts into account and remember that people believe, intend, desire, and do things under certain descriptions.[40] Thus if Paul believes that Cicero was a great orator, not knowing that Cicero is identical with Tully, it does not follow that he believes that Tully was a great orator. Similarly, if Melissa desires to smoke three packs of cigarettes a day, not knowing that heavy smoking causes lung cancer, it does not follow that she desires to get lung cancer. She desires to smoke large quantities of cigarettes under certain descriptions, for example, "source of pleasure," "enjoyable post-meal activity," and so on, but not under others, e.g., "probable cause of lung cancer," and "effective way of ending my life prematurely." In short, beliefs, intentions, desires, and actions may not legitimately be ascribed to people on the basis of descriptions they themselves would reject. To suppose otherwise is illegitimately to substitute

[39] The fallacy is widely recognized but variously labelled: "the fallacy of quantifying in psychological contexts" (Vlastos, 1991: 150), "the fallacy of misapplying the principle of the identity of indiscernibles to intentional mental acts" (C. C. W. Taylor, 1976: 180–81).

[40] My use of the concept of desiring under a description, and the related distinction between the intended and the actual object of a desire, is borrowed from Anscombe, 1963: 66: "We must always remember that an object is not what is aimed at *is*; the description *under which* it is aimed at is that under which it is *called* the object."

one intentional context for another, thereby arguing fallaciously. Socrates' argument is fallacious for precisely this reason. In claiming that "the pleasant" and "the painful" are simply alternative names for "the good" and "the bad," he illegitimately substitutes one intentional context for another.

Irwin[41] disagrees. According to his analysis, the hedonic equation of the pleasant and the good licenses Socrates' substitution because he has "made sure" that "the Many" accept the premises needed to refute their belief in *akrasia*. Unlike Melissa, who smokes large quantities of cigarettes, not believing that heavy smoking causes lung cancer, "the Many" *do* believe that the things they desire are pleasant and that pleasure is the highest good. Since this is so, Socrates can non-fallaciously substitute "good" for "pleasant." Is Irwin right?

He is not. For one thing, it is not clear that "the Many" really believe the premises which Socrates has "made sure" they "accept." But even if they do, it does not follow that anyone who desires what is pleasant desires what is good – much less that, in being overcome by pleasure, he is overcome by good. Even if Melissa desires to smoke large quantities of cigarettes, *believing* that heavy smoking causes lung cancer, this does not entail that she *desires* to get lung cancer. One might as well argue that the early Christians who desired to remain true to their faith, believing that doing so would cause them to be devoured by lions, entails that they desired to be devoured by lions. Melissa smokes for the sake of the pleasure it affords, believing that heavy smoking can cause lung cancer, but hoping that, in her case, it will not. Any adequate philosophy of action must distinguish between the action(s) a person intends to be performing (and sees himself as performing) and other action(s) which, given his beliefs, intentions, and desires, may be wrongly ascribed to him. Seated directly in front of you at the theater, I prevent you from seeing the stage. However, if you complain that I am blocking your view, I do not say, "I know, that is why I am sitting here"; I say, "Excuse me, I had no idea." Although I was, in fact, blocking your view, I was not performing the action of blocking your view (if there is such an action). I was merely sitting there waiting for the play to begin.

[41] 1995: 83–84.

Even if Socrates had shown that knowledge is a fine and power-ful thing which cannot be overcome by pleasure, he would still not have justified his more general claim that knowledge cannot be overcome by passion, pain, love, fear, *or anything else* (ὑπὸ τῶν ἄλλων ἁπάντων, 352c2). Insofar as the present argument focuses exclusively on pleasure, it ignores all these other potential knowl-edge overcomers.

Again abruptly changing the subject, Socrates asks Prodicus whether there is such a thing as the expectation of something bad – whether one calls it "apprehension," "dread," "fear," or any-thing else. He does. He also agrees that no one pursues what he fears when it is open to him to do the opposite; for to fear some-thing is to judge it bad, and no one voluntarily pursues what he judges bad.

The discussion suddenly takes an ominous turn. If the foregoing claims are true, how could Protagoras be right in claiming that although wisdom, temperance, justice, and piety resemble each other quite closely, courage is very different in that there are many people who are ignorant, intemperate, unjust, and impious, and yet very courageous? Having asked this question, the philosopher with the notoriously "poor memory" repeats almost *verbatim* Pro-tagoras' argument in support of this contention and asks whether he remembers having said this. He does. It does not take unusual perceptiveness to realize that trouble lies ahead.

Continuing his ominous line of questioning, Socrates asks whether Protagoras thinks the courageous and the cowardly are bold with respect to the same things? He does not. "With respect to different things then?" Socrates methodically inquires, leaving no logical stone unturned. "Yes." "What different things? Do the cowardly pursue things about which they are confident whereas the courageous pursue things about which they are fearful?" Pro-tagoras hedges: "So people say." Socrates does not care what "people" say. What does Protagoras say? (The sincere assent re-quirement is suddenly operative again.) Do the courageous pursue fearful things, *believing* them to be fearful, or do they pursue things which are *not* fearful? The second disjunct is ambiguous. Is Soc-rates asking whether the courageous pursue things which are *not* fearful or things which they *believe* are not fearful? The Greek pre-serves the ambiguity: do the courageous pursue ἐπὶ τὰ δεινά, ἡγουμένους δεινὰ εἶναι) or ἐπὶ τὰ μή (359d2)? Protagoras' response removes it: "By what you have just said (ἐν οἷς σὺ ἔλεγες τοῖς λόγοις), the former is impossible" (359d2–4). Interestingly, Socrates does not rebuke him on the ground that it was not he – Socrates – but his interlocutor – Protagoras – who advanced this claim. On the contrary, he says that Protagoras is right and concludes that if the foregoing argument is sound, no one pursues things which he *believes* (ἡγεῖται) to be fearful; on the contrary, everyone always pursues that about which they are confident. And if that is true, then it follows that the courageous and the cowardly pursue the same things (ἐπὶ τὰ αὐτά, 359d4–e1).

Stunned by this counterintuitive but apparently inexorable inference, Protagoras protests: surely the courageous and the cowardly do *not* pursue the same things; indeed, they pursue opposite things, for example, the former go willingly into battle whereas the latter do not. Socrates neither agrees nor disagrees. Instead, he advances an argument designed to prove that wisdom and courage are the same. The argument – 359e7–360e5 – is as follows:

(i)   The courageous go willingly into battle, which is noble and good – for whatever is noble is good.

(ii) But the cowardly do not.

(iii) Whatever is noble and good is also pleasant.

(iv) The cowardly are knowingly (γιγνώσκοντες) unwilling to pursue what is nobler, better, and more pleasant.

(v)   But the courageous always pursue these things.

(vi) The courageous have neither shameful fear nor shameful boldness; and whenever they are bold, their boldness is noble and good.

(vii) But the fear and boldness of the cowardly are shameful owing to their ignorance and error.

(viii) The cowardly are cowardly "by cowardice."

(ix) Moreover, they are cowardly because of their ignorance of what is (and is not) fearful.

(x)   Hence cowardice is ignorance of what is (and is not) fearful.

(xi) Courage and cowardice are opposites.

(xii) Hence wisdom, that is, knowledge, of what is (and is not) fearful is the opposite of ignorance of these things.

(xiii) And ignorance of what is (and is not) fearful is cowardice.

(xiv) Hence wisdom of what is (and is not) fearful is courage since it is the opposite of ignorance of these things.

(xv) Therefore it is impossible to be ignorant and courageous.

From which it follows that wisdom and courage are the same.

Of course, to schematize the argument in this way is to ignore the psychological dynamics between Socrates and Protagoras. Socrates' narration is generously sprinkled with self-congratulatory remarks about Protagoras' growing discomfiture. At first an eager participant in the discussion, he grows increasingly reluctant, lapsing into silence and simply nodding. He finally refuses even to nod. But Socrates will not be denied his pound of flesh. "What's this, Protagoras? Will you not say yes or no to my question?" "Answer it yourself," retorts the disgruntled sophist.[42] One more question: Does Protagoras still think people can be ignorant but exceptionally courageous? Protagoras accuses Socrates of arguing for victory but agrees to humor him (χαριοῦμαι) by giving the answer he wants: in view of their previous agreements (ἐκ τῶν ὡμολογημένων), this now seems to be impossible (360e3–5). And with this the discussion concludes.

Has Protagoras been refuted? He has not. Socrates' argument is unsound. It is not the case that no one ever pursues any course of action which he believes to be fearful, i.e., that everyone pursues those things and only those things about which they are confident. Protagoras is right: the courageous do pursue what they believe to be fearful, and the cowardly do not. Both know that the situation is fearful. Courage neither precludes nor banishes fear; on the contrary, being courageous and being fearful are perfectly compatible. Indeed, it is precisely because one is fearful that one needs courage – a virtue which enables the fearful to perform tasks from which they would otherwise shrink. A person who embarked on a course of action utterly devoid of fear would have no need of courage. The courageous go willingly into battle, not because they are fearless, but because they are courageous. The cowardly

---

[42] Even Vlastos, 1956: xxv, n. 4, confesses that by this point his sympathies "are wholly with Protagoras." Goldberg, 1983: 299–300, is more circumspect; whether one feels "a certain sympathy" for the defeated sophist depends on whether one agrees with Socrates or Protagoras. He adds that even if Socrates is rather hard on Protagoras, "perhaps he is still justified ... by the good he aims to do for Hippocrates."

shrink from battle, not because they are fearful, but because they are cowards. Courage is not the knowledge of what is to be feared and not feared; it is the resolution to do what must be done in spite of one's fear. Socrates' "intellectualist" view of courage invests it with a fear-dispelling power which it does not have and thereby confines the virtue of courage to precisely those people who have no need of it.

Furthermore, it is not the case that courage is wisdom and cowardice is ignorance. The cowardly are not those who are ignorant of what behavior is called for in any given situation. Nor are the courageous those who know what behavior is called for. If, at the beach, I notice that a child has been swept out by the tide and will surely drown unless I render aid but refuse to do so because of cowardice, would anyone say that my refusal is traceable to my ignorance of what I ought to do? Surely not. My refusal is not traceable to my lack of knowledge, but to my unwillingness to do what I perceive very clearly that I ought to do. Socrates' view of courage obscures this by defining courage in terms of knowledge of the long-range interest (or good) to be achieved. According to him, the courageous go willingly into battle because war is noble. Since whatever is noble is good, and since whatever is good is productive of pleasure, the courageous go willingly into battle for the sake of the pleasure it affords. The cowardly, on the other hand, are ignorant of the fact that going willingly into battle is noble. They are also ignorant of the fact that, by shrinking from battle and doing what is ignoble, they forfeit pleasure. However, were they to grasp this point, they too would go willingly into battle; for this knowledge would make them courageous. This is an implausible claim. Insofar as it construes courage as a form of knowledge – in particular, knowledge of what promotes the agent's long-range interests – it reduces courage to a means to an unabashedly egoistic end and thereby fails to explain why it is a virtue.

The implausibility of identifying courage with wisdom may also be seen by returning to the example of the drowning child. If, being both an expert swimmer for whom the sea holds no terrors and an unabashed hedonist who does what is noble and good because (and only because) it is productive of pleasure, I plunge into the raging surf and rescue the child, no one would praise me for my courage. And rightly so. My behavior was motivated by pure self-interest. According to Socrates, however, I *am* worthy of praise. Surely he is wrong. Having rescued a drowning child, the courageous person is praised for heroic conduct in the face of grave personal danger, not complimented for having maximized his long-range pleasure.[43]

Protagoras lodges none of these objections. Instead, he acquiesces to one dubious Socratic claim after another and finally lapses into silence. Savoring his apparent victory to the utmost and even pouring salt into Protagoras' dialectical wounds, Socrates wonders whether he still thinks that a person can lack all the other virtues but be courageous? Summoning his last ounce of civility, the sophist replies that, in view of his previous admissions, that now seems to be impossible, thereby tacitly acknowledging defeat in the presence of his long silent entourage which had so recently been enthralled by his apparent omnicompetence.

The dialectical gloom is minimally pierced by two tiny rays of Socratic "consolation." First, Socrates again assures Protagoras that his sole motive in conducting the investigation was to understand the relationship of the individual virtues to virtue and the nature of virtue itself. He had entered into the discussion believing that once these matters had been clarified, their disagreement about whether virtue can be taught could be resolved. However, he now recognizes that he had been guilty of an Epimethean-like blunder – the blunder of inadequate forethought. He had been proceeding with an inadequate philosophical methodology. Secondary questions about the relationships between the individual virtues and about whether virtue can be taught cannot be answered until one has answered the primary question of *what virtue is* (τὴν ἀρετὴν ὅτι ἔστιν, 361c5). The definitional question comes first. Until it has been answered, all other questions remain unanswerable (361c2–d6). Second, Protagoras is not the only person to have suffered a setback. So have "the Many." Indeed, so has Socrates. Whereas Protagoras entered the discussion believing

---

[43] Guthrie, 1975: 235, is one of the very few commentators who refuse to make excuses for Socrates and to find hidden virtues in his arguments. He acknowledges that the *Protagoras* often seems like "an irritating patchwork of niggling argument, irrelevant digressions, false starts, and downright fallacy." Having done so, however, he puzzlingly adds that, when read as a play in which the most outstanding and individual minds of a brilliant period engage in a battle of wits, which is how it should be read, it will give a different impression.

that virtue can be taught but now believes that it cannot, Socrates
entered the discussion believing that virtue cannot be taught but
now believes that it can. As a result of this reversal, both are pronounced "strange" (ἄτοποί) by the argument (τὸν λόγον) which
seems to be accusing and mocking (κατηγορεῖν τε καὶ καταγελᾶν)
them (361a3–6). Although Protagoras might have responded with
a threadbare smile, I cannot believe that he found this either terribly amusing or terribly consoling.

CHAPTER 14

Gorgias

The first of three increasingly intractable interlocutors in the dialogue which bears his name,[1] Gorgias the celebrated sophist[2] is visiting Athens and, as the dialogue begins,[3] has just completed an epideictic display. His audience includes his disciple Polus, a militant anti-democrat by the name of Callicles, and a crowd of anonymous auditors who periodically clamor for the discussion to continue and whose unobtrusive but ubiquitous presence[4] lends palpable concreteness to the dialogue's many allusions to shame (αἰσχύνη). Having arrived too late to enjoy this elegant "feast of words," Socrates blames Chaerephon for having lingered too long in the marketplace. In a misguided attempt to reinstate himself, Chaerephon offers to persuade Gorgias to give a repeat perfor-

---

[1] The similarity to *Republic* 1 has often been noted.

[2] The historical Gorgias was born *circa* 490 and reportedly lived to the ripe old age of 109 (Diogenes Laertius 8.58–59). A rhetorician and teacher of rhetoric, he was also the author of several treatises on the subject (of which fragments containing an encomium of Helen and a defense of Palamedes survive) as well as a more ambitious (but no longer extant) treatise entitled *On the Non-Existent*, or *On Nature*. Like many of the sophists, he was famous for his epideictic displays which he delivered in response to random questions from his audiences. Unlike the other sophists, however, he did not claim to be a teacher of virtue and laughed at those who did; he claimed only to make people clever speakers (*M.* 95c1–4) – a fact which prompts Dodds, 1959: 6–7; Canto, 1993: 27–30; and Irwin, 1995: 368, n. 8, to conclude that he was not a sophist at all. That Plato regarded him as one is clear from *HMa.* 282b4–5, where he is described as the sophist from Leontini, and from *Ap.* 19d8–20a2, where he is mentioned in the same breath as Prodicus and Hippias. As we have seen, Plato attached little importance to the difference between the rhetoricians and the sophists (*G.* 465c3–7, 520a6–8). For his real opinion of Gorgias, see *Phdr.* 267a6–b2 where he is numbered among those who love appearance more than truth and who make important things trivial and trivial things important by the power of speech. His vices are contagious: under his influence, Meno has fallen into the bad habit of answering questions confidently (*M.* 70b3–c3).

[3] Owing to its inconsistent historical allusions and occasional anachronisms, the *Gorgias* cannot be assigned a precise dramatic date. The possibilities range from 429 to 405. See A. E. Taylor, 1929: 104–5; Dodds, 1959: 17–18; and Irwin, 1979: 109–10.

[4] They are alluded to at 455c5–d1, 458b4–c2, 473e4–5, 487b5, and 490b1–2.

mance. But Socrates characteristically says that he would prefer a discussion to a speech,[5] for he is eager to understand the power (δύναμις) of Gorgias' art (τέχνη)[6] and to learn what he advertises and teaches (*G.* 447c1–4).[7] Since Gorgias has agreed to answer any question he is asked, Socrates instructs Chaerephon to ask Gorgias who he is (ὅστις ἐστίν, 447d1), that is, of which art he is the master.

But before he can do so, Polus intervenes to point out that Gorgias seems tired and suggests that Chaerephon question him instead. Perhaps suspecting that this intervention is prompted less by concern for the weary sophist than by the desire to outshine him, Chaerephon contentiously asks whether Polus thinks he can answer better than Gorgias. A flurry of petty personal and professional rivalry follows. Polus curtly retorts that it does not matter what he thinks so long as his answers are satisfactory. His irritation is understandable. After all, he never claimed that he could answer *better* than Gorgias. On the other hand, he does claim to know the same things that Gorgias knows (462a5–7), thereby implying that even if he does not regard himself as Gorgias' superior, he does regard himself as his equal. Chaerephon wisely drops the point and asks Polus to explain the nature of Gorgias' art and the name by which he should be called.

Having maneuvered himself into the spotlight, Polus insures his speedy exit by making a pompous and singularly uninteresting speech in which he notes that there are many *technai* which have been experientially devised by mankind – for experience guides our lives along the path of art whereas inexperience leads us along the path of chance – but of all the arts which can be learned and practiced by human beings, none is finer than Gorgias'. Socrates compliments Polus on his ability to make speeches but complains that he has not answered Chaerephon's question: instead of ex-

---

[5] Here as elsewhere, the distinction between a discussion (διάλεκτος) and a speech (μακρο-λογία) should be taken with a grain of salt. It is an exaggeration to say that in the *Gorgias* "sophistic rhetoric must justify itself before the bar of philosophy" (Friedländer, 1964, II: 248).

[6] Although Socrates later denies that rhetoric is a *technē* and demotes it to the status of a mere knack (ἐμπειρίαν, 462b6–c7), he describes it as a *technē* throughout the discussion with Gorgias.

[7] The sophists were very competitive and advertised their specialties in hopes of luring pupils away from their colleagues. Each found something grievously lacking in the others. Protagoras judged himself superior on the ground that he taught his pupils only what they wanted to know (*Pr.* 318d7–319a2). Gorgias' disavowal of being a teacher of virtue is also an implicit criticism of his more pretentious colleagues.

plaining Gorgias' art, he has merely praised it, thereby confusing what a thing *is* (τίς ... ὄντινα) with what it is *like* (ποία τις, 448e6–7). The point is lost on Polus, but the far-from-weary Gorgias rises to his disciple's defense and briskly suggests that, in that case, perhaps Socrates had better question Polus himself. Pouring fuel on the fire, Socrates retorts that since that Polus is obviously more skilled at rhetoric than at dialectic, he would rather question Gorgias, thereby unceremoniously dismissing the disciple from the discussion and irresistibly luring the master into it. Taking over for Chaerephon, Socrates puts the same questions to Gorgias who replies that he is skilled in the art of rhetoric and should, therefore, be called a rhetorician – a good one, he might add. He is equally skilled in making rhetoricians of others.

Perhaps fearing another "feast of words," Socrates asks whether Gorgias would be willing to dispense with speeches and to proceed by way of question-and-answer, "reminding" him that he had agreed to give brief answers to any question he was asked. Brevity, of course, was no part of Gorgias' original offer and he spots the addition at once, rightly pointing out that some questions require longer answers than others. However, he promises to be as brief as possible; for it is yet another of his many claims to fame that, however unsurpassed he may be at making long speeches, he is equally unsurpassed at making short ones.[8]

Since Gorgias has been severely censured, *inter alia*, for his "complacency," "pomposity," and "naive vanity,"[9] it is worth pausing for some preliminary stocktaking. An interlocutor's defects should not be swept under the rug, but neither should they be exaggerated and magnified out of all proportion. Although hardly a modest man, Gorgias need not be taken as advancing the foregoing claims arrogantly. However vain and self-congratulatory they might be in the mouth of an Ion or a Hippias, coming from the older and more seasoned Gorgias they seem more like expressions of supreme self-confidence – a very different thing from arrogance. If Gorgias had a big ego, he also had a big reputation. That his admittedly extravagant claims about himself are not idle

---

[8] At *Pr.* 329b1–5 and 334e4–335a3 Socrates ascribes the same two-fold ability – Dodds, 1959: 195, calls it the same "dual pretension" – to Protagoras.

[9] Dodds, 1959: 9. Dodds adds that Plato exposes Gorgias' character defects "by a series of small malicious touches" (194). Annas, 1981: 19, uses the same phrase to describe Plato's portrayal of Cephalus.

boasting is borne out by the fact that he can point to a long string
of sold-out performances and the enthusiastic testimonials of
countless transported and bewitched audiences. Accordingly, we
should not be too hard on Gorgias. Success is often as hard to
cope with as failure – sometimes harder. Gorgias' potentially off-
putting but, in themselves, harmless and (to the charitable eye)
endearing personal shortcomings are but a few of the many perils
of celebrity which have overtaken many others, before and since,
whose extraordinary talents but very ordinary characters have
rendered them unduly susceptible to admiration – not to mention
self-admiration.

At this point, the formal interrogation begins. Since Gorgias is
skilled in the art of rhetoric, it is important to be clear about the
subject matter with which it is concerned. Weaving is concerned
with making clothing, music with composing melodies. With what
is rhetoric concerned? With speech (περὶ λόγους), replies Gorgias
(449e1). Although his answer seems unobjectionable, Socrates finds
it hopelessly vague. What *kind* of speech? Surely not the kind
which enables the sick to get well, for that is the concern of the
doctor. Indeed, insofar as the various *technai* enable their practitioners to talk about the subject matter that falls under them, they
are all concerned "with speech." Gorgias has a reply. Unlike the
other *technai*, which make little (or no) use of speech and accomplish their ends wholly (or almost wholly) by means of manual
skills, rhetoric accomplishes its ends wholly by means of speech.
Socrates explains that while this is true of some *technai*, for example, painting and sculpture, it is not true of others, such as arithmetic and geometry. But surely Gorgias would not apply the term
"rhetoric" to them. So, again, how does he distinguish rhetoric
from these *technai*? Undaunted, Gorgias replies that rhetoric is concerned with what is greatest and best in human affairs (τὰ μέγιστα
τῶν ἀνθρωπείων πραγμάτων ... καὶ ἄριστα, 451d7–8).

At first glance, it seems that he has made the same mistake as
Polus. But if identical errors by Socratic interlocutors elicit identical objections from Socrates, that is not the case. For Socrates'
complaint is not that Gorgias has praised rhetoric instead of explaining it, but rather that his answer is unclear and debatable
(451d9–e1). There is wide disagreement about what is greatest and
best in human affairs – doctors think it is health, trainers think it is
a strong and beautiful body – and hence there is correspondingly

wide disagreement about the *technē* that produces it. Can Gorgias justify his contention that this coveted title belongs to rhetoric?

Gorgias asserts that the greatest good (μέγιστον ἀγαθόν) is the power of persuasive speech – in the lawcourts, the Assembly, or wherever people gather. The persuasive speaker gains freedom for himself and control over others; indeed, he has the power to make them his slaves. Rhetoric is supreme among the arts because it is the source of this power.[10] Socrates thereupon defines rhetoric as a producer of persuasion (πειθοῦς δημιουργός, 453a2) and adds that it has no other function. Gorgias accepts the definition.

A brief interlude follows during which Socrates interrupts his interrogation of Gorgias in order to describe himself and to explain his reason for engaging in philosophical debate. He is, he confides, a truth-seeker interested in understanding the subject under discussion – or so he persuades himself (ὡς ἐμαυτὸν πείθω, 453a8–b1) – and he hopes Gorgias is the same kind of man. His problem is this. Gorgias has agreed that rhetoric is a producer of persuasion, but he has not explained what *kind* of persuasion it produces or the subjects with which it is concerned. Although Socrates thinks he knows how Gorgias would answer these questions, he does not want to put words into his mouth and would prefer that he answer for himself:

It's not you I'm after, it's our discussion (τοῦ λόγου), to have it proceed in such a way as to make the thing we're talking about the most clear to us. (453c2–4)[11]

Dodds[12] thinks such passages reveal that Socrates is primarily concerned with the discovery of truth and that the refutation of the interlocutor is "incidental." I think Dodds is wrong about this. As we will see, Polus has a much clearer insight into what Socrates is up to in the discussion with Gorgias.

More questions follow. If someone described Zeuxis as a figure painter, it would be fair to ask what kind of figures he depicts; for other painters depict other kinds. Similarly, since rhetoric is not the only producer of persuasion, and since other *technai* produce other kinds (e.g., arithmetic produces persuasion about number),

---

[10] That the historical Gorgias held the same view is clear from *Philebus* 58a6–b3.

[11] Cf. *Ch.* 166c7–d4 where Socrates also claims to be pursuing the argument chiefly for his own sake, lest he falsely suppose that he knows something when he does not.

[12] 1959: 204.

it is also fair to ask what kind of persuasion rhetoric produces and about what?

There are obvious objections to both questions which do not occur to Gorgias – or, rather, which Plato does not put into his mouth. Instead of granting their legitimacy, Gorgias should have distinguished the art of speech-making from the subject matter spoken about. Armed with this distinction, he could have explained that rhetoric is content-independent and content-neutral: it is concerned with speech *qua* speech, not with speech *qua* vehicle for the communication of specific information. He could have then pointed out that the rhetorician *qua* rhetorician is not concerned with any specific subject matter and, therefore, does not have any specific substantive expertise; he simply teaches people to be better speakers and leaves the choice of subject matter to them – hardly a sinister enterprise. In short, there is a sense in which rhetoric *is* uniquely concerned "with speech." As we have seen in the chapter on Hippocrates, from the truism that all speech must be *about something*, it does not follow that the rhetorician must teach people to speak effectively *about something* and that he must, therefore, be an expert on that subject. In asking Gorgias to specify the subject matter peculiar to rhetoric, Socrates sends him on a wild goose chase. The unique subject matter he has been asked to identify does not exist.[13]

Instead of exposing the illegitimacy of Socrates' questions, Gorgias tries to answer them. He answers the first by repeating his earlier claim that rhetoric produces the kind of persuasion found in the lawcourts and other public forums; he answers the second by asserting that rhetoric is concerned with what is just and unjust (454b5–7). Socrates thereupon confesses that his suspicions have been confirmed. That is exactly what he thought Gorgias would say, but he wanted to be sure:

I'm asking questions so that we can conduct an orderly discussion. It's not you I'm after; it's to prevent our getting in the habit of second-guessing and snatching each other's statements away ahead of time. It's to allow you to work out your assumption in any way you want to. (454c2–5)

---

[13] See Vickers, 1988: 125: "Plato gives an account of his opponents' philosophy which is sufficiently detailed and close enough to its actual content as to make it seem reliable, yet he does so in such a way as to rob the original of its validity."

This ostensibly benevolent expression of goodwill towards Gorgias, yet another apparent indication of the importance of the sincere assent requirement, should be noted carefully – especially in view of the fact that Socrates will soon induce Gorgias to affirm propositions which he does not believe and thereby to contradict himself.

Having discovered the kind of persuasion Gorgias thinks rhetoric produces, Socrates sets out to discredit it. He begins by getting him to agree that there is a difference between learning something (μεμαθηκέναι) and believing something (πεπιστευκέναι) – a difference reflected by the fact that although there is such a thing as false belief (πίστις), there is no such thing as false knowledge (ἐπιστήμη). Yet the state of mind called "being persuaded" is common to those who know and those who believe. It seems, then, that there are two kinds of persuasion: the first produces belief without knowledge (πίστιν ... ἄνευ τοῦ εἰδέναι), the second produces knowledge (ἐπιστήμην, 454d1–e4).[14] Rhetoric produces the first kind. But if that is so, then the rhetorician does not inculcate knowledge about what is just and unjust; he merely inculcates belief. Gorgias concurs.

However, he should have protested. From the fact that the rhetorician does not inculcate knowledge about what is just and unjust, it does not follow that he inculcates belief and, therefore, produces persuasion without knowledge. The Athenian Assembly was not a gathering place for idiots who had no idea of what was going on and no knowledge of the issues about which the rhetoricians would try to persuade them. Many citizens were deeply immersed in Athenian political life and well informed about the issues. As a result, it was not necessary for the rhetoricians to pro-

[14] Dodds, 1959: 206, rightly notes that the Platonic distinction between knowledge and belief is "here formally drawn for the first time." However, in the early dialogues "knowledge" (ἐπιστήμη) and "belief" (πίστις or δόξα) are not technical epistemic terms which connote greater or lesser cognitive achievements on the part of their possessors and correspondingly greater and lesser degrees of epistemic reliability on the part of the propositions they affirm. In the *Crito* Socrates distinguishes between knowledge and belief, but only to remind Crito that he should ignore the unstable opinions of "the Many" and attend only to those who know and understand (τῷ ἐπιστάτῃ καὶ ἐπαΐοντι, 47a7–b11). Far from propounding an important epistemic distinction, he is simply trying to dispel Crito's worries about how his reputation will suffer among Athenian rumormongers chattering about his failure to arrange Socrates' escape from prison. In the *Gorgias* he employs the terms "knowledge" and "belief" to draw an equally non-technical distinction between two kinds of persuasion.

vide them with knowledge. Their task was not to instruct the citizenry, but to persuade it.[15] The historical Gorgias – an experienced and savvy public figure – would surely have registered this protest, but Plato's character, "dialectician's dummy that he is,"[16] placidly acquiesces in Socrates' parody.

The exchange between Socrates and Gorgias might very well have ended here. After all, from Socrates' point of view, what could be a more damaging objection to rhetoric than a rhetorician's admission that he inculcates belief *without* knowledge? But Socrates is not finished with Gorgias. Having impugned the epistemic status of the state of mind produced by the rhetorician, he next impugns his competence to speak authoritatively about anything in the first place. His reasoning, virtually identical to that which he employs against Protagoras at *Pr.* 319b5–d7, is as follows. When city planners deliberate about matters of public policy, for example, the building or fortifying of walls or harbors, they never solicit the advice of rhetoricians, but always consult skilled experts. So why *do* people consult Gorgias? About what *is* he competent to give advice? Only about what is just and unjust? Or about other matters as well? And if so, what other matters? This line of questioning is designed to demonstrate by the process of elimination that there is no subject matter which could possibly constitute Gorgias' area of expertise.

But Gorgias does not play into Socrates' hands. Unlike Protagoras, who concedes the point, Gorgias asserts that Socrates is wrong. As a matter of fact, people *do* consult rhetoricians about these matters. Has Socrates forgotten that massive public reconstruction was undertaken in response to the advice of Themistocles and Pericles?

Socrates' response is surprising. Having just denied that city planners consult rhetoricians about matters of public policy, he now admits that they do and implores Gorgias to explain the enormous power of rhetoric which suddenly strikes him as some-

---

[15] Vickers, 1988: 92, points out that no competent rhetorician would ever accept the claim that rhetoric inculcates belief without knowledge, and argues that Gorgias should have protested on the ground that, unlike the practitioners of the other *technai*, rhetoricians do not persuade by communicating information, but by "moving the will." Similar considerations are urged by Irwin, 1979: 117, 124.

[16] Vickers, 1988: 95. The language is strong, but the point is well taken.

thing superhuman (δαιμονία ... τις, 456a5). Oblivious to the irony, Gorgias obligingly explains that the power of rhetoric surpasses that of every other art. As proof of this, he recounts how he has persuaded many recalcitrant medical patients to undergo necessary surgery – something that many doctors, including his own brother, often cannot do. And he accomplishes this by no art other than that of rhetoric. Indeed, so great is the power of rhetoric that if a rhetorician and a doctor were to compete before the Assembly for the position of doctor, the rhetorician would win every time. The same thing would happen were he to compete for any other position. For there is no subject about which the rhetorician cannot speak more persuasively before a crowd (ἐν πλήθει, 456c4–6).

Having extolled the extraordinary power of rhetoric, Gorgias adds an important disclaimer. Although rhetoricians are capable of using their art for unjust purposes or personal gain, they ought not. Like every competitive skill (ἀγωνία), rhetoric has its proper uses. Just as boxers, wrestlers, and hoplites acquire their skills to be used against opponents and enemies and not against people indiscriminately, so also rhetoricians acquire their skills to be used properly. And just as it would be ludicrous to blame a boxing trainer if one of his pupils were subsequently to use his pugilistic prowess against his mother or father, thereby misusing the art of boxing, so also it would be ludicrous to blame a rhetorician if one of his pupils were subsequently to use his rhetorical skills for unjust purposes, thereby misusing the art of rhetoric. For the rhetorician imparted these skills to be used justly (ἐπὶ τῷ δικαίως χρῆσθαι, 456e3). In short, it is neither the teachers of these *technai* nor the *technai* themselves which are base and blameworthy, but those who do not use them rightly (οἱ μὴ χρώμενοι ... ὀρθῶς, 457a3–4). Ascriptions of blame for the misuse of a *technē* should be reserved for those who misuse it.

Inexplicably, it is often alleged that, in making this speech, Gorgias reveals that he has no interest in morality and merely imparts the "weapons"[17] of his trade, disclaiming responsibility for their subsequent conduct. Thus Friedländer[18] gravely observes that Gorgias "bears the stamp of *adikia* even though he is not con-

---

[17] The term is A. E. Taylor's, 1929: 109.
[18] 1964, II: 244.

sistent enough to admit that he belongs to the sphere of the law-less." Dodds goes much further:

> Gorgias puts a deadly instrument into unscrupulous hands for the cor-ruption of simple people who are morally only children. That is why the dialogue is called *Gorgias*, not *Callicles*: Gorgias' teaching is the seed of which the Calliclean way of life is the poisonous fruit.[19]

These somewhat overwrought assessments rely heavily on the first part of Gorgias' speech, in which he acknowledges that rhetoric can be used for unjust purposes or personal gain, but they ignore the second part, in which he denounces these misuses of his art. No one denies that rhetoric can be misused. And it is possible to cite passages from Gorgias' extant fragments which praise rhetoric for its power to persuade individuals and political bodies by means of dubious arguments – or non-arguments – and equally dubious rhetorical techniques. However, the issue is not whether rhetoric admits of abuse or whether the historical Gorgias advocated abus-ing it, but whether this is an accurate description of Plato's char-acter. The answer is that it is not. What he admires, practices, and urges his pupils to practice is not the ability to persuade *simpliciter*, considered in a moral vacuum and to be employed however they see fit, but the ability to persuade within the limits imposed by justice.[20] His remarks about ascriptions of blame need to be un-derstood in this light.[21] Having imparted the requisite skills and having exhorted his pupils to use them properly, the responsible rhetorician has done all that can reasonably be expected of him. In saying that the blame for misuses of rhetoric should be ascribed to those who misuse it rather than to their teachers, Gorgias is not "disclaiming responsibility" for his pupils' subsequent behavior; on the contrary, he is assigning responsibility to the true culprits. This is an eminently reasonable claim. A competent and conscien-tious instructor of rhetoric is no more responsible for his pupils' subsequent rhetorical violations than a competent and conscien-

---

[19] 1959: 15. Similar charges are levelled by A. E. Taylor, 1929: 109; Shorey, 1933: 135–36; Kahn, 1983: 84; Teloh, 1986: 140–41; and Rutherford, 1995: 142.

[20] A. E. Taylor, 1929: 109, grudgingly acknowledges that it is "important" to Gorgias that his pupils use rhetoric properly even though he does not explicitly teach them to do so. For more sympathetic estimates of Gorgias, see Guthrie, 1971a: 271; Irwin, 1979: 124–26; and Rankin, 1983: 43.

[21] Grote, 1867, II: 93, is one of the few commentators to have recognized this.

tious driving instructor is responsible for his pupils' subsequent traffic violations.[22]

Socrates takes no notice of this impassioned plea for the right use of rhetoric. He does not applaud Gorgias for the integrity with which he practices his art and for the determination with which he tries to inculcate it in his pupils. Nor does he acknowledge that Gorgias' distinction between just and unjust uses of rhetoric reveals that his own generic view of the sophists as unscrupulous practitioners of eristic who are uninterested in truth and argue for victory at any cost is overgeneralized and in need of qualification. Instead, he changes the subject. Again taking Gorgias aside, he confides that, as an experienced debater, he has noticed that people often have trouble expressing themselves clearly and, when criticized for their lack of clarity, they tend to become angry and to accuse their critic of contentiousness (φιλονικοῦντας, 457d4). This, he thinks, is unfortunate. For to resist criticism is to deprive oneself of one the chief services of philosophy. A Socratic meditation on the benefits of refutation follows.

Whenever Socrates waxes eloquent about the benefits of refutation, we can be sure that an interlocutor is about to be refuted. Although he usually prefaces an elenchus with elaborate assurances that refutation is the furthest thing from his mind, that is not the case here. In a rare display of strategic candor, he tells Gorgias that what he has just said does not seem to be entirely consistent or in accord with (οὐ πάνυ ἀκόλουθα ... οὐδὲ σύμφωνα, 457e2)[23] what he said earlier; however, he is reluctant to continue for fear that Gorgias will think he is being contentious. Accordingly, if the discussion is to continue, he must be assured that Gorgias is the same kind of man as he – a man who is happy to refute others if they say something false, but no less happy to be refuted himself if he says something false because it is a greater

---

[22] Irwin, 1995: 98, disagrees on the ground that Gorgias' admission that his pupils might use rhetoric for unjust purposes proves that his instruction about what is just and unjust "does not count as even trying to ensure" that they will use it justly. This is a puzzling claim. Does Irwin mean that a teacher's instruction counts as "trying" if and only if his pupils never disobey it? By that criterion, no teacher has ever tried to impart instruction to anyone.

[23] Following Robinson, 1953: 29, Irwin, 1979: 128, notes that Plato's logical vocabulary is "not sharp or specialized" and that it is, therefore, unclear whether Socrates is accusing Gorgias of straightforward self-contradiction or of some "looser mis-match."

good to be delivered of a false belief oneself than to deliver someone else of a false belief. So if Gorgias is the same kind of man,
the discussion may continue; but if he is not, it should be dropped.
Gorgias announces that he is indeed the same kind of man and
that he would like very much to continue the discussion – provided
that it will not tax the patience or the endurance of the others
present.[24] A spontaneous outburst of collective enthusiasm reveals
that his worries are groundless.

After all this fanfare about the benefits of refutation, it is surprising that Socrates does not try to demonstrate Gorgias' alleged
inconsistency until almost four Stephanus pages later. Instead, he
prefaces his elenchus by acknowledging that he might be taking
Gorgias' meaning in the wrong way (οὐκ ὀρθῶς ὑπολαμβάνω,
458e4–5)[25] – a significant remark to which I will return. He then
primes him for refutation by eliciting a series of admissions. Gorgias has said that he can make a rhetorician of anyone who comes
to him for instruction and that such a person will be able to produce conviction in his hearers about any subject: not by instruction, but by persuasion, for example, he will be able to speak more
persuasively about health than a doctor. Gorgias reaffirms this
claim, but again emphasizes that what he means is that a rhetorician can speak more persuasively than a doctor (or any other
practitioner of a *technē*) to a crowd (ἐν ... ὄχλῳ, 459a3).

By a "crowd," Gorgias means what people ordinarily mean – a
large group of people assembled together in one place – in the
lawcourts, the Assembly, or wherever people gather (452e1–4).
Defining a familiar and apparently harmless term like "crowd"
may seem like a paradigm case of belaboring the obvious, but it is
not. Socrates often refutes his interlocutors by employing familiar
terms but stripping them of their ordinary meanings and investing
them with very different ones. These subtle (and almost always
undetected) shifts of meaning predictably spell trouble for his
interlocutors. Gorgias is a particularly instructive example. Depriving the term "crowd" of its emotively neutral meaning and

---

[24] Even expressions of courtesy on the part of Socrates' interlocutors elicit criticism from
many commentators. Teloh, 1986: 134, thinks this remark reveals that Gorgias "values
rest over truth," while Rutherford, 1995: 142, thinks it is "probable" that Gorgias is trying to "ease out of the discussion without losing face."

[25] Lamb, 1925: 251, thinks that in this passage Socrates "hints" that he may not be treating
Gorgias fairly – a hint which is later confirmed when Polus protests the "unfair treatment of his master."

replacing it with a highly pejorative one, he redefines "crowd" as "those who do not have knowledge" (τοῖς μὴ εἰδόσιν), i.e., the ignorant masses (459a4). For surely, he adds, the rhetorician will not be able to speak more persuasively than a doctor to those who *do* have knowledge, that is, to other doctors, conveniently neglecting to point out that this redefinition logically commits him to defining "those who *do* have knowledge" as "those who avoid large groups of people assembled together in one place and congregate in small groups" – an implication which, however preposterous, is exactly the sort of entailment relation he himself would bring to light were one of his interlocutors to advance such a definition.

Armed with this redefinition of "crowd," Socrates interprets Gorgias as claiming that he who does not know (ὁ οὐκ εἰδώς) is more persuasive to those who do not know (οὐκ εἰδόσι) than he who does know (τοῦ εἰδότος, 459b3–4). More bluntly, the rhetorician is an ignorant man who dupes other ignorant men. Gorgias lamely concedes that, in the case of the doctor, that does seem to be the case. But he is in deeper water than he thinks. For Socrates now formulates this claim in full generality. Since, according to Gorgias, there is no subject about which the rhetorician cannot speak more persuasively than the practitioners of the corresponding *technai*, it follows that the rhetorician needs no substantive expertise whatever; all he needs is some persuasive device (μηχανὴν ... τινα πειθοῦς) which enables him to *seem* (φαίνεσθαι) to know more than those who do know (459b8–c2). In short, rhetoric is a "device" by which the non-expert passes himself off as an expert.[26]

Few rhetoricians would be happy with this account of rhetoric.[27] That Gorgias is not altogether happy with it is clear from the fact that he neither agrees nor disagrees, but simply wonders out loud whether it does not make things very simple (πολλὴ ῥᾳστώνη, 459c3) to be able to prevail over everyone by acquiring a single art. A more discerning interlocutor would have seen through Socrates' caricature of rhetoric as the art of seeming and of the rhet-

---

[26] Wardy, 1996: 72, mistakenly claims that Socrates deduces this conclusion "using only material supplied by Gorgias himself." As we will see, this conclusion is based on a tendentious misinterpretation of the "material" supplied by Gorgias.

[27] Vickers, 1988: viii, calls Plato "rhetoric's most influential enemy" and complains bitterly about his "violent travesty" of the subject which continues to influence "a majority of classicists and philosophers today." His book abounds with strong but eminently just criticism which should be pondered by all students of Plato.

orician as a seemer.[28] It is blatantly false to say that the rhetorician
exploits the ignorance of his audience by seeming, i.e., pretending, to know what he does not know. To say this is tantamount to
saying that rhetoric is dishonest in principle and that the rhetorician is similarly dishonest and motivated by the desire to deceive.
No one denies that some rhetoricians use their art for unjust purposes. Surely Gorgias does not deny it. But he believes that rhetoric itself is a noble art. Although unable to diagnose what is wrong
with Socrates' caricature, he rightly shrinks from the odious and
patently false implication that rhetoric is, by its very nature, a
form of seeming – a mask for falsity and pretense. He knows perfectly well that when he persuades his brother's medical patients
to undergo necessary surgery, he is neither trying to deceive them
nor pretending to know more than a doctor – much less pretending to *be* one.

More can be said on Gorgias' behalf. In saying that the rhetorician persuades by means of a single art, he is not driving a wedge
between rhetoric and morality; he is not even driving a wedge between rhetoric and the other *technai*. Socrates systematically overlooks the fact that although rhetoric has no specific subject matter
peculiar to itself, it is parasitic on the subject matter which falls
under those *technai*. The mere fact that the rhetorician has no substantive expertise *qua* rhetorician does not entail that he is universally ignorant *qua* human being. Nothing prevents him from
drawing upon the knowledge and expertise of others. Accordingly,
having discussed a recalcitrant patient's medical needs with a doctor, the rhetorician may try to persuade him to follow the doctor's
advice and undergo necessary surgery. To accomplish this, he
need not possess medical expertise himself; he need only consult
someone who has it and then try to effect persuasion. In doing so,
he is not a "seemer" devoid of every shred of integrity. Nor, *pace*
Socrates and legions of commentators, is he inculcating belief
without knowledge, thereby effecting (or trying to effect) persuasion in the patient without "proper grounds."[29] On the contrary,

[28] See Vickers, *ibid.*: 114–15: "This withholding of intelligence from Socrates' interlocutors
is something that any critical reader of Plato will have noticed." Cf. Poulakos, 1995: 78–
79: Plato "dresses [the sophists] up as incompetent dialecticians and ... denies them
their own intellectual identity and power. In their Platonic costumes, [they] are un-
recognizable and impotent because they are out of their element." For a more massive
critique, see Havelock, 1957: chs. 4, 7–9 *passim*.
[29] The terminology is Dilman's, 1979: 16.

he is providing the patient with the best possible grounds, namely, the authority of the doctor. Insofar as he succeeds in effecting persuasion, he does not cheat the patient by offering him a "semblance" of knowledge. Indeed, since the patient has already consulted with the doctor, he already knows what he must do to improve his condition. What he needs is not more *knowledge*, but someone to persuade him to act on the knowledge he already has. Gorgias is right: to effect persuasion in a patient, the rhetorician needs no art other than that of rhetoric – provided that he has previously consulted a doctor.

Deprived of these replies which would have rendered Socrates' criticisms impotent,[30] Gorgias is maneuvered into the awkward position of being the spokesman for, and the practitioner of, what is starting to look more and more like a pseudo-art – a mere knack (ἐμπειρίαν), as Socrates will soon describe it (462c3) – which is indifferent to truth and licenses clever ignorant men to deceive unclever ignorant ones. With his interlocutor now on the defensive, Socrates relentlessly presses his advantage by unleashing a cumulative barrage of questions – all of them heavily freighted with allusions to "seeming" and calculated to reinforce his earlier allegation of pretense and fraud: Does the rhetorician stand in the same dubious epistemic relation to what is just and unjust, noble and base, and good and bad? Need he know nothing about them either and merely employ other persuasive "devices" which enable him to *seem* knowledgeable to the ignorant? Or must he know something about them? And what about his pupils? If they do not know about these things, will he teach them? Or, since that is not part of his perceived task (οὐ γὰρ σὸν ἔργον, 459e4) – a subtle allusion to Gorgias' disavowal of being a teacher of virtue (*M.* 95c1–4) – will he merely teach them to *seem* to know (δοκεῖν εἰδέναι) what is just and unjust and, therefore, to *seem* to be good when, in fact, they are not (459c8–460a2)?

Gorgias is caught off guard by these questions and momentarily loses his poise. It is not clear why. In view of the highly publicized fact that he did not profess to be a teacher of virtue, the answers seem perfectly obvious. We expect him to say: "No. It is not necessary for the rhetorician to know these things, and I do not claim

---

[30] "The puppets are kept well under control," quips Vickers, 1988: 115, with characteristic but understandable pique.

to know them. Nor do I teach my pupils these things; I just teach them rhetoric." But he does not say this. Instead, he says: "Well ... I suppose that if [a pupil] really doesn't have this knowledge, he'll learn these things from me as well" (460a3–4) – thereby apparently contradicting himself.

I say "apparently" because there is no scholarly consensus about this. Commentators disagree: not only about whether Gorgias contradicts himself, but also about what the alleged contradiction is and how it is generated. According to Dodds[31] and Kahn,[32] he does contradict himself and his contradiction is two-fold: (i) his admission that he imparts moral instruction to pupils who lack it flatly contradicts his disavowal of being a teacher of virtue (*M.* 95c1–4); and (ii) it is also inconsistent with his (alleged) disclaimer of responsibility for their subsequent misuses of rhetoric. In offering this analysis, they follow Polus who thinks Gorgias is shamed into saying that he imparts moral instruction to pupils who lack it – an unfortunate admission which he could have avoided by acknowledging that he does not impart moral instruction to pupils who lack it. Dodds and Kahn take Polus' diagnosis seriously. Noting that it is "echoed" by Callicles (482c–d) and "confirmed" by Socrates (508c1–3), Kahn concludes that it is Plato's "signal" to the reader about how the refutation of Gorgias is to be understood. It follows, according to Kahn, that commentators who think Polus' diagnosis is a *mis*diagnosis[33] are rejecting Plato's diagnosis and tacitly implying that they have "understood Plato's argument better than Plato himself."

But perhaps they have. The possibility cannot be ruled out *a priori*. Let us examine these alleged contradictions.

First, (i). We should be wary of saying that, in simultaneously affirming and denying that he is a teacher of virtue, Gorgias contradicts himself. In making this allegation, to whom are we referring: the historical Gorgias or Plato's character? Although the former denied (or is reported by Meno to have denied) being a teacher of virtue, the latter does not. So the alleged contradiction is not traceable to contradictory statements that Plato's character makes about himself, but to a statement that Plato's character

---

[31] 1959: 216.

[32] 1983: 79–84.

[33] E.g., Irwin, 1979: 128; Allen, 1984: 195–96; and, before them, Grote, 1867, ii: 94.

makes about himself and a statement that Meno makes about his historical counterpart – a peculiar reason for accusing someone of self-contradiction.

But even if we waive this point and ascribe the historical Gorgias' disavowal of being a teacher of virtue to Plato's character, the charge of self-contradiction still does not follow. A person is guilty of self-contradiction if and only if he simultaneously affirms and denies the same proposition in the same sense. There is no compelling reason for thinking Gorgias is guilty of this. As Irwin rightly notes, in acknowledging that he imparts moral instruction to pupils who lack it, Gorgias need not be taken as claiming to be a teacher of virtue in the strong sense of "making people virtuous," but only in the weaker sense of teaching them "the sorts of things that are just and unjust," in teaching them "common beliefs" about justice and injustice.[34] Although the texts do not require this interpretation, neither do they preclude it. Since Gorgias is a fictional character, it is idle to speculate about what he "really" means; but is worth pointing out that this reply is open to him.

There is a further question. Why should Gorgias be ashamed to admit that he does not impart moral instruction to pupils who lack it? In view of his explicit disavowal of being a teacher of virtue – a fact reported by Meno and alluded to by Socrates – why should he be ashamed to admit something which was not only common knowledge but which also distinguished him from his more pretentious colleagues who did claim to be teachers of virtue and of whom he made fun? Moreover, the mere fact that he denies being a teacher of virtue in any official capacity entails neither that he has no beliefs about what is just and unjust nor that he never breathes a word about these subjects to his pupils. In denying that he is a teacher of virtue in the sense of "making people virtuous" and then simultaneously asserting that he imparts moral instruction to pupils who lack it, Gorgias no more contradicts himself than a person who disavows being a teacher of geography in the sense of "making people geographers" and then proceeds to give them directions about how to get from Athens to Sparta.

Nor need Gorgias' admission that he imparts moral instruction to pupils who lack it be taken as insincere and a mere face-saving

---

[34] 1979: 126. Irwin adds: "Learning this and acting justly or being just are, for Gorgias and for most people, two very different things."

device. In fact, he seems somewhat surprised that Socrates should envisage the possibility of such exceptional cases. Like Protagoras, he assumes as a matter of course that prospective pupils will already know what is just and unjust. Although not opposed to instructing those who do not, he clearly expects them to be few and far between. That this is so is clear from the language he employs: he supposes (οἶμαι) that a pupil who happens (τύχη) not to know these things will learn them from him, too (460a3–4).

I turn next to (ii). According to Dodds and Kahn, Gorgias' admission that he imparts moral instruction to pupils who lack it contradicts his (alleged) disclaimer of responsibility for their subsequent misuses of rhetoric. However, these claims are not sufficient to generate the contradiction. This charge can only be sustained if Gorgias also endorses the so-called "Socratic paradox" – the "moral paradox" – according to which a person who knows what is just cannot fail to *be* just. But although Gorgias is induced into affirming this thesis later, he does not affirm it here. So, at this point, nothing prevents him from saying, with the rest of the human race, that it is possible for a person to know what is just and unjust in the sense of knowing "the sorts of things that are just and unjust" and fail to *be* just.

Kahn[35] thinks Irwin's way out is "of no use" to Gorgias because, in claiming to teach his pupils what is just and unjust, he implies "that he trains only good men, who will not abuse their power." This contention is unanswerable if Gorgias says what Kahn says he says. But he does not. What he says is, first, that he "supposes" that a pupil who "happens" not to know what is just and unjust will also learn these things from him (460a3–4); and, second, that he imparts rhetorical skills *in the hope that* his pupils will not misuse them – a very different claim which does not commit him to saying that learning what is just is sufficient for *being* just. I conclude that insofar as it presupposes Socratic doctrine, unannounced by Socrates and unaffirmed by Gorgias, the second allegation of self-contradiction is as groundless as the first.[36]

---

[35] 1983: 82.
[36] Surprisingly, Kahn, 1983: 83, n. 13, agrees: "Of course no *logical* contradiction follows unless one adds the [Socratic] assumptions (i) that rhetoric is a *technē* that gives knowledge of its subject matter, and (ii) that knowledge of justice makes one a just person." However, instead of concluding that Socrates' argument fails, Kahn describes the charge of inconsistency "as an example of Socratic irony, which functions here proleptically."

Kahn is right in claiming that the fact that Polus' diagnosis is "echoed" by Callicles and "confirmed" by Socrates is fairly strong evidence that this is how Plato intends the refutation of Gorgias to be understood. But that is not sufficient to show that anyone who rejects Polus,' i.e., Plato's, diagnosis is wrong; perhaps Polus,' i.e., Plato's, diagnosis is a *mis*diagnosis that persists throughout the dialogue. In appealing to Plato's discernible intention as the decisive interpretive *datum*, Kahn is dubiously assuming that if Plato thinks that an argument shows something, that is necessarily what it shows.

At long last, Socrates turns to the task of demonstrating Gorgias' alleged inconsistency. It turns out to be this. In his speech about the persuasive power of rhetoric, Gorgias acknowledged that it is possible for rhetoricians to misuse their art for unjust purposes. This "surprised" Socrates (458e3) because Gorgias had previously claimed that rhetoric is concerned with speech about what is just and unjust. Socrates thinks these statements are inconsistent (457e1–3). But he is wrong. The propositions:

(A) Rhetoric is concerned with speech about what is just and unjust,

and

(B) Rhetoric can be misused for unjust purposes,

are not inconsistent. It is perfectly consistent for Gorgias to assert that a rhetorician can know that some particular rhetorical tactic is unjust (unfair, unscrupulous, shabby, and so on) but use it anyway. That this is so is also borne out by the fact that, in order to convict Gorgias of inconsistency, Socrates needs a further argument. It is this further argument which provides him with the additional premises needed to generate the inconsistency. I say "generate" rather than "demonstrate" because it is only by affirming these additional premises that Gorgias is guilty of inconsistency. In proposing them for Gorgias' assent, Socrates provides him with enough rope to hang himself. The argument – 460a5–c6 – is as follows:

(i) The prospective rhetorician must either already know what is just and unjust or learn it from Gorgias.

(ii)   He who has learned building, music, or medicine is a builder, a musician, or a doctor.

(iii) Similarly, he who has learned what is just *is* just.

(iv)   The just man not only does what is just, he also necessarily wishes to be just and never wishes to be unjust.

(v)   So the rhetorician who has learned what is just is just, necessarily wishes to be just, and never wishes to be unjust.

(vi)   Therefore, he will never wish to do wrong by misusing rhetoric for unjust purposes.

"Apparently not" (Οὐ φαίνεταί γε), replies Gorgias.

In affirming this conclusion, Gorgias is indeed guilty of inconsistency. In fact, he is guilty of straightforward self-contradiction; for he has simultaneously asserted that the rhetorician both can and cannot misuse his art for unjust purposes. Socrates thereupon claims victory and reminds Gorgias that if he is really the kind of man he said he was, he will welcome this refutation and count it a great benefit. Gorgias has no comment.

Dodds thinks Gorgias' silence shows that he is "a good loser" who accepts defeat in "dignified silence" and continues to take "a benevolent interest in the ... discussion."[37] But has he really been defeated? The only fair answer is: yes *and* no. Two points are worth emphasizing.

First, although Socrates prefaces his refutation with the assurance that a person can suffer no greater evil than to hold a false belief about a matter of great importance (458a8–b1), he has not purged Gorgias of any false beliefs; at best, he has demonstrated an inconsistency in his belief-set. That is what he originally set out to do when he said that Gorgias' statements did not seem to be "entirely consistent or in accord with" each other. And that is what he now claims to have done. However, to have demonstrated an inconsistency in someone's belief-set is not to have purged him of a false belief. It is merely to have demonstrated that the inconsistent beliefs cannot both be true.

Second, Socrates has not demonstrated an inconsistency in Gorgias' belief-set. Gorgias' logical difficulties are not traceable to inconsistency, but to inadvertence. Consistently believing that it is possible for a rhetorician to know that some particular rhetorical

---

[37] 1959: 9–10. Gorgias appears briefly at 463a5–464b1, 497b4–10, and 506a5–b4.

tactic is unjust (unfair, unscrupulous, shabby, and so on) but use it anyway, he carelessly assents to (iii) and (iv) – both of them theory-laden propositions heavily infused with contra-endoxic Socratic doctrine which he does not believe and which, given his speech about the uses and misuses of rhetoric, Socrates knows he does not believe. In view of the crucial role these premises play in Socrates' argument, it is surprising that he introduces them so casually. And in view of the fact that Gorgias' speech clearly pre-supposes that rhetoric can be misused, it is equally surprising that he assents to them so readily. They are, after all, Socratic, not Gorgianic, doctrine.[38] Had Gorgias not made these ill-advised ad-missions,[39] Socrates could not have generated the inconsistency.[40]

At this point, Polus reenters the discussion with a complaint about Socrates' dialectical tactics:

Really, Socrates? Is what you're now saying about [rhetoric] what you actually think of it? Or do you really think, just because Gorgias was too ashamed not to concede your further claim that the [rhetorician] also knows what's just, what's admirable, and what's good, and that if [the pupil] came to him without already having this knowledge to begin with, he said that he would teach him himself, and then from this admission maybe some inconsistency crept into his statements – just the thing that gives you delight (ἀγαπᾷς), you're the one who leads him on to face such questions – who do you think would deny that he himself knows what's

---

[38] Canto, 1993: 320, n. 32, finds Socrates' intellectualist contention that he who has learned what is just is just a bit surprising ("un peu surprenante"), but adds that nei-ther Gorgias nor Protagoras (*Pr.* 352c ff.) seem particularly surprised by it – a rejoinder which overlooks the fact that the *Gorgias* and the *Protagoras* are not transcriptions of actual conversations which preserve what these interlocutors actually said, but fictional-ized, dramatic works of art in which Plato can make them say whatever he wants them to say.

[39] Santas, 1979: 150–52, denies that they are ill advised and claims that Socrates' argument is "very strong" on the ground that mastery of a *technē* is "strong evidence" that one is a "qualified" and "successful" practitioner of it. He is, of course, right; but it is not a suf-ficient condition for being an infallible practitioner of a *technē* – which is what Socrates claims.

[40] Grote, 1867, II: 94, saw this very clearly: Gorgias "is now made to contradict himself – apparently rather than really – for the argument whereby Sokrates reduces him to a contradiction, is not tenable, unless we admit the Platonic doctrine that the man who has learnt what is just and unjust, may be relied on to act as a just man; in other words, that virtue consists in knowledge." See also Jowett, 1871, III: 12–13; Robinson, 1953: 29; and Arieti, 1991: 83. Irwin, 1977: 127–28, also thinks Socrates' argument "is illegitimate as it stands," since it depends on (iii) and (iv), according to which learning what is just is suffi-cient for being just. Irwin withdraws this claim in 1995: 98–99, and argues that the refu-tation of Gorgias does not rely solely on "a dogmatic appeal" to the Socratic view that knowledge is sufficient for virtue.

just and would teach others? To lead your arguments to such an outcome is a sign of great rudeness. (461b3–c4)[41]

Even if Polus is wrong in thinking that Gorgias was shamed into
saying that he imparts moral instruction to pupils who lack it, he is
right in tracing his inconsistency to Socrates. By proposing (iii)
and (iv) for Gorgias' assent, Socrates feeds him exactly the premises needed to refute him and thereby leads him into a carefully
prepared logical trap. In spite of his earlier "reluctance" to put
words into Gorgias' mouth, that is exactly what he does here. It
follows that the fact that he introduces these premises into the discussion so casually is, therefore, not really so surprising after all;
indeed, the refutation of Gorgias depends on his not noticing how
controversial, *and non-Gorgianic*, it is to assert that he who has
learned what is just *is* just and will never wish to be unjust.

At 458e4–5 Socrates acknowledged that he might be taking
Gorgias' meaning in the wrong way. At 460e2–461a7 we see that
he has:

[A]t the beginning of our discussion ... it was said that [rhetoric] would
be concerned with speeches ... about what's just and unjust ... [A]t the
time you said that, I took it (ὑπέλαβον) that [rhetoric] would never be an
unjust thing, since it always makes its speeches about justice. But when a
little later you were saying that the [rhetorician] could also use [rhetoric]
unjustly, I was surprised and thought that your statements weren't consistent ... But now ... you see for yourself that ... the [rhetorician] is
incapable of using [rhetoric] unjustly and of being willing to do what's
unjust.

Here is the key to what has gone wrong. When Gorgias said that
rhetoric is concerned with speech about what is just and unjust,
Socrates "took him to mean" that rhetoric can never be "an unjust
thing," – that it cannot be used for unjust purposes. But clearly
that is not what Gorgias meant.[42] For in the very next breath he

[41] Canto, 1993: 321, n. 34, rightly notes that the language with which Polus lodges his protest (461b3–c4) is chaotic, inelegant, and characterized by false starts and random
phrases over which he has increasingly less control ("qui lui échappe peu à peu"). Perhaps Plato is making a point here – satirizing the great rhetorician by portraying him
employing atrocious rhetoric. However, I prefer to focus on the cogency of the criticisms
Polus makes rather than on the language with which he makes them. Many good critics
express themselves poorly.
[42] This is overlooked by Allen, 1984: 194, who asks: "How is it possible to harmonize the
claim that rhetoric can never be unjust, since it ever makes speeches about justice, with
the claim that the orator may use his rhetoric unjustly?" The answer is that it is not possible. But Gorgias never said that rhetoric "can never be unjust." What he said was that
rhetoric is concerned with speech about what is just and unjust.

added that it often is. The contention that rhetoric cannot be used for unjust purposes is not what Gorgias said; it is Socrates' deliberate misinterpretation of what he said – a misinterpretation based on Socratic doctrine. The charge of inconsistency depends on the misinterpretation. For although it is not inconsistent simultaneously to affirm:

(A) Rhetoric is concerned with speech about what is just and unjust,

and

(B) Rhetoric can be misused for unjust purposes,

it is self-contradictory simultaneously to affirm:

(B) Rhetoric can be misused for unjust purposes,

and

(not-B) Rhetoric cannot be misused for unjust purposes.

Gorgias never affirmed (not-B), he affirmed (B). Hence the charge of inconsistency is unfounded. Unless, of course, he can be induced to affirm (not-B) – which is exactly what Socrates gets him to do by getting him to assent to (iii) and (iv) which entail it.[43]

Given his actual views, Gorgias should not have assented to (iii) and (iv). Asked whether he believes these propositions, he should have said: "No, Socrates; those are your doctrines, not mine. And until you provide me with some reason for affirming such counter-intuitive and contra-endoxic theses, I will not affirm them. I can, therefore, consistently affirm both that I impart moral instruction to pupils who lack it and that it is possible for them subsequently to misuse rhetoric for unjust purposes. Nor need I agree that when they do, it is I who is responsible." We can go further, if Socrates

---

[43] Teloh, 1986: 142–43, acknowledges that Socrates must "twist Gorgias' words" to generate the inconsistency, but denies that he is guilty of eristic on the ground that dialectic "is not a purely logical activity. What is essential ... is that the answerer concede the premises which lead to his refutation." Wardy, 1996, acknowledges that Socrates is agonistically competitive, but defends him on the ground that he is competing "for the truth, and not against Gorgias" (70). Unlike practitioners of eristic, whose motive is polemical and personal, Socrates' motive is philosophical and impersonal. Wardy vigorously denies that "anything goes" in Socratic dialectic; however, like many other commentators, he ultimately traces the difference between eristic and dialectic to a difference in motivation (120–24) – the unstated implication of which seems to be that anything *does* "go" – provided that the interlocutor's soul is "improved."

really cared about sincere assent and did not want Gorgias to affirm propositions he does not believe, he would never have fed him (iii) and (iv) in the first place.[44]

Like many Socratic interlocutors, Gorgias has not been refuted "from his own beliefs"; he has been dialectically ambushed. The fact that Socrates not only feeds him exactly the premises needed to refute him but also smuggles his own beliefs and assumptions into the discussion and interprets, i.e., *mis*interprets, Gorgias' statements in light of them raises serious doubts about his assurance that he enters into philosophical disputation only because he is trying to understand the subject under discussion and to discover truth. It raises equally serious doubts about Dodd's contention that the refutation of the interlocutor is "incidental." Far from being incidental, refutation seems to be the point of the whole discussion.

It might be argued that if an interlocutor assents to a proposition (or series of propositions) proposed for his assent, it does not matter whether he believes them or not; what matters is that he assented to them. And if they are inconsistent with his earlier assertions, it is perfectly legitimate for Socrates to charge him with inconsistency. But "perfectly legitimate" for what? For understanding the subject under discussion and arriving at truth? Or for winning the argument? To induce someone into affirming theses which he does not believe and which from his previous assertions one knows he does not believe but which enable one to defeat him in argument seems more like the eristic tactics of an agonistic sophist in search of victory than like the dialectical tactics of a moral gadfly in search of truth. Such tactics are sufficient to undo Gorgias. But that is a very different thing from improving his soul.

---

[44] I cannot endorse Irwin's contention, 1995: 97, that since each step of the argument is explicit and since Gorgias accepts them all, he "has no basis for complaint."

CHAPTER 15

Polus

The second of three increasingly intractable interlocutors in the *Gorgias*, Polus of Acragas is a disciple of Gorgias and a rhetorician and teacher of rhetoric in his own right. He has also written a treatise on the subject which Socrates has recently read.[1] Although he appears briefly at the beginning of the dialogue, his major contribution occurs at 461b3–481b5 where he abruptly breaks into the discussion to defend Gorgias. Socrates describes him as fresh and young – the name "Polus" means "colt" – young enough, in fact, to be his (or Gorgias') son. As things turn out, he is as dialectically unequipped as his mentor – in fact, more so;[2] but he is not nearly so courteous and urbane. He is also less inhibited about expressing his opinions which are more unconventional than Gorgias' albeit not so radical as Callicles'. Unlike Gorgias, who is enamored of the persuasive power of rhetoric but believes that it should be used to promote the interests of justice, Polus values rhetorical persuasiveness for its own sake.

In Plato's early dialogues, when one interlocutor succeeds or intervenes on behalf of another, it is often to lodge a protest – usually against Socrates. That is how the disgruntled Polemarchus succeeds Cephalus in *Republic* I, only to be succeeded a few pages later himself by the irate Thrasymachus who had been trying to

---

[1] At *Phdr.* 267b10 Socrates alludes to "the whole gallery of terms" that Polus and Thrasymachus employ in talking about good diction and effective speech (e.g., reduplication, speaking in maxims, images) by means of which rhetoricians manipulate the emotions of their audiences, raising them to high levels of excitement and then calming them down. He crudely adds that knowing how to produce these effects does not make one a true rhetorician any more than knowing how to raise and lower people's temperatures and how to make them vomit and move their bowels makes one a true doctor (268a8–b5).

[2] Thus Vickers, 1988: 97, declares: Polus is "so inept in dialectic ... that Socrates can exploit [his] ineptitude to deliver his most scathing attack on rhetoric."

break into the discussion for some time and even had to be restrained. Although Plato does not explicitly say so, the same seems to be true of Polus who bursts into the discussion with a speech "spluttering with indignation and anacoluthons."[3]

Like all Socrates' interlocutors, Polus has been showered with abuse. Vlastos[4] calls him "a dismal character" and an "impudent young upstart." Rutherford[5] judges him "something of a boor" – "crudely prudential" and "unwilling or unable to learn anything from Socrates." Dodds[6] dismisses him as an "intellectually and morally vulgar" young man whose "inferior manners" prompt him to treat Chaerephon and Socrates with "prickly resentfulness" and whose "unteachable stupidity" makes the "muddle-headed" Gorgias seem "quite intelligent" by comparison. The insults could be multiplied indefinitely. Little is known of the historical Polus. But if Plato's portrayal is accurate, he was a thoroughly disagreeable person. He is certainly one of the most disagreeable interlocutors in the early dialogues.

Before making too much of this, however, several points should be noted. First, Polus' initial belligerence is prompted by his belief – correct, in my opinion – that Socrates has not played fair with Gorgias. Second, his escalating disagreeableness is largely traceable to the hostile treatment he receives at the hands of Chaerephon, who is out of patience with him from the beginning, and to the patronizing remarks of Socrates, whose attitude towards him – withering sarcasm bordering on overt contempt – is strikingly different from his (at least superficially) deferential attitude towards Gorgias. Polus is rebuked for verbosity and accused of a serious misunderstanding the minute he opens his mouth. Within the space of a few paragraphs, he is also accused of contriving to upstage his teacher, berated as dialectically inept, and mocked as an unlikely source of enlightenment. Accordingly, before heaping further abuse upon him, we should acknowledge that he finds himself cast in the thankless role of Socrates' dialectical whipping-boy and is understandably unhappy with the part. Yet, however unlikable his

---

[3] The delicious language is Shorey's, 1933: 137.
[4] 1991: 147–48.
[5] 1995: 150–51, 154.
[6] 1959: 11.

character and however non-existent his dialectical ability, his criticisms of Socrates are mostly on target.[7]

The foregoing argument had yielded the conclusion that since he who knows what is just *is* just, and never wishes to be unjust, it follows that the rhetorician who knows what is just will never use the art of rhetoric for unjust purposes – a possibility for which Gorgias had originally allowed. On the strength of this argument, Socrates had accused him of inconsistency. Polus is irritated – if "irritated" is not too mild a term – because he does not think Gorgias has been legitimately refuted. As he sees it, Socrates has not demonstrated that Gorgias' beliefs are inconsistent; he has merely shamed him into inconsistency by inducing him to say – falsely, according to Polus – that he imparts moral instruction to pupils who lack it – an inconsistency which Gorgias could easily have avoided by candidly admitting that he does not teach his pupils what is just, noble, and good because he does not think that is part of his educational task – which is simply to make people clever speakers.

In the previous chapter, I argued that Polus is wrong about this. Gorgias is not shamed into inconsistency. His inconsistency is traceable to the fact that Socrates has induced him into affirming two propositions which he does not believe and which Socrates knows he does not believe. It is Gorgias' ill-advised (and insincere) assent to these propositions which traps him into "agreeing" that the rhetorician who has learned what is just *is* just and will never use the art of rhetoric for unjust purposes – a proposition which contradicts his original claim that the rhetorician can misuse the art of rhetoric. But although Polus is wrong in thinking that Gorgias has been shamed into inconsistency, he is right in thinking that his inconsistency is traceable to Socrates who *leads* him into inconsistency by feeding him the premises which generate it.

As usual, Socrates refuses to acknowledge that he is guilty as charged; instead, he assures Polus that *if* he has treated Gorgias unfairly, it was unintentional. In short, instead of taking Polus' criticism seriously and rendering himself a candidate for that dis-

---

[7] See Méron, 1979: 66: "[S]'il [Polos] est un mauvais dialecticien, sa fougue en est coupable, mais il lui suffit d'être attentif pour définir un problème ou discerner avec acuité les points faibles d'une argumentation."

turbing but humbling kind of self-knowledge which he is forever recommending to others, Socrates dodges the issue and quips that the old are grateful to the young for coming to their aid when they stumble. He adds that if Polus can persuade him that anything has been wrongly admitted, he will gladly withdraw it. He has only one condition: Polus must refrain from making long speeches.

This request does not sit well with Polus. Like Gorgias, he loves to talk; unlike Gorgias, however, he is not nearly so willing to abandon the method of speech-making in favor of the method of question-and-answer. He, in fact, resents this seemingly arbitrary restriction and accuses Socrates of depriving him of freedom of speech. It is only when Socrates points out that the same freedom which entitles Polus to make long speeches entitles him to stop listening and even to leave that Polus grudgingly relents.[8] The prospect of someone walking out during one of his magnificent epideictic displays is more than he can bear. So the brevity requirement prevails.

Of course, Socrates has no intention of withdrawing anything. That this is so is borne out by the fact that he does not invite Polus to pursue his objection further to determine whether there is anything to it; instead, he browbeats him into submission by telling him that if he really cares about the discussion, he will either assume the role of questioner and refute Socrates or agree to be questioned and, if necessary, be refuted himself. Like most Socratic interlocutors, Polus allows himself to be sidetracked. Dropping his protest, he is maneuvered into the role of questioner, thereby failing to follow through on a legitimate insight and forgetting that he had originally entered the discussion to defend Gorgias. Invited by Socrates to ask any question he wishes – a thinly disguised parody of Gorgias – Polus queries him about his view of rhetoric. Socrates counters with a question of his own: Is Polus asking what *technē* he thinks rhetoric is? If so, his question is easily answered: it is not a *technē* at all; it is merely a certain knack (ἐμπειρίαν ... τινα, 462c3), that is, an empirically acquired know-how.[9]

---

[8] As we have seen, at *Pr.* 335c3–6 Socrates actually does threaten to leave.
[9] On the difference between a *technē* and an *empeiria*, see Dodds, 1959: 228–29; and Irwin, 1979: 130–31.

Polus is stunned and momentarily at a loss for words. "A knack?" he muses, reeling in disbelief.[10] "A knack for what?" "For producing a certain gratification and pleasure" (χάριτός τινος καὶ ἡδονῆς, 462c7), replies the philosopher whose wisdom consists in the fact that he knows nothing.[11] When Polus wonders whether it is not a fine (καλόν) thing to gratify people, he is rebuked for proceeding too quickly. Before we can judge whether something is fine, we need to know what it is (ὅτι ἐστίν, 463c5). A Socratic analysis of the nature of rhetoric follows. As a knack, rhetoric resembles cookery which is the knack of providing gastronomical pleasure. This does not mean that rhetoric and cookery are the same thing, but it does mean that they are parts of the same practice (τῆς αὐτῆς ... ἐπιτηδεύσεως μόριον, 462e3–4), namely, the practice of flattery (κολακείαν, 463b1). By "flattery," Socrates does not mean bestowals of excessive and insincere praise; he means appeals to the emotions and other non-rational "parts" of the soul of the person flattered. As such, flattery implies a certain "moral baseness"[12] on the part of the flatterer who is operating with covert (and presumably sinister) motives.

Having set forth this decidedly uncomplimentary view of rhetoric, Socrates again faults Polus – this time for failing to ask what *kind* of flattery Socrates thinks rhetoric is, thereby implying that, in addition to being inept at answering questions, he is equally inept

[10] Rutherford, 1995: 151, notes that Polus' reactions to Socrates' claims are not reasoned responses but "exclamations of incredulity," thereby making him an ancestor of the "I can't believe I heard you say that" school of criticism which tries to rebut error by recoiling in horror. However, Rutherford fails to add that, as the discussion progresses, Socrates' claims become increasingly extreme and counterintuitive, and that Polus' incredulous responses are perfectly understandable.

[11] Guthrie, 1975: 295, thinks this passage is unprecedented in the early dialogues. Unlike the Socrates of the *Euthyphro*, the *Laches*, and the *Charmides*, who does not know what piety, courage, and temperance are, the Socrates of the *Gorgias* does know what rhetoric is; this Socrates is no longer a morally ignorant searcher, but a "transformed" Socrates who possesses knowledge and is willing to impart it. Kahn, 1996: 93–94, is less impressed. He agrees that Socrates does indeed define rhetoric in the *Gorgias*, but he argues – rightly, in my opinion – that his definition of "rhetoric" as "a producer of persuasion" (453a2) is not the answer to a *bona fide* "What-is-F?" question on the ground that it "does not claim any kind of epistemic priority or metaphysical depth"; nor does it reveal "the explanatory essences or natures of things." He would presumably say the same thing about the view of rhetoric Socrates advances in this passage. See also Méron, 1979: 46, n. 18, according to whom Socrates' definition of rhetoric "est plutôt un jugement de valeur qu'une définition."

[12] The term is Dodds's, 1959: 225.

at asking them.[13] When Polus dutifully asks what kind, he learns that rhetoric is a counterfeit – or semblance (εἴδωλον, 463d1–2) – of a branch of politics; for politicians also flatter their constituencies by pandering to them, thereby gratifying their decadent taste instead of improving and ennobling it. Since this is so, it follows that rhetoric is not fine, but shameful (αἰσχρόν). When Polus confesses that he is puzzled by Socrates' analysis of the nature of rhetoric, Socrates attributes his lack of understanding to youth and inexperience; but when Gorgias confesses that he is puzzled too, Socrates realizes that he must explain himself more clearly. He sarcastically adds that Polus will refute him should he again go astray.

He begins by getting Gorgias to agree to three propositions: (i) that there is a distinction between the body and the soul,[14] (ii) that the body can seem healthy when it is not, and (iii) that the same is true of the soul. Having just forbidden Polus to make long speeches, Socrates spends the next three Stephanus pages making a speech of his own in which he sets forth his view of rhetoric as a pseudo-*technē* (464b2–465d6) based on the foregoing distinction between the body and the soul and the *technai* or practices (παρασκευαί)[15] which care for them. The *technai* which care for the body are gymnastics and medicine, and the *technē* which cares for the soul is politics. It consists of two parts: the first, which corresponds to gymnastics, is legislation; the second, which corresponds to medicine, is justice. There are, then, four genuine *technai* which divide into two pairs: gymnastics and medicine, on the one hand, and legislation and justice, on the other. Although each is distinct from the others, they are alike in that each aims at what is best (τὸ βέλτιστον, 464c4). Flattery, on the other hand, is a pseudo-*technē* which imitates the genuine ones. It differs from them in two ways: first, it does not aim at what is best, but at what is pleasant; second, it cannot give an account (λόγον) of what it does (465a3).

---

[13] Although it is natural to suppose that it is easier to ask questions than to answer them, sometimes the opposite is true. As Cazeaux, 1996: 41, n. 3, astutely notes, if questioning is to lead anywhere, the questioner must know where he is going, and Polus clearly does not.

[14] According to Dodds, 1959: 231, "[t]he sharp Platonic antithesis" between mind and body is here set forth for the first time – a claim denied by Irwin, 1979: 133, on the ground that in this passage (and in the early dialogues generally) the term "soul" is not burdened with any metaphysical baggage, but simply means the "source" or "principle" of life.

[15] A value-neutral term, according to Dodds, 1959: 318, which covers both empirically acquired knacks and genuine *technai*.

Thus cookery imitates medicine by providing food which is tasty rather than nourishing, and cosmetics imitates gymnastics by providing beauty which is artificial rather than natural. Analogously, sophistry imitates legislation, and rhetoric imitates justice. Both have the same debilitating effect on the soul that cookery and cosmetics have on the body. Mathematically expressed, sophistry is to legislation as cosmetics is to gymnastics, and rhetoric is to justice as cookery is to medicine. Since all these pseudo-*technai* are a species of flattery, all are shameful.

Having made this long speech, Socrates realizes that he has broken his own rule and sheepishly excuses himself on the ground that, when he spoke briefly, Polus did not understand him. In fairness, it should be added that he thereupon extends the same privilege to Polus who may also speak at greater length if he has trouble making himself understood.

Obviously disturbed by this Socratic disparagement of the art (or alleged art) of which he and Gorgias are the consummate masters, Polus responds with a capsule summary: "So you think rhetoric is flattery?" "No. A *part* of flattery," retorts Socrates, deploring Polus' poor memory, thereby providing him with a golden opportunity to demand that Socrates refrain from making long speeches – an opportunity of which, needless to say, Polus does not avail himself. Instead, he vacantly asks whether rhetoricians are considered to be flatterers in their own cities and held in low esteem. "Is this a question you're asking, or some speech you're beginning?" replies the philosopher who had just lifted the ban on speech-making if it promotes the interests of clarity. Assured that it is a question, Socrates explains that rhetoricians are not considered to be flatterers in their own cities because they are not considered at all.[16] Polus is again puzzled: do not rhetoricians have the greatest power in their cities? Socrates does not think so – at least not if, by "power," one means something that is good for the person who has it. Is that what Polus means by the term? It is.

Socrates does not ask this question for informational purposes, but for polemical ones. Had he asked, "What do you mean by

[16] The claim is demonstrably false. See Grote, 1867, II: 96, n. t: "[A]s a matter of fact, the Rhetors ... had considerable importance, whether they deserved it or not ... How little Plato cared to make his comparisons harmonize with the fact, may be seen by what immediately follows – where he compares the Rhetors to Despots; and puts in the mouth of Polus the assertion that they kill or banish anyone whom they choose."

'power' "?, Polus could have produced his own definition, thereby saying what he really believes. In asking, "By 'power', do you mean something that is good for the person who has it?", he not only invites an affirmative answer to his question – Polus could hardly reply, "No, I mean something that is bad for the person who has it" – he also surreptitiously introduces peculiarly Socratic notions of "power" and "good" into the discussion without making this clear to Polus, thereby again priming his interlocutor for refutation by employing familiar terms but stripping them of their ordinary meanings and investing them with very different ones. Instead of agreeing that power is good for the person who has it, Polus should have pointed out that "power" and "good" are ambiguous terms and asked Socrates to explain exactly what he means by them. At the very least, he should have said that, in agreeing that power is good for the person who has it, he means what Gorgias means, namely, that power is good because it enables the rhetorician to persuade others and thereby gain control over them. In assenting to the Socratically proposed thesis that power is good for the person who has it without being allowed to explain what he means either by "power" or by "good," Polus endorses a thesis which, although verbally identical with his own, means something very different.

In addition to these logical objections, Polus should have lodged a methodological one. In asking whether power is good for those who have it, Socrates is guilty of the same mistake of which he had previously accused Polus – the mistake of trying to answer the secondary question of what something is *like* without having answered the more fundamental question of what it *is*. If it is impossible to determine whether rhetoric is fine until we have determined what rhetoric is, it is equally impossible to determine whether power is good for the person who has it until we have determined what power is. "Power is good for the person who has it" may be a true statement about power, but it is not a definition of "power."

Having agreed that power is good for the person who has it, Polus is baffled to learn that Socrates not only denies that rhetoricians have the greatest power in their cities, but thinks that they have the least power (466b9–10). How could he possibly think such a thing when everyone knows that, like tyrants, rhetoricians can do whatever they wish – including banishing people, confiscating their property, and even putting them to death?[17] Socrates thereupon points out that Polus is not asking one question but two[18]: (i) Do rhetoricians have the greatest power? and (ii) Can rhetoricians do whatever they wish? According to Socrates, the answer to both is, No. Rhetoricians have the least power because they do nothing that they wish (βούλονται), but only what seems best (δόξη βέλτιστον εἶναι) at any given moment (466e1–2). Polus thinks that is exactly what "having the greatest power" means; but Socrates again begs to differ. If power is good for those who have it, as Polus has agreed, then he must also agree that it is not good for a person devoid of intelligence to do what seems best at any given moment. Hence Polus must either refute Socrates by proving that rhetoricians are intelligent and that rhetoric is a genuine *technē* or he must admit that rhetoricians do what seems best without intelligence and therefore have no power and attain no good for themselves (466e13–467a6).

Polus is irritated by these claims and pronounces them shocking and absurd. Although Socrates dismisses this objection as mere verbal abuse, Polus has a legitimate complaint. Ordinarily, we would say that, in banishing people, confiscating their property, and putting them to death, tyrants are doing exactly what they wish and achieving exactly what they want. It is paradoxical in the extreme to say that, in murdering millions of Jews during the Holocaust, Hitler was not doing exactly what he wished and, to an appalling degree, achieving exactly what he wanted. Yet that is apparently what Socrates would say.[19] However, in saying it, he is not so much denying Polus' contention as redefining "doing what one wishes" in light of Socratic doctrine. Only by defining "doing what one wishes" as "achieving some end which is beneficial to one's soul and enables one to achieve what one 'really' wants" is it

[17] Vickers, 1988: 99, protests: "Once again Plato has sabotaged the defence of rhetoric by giving its proponent an outrageous claim." Even the usually imperturbable Grote, 1867, II: 145, responds to this comparison with something akin to horror: "Perikles would have listened with mixed surprise and anger, if he had heard anyone utter the monstrous assertion which Plato puts into the mouth of Polus ..."

[18] A sophistical technique, according to Aristotle (*S.E.* 167b38–168b17), but one of which Polus is unaware, according to Canto, 1993: 322, n. 45, since he cannot distinguish between the true object of desire and the object of immediate pleasure, i.e., between what he really wants and the immediate gratification of some momentary desire.

[19] Irwin, 1979: 141, notes that Polus is rightly puzzled by Socrates restriction "on the ordinary range of 'want'."

even remotely plausible to say that tyrants and rhetoricians do nothing that they wish, achieve nothing that they want, and, therefore, have the least power in their cities. Although there is a genuine conceptual distinction between doing what seems best at any given moment and doing what one really wants, Socrates' employment of it is so theory-laden and so heavily freighted with metaphysical baggage that it is either inapplicable to ordinary situations or applicable only by equivocating on "doing what one 'really' wants." In the first case, the inference is false; in the second, it is fallacious.

Unlike Gorgias, who is not told that his refutation depends on his unwitting endorsement of Socratic doctrine, Polus receives a detailed explanation of the Socratic theory of voluntary action on which the foregoing claims are based. This "apparent tangent"[20] allows Socrates to expound the distinction on which the so-called "prudential paradox" – according to which all desire is for the good – depends.

Whenever human beings act, they do what they do, not for its own sake but for the sake of an end to which the action is (or is believed to be) a means (ἕνεκα πράττουσιν τοῦθ' ὃ πράττουσιν, 467c6–7), for example, the sick take medicine because they want to get well. Formulated in full generality, whenever A does X, which leads to Y, it is because he wants Y, not because he wants X. Indeed, according to Socrates, he does *not* want X (οὐ τοῦτο βούλεται, 467d7).[21] Socrates elaborates this theory of voluntary action by producing a threefold classification of existing things (τι τῶν ὄντων, 467e1–2): (i) things that are good, for example, health and wealth; (ii) things that are bad, e.g., disease and poverty; and (iii) things that are neither good nor bad but "partake" (μετέχει)

---

[20] The terminology is Vickers's, 1988: 99. Dodds, 1959: 232, calls it an "apparently senseless distinction."

[21] Vlastos, 1991: 150, n. 77, and 303–4, rejects this interpretation on the ground that, according to Socrates, a person can want something *both* for the sake of the end to which it is a means *and* for its own sake. In support of this contention, he cites *G.* 468c3–4 where Socrates says: "[B]ut if these things [*sc.* things we want for the sake of something else] are advantageous, *we do desire them.*" Vlastos is right. Socrates does say this. But, as is clear from *G.* 467d1–6, what he means is that we desire such things solely for their advantages. The same claim is repeated at *G.* 468b8–c1. Vlastos denies this (in the same note) on the ground that although Socrates does not "formally" state the "vital qualification" that we do not want these things "just" (ἁπλῶς οὕτως), that is solely, for their own sake, it is "clear" that he "does intend it." I do not think this is "clear" at all. Neither do Irwin, 1979: 141; and Dodds, 1959: 237.

sometimes of the one and sometimes of the other, for example, running, walking, and sailing (467e1–468a4). He thereupon gets Polus to agree that we perform these "intermediate" actions (τὰ μεταξύ) not just for the sake of some end judged to be good, but judged to be good *for us*. In short, all desire is for the good *of the moral agent*. It follows that tyrants who put people to death for the sake of some end which they think good and beneficial (ὠφέλιμα) for themselves, but which is, in fact, bad and harmful (βλαβερὰ) do what seems best but not what they wish, since no one wishes to be harmed. Socrates thereupon concludes that if power is good for those who have it, as Polus has agreed, then, by his own admission (κατὰ τὴν σὴν ὁμολογίαν), these mistaken tyrants have no power in their cities (468a5–e3). Hence what *Socrates* has said is true ('Ἀληθῆ ἄρα ἐγὼ ἔλεγον, 468e3)[22]: it is possible for a person to do what seems best but not to do what he wants (468e3–5). Polus grudgingly concurs.

But he has accepted Socrates' classification of "existing things" too quickly. Although few would dispute that some things are good and others bad, the contention that no one performs "intermediate" actions for their own sake but only for the sake of the end (or good) which they promote (or are believed to promote) is eminently disputable. As Irwin[23] rightly points out, Socrates has given no argument for his contention that if A does X, which leads to Y, it is because he wants Y, not because he wants X. In fact, the plausibility of this contention depends on a judicious selection of examples. It is unobjectionable to say that the sick do not (usually)[24] want to take medicine and take it only because they want to get well. But it is highly objectionable to say that concert-goers do not want to go to concerts and go because they want to expand their knowledge of the symphonic repertoire or because they are in quest of some other extra-musical benefit. The typical concert-goer is a music lover for whom listening to music is an intrinsically enjoyable experience – not a means to a non-musical end, but an end in itself and something worth doing for its own sake. Insofar as he thinks of extra-musical benefits at all, he thinks of them as

---

[22] This is yet another passage in which it is not the interlocutor but Socrates himself who advances a thesis.

[23] 1979: 141.

[24] The qualification is necessary. Some medicine is delicious and taking it is a thoroughly (and even intrinsically) enjoyable experience.

incidental by-products of concert-going, not as his reason for going – much less, his sole reason. The tyrant is a particularly interesting example because it fits neither model. Unlike the medical patient, who does not want to take medicine and takes it only because he wants to get well, the tyrant *does* want to banish people and put them to death. He does not say, "I do not want to do these dreadful things; I do them only because they enable me to attain my ends." On the other hand, unlike the concert-goer, who wants to go to concerts for its own sake rather than for the sake of extramusical benefits, the tyrant *is* in quest of benefits. In short, he wants *both* to perform the "intermediate" actions *and* to attain the ends to which they lead (or to which he believes they lead). Insofar as he does the former, he attains the latter. Instead of accepting Socrates' three-fold classification of "existing things," Polus should have rejected it on the ground that it does not explain what it purports to explain.

He should also have denied his patently false contention that rhetoricians have no power in their cities. At the very least, he should have asked: no power *to do what*? Even if, devoid of intelligence and ignorant of what is in their own interests, rhetoricians have no power to do what they wish in Socrates' sense of "doing what one wishes," thereby doing what is good and beneficial for their souls, it does not follow that they have *no* power. Presumably not even Socrates would deny that rhetoricians and tyrants have power to banish people and put them to death. It is one thing to say that rhetoricians have enormous power which, owing to their ignorance, they systematically abuse; it is something else to say that, insofar as they are ignorant of what they "really" want, they have no power at all. There is a distinction between having power and using it rightly. Such arbitrary re-definitions clarify nothing and obscure a great deal.

Instead of critically examining Socrates' argument and showing what is wrong with it, Polus merely retorts *ad hominem* that, given the choice, Socrates would welcome the opportunity to do what seemed best and envy others who did – whether their conduct was just or unjust. In a reply which is unprecedented in the early dialogues, Socrates tells Polus to be quiet (469a2) and admonishes him not to envy the unenviable and the wretched but to pity them; for those who act unjustly are wretched and pitiable. Polus disagrees. It is those who are unjustly put to death rather than those

who unjustly put them to death who are most wretched. Socrates
rejects this claim on the ground that those who are wronged are
less wretched than those by whom they are wronged. For those
who are wronged merely suffer wrongdoing whereas those who
wrong them commit it. And to do wrong is the greatest of evils
(469b8–9). Polus again disagrees: Is it not worse to suffer injustice
than to commit it? Socrates thinks not. Although he himself would
wish to do neither, if he had to choose, he would rather suffer injustice. That is why he would not want to be a tyrant; for tyrants
have no power to do what they wish.

At this point, Polus qualifies his original claim by defining
"power" as the ability to do what seems best with the built-in
guarantee that one will escape detection and thereby escape punishment.[25] Confronted with this amended view of power, Socrates
gets Polus to agree that there are times when it is better to put
people to death and times when it is worse. Asked how he draws
the line (ὅρον ὁρίζῃ, 470b10) between the two,[26] Polus suggests that
Socrates answer that question himself. Surprisingly, he obliges: it
is better to put people to death justly than unjustly. Polus sneers at
this contention and claims that any child could refute it. Socrates
thereupon invites Polus to refute him and thereby purge him of a
false belief. In a feeble attempt at cogency, Polus introduces empirical evidence, citing the tyrant Archelaus who had recently
usurped the Macedonian throne and asking whether Socrates
thinks he is happy. Socrates unhelpfully replies that he has no
idea; he does not know the man. Whether he is happy or miserable
depends on how he was educated and how he stands in relation to
justice: a noble and good (καλὸν καὶ ἀγαθόν) man or woman[27] is
happy whereas an unjust and base (ἄδικον καὶ πονηρόν) one is not.
So if Archelaus is just, he is happy; but if he is unjust, he is wretched
(470e6–11).

---

[25] This passage is one of many that could be cited as evidence of Polus' fundamental intellectual and moral dishonesty. See Canto, 1993: 37: "Le Polos du Gorgias est donc le rep-
résentant d'une form d'hyprocrisie sociale contre laquelle Socrate s'est battu avec une
grande énergie."
[26] The Greek is hard to render felicitously. Witness Irwin's uncharacteristically awkward
"Tell me what definition you define" (1979: 40). Although ὅρος can mean "definition,"
its use is often wider and less technical. It can also mean "boundary" or "line of demar-
cation." Here it simply means: "How do you tell them apart?"
[27] Dodds, 1959: 243, notes that, to his knowledge, this is the only application of this phrase
to women in the early dialogues.

Polus is astonished. Does Socrates really believe that whether one is happy depends *solely* on whether one is just? He does. Taken aback by this startling claim, Polus proceeds to review Archelaus' political career and concludes that in view of his unprecedented wrongdoing – which Polus enumerates in gruesome detail – he is surely the most unjust man in Macedonia. Yet he is supremely happy. Or so people say. Is Socrates prepared to deny what everyone else affirms? If so, he will find himself in a tiny minority – indeed, in a minority of one.

Socrates again compliments Polus on his ability to make speeches, but complains that his long-windedness is an impediment to productive discussion. Having registered this complaint against speech-making, he makes a much longer one himself – not about the benefits of refutation, as he did with Gorgias, but about its proper method. Polus is trying to refute him like the rhetoricians in the lawcourts who produce many witnesses to corroborate their claims while the other party has only one witness or none. But although this method may be effective in court, it is worthless for getting at the truth. It does not matter how many people agree with Polus. It does not even matter if everyone agrees with him. Socrates has no interest in polling "the Many." Nor is he trying to refute everyone. He is trying to refute Polus who is the only witness he needs. Accordingly:

[I]f I don't produce you as a single witness to agree with what I'm saying, then I suppose I've achieved nothing worth mentioning concerning the things we've been discussing. And I suppose you haven't either, if I don't testify on your side, though I'm just one person, and you disregard all these other people. (472b6–c2)

The only kind of refutation that Socrates cares about is the kind in which his interlocutor bears witness to (and ultimately against) himself.

Socrates and Polus disagree about two things: (i) Which is worse: to suffer injustice or to commit it? and (ii) Who is happier: the punished or the unpunished wrongdoer? Polus believes that it is worse to suffer injustice and that the unpunished wrongdoer is happier; Socrates believes the opposite. Polus thinks that Socrates' views are not only false, but preposterous. Does he really believe that the wrongdoer who is placed on the rack, blinded, castrated, crucified, and finally burned alive is *happier* than the wrongdoer who lives out his days in luxury surrounded by servants who cater to his every whim?

Monumentally unimpressed, Socrates quips that whereas Polus had previously tried to refute him by invoking the opinions of "the Many," he is now trying to refute him by making his flesh creep. But his criticism is wide of the mark. Polus is merely underscoring the absurdity of Socrates' claim that punished wrongdoers are happier than unpunished ones by embellishing it with concrete details. When Socrates reaffirms that an unjust man cannot be happy, Polus laughs in his face. Advised that laughing at one's opponent is not to be confounded with refuting him,[28] Polus adopts a hectoring tone and suggests that, in affirming a thesis which is so bizarre that everyone would reject it out of hand, Socrates has refuted himself. Socrates retorts that if that is the best Polus can do by way of refutation, he will resume the role of questioner himself and produce a witness who will testify to his "bizarre" view, namely, Polus. He thereupon sets out to prove not only that it is worse to commit injustice than to suffer it, but also that Polus and everyone else really believe the same thing – albeit without realizing it.

The refutation that follows is strikingly different from any we have seen so far. Instead of trying to demonstrate that Polus' thesis is false (or that it is inconsistent with his other beliefs), Socrates tries to demonstrate that Polus does not really believe what he says he believes. His argument – 474c4–475e6 – is as follows:

(i) It is worse to suffer injustice than to commit it.
(ii) But it is more shameful to commit injustice than to suffer it.[29]

That is, it is not the case that if action A is more shameful than action B, it is also necessarily worse than action B; the class of evil (κακόν) actions is not coextensive with the class of shameful (αἰσχρόν) ones. Nor is the class of fine (καλόν) actions coextensive with the class of good (ἀγαθόν) ones. Furthermore, in judging things to be fine, it is not the case that we look to nothing (εἰς οὐδὲν ἀποβλέπων, 474d4–5), that is, it is not the case that we employ no standards or criteria; on the contrary, we employ very specific ones:

---

[28] According to Aristotle (*Rh.* 1419b5), the historical Gorgias advocated laughter as a form of refutation: "You should kill your opponents' earnestness with jesting and their jesting with earnestness."

[29] Callicles later traces Polus' difficulties to his acceptance of this proposition.

(iii)	We judge things to be fine insofar as they are useful (χρήσι-
μον) or provide some pleasure (ἡδονήν τινα) for the beholders
(τοὺς θεωροῦντας, i.e., for those who view, hear, or contemplate them (474d5–e1).[30]

For example, a painting is judged fine insofar as it provides pleasure to the viewer, a musical composition is judged fine insofar as
it provides pleasure to the hearer, and so on. Polus agrees that
these are indeed the criteria we employ.

(iv)	Hence if one thing is judged finer than another, it is because
it surpasses it in one (or both) of these respects, i.e., it is either
more beneficial or it affords greater pleasure to the viewer,
hearer, etc. (or both).
(v)	Similarly, if one thing is judged more shameful than another,
it is because it surpasses it either in pain or in evil (or in both).
(vi)	Those who commit injustice do not surpass those who suffer
it in pain.
(vii)	But they do surpass them in evil.
(ix)	Hence insofar as committing injustice surpasses suffering it in
evil, it is worse.
(x)	Since Polus has agreed that committing injustice is more
shameful than suffering it, he must either opt for more evil
and shame rather than less or concede that committing injustice is also worse than suffering it.
(xi)	He would not opt for more evil and shame rather than less.
(xii)	Therefore he must concede that it is worse to commit injus-
tice than to suffer it.

Polus does concede this – albeit very reluctantly, thereby testifying
against himself and (apparently) becoming a witness to the truth of
Socrates' view.

I say "apparently" because the argument is fallacious. Polus has
said that it is worse to suffer injustice than to commit it and that it
is more shameful to commit it than to suffer it. But worse and
more shameful *for whom?* The obvious answer is that it is worse for

---

[30] Irwin, 1979: 156, thinks that, owing to the vagueness of the term ὁρίζω, it is not clear that
Socrates intends to be offering a definition of the fine (καλόν). But this seems overly cautious. Although Socrates does not explicitly say that he is offering a definition, he does
say that being beneficial or a source of pleasure is what makes fine things fine. In the
language of the *Euthyphro*, the standard (παράδειγμα) to which we look in distinguishing
what is fine from what is not is that "by which" they are fine (*Eu.* 6e3–6).

the person who *suffers* injustice and more shameful for the person who *commits* it. Socrates and Polus agree about the second claim, but they disagree about the first. Socrates thinks that committing injustice is worse for the wrongdoer than for the person wronged. But his argument is flawed.

In assenting to (vi), Polus agrees that those who commit injustice do not surpass those who suffer it in pain. He is right. But the correctness of the answer obscures the fact that there is something very peculiar about the question. According to (iii), things are judged fine insofar as they are useful or provide some pleasure for those who view, hear, or contemplate them. According to (iv), one thing is judged finer than another because it surpasses it in one (or both) of these respects, that is, it is either more beneficial or it affords greater pleasure (or both); and, according to (v), one thing is judged more shameful than another because it surpasses it either in pain or in evil (or both). In short, from (iii) to (v), the criterion of what is fine or shameful is its effect *on those who view, hear, or contemplate it*. However, at (vi) this criterion is quietly abandoned and replaced by a very different one. In asking who experiences more pain: the person who commits injustice or the person who suffers it?, Socrates surreptitiously substitutes different referents for pain. He is no longer asking a question about the respective degrees of pain experienced by those who *view* an act of injustice perpetrated by one person on another. Indeed, he is no longer employing the criterion of the pleasure or displeasure of the viewer at all; he is employing the very different criterion of the pleasure or displeasure of the wrongdoer and his victim, that is, the pleasure or displeasure *of the persons viewed*. He is also asking a very different question – a question about the respective degrees of pain experienced by them. Instead of answering it, Polus should have pointed out that Socrates has shifted ground. Of course it is more painful to *be* tortured than to torture someone else! But given the previously announced criteria for judging what is fine and shameful – the pleasure or pain that fine and shameful things afford for those who view, hear, or contemplate them – the pleasure or pain of the person contemplated is completely irrelevant. I conclude that Polus has not been refuted.[31]

---

[31] Allen, 1984: 211, disagrees: "In dialectic, playing by the rules of the game, he had his mouth stopped in argument ... This is dialectical checkmate, and Polus has lost."

The foregoing analysis is heavily indebted to Vlastos's critique of Socrates' "thoroughly unsound argument."[32] Having shown that it is unsound, however, Vlastos adds that the mistake is inadvertent and that the argument can be patched up.[33] The apologetically motivated way in which he "corrects" it is an illuminating example of the standard picture at work and, therefore, worth quoting at some length:

> Bodies are said to be beautiful ... if (and only if) they are beneficial for their respective purpose or if they give *the viewer* "a certain pleasure" *in viewing them*" ... There can be no reasonable doubt that the same qualification is understood to apply to the pleasure we derive from beautiful figures [and colors and sounds]. A close reading of the text should convince anyone that this is indeed what is meant. It is only for stylistic reasons that the phrase "because of a certain pleasure if they delight their beholder in beholding them" is not repeated ... [T]he pace is quick and Socrates clips his sentences, reducing verbal baggage to the minimum ... [But] he does expect the sense of the omitted phrase to be supplied ... Socrates is represented as working with elliptical expressions for what he means, drawing inferences which are perfectly valid for what is *said* in this abbreviated form, though invalid for what is *meant* ... Plato evidently feels that the shortened form of the question he puts into his text [i.e., which is more painful: to commit injustice or to suffer it? *without adding* "for the beholder"] is so clear by itself that it would be superfluous to add all those extra words to make it clear ... The omissions would be blameless if they did not trip up his reasoning at an unguarded moment ...[34]

"The pace is quick"? "Superfluous to add all those extra words"? "Expects the sense of the omitted phrase to be supplied"? These are strange claims coming, as they do, from the foremost defender of the thesis that the early dialogues are not stenographic transcripts which preserve the *ipsissima verba* of actual conversations to which Plato was privy, but invented conversations in which Plato, "sharing Socrates' basic philosophical convictions, sets out to think through for himself their central affirmations, denials, and

---

[32] 1991: 144. For the critique itself, see 140–44 – an earlier version of which is found in 1967: 454–60.

[33] Irwin, 1979: 157, is less inclined to rush to Socrates' defense: "Socrates has either a valid argument with an implausible and undefended premise ... or a more plausible premise ... and an invalid argument."

[34] 1991: 141–46 *passim*. See also 148, n. 68: "Let us bear in mind that Plato is simulating a live conversation. When people are arguing on their feet not all of their arguments can be expected to come through in apple-pie order."

reasoned suspensions of belief by pitting them in elenctic encounter against the views voiced by a variety of interlocutors."[35] In thus defending Socrates, Vlastos confuses art with life. He also overlooks a point of considerable philosophical importance, namely, if we *do* supply "the sense of the omitted phrase," the argument collapses. The conclusion "follows" only if Polus does not spot what has happened. And, of course, he does not.

Having again announced that, in testifying against himself, Polus is a witness to the truth of his own view, Socrates next sets out to prove that punished wrongdoers are happier than unpunished ones. His argument – 476a7–479e9 – is as follows:

(i)   Paying a just penalty and being justly punished are the same.

(ii)   Just things are fine insofar as they are just.

It should be noted that, in asserting that insofar as things are just, they are fine, without having discovered (or even asked) what justice is, Socrates is again guilty of the same mistake for which he has twice faulted Polus – first, for claiming that rhetoric is fine without having discovered what it is (448d1–e7), and, second, for claiming that power is good for those who have it without having determined what power is (462c10–d2).[36]

(iii)   Whenever an action is performed, someone (or something) is necessarily acted upon, e.g., if someone strikes a blow, someone (or something) is necessarily struck.

(iv)   The person (or thing) acted upon necessarily experiences an effect which is qualitatively the same (τοιοῦτον) as the agent's action, e.g., if the striker strikes with great force, the person (or thing) struck is struck with great force.

---

[35] *Ibid:* 50. Cf. 1956: xxxv, where Vlastos acknowledges that Socrates makes "a definite error" in the *Protagoras*, but defends him on the ground that it "is one that he could easily have detected when he got the chance to think out his moves in a more leisurely moment."

[36] Irwin, 1979: 167, denies that Socrates violates the so-called "priority of definition" thesis on the ground that he does not claim to *know* what justice is, but is merely arguing from "some beliefs" about justice. This appeal to the distinction between knowledge and belief in their epistemically relevant senses, a distinction which is never explicitly made in the early dialogues, strikes me as yet another *ad hoc* attempt to defend Socrates against the charge of inconsistency. But even if it is not, is not the same defense open to Polus? Could he not say that, in asserting that rhetoric is fine, he is not claiming to *know* what rhetoric is, but merely arguing from "some beliefs" about rhetoric?

(v)   To be punished is to be acted upon, i.e., to suffer some-
         thing, i.e., the punishee acted upon experiences the punish-
         ment administered by the punisher.
(vi)   He who punishes someone rightly punishes him justly and,
         therefore, does what is just.
(vii)   Hence, by (iv), he who is justly punished experiences what is
         just, i.e., he experiences just punishment.

That is, since, by (iv), the effect produced on the patient by the
agent is necessarily "of the same kind" as the action of the agent,
if the affliction of punishment is just, the experience of being punished must also be just.

(viii)   Since, by (ii), whatever is just is fine and good, insofar as the
         punisher does what is just, he does what is fine and good;
         and insofar as the punishee suffers what is just, he suffers
         what is fine and good, and is, therefore, benefited.
(ix)   To be benefited is to become better in soul and to be ridded
         of evil of soul – which is the greatest evil.

Before eliciting Polus' assent to (ix), Socrates tries to remove its
sting by getting him to endorse several less controversial theses
which he thinks are analogous to it, for example, from a financial
point of view, there is no greater evil than poverty; from a medical
point of view, there is no evil greater than disease; and so on.
Accordingly:

(x)   There are also evils in the soul, namely, injustice, igno-
         rance, and cowardice.
(xi)   Of these evils, injustice is the most shameful because it is
         the vice of the soul (ἡ τῆς ψυχῆς πονηρία).
(xii)   Since injustice is the most shameful, it must also be the
         most evil and, therefore, must produce the worst pain or
         the worst harm (or both).
(xiii)   Since it does not produce the most pain, it must produce
         the most harm.
(xiv)   Whatever surpasses all else in harm must be the greatest
         evil.
(xv)   Hence injustice is the greatest evil.

But the argument is not yet complete. Just as money-making and
medicine are the *technai* which rid people of poverty and disease,

so there must be a *technē* which rids the soul of evil and injustice. Hence:

(xvi)   Just as the diseased must be taken to the doctor, so also the unjust and the evil must be taken to the court of justice.

(xvii) And just as those who undergo medical treatment find it unpleasant but submit because it is beneficial, so also those who undergo punishment find it unpleasant but submit for the same reason.

(xviii) And just as those who avoid medical treatment are more wretched than those who submit to it, so also those who escape punishment are more wretched than those who submit to it.

For insofar as punishment improves the soul by ridding it of evil, it is the medicine for evil and injustice. Socrates thereupon qualifies a claim that he had made earlier. To do wrong is not the greatest of evils, as he had claimed at 469b8–9; it is the second greatest evil. The greatest is to do wrong and not to pay the penalty for one's wrongdoing and thereby remain permanently tainted by one's wrongdoing (479d4–6).

(xix)   Hence the happiest man is the one who has no evil in his soul, but the next happiest man is the one who has been purged of evil by being punished.

(xx)   Therefore the unhappiest man is the one who has evil in his soul and who has not been punished.

It follows that since Archelaus has not been punished for his wrongdoing, he cannot be happy.

Polus assents to each step of the argument (or says he does) – albeit very reluctantly: "Apparently" (φαίνεται), "So it seems" ("Εοικεν), and so on. And with good reason. Why should he agree that just things are fine insofar as they are just? Does this mean that being just is a sufficient condition for being fine? Surely it is not a necessary condition; for, as Socrates argued earlier, things are fine (or, at least, judged fine) insofar as they are either useful or a source of pleasure. Furthermore, why should Polus agree that whatever is fine is necessarily good? Good in what sense? And for whom? Or that there is any analogy between things which are bad for the body, e.g., disease, and things which are bad for the soul, e.g., injustice? Or that punishment necessarily has a remedial effect on the soul of the person punished? Above all, why should he agree that a person (or thing) acted upon necessarily experiences an effect which is qualitatively the same as the agent's action?

Arguments based on "correlative ideas" – the term is Aristotle's (*Rh.* 1397a25) – are slippery and need to be employed with caution. It is true that if A treats B nobly and justly, then B is nobly and justly treated by A; if it is right for A to command B, then it is right for B to obey A, and so on. However, having noted these (and other) uncontroversial cases, Aristotle adds:

> But it is possible to draw a false conclusion here. It may be just that A should be treated in a certain way, and yet not just that he should be so treated by B. Hence you must ask yourself two distinct questions: (1) Is it right that A should be thus treated? (2) Is it right that B should thus treat him? and apply your results properly, according as your answers are Yes or No. Sometimes in such a case the two answers differ ... (*Rh.* 1397a29–1397b4).

Aristotle's analysis yields interesting results when applied to punishment. Before investigating this, however, it is worth noticing a preliminary point. Contrary to what Socrates implies, "punishing" is not the name of an action. We punish people by performing particular actions which, if performed by certain people (but not others), under certain descriptions (but not others), and in certain contexts (but not others), count as punishing: for example, we fine them, send them to their rooms, imprison them, and so on. It is trivially true that if A punishes B by striking him with great force, thereby inflicting severe pain, then B is punished by A by being struck with great force and experiences severe pain. It is also trivially true that if A justly punishes B by striking him with great force, thereby inflicting severe pain, then B is justly punished by A by being struck with great force and experiences severe pain. But he does not experience severe pain *justly inflicted*. Even if B believes that his punishment is justly inflicted, the recognized justice of his punishment is not a perceptual component of the pain he experiences. The justice of the punishment is a property neither of the pain inflicted by A nor of the pain experienced by B. One might just as well argue that if A reluctantly strikes B with great force, thereby inflicting severe pain, then B experiences severe pain reluctantly inflicted by A. If this is true, then it follows that the most crucial premise in Socrates' argument is false. It is not the case that a person acted upon necessarily experiences an effect which is qualitatively the same (τοιοῦτον) as the agent's action. The argument, therefore, fails.

The discussion with Polus concludes with a question: What, then, are the proper uses of rhetoric? According to Socrates, they are as follows. So far as injustice is concerned, rhetoric has no proper uses. So far as justice is concerned, however, it has one very important use. Everyone should be eternally diligent to avoid wrongdoing. If a person is guilty of wrongdoing, he should voluntarily turn himself in and submit to punishment in order to prevent the disease of injustice from spreading and becoming chronic. But what if he refuses? In that case, his friends and relatives should not conceal his wrongdoing, but bring it to light, employing their rhetorical powers to the fullest by urging, entreating, and even compelling (ἀναγκάζειν, 480c5) him to turn himself in. Far from protecting friends and relatives who are guilty of wrongdoing, one should be the first to accuse them, thereby following the example of Euthyphro.[37]

Having assented (with varying degrees of conviction) to each step of the argument and having (apparently) accepted its conclusion, Polus cannot endorse this call to incarcerate one's friends and relatives. Indeed, he pronounces it absurd. Ignoring Polus' protest, Socrates confronts him with a dilemma: either the conclusion does not follow and the argument should be abandoned (λυτέον) or the conclusion follows necessarily (ἀνάγκη συμβαίνειν) and the argument stands (480e3). This singularly unhelpful remark[38] suggests that Socrates no longer cares whether Polus has been persuaded. But if that is so, what was the point of the foregoing discussion?

Socrates concludes by deducing a corollary which has prompted considerable scholarly discussion. If it is ever just to harm anyone, the best way would be by doing everything in one's power to prevent a wrongdoer's crimes from coming to light; for this would insure that he would never come to trial and, therefore, never be punished. If he is tried and found guilty, one should do everything in one's power to arrange for his escape, thereby again preventing

---

[37] Dodds, 1959: 258, is mistaken in claiming that Socrates "stops short" of requiring people to insure that unjust friends and relatives are prosecuted and punished.

[38] See Irwin, 1979: 168: "Socrates ... notices the danger of false premises, but neglects the possibility of fallacious inference."

him from being punished and insuring that he will live the rest of his days in wretchedness (480e5–481b1)[39] – from which it seems to follow that rhetoric has some unjust uses after all. At this point, Polus relinquishes his role as Socratic interlocutor and is succeeded by the no-nonsense and far more formidable Callicles.

---

[39] It should not be inferred that, in saying this, Socrates is endorsing the *lex talionis*, thereby renouncing his interdict on retaliation (*Cr.* 49b10–11) and opting for the Simonidean – Polemarchian view of justice as helping one's friends and harming one's enemies. The entire speech is predicated on a condition: *if* (εἰ) it is ever just to harm anyone (480e5–6). See also *HMi.* 376b5–6. Socrates is, of course, persuaded that it is never just to harm anyone. Dodds, 1959: 259, describes this passage as "a piece of comic fantasy," thereby overlooking the fact that it has a deeper and more unsettling implication. Those who do cover up for their friends and relatives by failing to prosecute them and by helping them to escape punishment, are, in fact, harming them and thereby treating them *as if* they were enemies.

CHAPTER 16

Callicles

The third of three increasingly intractable interlocutors in the *Gorgias*, Callicles of Acharnae[1] is one of Plato's great achievements – perhaps (after Socrates) his greatest achievement. Dramatically considered, he is one of the most highly developed and finely wrought interlocutors in the early dialogues; only Protagoras is portrayed with comparable thoroughness and attention to detail, but he is much less interesting. Philosophically considered, he is Socrates' most formidable opponent and his most unyielding critic – the only interlocutor that Socrates does not claim to have refuted. He is also the interlocutor whose dialectical encounter with Socrates contains Plato's deepest pre-middle period insights into moral psychology – particularly, into the psychology of intellectual and moral recalcitrance.

The Platonic counterpart of the Nietzschean Übermensch,[2] "beyond" what is good and evil by convention (κατὰ νόμον) and enamored of what is good by nature (κατὰ φύσιν), Callicles is the incarnation of everything that Plato thought corrupt, dangerous, and "modern" in Athenian life. At the same time, some commentators think that Plato felt a certain affinity towards Callicles and that his portrayal of him was, in part, a retrospective self-portrait. In support of this contention, they point out that there are striking parallels between this young Athenian aristocrat, aspiring to a political career and openly critical of democracy, and the young Plato, who entertained similar ambitions and harbored similar

---

[1] Although Callicles is often regarded as a fictional character, his historicity is implied in several passages: at *G.* 481d1–482a2 where his lover and his behavior in the Assembly are alluded to, at 487c1–4 where his friends (who were historical persons) are mentioned, and at 495d3 where his deme is identified.

[2] A claim endorsed by many commentators, but disputed by Allen, 1984: 220, who thinks that Callicles and Nietzsche differ radically in their basic assumptions and that Callicles is the better philosopher.

sentiments. If they are right,[3] Callicles represents "the anti-Plato in Plato" – "something which Plato had it in him to become (and would perhaps have become, but for Socrates)."[4]

A. E. Taylor[5] once remarked that Calliclean immoralism has a "certain largeness about it which gives it a dangerous fascination." There is also a "certain largeness" about Callicles himself. Although often described as a sophist, he is not; in fact, he has nothing but contempt for these "completely worthless people" (*G.* 520a1–2). Like Thrasymachus, with whom he is sometimes mistakenly identified,[6] Callicles repudiates conventional ideas of justice; but, unlike Thrasymachus, he does not advocate the life of injustice. His repudiation of conventional morality is not a repudiation of morality as such, but of "slave morality" – that sickly moral code rooted in fear and resentment by which the many weak restrain the few strong and which he wants to replace with a "master morality" worthy of superior natures capable of casting off all "unnatural" restraints and living according to the dictates of natural justice.

Callicles is a fascinating and complex character. On the one hand, he is one of the most unlikable (and unliked) interlocutors in the early dialogues; and he has been deluged with the choicest scholarly pejoratives: he is "insufferably patronizing" and "unpleasantly rude,"[7] "shrilly abusive and indignant,"[8] "intelligent, though potentially ruthless,"[9] – a man of "egoistical ambition" who advocates a "bestial society" ("une société animale") based on brute force.[10] On the other hand, he seems to have engaged Plato's philosophical imagination as no other Socratic interlocutor. Plato's apparent fascination with him might have been partly traceable to his undisguisedly elitist beliefs and the outspokenness with which he expresses them – a far from ignoble (οὐκ ἀγεννῶς) intellectual honesty which elicits one of Socrates' rare, non-ironic

[3] Not everyone thinks they are. The "curious" theory that Plato felt "a secret sympathy" for Callicles, "who stood for something deeply implanted in his own nature," is contested by Guthrie, 1971a: 106.
[4] Dodds, 1959: 14, 387.
[5] 1929: 116.
[6] See, e.g., Hamilton and Cairns, 1961: 15: "Thrasymachus ... is simply Callicles under another name"; and Adkins, 1960: 274: Thrasymachus is "Callicles *redivivus*."
[7] Dodds, 1959: 14.
[8] Rutherford, 1995: 161.
[9] Rankin, 1983: 69.
[10] de Romilly, 1992: 120.

compliments: Callicles says what others think but are ashamed to say (492d1–3). The nostalgic wistfulness, expressive of regret for what might have been, with which the closing pages of the *Gorgias* are infused suggests that Plato's apparent fascination with Callicles might have also been partly traceable to his belief that the greater the initial promise, the greater and more lamentable the failure when proper education and habituation are lacking (*R.* 491e1–495b7).

Callicles enters the discussion sneeringly but perceptively. Having just witnessed Socrates arguing that it is better to suffer injustice than to commit it and that punished wrongdoers are happier than unpunished ones, Callicles can hardly believe his ears. Is Socrates serious or joking? If he is serious and if what he says is true, human life would be turned upside down; for our conduct would be exactly the opposite of what it ought to be (481c1–4) – a remark which reveals that, unlike Polus, who had merely found Socrates' claims bizarre, Callicles grasps their revolutionary implications.

Socrates responds by drawing a parallel between Callicles and himself which, although based on a pun and "partly playful,"[11] is so demeaning to Callicles that it seems like an act of deliberate provocation. Both are lovers. But whereas Callicles loves the Athenian public (τοῦ ... Ἀθηναίων δήμου) and Demos, the son of Pyrilampes,[12] catering to their every whim and accommodating himself to their constantly changing opinions, Socrates loves the equally unstable Alcibiades and philosophy which is always the same. It was, in fact, not Socrates but philosophy that advanced the claims which so astounded Callicles (482a2–b2). So he must either "refute philosophy" by demonstrating that wrongdoing and escaping punishment for one's misdeeds are not the greatest evils that can befall a person or he must persist in his erroneous views and live in perpetual discord (διαφωνήσει) with himself his whole life long (481d1–482c3).

Rutherford[13] thinks Socrates is referring to Callicles' incompatible ambitions: on the one hand, he claims to be a "superior nature" who is contemptuous of the Athenian public as convention-bound weak-

---

[11] Irwin, 1979: 169.
[12] Plato's stepfather and the maternal uncle of Charmides (see *Ch.* 158a1–2).
[13] 1995: 158–59.

lings; on the other hand, he is an aspiring politician who must court the favor of the very people he despises. The point is well taken, but the "discord" of which Socrates speaks goes deeper: according to Socrates, Callicles does not just have incompatible ambitions; he also holds inconsistent beliefs. Hence no matter how strongly he disagrees – or claims to disagree – with the theses Socrates has just advanced, he will always believe them – or propositions which entail them.

Callicles finds Socrates' parallel offensive. And with good reason. How could it be anything but offensive to be described as putty in the hands of a fickle lover and a panderer to the masses, and then unfavorably compared to Socrates, lover of philosophy and servant of truth? Callicles' antagonism is evident from the vehemence with which he criticizes Socrates' polemical tactics as well as from the relish with which he accuses him of behaving like a mob-orator. According to Callicles, although Socrates claims to have refuted Polus, he has actually done the same thing to him that he had done (and had been rebuked by Polus for doing) to Gorgias: he has merely shamed him into saying that it is worse to commit injustice than to suffer it – a proposition which is only true by convention and which Polus does not believe. By nature, it is worse to suffer injustice. That is what Polus really believes. Since nature and convention are opposed, anyone who is ashamed to speak his mind will sooner or later contradict himself – which is exactly what happened to Polus. Furthermore, Socrates made sure that it happened. Whenever Polus spoke according to convention, Socrates questioned him according to nature; and whenever he spoke according to nature, Socrates questioned him according to convention.[14] Like Thrasymachus, Callicles sees Socrates' tactics for what they are and will not allow him to get away with them. Although ostensibly an honest inquirer in search of truth, he is actually a dishonest debater who prevails by means of dialectical trickery (482c4–483a8).

The vehemence with which Callicles lodges these objections

---

[14] Aristotle identifies this ground-shifting technique as a species of sophistical refutation and cites this very passage from the *Gorgias* as a prime example (*S.E.* 173a13–16). Throughout the *Gorgias* Callicles repeatedly accuses Socrates of unfair argumentation bordering on sophistry. Like many commentators, Canto, 1987: 349, points out that this criticism is common in the early dialogues. She is, of course, right. The more interesting question, however, is not whether the criticism is common, but whether it is accurate. It seems to me that it usually is.

should not obscure the fact that the objections themselves are on target. That this is so is borne out by the response which Plato puts into Socrates' mouth. Instead of replying to Callicles' objections, Socrates concedes them *in toto*: he acknowledges that he employed shame tactics against Gorgias and Polus who are indeed overly susceptible to shame and whose inconsistencies are traceable to their inability to say what they really believe (487a7–b2).[15] These concessions are unprecedented in the early dialogues. Socrates rarely acknowledges the cogency of the criticism lodged against him, but he does here. These admissions cast further doubt on the methodological importance of the sincere assent requirement. Although officially insisting on sincere assent, Socrates is often willing to waive the requirement, as he did, and now acknowledges having done, with Gorgias and Polus.[16] In Callicles, he encounters an interlocutor who is astute enough to perceive that psychology is not to be confounded with logic and bold enough to say that he will never be shamed into submission.

The examination of Callicles is prefaced by a restatement of his theory of natural justice, apocalyptically announced earlier, according to which the better should rule the worse, the superior should despoil the inferior, and the stronger should have more than the weaker. The discussion begins and ends on a note of uncommon solemnity, and it abounds with Socratic homilies about the momentous importance of the questions being discussed – questions about justice, happiness, and how to live. But it is often a mock solemnity. Although Socrates thinks Callicles' views are not only false but potentially dangerous, his initial arguments against them are so inconsequential, unconvincing, and based on such deliberate misunderstanding that he seems to be toying with his interlocutor rather than seriously trying to refute him.

Since Callicles has been using the terms "better," "superior," and "stronger" more or less interchangeably, Socrates asks

---

[15] This single passage is sufficient to discredit Teloh's (so far as I know unchallenged) contention, 1986: 1, 18, 142, that Socratic dialectic should not be judged "primarily by the excellence of its logic," and that shaming an interlocutor into submission is just as legitimate as refuting him.

[16] Ryle, 1966: 206, thinks passages like this one testify to Plato's growing awareness of the difference between a cogent argument, which refutes an interlocutor, and an unrebutted argument, which merely silences him. See also Irwin, 1979: 170, according to whom Plato periodically employs Callicles to criticize the methods and assumptions of the Socratic elenchus.

whether he thinks they are the same (ταὐτὸν, 488d2). He does. "The same" in what sense? According to Irwin,[17] the question does not admit of a confident answer: Socrates could be asking (i) whether superior people are better and stronger than inferior ones (an empirical question), (ii) whether the terms "superior," "better," and "stronger" all mean the same thing (a definitional question), or (iii) whether these three terms all refer to the same property (a quasi-scientific question). Irwin cautiously opts for (iii) on the dual ground that Socrates hardly ever asks empirical questions and that it is implausible to say that these terms all have the same meaning.

But Socrates' question is not as ambiguous as all that. He is obviously asking whether Callicles thinks that the terms "superior," "better," and "stronger" all mean the same thing: at 488c8–d1 he asks whether they all have the same definition (ὁ αὐτὸς ὅρος), and at 491b5–c4 he complains that whereas Callicles had previously defined (ὡρίζου) "the superior" and "the better" as "the stronger," he is now defining them differently. When Callicles asserts that he does think "the superior," "the better," and "the stronger" are the same in this sense, Socrates thereupon sets out to prove that they are not. His argument – 488d5–489b1 – is as follows:

(i)   By nature, the many weak are numerically superior to the few strong and enact laws to restrain them.
(ii) Since the superior are the same as the better, the laws of the superior are the laws of the better.
(iii) Since the superior and the better are superior and better by nature, their laws are fine by nature.
(iv) The many weak believe that justice consists in having an equal share and that it is more shameful to commit injustice than to suffer it.
(v)   Hence it is not only by convention but also by nature that justice consists in having an equal share and that it is more shameful to commit injustice than to suffer it.

Socrates thereupon concludes that Callicles is wrong on two counts: first, in claiming that nature and convention are opposed; second, in accusing him of being an unscrupulous debater who shifts back and forth between what is true by nature and what is true by convention. How can one shift back and forth between nature and convention when they are one and the same?

[17] 1979: 184–85.

Although many commentators think Socrates' argument exposes a fatal flaw in Callicles' theory of natural justice,[18] Callicles dismisses it as a piece of semantic quibbling (ὀνόματα θηρεύων) which takes unfair advantage of a mere verbal slip (τις ῥήματι ἁμάρτῃ, 489b8–c1). By "the superior," "the better," and "the stronger," he did not mean "the physically or the collectively stronger." If a mob of slaves (or other worthless people) were to convene and issue statements about public policy, does Socrates really think that he would argue that the mere fact that they were superior in physical strength or in number would elevate their utterances to the status of law?

Callicles' point is well taken. Those who think that Socrates has demolished his theory of natural justice have misunderstood the logical status of the concepts of "nature" and "by nature" in Calliclean philosophy. According to Callicles, the few strong are superior to the many weak by nature and should rule over them. He acknowledges, of course, that this natural order is reversed in most existing societies owing to the fact that, in banding together, the many weak have acquired a collective strength which each lacks individually. But this purely contingent fact has no relevance to his theory of natural justice. In saying that something is true "by nature," Callicles is not talking about what is true as a matter of fact; he is not talking about what *is*, but about what *ought* to be. It follows that something can be "according to nature" in the first sense but "contrary to nature" in the second. Socrates' argument ignores this distinction. Thus having conceded that "by nature," that is, as a matter of fact, the collective strength of the many weak enables them to restrain the few strong and to rule over them, Callicles can consistently assert that "by nature" – in his sense of "nature" – they should be ruled by them.

Instead of taking Callicles' position seriously, Socrates makes fun of him and marvels at how he reduces people to guessing at what he means. Having done so, he wonders whether, by "the superior" and "the better," Callicles means "the wiser" (τοὺς φρονιμωτέρους, 489e7–8). Assured that he does, Socrates asks whether he agrees that one wise man is superior to ten thousand fools and should have more than they (490a1–4). Unaware that he is being invited to walk into another verbal trap, Callicles does agree.

---

[18] "Callicles' position collapses at a touch," exults Allen, 1984: 217–18; cf. Irwin, 1979: 185; and Gentzler, 1995: 32–33.

A piece of Socratic mischief follows. Does Callicles mean that a doctor who is wiser about dietary matters than many non-doctors should have more food? Callicles finds the analogy absurd. He was not talking about doctors. Irwin comments: "Socrates takes Callicles to mean that if *A* is wiser than *B* about *F*s, *A* is entitled to more *F*s than *B*."[19] He acknowledges that this general principle is not implied by what Callicles has said, but he insists that *some* justifying principle is needed and that it is therefore "fair" for Socrates to look for it. Irwin is right. Some justifying principle *is* needed. However, in asking whether the doctor's medical knowledge entitles him to more food, Socrates is not making a serious attempt to uncover the intended but unspecified general principle underlying Callicles' remarks; he is introducing an obviously unintended principle from which he proceeds to deduce an equally unintended and patently absurd consequence.[20]

Understandably annoyed, Callicles retorts that he meant nothing of the kind. Socrates continues to feign puzzlement: "But didn't you just say that the wiser and the better should have a larger share?" "Yes, but not of food," snaps Callicles. "Of clothes then?" asks the increasingly insufferable Socrates. "And should the wisest and best weavers and cobblers have the most elegant clothing and the finest shoes?" In response to this string of irrelevancies the exasperated Callicles accuses Socrates of being obsessed with doctors, weavers, and cobblers, and of always saying the same thing. He thereupon explains that the superior people he is talking about are not craftsmen who are wise about their respective *technai*, but political men who are wise about public affairs – and not only wise, but courageous and able to accomplish their purposes without faltering through weakness of soul (491a7–b4).

Having just been accused of always saying the same thing, Socrates now proceeds to accuse Callicles of never saying the same thing, sometimes defining "the superior" and "the better" as "the stronger" and other times as "the wiser" and "the more courageous." The accusation is not wholly false. But neither is it wholly

---

[19] 1979: 188.
[20] Gentzler, 1995: 35, acknowledges that, in deducing this "ridiculously absurd" consequence, Socrates misrepresents Callicles' position; however, like many other commentators, he denies that Socrates is guilty of sophistry on the ground that the difference between dialectic and eristic is, at bottom, a difference in motive: sophists argue for victory; Socrates argues for truth.

true. It is one of those Socratic half-truths which routinely pass for cogent criticism – a half-truth which underscores the fact that Callicles has indeed defined the crucial terms under consideration in a variety of ways, but which also obscures the fact that he had not volunteered any of these opinions but had produced them in response to Socrates' questions: Are the superior the better and the wise? He could hardly have replied, "No, they are the worse and the foolish." Again asked what he means by "the superior" and "the better" – and superior and better *at what* (εἰς ὅτι, 491c5) – Callicles rightly points out that he has already answered both questions: he means those who are wise and courageous about public affairs (491c6–7). This reply – identical to the one he gave at 491a7–b4 – discredits Socrates' accusation that Callicles never says the same thing.

At this point, another gratuitous Socratic complication threatens to arise which Callicles astutely avoids by rejecting the assumption on which it is based. In response to Callicles' contention that the superior should rule the inferior and have more than they, Socrates obscurely asks whether this means that the superior should have more than themselves (491d4–5). When Callicles fails to see what he is driving at, Socrates offers the following "explanation." If Callicles' rulers are temperate, then, in addition to ruling others, they must also rule themselves and be the masters of their own desires. So if rulers should have more than the ruled, it would seem to follow that, insofar as temperate men rule themselves, they should have more than themselves. But before Socrates can draw this preposterous inference, Callicles undercuts his argument by rejecting the idea of self-rule: by "temperate" men, Socrates obviously means fools; for only a fool would voluntarily fail to satisfy a satisfiable desire. "There's no one who'd fail to recognize that I mean no such thing" (491e3–4), retorts the philosopher who has been deliberately misunderstanding his interlocutor since the discussion began. Callicles is unmoved. The superior man is ruled by no one – not even by himself; on the contrary, he cultivates and gratifies his desires to the fullest in accordance with the dictates of natural justice. The many weak are incapable of this and conceal their weakness by inventing bogus virtues like temperance and justice by which to restrain the few strong. But these "virtues" have no foundation in nature; they are merely symptoms of the sickliness of their convention-bound inventors.

Socrates acknowledges the "certain largeness" of Callicles' views and applauds the candor with which he says what others think but are ashamed to say. However, he cannot agree that the happy life is the intemperate and self-indulgent life; if it were, the common view that happiness consists in wanting nothing would be false. Callicles thinks it *is* false; if it were true, stones and corpses would be supremely happy.

Before arguing against this Calliclean view of happiness, Socrates recounts a remark he once heard from a wise man who believed that human beings are already dead and that their bodies are the tombs in which their souls, as the seat of desire, are housed – a remark which was later embellished in the form of a myth in which the souls of the foolish in the hereafter are likened to leaky jars which can never be filled in spite of the continual efforts of the foolish to fill them by fetching water in leaky sieves. Monumentally unimpressed, Callicles retorts that no amount of these quaint little stories will ever induce him to change his mind.

Socrates tries again. Imagine two men with many jars. The first man is temperate and his jars are sound and constantly full, whereas the second man is intemperate and his jars are leaky and in need of constant replenishment. Does Callicles not agree that the first man is happier? He does not. Since the first man wants nothing, he is capable neither of present nor of future pleasure; for pleasure is the filling of a void. On the other hand, the second man is in a state of constant want and therefore also in a state of constant pleasure and anticipation of future pleasure. Happiness is not a static state in which all want has been banished; it is a constant process – an endless succession of wants and satisfactions which requires the largest possible inflow (ἐν τῷ ὡς πλεῖστον ἐπιρρεῖν, 494b2). Socrates thereupon points out that if happiness requires the largest amount of inflow (ἐπιρρέη), it must also require the largest amount of outflow (ἐκροαῖς) too (494b3–4) – a state of affairs which he crudely likens to the digestive process of the torrent-bird, a gluttonous creature "of messy habits"[21] who excretes its food immediately after consuming it.[22]

---

[21] The exquisite euphemism is Dodds's, 1959: 306.
[22] See *Tim.* 72e4–73a10 where Timaeus solemnly explains that to deliver rational creatures from insatiable gluttony the gods equipped them with long intestines which, by prolonging the digestive process, provide them with sufficient between-meal leisure for intellectual pursuits and thereby prevent them from becoming enemies to philosophy and music.

Having just applauded Callicles for the candor with which he expresses his views, Socrates now proceeds to travesty them. Does Callicles mean that the pleasant and happy life consists in eating and drinking when one is hungry and thirsty? He does. And in having and satisfying all (ἁπάσας) one's other desires too? Yes. Ever the literalist, Socrates pounces on the word "all" and invests Callicles' admission with an obviously unintended universality. *All* one's other desires? Including the desire to scratch when one is itchy? The increasingly irritated Callicles again calls Socrates a mob-orator. Again he is right. The logic of standard form universal affirmative categorical propositions aside, the typical use of "all" does not imply unrestricted universality and commit its user to the most idiotic implications his hearer can think of. The prospective diner who replies to the question, "What kind of food do you like?" by saying "All kinds" is not thereby logically committed to acknowledging that he has periodic cravings for chilled fish-heads and grilled rattlesnake. His response is a casual one – an expression of gastronomic adventurousness, not a confession of indiscriminate consumption.

So, too, here. In saying that the pleasant and happy life consists in cultivating and satisfying all one's desires, Callicles is not logically committed to acknowledging that he holds exaggerated beliefs about the ecstacy-inducing potential of scratching his itches. Only a practical joker would draw such an inference. Callicles' meaning is contextual and perfectly clear. In saying this, he is trying to supplement the tiny list of satisfactions supplied by Socrates (eating when hungry and drinking when thirsty) and thus provide the happy man with a richer and more diverse set of pleasures. To claim, with many commentators, that Socrates' example of pleasurable scratching confronts Callicles with a scandalous and hitherto unrecognized implication of his "animalistic" view of happiness signals a failure of imagination. Socrates' trivial and far-fetched example is another attempt to put words into Callicles' mouth.

In saying this, I am not objecting to trivial and far-fetched examples as such. On the contrary, they are often very telling and can be employed with devastating effect. Insofar as their specificity and concreteness yield flashes of illumination which instantly expose deficiencies in claims which seem unobjectionable when formulated at a higher level of generality, trivial and far-fetched examples are often the most effective kind – particularly when employed as counterexamples or in *reductio ad absurdum* arguments. But they also admit of less salutary uses. And that is my complaint. Light can illuminate, but it can also blind. Socrates often employs trivial and far-fetched examples not to enlighten his interlocutors, but to confuse them. Although they are reduced to *aporia*, it is not philosophically fruitful *aporia* which plunges them into genuine perplexity and impels them to search for a solution, but philosophically pointless *aporia* which plunges them into bogus perplexity and renders them liable to careless assertion.

That is exactly what happens to Callicles. Having introduced the example of pleasurable scratching, Socrates does everything in his power to get Callicles to assert that the scratcher is happy. Within the space of a single Stephanus page, the philosopher who had emphatically denounced rhetoric as a form of flattery which gratifies the existing desires of its audience flatters his interlocutor by making no less than three appeals to his shamelessness: at 494c4 he applauds the uninhibitedness with which Callicles had asserted that the pleasant and happy life consists in cultivating and satisfying as many desires as possible; at 494c4–5 he prefaces the question: Is the scratcher happy? by saying: "Do carry on the way you've begun, and take care not to be ashamed"; and at 494d2–4 he responds to the charge of being a mob-orator by paying Callicles a further "compliment": "That's just how I just shocked Polus and Gorgias and made them be ashamed. You certainly won't be shocked, however, or ashamed, for you're a brave man." Callicles succumbs: "I say that even the man who scratches would have a pleasant life" (494d6). Hence in spite of his earlier resolution to abandon psychological warfare and play fair, Socrates is back to his old tricks, again manipulating his interlocutor into saying what he wants him to say. Having (according to many commentators) previously shamed Gorgias and Polus into saying what they do not believe, Socrates here flatters Callicles into saying what (according to many commentators) he does believe, namely, that the scratcher lives a pleasant and happy life.

But Callicles does not believe this at all. That is why he becomes indignant, calling the proposition absurd and again accusing Socrates of being a mob-orator. Furthermore, having just moments ago heard Callicles set forth his actual position, Socrates knows perfectly well that he does not believe it. That is why he has to work so hard to get him to assert it. If Gorgias and Polus are overly susceptible to shame, Callicles is surely overly susceptible to flattery. Having promoted himself as a shameless man, he is a sitting duck for every shameful thesis that comes along. He has a reputation to protect. So if it is shameful to assert that the scratcher lives a pleasant and happy life, he will assert it.

With his interlocutor on the defensive, Socrates presses his advantage: "Suppose the scratcher scratches only his head. Would he not experience more pleasure if his scratching extended to other parts of his body? How would you answer if someone were to ask all the questions that naturally come to mind?" (494e1–3). At this point, even Socrates realizes that the limits of propriety have been reached and that a detailed enumeration of other bodily parts in need of scratching would be going too far. Yet what he cannot bring himself to describe in scintillating detail he nevertheless manages to convey in more general terms by asking whether Callicles' admission does not lead inexorably to the conclusion that the catamite is the happiest of men – thereby incurring a severe rebuke for leading the discussion in such an unsavory direction (494e7–8).

"The unshockable Callicles is shocked at last" upon realizing that his theory of natural justice entails conclusions which are "repugnant to ethical common sense," exclaims Dodds[23] – thereby missing the point of Callicles' remark which is a rebuke of Socrates' crudity. "Ethical common sense" has nothing to do with it. Callicles is shocked: not because Socrates has shown that his position entails a "repugnant" conclusion, but because he is apparently prepared to do anything to win an argument. Characteristically absolving himself of all responsibility, Socrates claims that it was not he but Callicles who led the discussion in this unsavory direction by asserting without qualification (ἀνέδην οὕτω) that anyone who experiences any pleasure, whatever it may be, is happy, and thereby failing to distinguish good from bad pleasures (494e9–495a2).

Socrates is wrong on both counts. Callicles never said that anyone who experiences any pleasure, whatever it may be, is happy. That is not Callicles' thesis; it is a thesis which Socrates deduced from his admission that the scratcher lives a pleasant and happy

---

[23] 1959: 307. Vickers, 1988: 104–5, makes the same mistake.

life. Although Socrates had induced him to affirm this thesis, he did not thereby reveal the triviality of Callicles' view of happiness;[24] he misrepresented it. Callicles believes that "superior natures" should cultivate and satisfy as many desires as possible, that is, the happy life is the appetitive life conducted on the grandest possible scale – a life in which one's degree of happiness is in exact correlation to the number of desires one has cultivated and satisfied. Socrates misrepresents his position by focusing on one trivial desire – the desire to scratch an itch – and by luring him into concluding that since the happy man cultivates and satisfies all his desires, and since the urge to scratch an itch is a desire, it follows that the scratcher is happy – and the more he scratches, the happier he is. Callicles should have disputed this conclusion. Two replies are open to him. First, he could have pointed out that although scratching one's itches is sometimes (though hardly always) pleasurable, it is a trivial pleasure unworthy of the "superior natures" he envisages. Second, he could have pointed out that although scratching one's itches may *contribute* to one's happiness, it is not *constitutive of* it. Scratching one's itches is, at best, a necessary condition for happiness; it is not a sufficient condition.

But does Callicles even think that it is a necessary condition? Surely not. If he did, why would the mere mention of inordinate scratching prompt him to object to the unsavory direction in which Socrates has led the discussion? A possible answer – Dodds's[25] – is that Callicles objects because he is revolted by the hitherto unrecognized and "repugnant" implication of his own theory. But why say that? Why not say that he objects because he does not hold this theory and because Socrates has parodied his actual position beyond recognition? Callicles clearly believes that pleasure is a necessary condition for happiness, but he does not believe that any *particular* pleasure is. He also believes that "superior natures" are a breed apart – wise about public affairs and sufficiently powerful and courageous to achieve their ends, thereby enjoying what natural justice decrees as rightfully theirs. Whatever one may think of this view, it cannot be refuted by parody and ridicule. Surely the Calliclean man would not be sidetracked by a

---

[24] As Allen, 1984: 219, implies when he jubilantly asserts: "It is to this that Callicles' good by nature has been reduced. It is the result of claiming that those who attain pleasure, whatever the pleasure, are happy."

[25] See n. 23.

scratching compulsion – much less rank scratching his itches among life's most coveted pleasures.

Socrates is also wrong in claiming that Callicles fails to distinguish good pleasures from bad, thereby committing himself to unrestricted hedonism – the view that whatever is pleasant is good and that the goodness of anything is to be judged solely in terms of its pleasure-producing capacity. In fact, he explicitly rejects this view at 499b6–8 where he categorically states that some pleasures are better (βελτίους) and others worse (χείρους). Since Socrates later accuses him of changing his mind – a criticism endorsed by every commentator I have consulted[26] – it is important to be clear about what Callicles actually does believe.

It is true that at 495a5–6 Callicles asserts that the good and the pleasant are the same (τὸ αὐτό). But his reason should not slip by unnoticed: he does so to avoid inconsistency (ἵνα ... μοι μὴ ἀνομολογούμενος ᾖ ὁ λόγος, 495a5). He adds that were he to assert that they are different – which is his actual view – he would be advancing a thesis which is inconsistent with his previous assertion that the scratcher is happy – an unfortunate admission which now comes back to haunt him.[27] Socrates knows that these propositions are inconsistent. That is why he was so intent on inducing Callicles to assert that the good and the pleasant are the same. Having asserted it, he cannot now consistently say that they are different. So to avoid inconsistency he says that they are the same – only to be told that he cannot advance a thesis simply to avoid inconsistency. He must say what he really believes. Failure to do so renders him an unfit dialectical partner (495a8–9).

This is yet another of those periodic Socratic assurances of seriousness which is often wrenched from context and cited as evidence of the importance of the sincere assent requirement. In fact, it is an eristic trick by which Socrates prevents Callicles from saying what he really believes. Trapped by his own previous admissions, he now faces a dilemma: he must either say what he really

---

[26] Irwin's gloss is representative: Callicles "pretends that he was not serious in his previous endorsement of hedonism ... But his pretence is useless" (1986: 69). Cf. Guthrie, 1975: 303; Santas, 1979: 256–57; and Kahn, 1983: 76.

[27] Irwin, 1986: 65–66, is mistaken in claiming that Callicles is "persuaded" that his advocacy of the unrestrained satisfaction of desire commits him to hedonism. He is also mistaken in claiming that Socrates "makes sure" that Callicles sincerely assents to hedonism "in full recognition of [its] shameful consequences."

believes – that the good and the pleasant are different and that the scratcher is not happy, thereby asserting inconsistent propositions – or he must avoid inconsistency by saying what he does not believe – that the scratcher is happy, and that the good and the pleasant are the same. Shrinking from the first alternative and forbidden from opting for the second, he stalls for time. In the meantime, he fights back by accusing Socrates of speaking contrary to his convictions himself (495b1) – an accusation to which I will return.

Socrates induces Callicles to opt for the second horn of the dilemma by administering yet another heavy dose of flattery, assuring him that anyone who asserts that the good and the pleasant are the same must face a series of shameful consequences. Callicles could not be more pleased and instantly asserts this shameful proposition, thereby feigning sincere assent with the full cooperation of Socrates who again knows perfectly well from Callicles' previous remarks that this is not what he really believes. Socrates thereupon implicates himself still further in the charade by requiring Callicles to certify that what he has just said *is* what he really believes (495b8) and that he will be arguing in earnest (σπουδά-ζοντος, 495c1). Although Callicles obliges him, it is abundantly clear from the context that it is not. Accordingly, when he subsequently denies that the good and the pleasant are the same and affirms that there is a difference between good and bad pleasures, he is not changing his mind, as Socrates falsely alleges; on the contrary, he is saying what he really believed all along, but had been forbidden to say. In short, although ostensibly forbidding Callicles to say what he does not believe, Socrates actually requires him to do so and then faults him for changing his mind when he finally says what he does believe. It is not Callicles' actual view but his momentary, *and Socratically-induced*, abandonment of it which generates the inconsistency. He could, in fact, have avoided the whole problem. Instead of initially asserting that the scratcher is happy and denying that the good and the pleasant are different, he should have asserted that the good and the pleasant are different and denied that the scratcher is happy, thereby saying what he really believed at the outset and forestalling Socrates' criticism.

Having induced Callicles to assert that the good and the pleasant are the same, Socrates advances three arguments designed to prove that they are not. In the process, he spells out the shameful consequences which must be faced by anyone who holds this view. Unlike the foregoing skirmish, which often borders on the comical, these arguments are completely serious. The first – 495c3–497a5 – is as follows:

(i)   There is something called knowledge.
(ii)   There is also a kind of courage which accompanies it.
(iii)   Knowledge and courage are different.
(iv)   Knowledge and pleasure are also different.
(v)   Therefore courage and pleasure are different.
(vi)   Those who are happy are in the opposite condition of those who are unhappy.
(vii)   Since happiness and unhappiness are opposites, they necessarily exclude one another.
(viii) Hence just as a person cannot simultaneously be healthy and diseased, so also he cannot simultaneously be good (happy) and evil (and unhappy).
(ix)   Hence if there is anything which a person can simultaneously have and not have, it cannot be good and evil.
(x)   Like all lacks, hunger and thirst are painful; but eating and drinking when one is hungry and thirsty are pleasant because they are the filling of a lack.
(xi)   To drink when one is thirsty is to drink when one is in pain.
(xii)   But it is also to fill a lack and, therefore, pleasant.
(xiii) Hence, in drinking, pain and pleasure are simultaneous.
(xiv)   Since it is impossible simultaneously to be happy and unhappy but possible simultaneously to experience pain and pleasure, pleasure and pain cannot be the same as happiness and unhappiness.
(xv)   Therefore the good is not the same as the pleasant.

Callicles disputes this conclusion: not by finding fault with the argument which generates it, but by feigning puzzlement and accusing Socrates of sophistry. In turn, Socrates accuses Callicles of dissembling. Did he not just agree that the cessation of thirst coincides exactly (ἅμα) with the cessation of drinking? Has he changed his mind during this short interval?

Before proceeding to Socrates' second argument, it is worth noticing that the first is fallacious. There is a distinction between drinking *as a cause* of pleasure and drinking *as pleasurable*. Drinking ice-cold lemonade on a blistering summer day is not a mere means

to the end of quenching one's thirst; it is also an intrinsically pleasurable experience and an end in itself. Furthermore, in saying
that the cessation of thirst (which is painful) coincides exactly with
the cessation of drinking (which is pleasurable), Socrates is advancing a temporal rather than a causal claim. Stated in full generality,
the cessation of pain always coincides exactly with the cessation of
the activity which alleviates it. This claim comes perilously close to
being tautological. Whatever non-tautological plausibility it has
depends on a judicious selection of examples. But counterexamples spring readily to mind. The cessation (or diminution) of
pain never coincides exactly with the administration of a pain kill-
er. There is always a temporal interval, however brief, between
the administered remedy and the experienced relief. The cessation
(or diminution) of pain is always gradual. But even when it is no
longer excruciating, diminished (or diminishing) pain is often still
very hard to endure. Neither third-person descriptions of diminishing pain nor first-person reports of it employ "pleasure" and
"pain" as correlative terms. To say "I am experiencing less pain"
is not tantamount to saying "I am experiencing more pleasure."

Socrates' second argument – 497b4–d8 – follows:

(i)   Since the cessation of the pain of thirst coincides exactly with
      the pleasure of drinking, pain and pleasure can coexist simul-
      taneously.
(ii) But good and evil cannot.
(iii) Therefore the good and the evil are not the same as the
      pleasant and the painful.

Before Callicles can agree or disagree, Socrates launches his third
argument – 497e3–499b3 – a *reductio ad absurdum* designed to demonstrate that the identification of the good and the pleasant leads
to a paradoxical conclusion. However, before he can generate the
paradox, he must elicit Callicles' assent to the premises which
entail it – something easier said than done. The psychological dynamics between them shed light on the importance – or, rather,
the non-importance – of the sincere assent requirement.

Callicles agrees that the good and the beautiful are so designated
because goodness and beauty are present in (παρουσίᾳ) them. He
also agrees that the term "good" is not predicated of the foolish
and the cowardly, but of the wise and the courageous, and that
both the foolish and the wise experience pleasure and pain. How-

ever, when asked who experiences *more* pleasure or pain, he replies that there is not much difference (498a4–5). That, of course, is not the answer Socrates wants; so he changes his line of questioning: Who experiences more pleasure when the enemy retreats: the cowardly or the courageous? Callicles replies that both experience it about equally (παραπλησίως, 498b1), again disappointing Socrates who immediately opts for a third line of questioning: Who experiences pain when the enemy advances: the cowardly or the courageous? Callicles again replies that both experience it. Only when asked whether both experience it equally does he finally concede that *perhaps* (ἴσως) the cowardly experience more pain when the enemy advances, just as *perhaps* they experience more pleasure when the enemy retreats (498b5–7). This reply – the one for which Socrates has been fishing for almost two Stephanus pages – enables him to generate the paradox. For if the pleasant and the good are the same, then, insofar as the cowardly experience more pleasure than the courageous when the enemy retreats, they also experience more good and are therefore better.

I am not disputing that the conclusion follows from the premises to which Callicles "assents." But I am disputing that he believes them.[28] As is clear from the overall context, what he actually believes is that in the situations Socrates has described the courageous and the cowardly experience pleasure and pain *about equally*. Since that is not the answer Socrates wants, he brushes it aside and continues asking questions until he gets the answer he does want, that is, the one he needs to generate the paradox.[29] Throughout the discussion, he is ostensibly trying to determine what Callicles really believes, and Callicles is telling him. But he ignores what Callicles says, puts words into his mouth, and overlooks the patently obvious fact that he finally "agrees" that *perhaps* the cowardly experience more pain than the courageous when the enemy advances because he has grown weary of the "discussion" and will say anything Socrates wants him to say. His reason, al-

---

[28] Gentzler, 1995: 39, acknowledges that Socrates induces Callicles to endorse theses which are incompatible with his actual position.

[29] In view of his usual dispassionate, non-apologetic, and critical approach to the Platonic corpus – rare virtues among traditional and contemporary Anglo-American commentators – I am baffled by Irwin's claim, 1986: 68, that Socrates "never interferes" with his interlocutors' attempts to articulate their views and never employs "eristic coercion," that he allows Polus "full freedom" to say whatever he wants to say, and that he tries "even harder" with Callicles.

though grumpily expressed, is exactly on target: since Socrates has been feeding him premises all along, he might as well assert them himself and abandon the charade of a "joint" search. Which he subsequently does.

Gloating over his apparent victory, Socrates asks Callicles whether it does not follow from "his" admissions that the coward is the better man. Callicles is amused by the childish delight with which Socrates' pounces on his opponent's slightest concession – even if made in jest – and thereupon announces that he had been joking when he said that the good and the pleasant are the same; actually, like most people, he thinks that they are different and that some pleasures are better and others worse (499b6–8).[30] In saying this, he trivializes his earlier contention that he had said the good and the pleasant are the same only to avoid inconsistency. Unlike that contention, an honest one which revealed that he believed all along that the good and the pleasant are different, the contention that he had only been joking is a dishonest one which enables Socrates falsely to accuse him of having changed his mind.

Having finally said what he believed all along – that there is a difference between good and bad pleasures – Callicles now makes a series of damaging admissions: (i) that there is a distinction between good and bad pleasures; (ii) that good pleasures are beneficial (ὠφέλιμοι) whereas bad ones are harmful (βλαβεραί); (iii) that pleasures are good because they are beneficial and bad because they are harmful; (iv) that some pains are worthy (χρησταί) and others base (πονηραί); (v) that one ought always to choose the former and never the latter; (vi) that since the good is the end of all human action, one ought to choose pleasant things for the sake of the good, not good things for the sake of the pleasant; and (vii) that not everyone can distinguish good from bad pleasures, and to do so requires expertise (499c6–500a6).

Socrates thereupon reminds Callicles of a point made during the discussion with Polus (464c3–d3), namely, that there are some practices, for example, cookery, which are mere "knacks" and concerned only with pleasure, whereas there are others, for example medicine, which are genuine *technai* and concerned with what

---

[30] Since, according to Callicles, some pleasures are worse than others, they should be avoided. It follows that, *pace* Irwin, 1979: 206, in calling temperate people "fools," Callicles is not rejecting temperance *simpliciter*; he is only rejecting the "unnatural" view of temperance embodied in conventional morality.

is good. He then reinstates the sincere assent requirement and forbids Callicles to answer jokingly, capriciously, and contrary to his real opinion (500b5–c1). Having done so, he asks whether Callicles thinks there are analogous practices which have to do with the soul, some concerned only with its pleasure and others concerned with its moral improvement. Callicles does not think so, but he is willing to concede the point for the sake of the argument and to please Gorgias. Surprisingly, Socrates does not protest. Ignoring his interlocutor's withholding of sincere assent, he continues with his line of questioning. Is this tendency to gratify the existing desires of the soul without regard for its true interest confined to single individuals or is it also practiced by groups of individuals and even by whole assemblies? The argumentatively detached Callicles "agrees" that it is also practiced by the latter. He also "agrees" that there are many other practices, for example, instrumental and vocal music, dithrambic poetry, and tragedy,[31] which also aim at gratification and pleasure and are therefore also forms of flattery.

Returning to the subject of rhetoric, Socrates asks whether rhetoricians try to improve the citizenry or whether they, too, aim only at gratification and pleasure? Callicles does not think this question can be answered *in general*; there are rhetoricians who fall into both categories. Clearly, Pericles, Themistocles, Miltiades, and Cimon fall into the former. Socrates is skeptical. If true virtue consists in making oneself and others as good as possible, then these were not good men; for just as the craftsman does not work haphazardly but in accordance with specialized knowledge which enables him to impose form on his materials, so also the good man aims at what is best (ἐπὶ τὸ βέλτιστον), and looks to something (ἀποβλέπων πρός τι), that is, to some standard, which enables him to regulate and to control his own desires and the desires of others. Just as health and strength are the properties of the well-formed body, so also there are analogous properties of the well-

---

[31] Socrates' contention that tragic poetry exists to gratify the corrupt tastes of "the Many" is defended by Dodds, 1959: 320–21, on the ground that Euripides' tragedies are sometimes guilty of "pander[ing] to the prejudices of an ignorant audience." Vickers, 1988: 106, is shocked that so great a scholar and so acute a critic of Greek drama should have defended Socrates on this point. Plato makes the same criticism at *Laws* 659b5–c3 where the Athenian Stranger asserts that the tragedians write in order to gratify "the depraved tastes" of their audiences – an unfortunate state of affairs which reveals that, instead of instructing their audiences, they are instructed by them.

formed soul. Can Callicles identify them? Like many hard pressed interlocutors, Callicles prefers that Socrates answer this question himself. Surprisingly, given his disavowal of moral knowledge, he complies. The properties of the well-formed soul are lawfulness and law (νόμιμόν τε καὶ νόμος), that is, justice and temperance (504d1–3). "Let it be so" (Ἔστω), retorts Callicles.

Let what be so? To what is Callicles paying lip-service? What he grudgingly "affirms" is the Socratic thesis that the healthy soul is the lawful one – a thesis which Socrates had previously derived from a series of premises to which Callicles had insincerely assented after having announced that he was dropping out of the discussion as a serious participant but that he would continue to function as Socrates' straightman in deference to Gorgias' wishes. Socrates paid no attention to that announcement then, and he pays no attention to it now. It is easy to see why. Only by ignoring it can he conceal the fact that he is conducting a mock elenchus.[32] As the discussion proceeds, it becomes increasingly hard for him to extract even token concessions from Callicles. The discussion has degenerated into a competitive eristic contest – albeit about "a matter of the greatest importance."

Proceeding as if Callicles were hanging on his every word, Socrates unleashes a series of (mostly rhetorical) questions: Will the true rhetorician not try to implant justice and temperance in the souls of his hearers? And will he not also try to uproot injustice, intemperance, and every other vice? And does it not follow that, like a diseased body, a diseased soul should not be allowed to gratify its desires at will, but only those which are beneficial for it? Callicles retorts that he has no idea what Socrates is talking about, reiterates that he is playing along only to please Gorgias, and finally urges him to interrogate someone else – himself, if need be. Although Socrates reacts as if that would be nothing short of a calamity, it is exactly what he has been doing ever since Callicles dropped out of the discussion as a serious participant. Required to interrogate himself, he agrees, prefacing his self-examination by reminding everyone that they must be contentious (φιλονίκως) to know what is true and false and by urging them to refute him if any of the admissions he makes to himself seem to them dubious.

---

[32] Brickhouse and Smith, 1995: 14, n. 21, are mistaken in claiming that the conclusions at which Socrates arrives "derive plainly" from admissions Callicles had made before dropping out of the discussion. Irwin, 1986: 69–70, makes the same mistake.

And if Callicles (or anyone else) can refute him, he will consider him his greatest benefactor. Callicles dourly tells him to get on with it.

Socrates thereupon sets out to prove that it is the temperate rather than the intemperate who are happy. Asking and answering his own questions – 506c5–507c7 – he proceeds as follows:

(i) The pleasant and the good are not the same.
(ii) The pleasant should be done for the sake of the good, not the good for the sake of the pleasant.
(iii) The pleasant is that which gives pleasure, but the good is that which makes us good.
(iv) Everyone is good insofar as virtue is present in him.
(v) Virtue is not present randomly, but by order, rightness, and art.
(vi) Hence an ordered and good soul is better than a disordered and bad one because it is temperate, whereas a disordered and bad soul is intemperate.
(vii) The temperate do what is fitting (τὰ προσήκοντα) towards gods and men, i.e., they are pious and just; they are also courageous, pursuing and avoiding what should be pursued and avoided.
(viii) Therefore since the temperate are just, courageous, and pious, they do what is good and noble, and are happy; and since the intemperate do what is evil and shameful, they are wretched.

This is Socrates' view, and he thinks it is true (ἀληθῆ, 507c8–9). In saying that his beliefs are true, Socrates means that they are held fast by arguments of steel and adamant (σιδηροῖς καὶ ἀδαμαντίνοις) – or so it would seem (ὡς γοῦν ἂν δόξειεν οὑτωσί, 509a1–2). And unless Callicles (or someone even more vigorous) can undo them, anyone who says anything else must be wrong. Although Socrates does not claim to *know* that his beliefs are true, he does know that anyone who has ever denied them ended up looking ridiculous (καταγέλαστος, 509a7).

Since wrongdoing and escaping punishment for one's misdeeds are the two greatest evils that can befall a person, and since one cannot avoid these evils just by wishing to avoid them, it follows that one must possess some power and art (δύναμίν τινα καὶ τέχνην, 510a4) which enables him to avoid both *being* wronged and *doing* wrong. At this point, Socrates seems genuinely troubled by Callicles' argumentative detachment and blurts out that he really must know whether he agrees that all wrongdoing is involuntary. Callicles glibly chirps that Socrates may believe that if he wishes.

Again ignoring his interlocutor's withholding of sincere assent, Socrates addresses himself to the first question: How can a person avoid *being* wronged, that is, suffering injustice? His answer should be noted carefully because it is contrary to *his* real opinion – a fact which reveals that Callicles was right when he accused him of sometimes speaking contrary to his own convictions himself (495b1). To avoid being wronged, Socrates falsely declares, one must either be a tyrant oneself or be closely associated with one; for only then will one have sufficient power to avoid suffering injustice (509d3–510a9). Temporarily back in the discussion, Callicles agrees and adds that he stands ready to praise Socrates whenever he talks sense.

Socrates thereupon proceeds to the second question: Does being or being associated with a tyrant also enable one to avoid *doing* wrong, that is, to avoid *committing* injustice? Will it not rather equip one with the power to commit injustice with impunity and thus become as bad as the tyrant?

The temporarily engaged Callicles realizes that he has been tricked. Marveling at Socrates' uncanny ability to twist the argument to his own advantage, he responds with a question of his own: Does Socrates not know that people who associate with or imitate tyrants protect themselves by killing all non-imitators? Socrates is unimpressed. All that shows is that some base men are willing to murder others who are noble and good. Callicles agrees and adds that it is precisely that which makes their behavior so deplorable. This remark may come as a surprise to readers who suppose that Callicles identifies justice with power and, like Thrasymachus, believes that might makes right. But he does not. Callicles deplores this state of affairs every bit as much as he thinks Socrates does. However, to Callicles' (and perhaps the reader's) surprise, Socrates does not deplore it. As he sees it, the rational person (νοῦν ... ἔχοντι, 511b7) does not try to avoid *being* wronged in hopes of living as long as possible; he tries to avoid *doing* wrong and sets little store by his life. That is to say, true virtue does not consist in preserving one's life, but in cultivating one's character. That is why he thinks no politician can be truly virtuous. And if Callicles thinks he can become one without conforming to popular criteria for political success, he is deluding himself. Callicles' reply is noteworthy:

I don't know how it is that I think you're right, Socrates, but the thing that happens to most people has happened to me: I'm not really persuaded by you (οὐ πάνυ σοι πείθομαι). (513c4–6)

Socrates' reply is even more noteworthy. First, he explains that Callicles' lack of persuasion is traceable to his love of Demos (ὁ δήμου ... ἔρως)[33] which has taken root in his soul and causes him to resist (ἀντιστατεῖ); second, he assures him that if they examine these matters "often and in a better way," he will be persuaded (513c7–d1).

Returning to the distinction between practices which aim at moral improvement and those which aim only at gratification and pleasure, Socrates observes that since the latter are forms of flattery, they are base and of no account. The defensively retrenched Callicles perfunctorily concurs: "Let it be so" (Ἔστω). Again ignoring his interlocutor's withholding of sincere assent, Socrates asserts that it is the former which must be possessed by the true politician who cares about the city. So before he can endorse Callicles' intended entry into public life, Socrates needs to know whether he has improved anyone. That is to say, is there anyone who was previously bad, unjust, undisciplined, and foolish, but who is now admirable and good because of his association with Callicles? (515a5–b2)[34]

Callicles is annoyed by the question and accuses Socrates of contentiousness. Socrates ignores the charge and insists that he is merely trying to find out how Callicles views the politician's task. Have they not agreed that the true politician is not a flatterer but strives to make the citizenry as good as possible? When Callicles refuses to answer, Socrates answers for him: we have agreed (515c3–4). But was this the goal of Pericles and the other politi-

---

[33] It is unclear whether Socrates is referring to Callicles' lover – Demos (see *G.* 513b5–6) – or to the Athenian public (or both).

[34] Arieti, 1991: 89–90, faults Socrates for his "nastiness" and "rudeness" in asking Callicles this question – especially in view of his own failure to improve Alcibiades. Refreshingly free of the apologetic tendency to find excuses for Socrates' often unscrupulous dialectical conduct, Arieti candidly acknowledges his logical and psychological shortcomings throughout the discussion with Callicles and contends that they were among the principal causes of his failure. He concludes that Plato does not expect his readers to be filled with admiration for Socrates in this dialogue, but rather to see him as "bull-headed, tricky, abusive, and wholly indifferent to reality."

cians upon whom Callicles has just heaped such lavish praise? Callicles thinks so, but Socrates disagrees. If Pericles had been a good politician, the citizenry would have been better at the end of his tenure than it was at the beginning; in fact, it was worse. Pericles made the people idle, cowardly, talkative, and covetous. Callicles disparages this assessment on the ground that Socrates' source of information is obviously the people with battered ears (515e11).[35] Socrates thereupon points out that the Athenian citizenry thinks the same thing. Asked whether the fact that the Athenian citizenry thinks that Pericles was a villain entails that he was a villain, Socrates replies with an analogy. What would Callicles think of an animal keeper whose charges responded cordially to him at first, but were soon kicking, butting, and biting him? Callicles agrees that such a man would not be a good animal keeper – but only to gratify (χαρίσωμαι) Socrates. "Then gratify me some more," (Καὶ τόδε τοίνυν μοι χάρισαι, 516b5–6), replies the philosopher who will allegedly tolerate nothing less than complete sincerity from his interlocutor. If Pericles had been a good keeper of men, his charges would have become more just; in fact, they became less just. So he was not a good keeper of men. "In your opinion," snaps Callicles. "In yours too, by Zeus, given your previous agreements" (ἐξ ὧν ὡμολόγεις, 516d5), retorts Socrates, again holding Callicles responsible for his previous admissions in spite of the fact that he has repeatedly announced that they were perfunctory and non-committal.

Having disposed of Pericles, Socrates makes equally short work of the rest and summarily concludes that recent Athenian history does not yield a single example of a good politician.[36] A long diatribe follows in which the man who cannot tolerate long speeches spends the next three Stephanus pages railing against politicians, past and present, who wasted their time on trivialities and who gratified the existing desires of the citizenry instead of inculcating nobler ones and making it temperate and just. He concludes that they were all pretenders to the title of politicians, just as the sophists are pretenders to the title of teachers of virtue. Surely I am not the only reader who has wished that Callicles had responded

---

[35] The allusion is to the young, oligarchic Athenians whose cauliflower ears bore witness to their Spartan sympathies and addictions among which was boxing (see Dodds, 1959: 357).

[36] Curiously, in the *Meno* Socrates says exactly the opposite: at 93a5–6 he acknowledges that Athens presently has good politicians and that it also had good ones in the past; and at 94a7–b2 he includes Pericles among them.

to this tiresome harangue by bemoaning his "poor memory" and by confessing that Socrates had lost him pages ago. Astonishingly, having gone on at such length, Socrates proceeds to blame Callicles who "forced" him to make a speech by refusing to answer his questions (519d5–7).[37] But Callicles knows better. When he sarcastically taunts him as the man who could not speak unless someone answered him, Socrates flippantly retorts, "Evidently I could" (519e1).

Having denounced every politician in recent Athenian history, Socrates claims that he alone practices the true political art (ἀληθῶς πολιτικῇ τέχνῃ, 521d6–7), refusing to flatter his contemporaries and trying to improve them by directing them to what is best. And if he is accused of speaking harshly about the old and of corrupting the young, he will be powerless to defend himself. Asked whether it is desirable for a man to be in such a position, he replies that the best defense is to be guilty of no wrongdoing; for that alone enables one to bear death easily. The rational man does not fear death; what he does fear is arriving in the next world with an unjust soul. Asked whether he would like to know why Socrates believes this, the eschatologically indifferent Callicles briskly replies that since Socrates has had the last word on every other subject, he might as well have it on this one, too. The Great Myth follows (523a3–526d2).

According to Homer,[38] after death[39] the souls of the just depart

---

[37] Instead of faulting Socrates for this childish ascription of blame – "It's *your* fault" – most commentators agree with him. Coventry's opinion is representative: "[I]n an imperfect world ... confrontation with an obdurate interlocutor may necessitate a compromising of [the dialectician's] principles" (1990: 184, n. 29).

[38] Socrates' uncritical reliance on Homer throughout this passage is unprecedented in the early dialogues. It is also glaringly inconsistent. He never allows his interlocutors to defend their views by invoking Homeric authority and periodically expresses grave reservations about Homeric theology.

[39] Death is the separation (διάλυσις) of soul and body (524b2–4). Although this passage contains the first explicit statement of Plato's metaphysical dualism, the seeds of this view are already present at *Ap.* 40e4–7 and *Cr.* 54c6–8 where the *possibility* of a final judgment is envisaged. However, since the first passage is qualified by skeptical doubts as to whether there is a hereafter and since the second is part of a speech which Socrates puts into the mouth of the personified Laws of Athens, most commentators are wary of investing him with any explicit eschatological beliefs. This excessively cautious attitude was challenged years ago by A. E. Taylor, 1911: 31: "It is still common to say that Socrates took up a purely agnostic position with respect to immortality ... but it requires a singularly dull and tasteless reader not to see that his own sympathies are with the hope of a blessed immortality." Although a hope is not the same thing as a belief, it seems to me that Taylor's remark is a salutary corrective to the still prevalent tendency on the part of many commentators to over-emphasize the differences between Socratic and Platonic philosophy.

to the Isles of the Blessed where they dwell in perpetual happiness; but the souls of the unjust are consigned to the prison of Tartarus where they are punished for their misdeeds. Since I have already discussed this myth and Socrates' reasons for employing it in the chapter on Cephalus, it will be sufficient to reiterate the main points here.

The purpose of the terrible punishment to which the wrongdoer is subjected in the hereafter is not retributive but remedial. For it is only by being punished that he can be purged of the effects of his wrongdoing – provided, of course, that he is curable. Not all wrongdoers are. If he is not, he is still punished; but his punishment has a different justification. Incapable of improvement himself, the incurable wrongdoer is punished in hopes of deterring other curables who, by contemplating his awful suffering, will be afraid (φοβούμενοι) and become better (*G.* 525b3–4).[40] Such is the fate awaiting all whose lives have been unjust – not only Archelaus and other tyrants like him, but also the great mass of mankind. For given the opportunity to commit injustice, few will opt for justice. Although Callicles may dismiss all this as an old wife's tale, Socrates offers it as an account (λόγον), i.e., as true (ὡς ἀληθῆ, 523a2).[41] He belabors this point by repeating it twice – at 524a8–b1 and at 526d3–4. It is because he is persuaded (πέπεισμαι) by it (526d4) that he has spent his life trying to become as good as possible so as to present his soul to the judges in the best possible condition and avoid punishment. And he calls all men to this life

---

[40] I cannot accept Allen's contention, 1984: 229, that Socrates is trying to make Callicles fear injustice rather than punishment. It seems to me that he is trying to make him fear punishment *for* his injustice.

[41] "True" in what sense? According to Dodds, 1959: 376–77, the Great Myth does not convey a "philosophical truth" but a "truth of religion" expressed "in imaginative terms"; Allen, 1988: 229, thinks it conveys a "moral truth"; Dilman, 1979: 185, thinks that, in calling the myth "true," Socrates is making a "*grammatical* or conceptual" remark. Plato is less embarrassed and less obscure. Socrates gives three reasons for thinking that the myth is true: (i) the discussion has yielded nothing better; (ii) no one else has shown that any other life is more advantageous (σύμφερον); (iii) every other thesis has been refuted and Socrates' alone remains unshaken (527a5–c4). The qualification "Socrates" appends to the (in many respects similar) eschatological myth of the *Phaedo* provides further Platonic commentary on the concept of mythical truth: although no intelligent person will believe that the factual details are exactly as he has described them, "this or something like it" (ἢ ταῦτ' ἐστιν ἢ τοιαῦτ' ἄττα) seems to be the truth and, therefore, worthy of being believed (*Ph.* 114d1–6). See also Canto, 1987: 359: n. 281: "[L]'évidence du mythe est à accepter faute de mieux. C'est une forme de protreptique (ou morceau d'exhortation à la sagesse et à la vertu) que Platon développe ici."

which is of more worth than any other. By contrast, the life advocated by Callicles is worthless. On this solemn eschatological note, the dialogue concludes.

After playing major roles as interlocutors, Polus is heard from no more and Gorgias makes only a few brief appearances – each time urging Socrates to complete the discussion. It is significant that it is Gorgias who makes these appeals: first, because the unifying theme of the dialogue is the nature and uses of rhetoric, and Gorgias is a rhetorician; second, because having been criticized by Polus for being shamed into making an insincere admission and having witnessed Callicles criticize Polus for doing the same thing and then announce that he is incapable of being shamed, Gorgias is interested in seeing how Callicles will fare. How does he fare?

One's answer to this question depends on what one thinks of Socrates' arguments. I have been quite critical of them and claimed that Callicles has not been persuaded. Socrates agrees. However, he implies that he should have been and adds that he would be if they examined these matters "often and in a better way." What is Callicles being urged to do here?

Irwin[42] thinks he is being urged to review the argument thoroughly to satisfy himself that it contains "no tricks" and that Socrates' position really follows from his – Callicles' – own basic convictions; although Socrates thinks Callicles' desires are misdirected, he does not think he is "unreachable by rational argument" and "still insists that rational persuasion can make [him] re-direct his desires." On the other hand, Dodds[43] thinks Callicles *is* beyond rational persuasion and that Socrates' remark about his "false loves" (513c7–8) should be taken "as expressing Plato's recognition that basic moral attitudes are commonly determined by psychological, not logical reasons."

There are two questions here. First, should Callicles have been persuaded? Second, is he beyond rational persuasion?

It will come as a surprise to no one to learn that my answer to the first question is, No. Socrates' arguments are singularly unconvincing; indeed, most of them are demonstrably fallacious or

[42] 1979: 233.   [43] 1959: 352.

unsound. However, the answer to the second question is more complicated. In fact, I think the *Gorgias* contains two answers to this question: the answer of Socrates, who thinks Callicles is not beyond rational persuasion, and the answer of Plato, who thinks he is. (Irwin gives the Socratic answer; Dodds gives the Platonic one.) My reasons for thinking this are as follows.

Having been assured that he would be persuaded if he examined these matters "often and in a better way" and having examined them further, Callicles remains unpersuaded. There is nothing surprising about that. Socrates' interlocutors almost always remain unpersuaded. What *is* surprising is Socrates' response. Instead of bemoaning their individual and joint failure and either suggesting that they start all over again or allowing the dialogue to end inconclusively, as he does in all the pre-*Gorgias* dialogues, he tries once more to persuade his interlocutor: not by advancing yet another argument, but by making a long speech about the unjust life, the effects of injustice on the soul of the unjust man, and the punishment awaiting him in the hereafter. It is as if the foregoing discussion has convinced him that if he is ever to persuade Callicles to opt for the just life, he must abandon rational argumentation in favor of a different strategy. The Great Myth embodies that strategy.

The presence of this myth, awkwardly "tacked on" to the dialogue like a clumsy appendix, as some commentators have mistakenly suggested, has prompted a good deal of speculation. What is it doing there? Whose views does it express: Socrates' or Plato's? If the former's, how can they be reconciled with his agnosticism about the immortality of the soul (*Ap.* 40c5–e4)? If the latter's, how can they be reconciled with the widely accepted hermeneutical principle that the views espoused by the Socrates of the early dialogues – of which the *Gorgias* is one of the last (perhaps *the* last)[44] – are those of the historical Socrates whereas the views espoused by the "Socrates" of the middle dialogues are those of Plato? These are important questions, and anyone who rejects the answers of others is obliged to offer something in their place.

I began this chapter by saying that the dialectical encounter between Socrates and Callicles contains Plato's deepest pre-middle period insights into moral psychology – particularly, into the psy-

---

[44] See Vlastos, 1983a: 27, n. 2; and Santas, 1979: 219.

chology of intellectual and moral recalcitrance. What are those insights?

The Socrates of the pre-*Gorgias* dialogues thought that his inter-locutors' *beliefs* were the appropriate starting point of philosoph-ical discussion. He also thought that, in getting them to say what they believe, he was getting them to lay their lives (and their deepest selves) on the line. Hence to demonstrate that a person's beliefs are false (or inconsistent) is to refute him. And to do this is tantamount to improving his soul. Once the elenchus has done its work, moral improvement will take care of itself. The man who has come to see that he does not know what he thought he knew will be appalled by his ignorance and become a truth-seeker.

By the time Plato wrote the *Gorgias*, he had come to believe that genuine and lasting persuasion cannot be effected in this way. One cannot "win over" a person simply by eliciting his assent to a series of premises and deducing conclusions to which he is logically committed on penalty of inconsistency or self-contradiction. Such an approach may enable one to reduce one's opponent to silence and to score a resounding dialectical victory. But what is such "victory" worth if the opponent remains unpersuaded and un-touched? Initially enamored of the Socratic elenchus, Plato came to have grave doubts about it and eventually abandoned it because he had come to believe that the self revealed in a person's beliefs – even in his sincerely held beliefs – is not the deepest self. In short, by the time he wrote the *Gorgias*, Plato had come to recognize that "peirastic" argumentation – in which the interlocutor is refuted "from his own beliefs" – is much more problematic than Socrates (and perhaps he himself) had initially supposed.

The end of the *Gorgias* marks a turning point in Plato's philo-sophical development – a radical break with Socratic moral psy-chology and the emergence of an innovative Platonic alternative based on an equally innovative diagnosis of intellectual and moral recalcitrance. Without so much as mentioning that it is innovative – much less that it is a diagnosis based on a rejection of the Soc-ratic one – Plato accounts for Callicles' recalcitrance not in logical or epistemic terms, but in psychological ones. Callicles' recalci-trance is not traceable to his lack of knowledge or to his inability to follow an argument, but to his "false loves." His problem is not lack of understanding, but resistance to things understood. Such recalcitrance cannot be overcome by examining important matters "more and in a better way." This is Plato's deepest pre-middle period insight into the psychology of recalcitrance. To say that Callicles resists only because he is presented with fallacious and unsound arguments is to assign too much blame to Socrates. But to say that he resists only because he is determined to resist is to assign too much blame to Callicles.

In fact, both are to blame. One failure is Callicles'. In spite of his elaborate assurances that he cannot be shamed into submission and that he will never say anything less than what he really thinks, he is, in some respects, an intellectually dishonest dialectical partner. Having embarked on the discussion as a willing and active participant, he is gradually transformed into a detached and cynical observer, authorizing Socrates to say whatever he wishes and perfunctorily "assenting." It is easy to berate him for this, and few have resisted the temptation.[45]

However, the other failure is Socrates'. Rebuked by Callicles for the shame tactics he had employed with such apparent success against Gorgias and Polus, he owns up to his dialectical shortcomings and "resolves" to do better. For a few pages he is on his best behavior, but soon he is back to his old tricks, deliberately misunderstanding Callicles' theses and deducing absurd and obviously unintended inferences from them, periodically confronting him with bogus ambiguities, falsely accusing him of changing his mind, alternately enforcing and waiving the sincere assent requirement, and surreptitiously feeding him the premises he needs to refute his own elaborately constructed Calliclean straw men. As the premises become more and more outrageous, he induces Callicles to affirm them by reminding him of his shamelessness – the Gorgias–Polus shame tactic in reverse. But although Callicles "assents" to these premises, he does not believe them. Nor does he accept the conclusions Socrates deduces from them. "Draw your tidy little inferences," he taunts, "you will never persuade me." The argumentative chain, so meticulously constructed, seems to be intact, its "steel and adamant" binders apparently as strong as ever. But it "binds" only its own conclusions; it does not "bind" Callicles. The allegedly irresistible and life-altering power of the

---

[45] Irwin is one of the few commentators who tries hard to understand Callicles and to do justice to him, but even he ends up minimizing the force of his objections and accounting for his recalcitrance by saying that he is "ill-tempered" (1986: 71).

logos has been resisted, and Callicles remains as he was. The game is over, and the result is not checkmate but stalemate. No amount of Callicles-bashing can conceal the fact that Socrates has failed. Callicles exits the discussion as impervious to the call of virtue as when he entered.

What can be done for such an interlocutor? If the Socratic elenchus is not efficacious, what is? This is the Socratic problem to which the Great Myth contains the seeds of the Platonic solution – a solution which Plato develops into a full-blown theory of early education in *Republic* II–III.

It is impossible to know whether (or to what extent) Plato would have agreed with my criticisms of the arguments he puts into the mouth of Socrates in the early dialogues. But even if he thought Socrates' arguments were logically impeccable, the fact remains that the *Gorgias* culminates in the discovery of a more fundamental problem: deep within Callicles – and, by implication, everyone – there is an inner core of psychological resistance which rational argumentation cannot penetrate. This is not a recognition of the limitations of faulty argumentation, but a recognition of the limitations of argumentation itself. Socrates apparently thought it was possible to enter into dialectical disputation with a fully formed adult with fully formed beliefs, values, attitudes, and practices – a person like Callicles or Euthyphro or Cephalus – or with a partially formed young adult with partially formed beliefs, values, attitudes, and practices – a person like Charmides or Alcibiades – and, by eliciting his sincere assent to a series of premises, induce him to renounce all this and to embark on a philosophical quest for the knowledge he lacks. This struck middle-period Plato as psychologically naive – a philosophical program which is foredoomed to fail because it is based on a methodology which does not recognize the true determinants of moral conduct.

The encounter with Callicles documents Plato's recognition of the futility of trying to put an interlocutor – any interlocutor – on the road to virtue simply by refuting him "from his own beliefs." To attempt this is to begin in the wrong place. Genuine and lasting persuasion requires something more fundamental than *belief* – something even more fundamental than *true* belief. Before the interlocutor's mind can be changed and his behavior improved, his desires must be redirected. He must be delivered from his "false loves." That is the discovery of the *Gorgias*. In meticulously

depicting the psychological dynamics between Socrates and Callicles, Plato reveals the inefficacy of the Socratic elenchus and, in
the process, shows not only *that* Socrates failed but *why* he failed. It
is as if he were saying in retrospect, "Look, again and again, in
one conversation after another, Socrates is trying to awaken his
interlocutors to the call of morality by refuting their false beliefs,
thereby exposing their ignorance and motivating them to take up
the philosophical quest for the knowledge they lack. But it cannot
be done."

Plato revered knowledge every bit as much as Socrates. Perhaps
more. But he gradually came to believe that Socrates had greatly
overestimated its motivational efficacy. Unlike Socrates, who believed that, given the universal desire for happiness, knowledge is
both necessary and sufficient for virtue, Plato came to believe that
it is neither. The *Gorgias* marks the beginning of the end of the
Socratic elenchus and the moral psychology on which it is based.
It is replaced by a new moral psychology of which the Great Myth
is an early expression. Firmly believing in the immortality of the
soul and of the necessity of remedial punishment in the next life
for injustices committed in this one, Plato anachronistically ascribes these beliefs to Socrates in the *Gorgias*. Making no attempt
to demonstrate that they are true, he makes Socrates express his
belief that they are and then try once more to persuade Callicles
to opt for the just life by dwelling on the torments awaiting the
unjust man in the hereafter. Although admittedly an appeal to
fear and hence, at bottom, psychological, it is not an appeal to
mere fear, as the appeal to shame in the arguments with Gorgias
and Polus is an appeal to mere shame. Insofar as Socrates is convinced that the beliefs he has expressed are true, he is also convinced that the emotions he is trying to inculcate in Callicles have
a cognitive base and even a cognitive component and that the fear
he is trying to inculcate is therefore a rational fear. In view of the
periodic rebukes with which Socrates is upbraided by Polus and
Callicles, Plato apparently disapproves of appeals to irrational
emotions like shame – particularly shame in the eyes of people
whose opinions do not matter (*Cr.* 46d7–47a12). But he clearly
does not disapprove of appeals to rational emotions like fear of
punishment to be meted out in the hereafter by "true judges"
whose opinions matter profoundly. Indeed, he exploits them to

the hilt in the *Gorgias* and makes their inculcation the basis of his theory of early education in *Republic* ii–iii.

At the heart of that theory is the radically innovative (and decidedly un-Socratic) thesis that the young are to be sheltered from all that is ignoble and base and surrounded from the cradle with objects and persons worthy of imitation and thereby assimilate beauty and goodness into their innermost souls (*R.* 395b8–d3) so that, when reason comes (ἐλθόντος ... τοῦ λόγου), they will have been emotionally prepared by proper habituation (δι' οἰκειότητα) to welcome its precepts (*R.* 401d5–402a4). Although these Platonic graduates cannot "give an account" of their moral beliefs and could not survive Socratic interrogation any better than the interlocutors of the early dialogues, they remain steadfast: not because their beliefs are "bound by arguments of steel and adamant," but because, like carefully selected and pre-treated wool, their souls have been permanently imbued with the indelible dye of virtue which nothing can rinse out (*R.* 429d4–430b2). Having been habituated to virtue during their early years, there is little danger of their being seduced by "false loves" in their later ones. Moral resistance can only develop and take root in unhabituated souls – souls like Callicles'. Educationally neglected and irreparably damaged, such souls cannot be rehabilitated – either by logical demonstrations, however cogent, or by emotional appeals, however sublime. Their only hope is remedial punishment in the hereafter. And even then some are incurable.

It is not that middle-period Plato despairs of attaining the knowledge for which the Socrates of the early dialogues searched. It is rather that he thinks it is beyond the reach of most people and accessible only to the gifted and properly habituated few. Those who cannot attain it must be provided with an education which shapes them into persons who are able to appropriate it in the form of true beliefs from those who can. In the *Republic*, true belief is no longer the theoretically ungrounded and morally precarious state of mind to which "the Many" are forever doomed; it is a *laudable* state of mind which is to be inculcated in all but the select few – and even in them during the early stages of their education. This Socratic heresy is forecast in the *Meno* where "Socrates" makes the unprecedented statement that, so long as one person has a true belief (ὀρθὴν δόξαν) *on a subject about which another* (ὁ ἕτερος) *has knowledge* (ἐπιστήμην) – the qualification is crucial – he will be as good a guide to right action as a person who has knowledge (*M.* 97b5–7). In short, for the purpose of acting rightly, true belief is no worse (οὐδὲν χεῖρον) than knowledge (*M.* 98b7–9). Such views are utterly foreign to the Socrates of the early dialogues who would have repudiated the central moral thesis on which the entire *Republic* is based – that virtue is attainable without knowledge by holding true moral beliefs on the authority of the philosopher-king and by performing one's function in the ideal state.

Unlike the Socrates of the early dialogues, who reposes no confidence in belief – even true belief – without knowledge and is still censuring rhetoricians for inculcating it in their hearers in the *Gorgias* (454e3–455a2), the "Socrates" of the *Republic* builds his ideal society on the foundation of belief without knowledge and invests the philosopher-king with the responsibility for inculcating it. The crucial difference is this. Unlike the belief without knowledge inculcated by the rhetorician, which is *mere* belief and whose truth-value is unknown to him (or to anyone else), the belief without knowledge inculcated by the philosopher-king is *true* belief and known to be such by the philosopher-king. Yet however different the respective content of the beliefs imparted, the epistemic status of the beliefs themselves is the same: both are belief without knowledge. Thus by an unexpected irony, the philosopher-king in the *Republic* inculcates exactly the same state of mind as the rhetorician in the *Gorgias*.

Thus Plato deprives true belief of (what Socrates thought was) its irremediable and fatal instability. He does so, not by replacing true belief with knowledge which enables its possessor to "give an account" and which is sufficient for virtue, but by inculcating true beliefs grounded in rational emotions (and what Aristotle was later to call "fixed dispositions") which enable their possessor to do what, according to Socrates, could not be done, namely, to be virtuous and attain happiness without having attained knowledge.[46] In short, the theory of early education set forth in the *Republic* renders the Socratic elenchus superfluous. Unlike the *Gorgias*, in which the appeal to rational emotions is a last-ditch effort – an

---

[46] This point is emphasized by Vlastos, 1981d: 136, n. 73: "True belief is quite sufficient for virtue in the *Republic*."

eleventh-hour attempt to produce a psychological effect which has not been (and, presumably, cannot be) produced by rational argumentation alone – the middle books of the *Republic* advocate a program of emotional habituation which *precedes* rational argumentation and is one of the conditions on which genuine and lasting persuasion depends. Without properly trained emotions, reason remains inefficacious and the dialectician argues in vain.

So again: what can be done for an interlocutor like Callicles? By the time Plato wrote the *Republic*, his answer seems to be, Nothing. Given his defective early education and resultant insusceptibility to the call of virtue, it is too late for Callicles. Like corrupt political institutions, he is beyond remedy – the paradigmatically recalcitrant interlocutor. Little wonder that Plato soon abandoned the Socratic elenchus. Insofar as its intended effects are systematically undercut by a deficient moral psychology, it fails when you need it most. If the Callicleses of this world have not been properly fashioned in childhood, they cannot be *re*-fashioned in adulthood. The bravado with which they herald the emergence of a new breed pursuing a morality rooted in *phusis* rather than in *nomos* is merely a mask through which peers an emotionally atrophied soul. A Socrates on every street corner, underwritten by Athens and awarded publicly subsidized housing at the Prytaneum, would not make a dent in the heavy armor in which these intellectual hoplites have encased themselves, Unlike the notorious jury, which found Socrates dangerous, subversive, and worthy of death, Callicles merely finds him quaint, old-fashioned, and a bit of a bore.

Plato, of course, disagrees. At the same time, the *Gorgias* reveals that his enthusiasm for and confidence in the Socratic elenchus have waned. Although he would always share the moral vision that inspired it, he was increasingly plagued by doubts (which subsequently gave way to the conviction) that the Socratic elenchus was methodologically flawed. It was based on an overly optimistic theory of human nature and its capacity for moral reform, and it had been applied to people whose early education had not prepared them to benefit from it. If elenchus was still valuable – something Plato never doubted – it had to be completely rethought. In the opinion of middle-period Plato, it required a different kind of practitioner – one who possessed moral knowledge – and a different kind of interlocutor – one who had undergone intensive and prolonged immersion in the rigors of mathematics, geometry, astronomy, and harmonics, and by equally intensive emotional habituation. Only such a person could benefit from the aporetic effects of the equally rigorous but more selectively applied elenchus and be rendered receptive to the moral instruction subsequently imparted by the elenctic practitioner.

The "Socrates" of the *Republic* (and of the middle dialogues generally) no longer discharges his divine mission by haunting the marketplace and entering into debate with all comers in hopes of exposing them as fraudulent claimants to wisdom. The original philosophical task has been abandoned and replaced by a very different one which is conducted in a very different locale. The enormous distance between this "Socrates" and the Socrates of the early dialogues is evident in many ways. But none is more striking and more poignant than the fact that, according to the former, the true philosopher is so uninterested in and detached from his surroundings that he does not even know the way to the marketplace (*Th.* 173c8–d1).

It is often said[47] that the *Gorgias* presents us with an embittered Socrates filled with undisguised contempt for the city in which he had willingly spent his life. The usual authorial inference is that these Socratic character traits are symptomatic of Plato's own escalating disenchantment with the city in which he had once aspired to a political career but which he had come to view as corrupt and as having compounded its corruption by executing Socrates. There is every reason for thinking that this inference is warranted. What is not so often said is that the *Gorgias* also presents us with a Plato whose personal attachment to Socrates persists in spite of his waning philosophical attachment to his method. The Great Myth reveals a philosophically divided Plato with one foot tenuously resting on a Socratic foundation which has turned to sand and with the other desperately groping for bedrock – a Plato on the threshold of a radically novel conception of philosophy and an equally novel educational theory destined to invert Socratic moral psychology by assigning much less importance to Reason and much more importance to moral habituation. He has discovered his tool of moral reform, but he does not yet fully understand how – and, more important, when – to use it.

---

[47] See Dodds, 1959: 16–19.

CHAPTER 17

The last days of the Socratic interlocutor

Plato's earliest philosophical views and his initial conception of philosophy itself were decisively influenced by Socrates – a fact which has prompted many commentators to think that the early dialogues document a "Socratic" period in his philosophical development in which he "is imaginatively recalling, in form and substance, the conversations of his master without as yet adding to them any distinctive doctrines of his own."[1] As his thought develops, he advances many innovative epistemological, metaphysical, political, and educational theories, some of them built on his Socratic foundations, others without precedent in Socratic thought and, on occasion, incompatible with it – a fact which has prompted many of these same commentators to think that the views set forth in the transitional and middle dialogues should not be ascribed to the historical Socrates, but to the mature Plato. The methodology also changes. The Socratic elenchus, ubiquitously present in the early dialogues, is completely absent from most of those which follow – the *Meno* and the *Theaetetus* being conspicuous exceptions.

In the process, the character of Socrates undergoes a striking identity change. No longer the moral gadfly who disavows all knowledge, confines himself almost exclusively to ethical questions, and relentlessly interrogates his interlocutors in hopes of convincing them that they do not know what they think they know, he is gradually transformed into a philosopher in possession of a great deal of positive doctrine which encompasses practically every branch of philosophy and which he is eager to impart.

This transformation of Socrates is accompanied by an equally striking identity change on the part of his interlocutors. Unlike the active, recalcitrant, unpersuaded, and occasionally unpersuadable dialectical partners of the early dialogues, the interlocutors of the

[1] Guthrie, 1975: 67.

377

middle and late dialogues are (for the most part) passive, cooperative, and eminently persuadable auditors who listen attentively
and dutifully nod in agreement. Disinclined to lock horns with
"Socrates" and to engage in adversarial dialectical interaction
with him, they are not so much participants in a joint search as
witnesses to a series of solitary discoveries. In the process, they
cease to be recognizable individuals with minds of their own and
tend to be faceless straightmen who can be relied on to produce
the desired response. Everyone remembers Euthyphro, Crito, Ion,
Hippias, Callicles, and Thrasymachus. But who has vivid memories of Cebes, Phaedrus, Clinias, Megillus, Protarchus, or even
Theaetetus? Their substantively marginal contributions, largely
confined to enthusiastic endorsements of Platonic doctrine or pedagogically motivated requests for further clarification, neither
advance nor impede the flow of the argument; and their dialectical roles become increasingly perfunctory and, in the end,
non-existent. Even in the *Meno* and the *Theaetetus*, transitional and
middle dialogues respectively in which the Socratic elenchus temporarily resurfaces, the interlocutors either immediately agree
with "Socrates" or are easily persuaded. Although the dialogue
form is nominally retained, it becomes increasingly external; and
one often comes away thinking that Plato could have abandoned it
altogether and presented his views in the form of systematic treatises – which he, in effect, does in the *Timaeus*, the *Laws*, and much
of the *Parmenides* in which the interlocutors are silent and all-but-
forgotten for pages on end. Once an indispensable ingredient in the
activity of philosophizing, the interlocutor has become dispens-
able. The Socratic interlocutor has become the Platonic disciple.

This transformation of the interlocutor from a resistant and
protesting opponent into a congenial and accommodating Yes-
man has disappointed some commentators and embarrassed (and
even annoyed) others. It has been explained in a variety of ways.
One of the most common explanations is that, as the death of
Socrates receded into the past and Plato came of age as a philosopher, his enthusiasm for writing philosophical Socratic dramas
gradually waned; and he embarked on philosophical investigations
of his own – investigations of increasing complexity which did not
lend themselves to conversational treatment and rendered character depiction superfluous.

Although this is undoubtedly part of the story, it is not the
whole story. It is not even the most important part. Ultimately, the

radical difference between the interlocutors of the early dialogues and those of the middle and late ones is not traceable to dramatic or stylistic considerations, but to philosophical and methodological ones. That this is so is borne out in the opening pages of the *Sophist* where the qualities looked for in an interlocutor are spelled out very clearly. Asked whether he would prefer to make a long speech or to enter into discussion and ask questions, the Athenian Stranger replies:

> It's easier to do it the second way ... if you're talking with someone who's easy to handle and isn't a troublemaker (ἀλύπωσ τε καὶ εὐηνίως ... ῥᾷον). Otherwise it's easier to do it alone. (*S.* 217d1–3)

In short, the radical difference between the interlocutors of the early dialogues and those of the middle and late ones is traceable to the radical difference between the Socratic and the Platonic conceptions of philosophy, how best to pursue it, and with whom. The early dialogues embody the Socratic conception; the middle and late dialogues embody the Platonic.

As we have seen, by the time he wrote the *Gorgias* Plato had come to believe that the Socratic elenchus was based on an inadequate moral psychology and that genuine and lasting persuasion cannot be effected by refuting a person "from his own beliefs." And by the time he wrote the *Republic* he had come to believe that there was something radically wrong: not only with the Socratic elenchus, but with the whole Socratic conception of philosophy – a change of mind of such magnitude that, in describing its relation to his earlier view, commentators employ heavy-duty terms like "reversal" and "antithesis."[2]

But the "Socrates" of the middle books of the *Republic* not only thinks that the Socratic elenchus is psychologically inefficacious; he also thinks that it is morally harmful unless its application is carefully supervised and confined to people whose early education has prepared them to benefit from it. In his ideal society, dialectic may be conducted only by certified practitioners who possess the requisite knowledge; and it may be applied only to intellectually gifted and hand-picked people over the age of thirty who have been immersed in the rigors of mathematics, geometry, and harmonics, and who have undergone an intensive program of psychological and emotional habituation which insures that they have the kind of character which will make them amenable to refutation

---

[2] See, e.g., Grote, 1867, III: 236–40; Nussbaum, 1980: 43–97; and Vlastos, 1991: 110.

and receptive to the true moral beliefs which will subsequently be imparted to them by those who have moral knowledge (*R.* 537c9–d6).[3] In a word, philosophy is not for everyone. To reduce the theoretically unprepared and the emotionally unhabituated to the allegedly salutary state of mind called *aporia* is dangerous and ill-advised. Indeed, for such people, the experience of *aporia* is not salutary; it is the worst thing that could happen to them. Indiscriminate exposure to dialectic does not prompt people to think harder about morality; it undermines morality:

> We hold from childhood certain convictions about just and fine things; we're brought up with them as with our parents, we obey and honor them ... And then a questioner comes along and asks someone of this sort, "What is the fine?" And, when he answers what he has heard from the traditional lawgiver, the argument refutes him, and by refuting him often and in many places shakes him from his convictions, and makes him believe that the fine is no more fine than shameful, and the same with the just, the good, and the things he honored most ... Then, when he no longer honors and obeys those convictions and can't discover the true ones, will he be likely to adopt any other way of life than that which flatters him? ... And so ... from being law-abiding he becomes lawless. (*R.* 538c6–539a3)

The educational theory set forth in the middle books of the *Republic* casts an eerie retrospective light on the dialectical encounters depicted in the early dialogues. The inescapable implication is that, like theoretically unprepared and emotionally unhabituated people generally, Socrates' interlocutors have been methodologically short-changed, educationally mistreated, and (inadvertently) morally harmed. And insofar as Socrates indiscriminately applied the elenchus to all comers, he is no longer a moral gadfly tirelessly discharging his divine mission, but an irresponsible practitioner of dialectic of whom "corruptor of the youth" would not be a wildly implausible description.[4]

---

[3] At *Th.* 145c2–d3 "Socrates" praises Theaetetus' character (τρόπος) and prefaces his interrogation by pointedly asking whether he is learning geometry, mathematics, astronomy, and harmonics from Theodorus. Theaetetus obligingly replies that he is doing his best.

[4] Middle-period Plato would have been in full agreement with Geach, 1972: 39–40: "Socrates used to maintain that nobody has the right to maintain a thesis unless he is prepared (if challenged) to produce a definition of the key words used in stating [it]: inability to do this means that you didn't know what you were talking about ... In concrete instances, the Socratic demand is preposterous ... Socratic dialectic was believed at the time to be morally pernicious. One can indeed well imagine that a man might be harmed if he decided that he must suspend judgment as to whether swindling is unjust until he has watertight definitions of 'swindling' and 'unjust'."

This remarkable change of attitude is already apparent at the beginning of *Republic* II. Before embarking on a long discussion about the nature of justice designed to demonstrate that the just life is superior to and more profitable than the unjust, "Socrates" heaps lavish praise on Glaucon and Adeimantus[5] – the interlocutors with whom he will subsequently be dealing. Since even the most tepid and qualified praise of an interlocutor is unheard of in the early dialogues, it is worth noticing what elicits this high compliment. What impresses "Socrates" is this. Although Glaucon and Adeimantus feel the full impact of the opposing view, as championed by Thrasymachus, and even strengthen his case by citing many other popularly held reasons for thinking that the unjust life is more profitable, they are still inclined to be just – a fact which prompts "Socrates" to admire their nature (τὴν φύσιν, 367e6), that is, their moral character, and to suggest that they must have been "touched by the divine" (πάνυ ... θεῖον πεπόνθατε, 368a5–6). For the "Socrates" of the *Republic* (and the middle dialogues generally), this pre-reflective orientation to moral goodness – and resultant disposition to be just – is much more important than mere theoretical ability. It is precisely that which makes Glaucon and Adeimantus more amenable to the claims of Reason than Polemarchus, Thrasymachus, and the interlocutors of the early dialogues generally whose character flaws are often depicted in considerable detail, but never ascribed such decisive importance.

If elenchus is still valuable – something Plato never doubted[6] – its nature and purpose had to be completely rethought. The question that exercised him was not: Is elenchus valuable? but: Valuable *for whom* and *for what*? The conclusions at which he ultimately arrived were radically un- and even anti-Socratic.

Unlike the Socrates of the early dialogues, who proceeds as if philosophical argumentation takes place in a psychological and contextual vacuum, the "Socrates" of the *Republic* recognizes the decisive importance of attitudinal, affectional, and dispositional tendencies. In his opinion, it is futile continually to refute people and then exhort them to "start all over again" in hopes of hitting upon a more defensible thesis; for no matter how different the thesis advanced, the person advancing it remains the same. Theoretical assent is parasitic on affectional response. That is the dis-

---

[5] The historical Glaucon and Adeimantus were Plato's brothers.
[6] See, e.g., *S.* 230a5–e6.

covery of the *Gorgias* – a discovery which is fully elaborated in the *Republic*. The young should not be refuted and then, with their ignorance exposed, provided with an incentive to search for the knowledge they lack; they should be surrounded with beauty and goodness on every side so that the knowledge later imparted by the philosopher-king will find psychologically fertile soil in which it can take root and flourish.

If the conclusions at which Plato arrived were radically un- and even anti-Socratic, the attitude he displayed in arriving at them was refreshingly so. Unlike Socrates, who unabashedly admits that refuting the ignorant has its amusing side (*Ap.* 33b9–c4), especially if carried out in the presence of others who share in the amusement, Plato came to believe that the refutation of the ignorant, the unprepared, and the unhabituated was no laughing matter. To apply the elenchus to such people is not a strategy for moral progress; it is a recipe for moral disaster. However he may have reacted as a young man, by the time he wrote the *Republic* Plato was no longer inclined to participate in the hectoring snickers and reinforcing laughter of those amused onlookers who take their cues from Socrates as he demolishes his interlocutors. Neither should we.

But our severest criticism should not be reserved for them. For it is Socrates who orchestrates and directs these productions. His patronizing and deflating laughter is more than enough to paralyze the minds and to deflate the spirits of those helpless dialectical victims whose inability to answer his questions allegedly reveals that their lives are unexamined and, therefore, not worth living. If we listen carefully, we can still hear it echoing down the corridors of time, daring people to advance a thesis and then bludgeoning them into submission in the name of philosophy. Of the many labels that could be applied to such tactics, "moral education" and "soul-care" are not among them. In assessing the views, the characters, and the dialectical performances of these ill-prepared and (often) pathetic victims, we should abandon the example of Socrates in favor of that of middle-period Plato who reserved his severest criticism not for the demolished but for the instrument of demolition and those who indiscriminately wield it.

The middle and late dialogues were written by a philosopher who had taken a hard look at his beloved mentor and friend. That Plato had been captivated and enthralled by the Socratic conception of philosophy cannot be doubted. That he came to see its deficiencies and potential dangers cannot be doubted either. Nor need we deny that, having see them, he continued, in some sense, to be captivated and enthralled. Why else would he have retained the *persona* of "Socrates" as his mouthpiece? In the end, however, he parted company with him. Attracted by the Socratic vision of the good life but repelled by the method by which he tried to achieve it, he could opt for neither. The Socrates portrayed in the early dialogues is a Socrates with whom Plato came to have deep philosophical, methodological, and educational disagreements. In arriving at his final estimate, he took Socrates' interlocutors very seriously. So should we.

Bibliography

Adam, J. (1888). *Plato Crito*, 2nd edn., Cambridge

    (1890). *Platonis Euthyphro*, with introduction and notes, Cambridge

    (1894). *Platonis Apologia Socratis*, with introduction, notes, and appendices, new edn., Cambridge

    (1938). *The Republic of Plato*, edited with critical notes, commentary, and appendices, 2 vols., Cambridge

Adam, J., and Adam, A. M. (1893). *Platonis Protagoras*, with introduction, notes, and appendices, 2nd edn., Cambridge

Adkins, Arthur W. H. (1960). *Merit and Responsibility: A Study in Greek Values*, Chicago

Allen, R. E. (1970). *Plato's "Euthyphro" and the Earlier Theory of Forms*, London

    (1980). *Socrates and Legal Obligation*, Minneapolis

    (1984). *The Dialogues of Plato*, vol. I: *Euthyphro, Apology, Crito, Meno, Gorgias, Menexenus*, translated with analysis, New Haven

    (1996). *Plato*, vol. III: *Ion, Hippias Minor, Laches, Protagoras*, translated with comment, New Haven

Angélopoulos, Elie J. (1933). *Aristophane et ses idées sur Socrate*, Athens

Annas, Julia (1981). *An Introduction to Plato's Republic*, Oxford

    (1982). "Plato's myths of judgment," *Phronesis* 27: 119–43

    (1992). "Plato the sceptic," *Oxford Studies in Ancient Philosophy* Supplementary Volume: 43–72

Anonymous (1768). *Socrates Diabolicus: or, The Old Man Exploded. A Declamation Against Socrates*, London

Anscombe, G. E. M. (1963). *Intention*, Oxford

Anselm, St. (1974–76). "Why God became Man" (*Cur Deus Homo*) and "On Truth" (*De Veritate*), in *Anselm of Canterbury*, 4 vols., edited and translated by Jasper Hopkins and Herbert Richardson, Toronto

Apelt, Otto (1912). *Platonische Aufsätze*, Leipzig

Arieti, James A. (1991). *Interpreting Plato: The Dialogues as Drama*, Savage

Aristophanes (1924). *The Birds, The Frogs*, with the English translation by Benjamin Bickley Rogers, London

    (1927). *The Clouds*, with the English translation by Benjamin Bickley Rogers, London

Aristotle (1935). *Metaphysics*, 2 vols., translated by Hugh Tredennick, London

(1947). *Nicomachean Ethics*, translated by H. Rackham, London

(1957). *Rhetoric*, translated by John Henery Freese, London

(1976). *Topics*, translated by E. S. Forster, London

(1978). *On Sophistical Refutations*, translated by E. S. Forster, London

Athenaeus (1933). *The Deipnosophists*, with an English translation by Charles Burton Gulick, 7 vols., London

Augustine, St. (1953). "On Free Will" (*De Libero Arbitrio*) and "The Teacher" (*De Magistro*), in *Augustine: Earlier Writings*, selected and translated with introductions by John H. S. Burleigh, Philadelphia

Austin, J. L. (1961). *Philosophical Papers*, Oxford

(1962). *How to do Things with Words*, Oxford

Baccou, Robert (1966). *La République*, introduction, traduction, et notes par Robert Baccou, Paris

Bain, Alexander (1880). *The Emotions and the Will*, London

Benardete, Seth (1991). *The Rhetoric of Morality and Philosophy*, Chicago

Benson, Hugh H. (1989). "A note on eristic and the Socratic elenchus," *Journal of the History of Philosophy* 27: 591–99

(1990). "The priority of definition and the Socratic elenchus," *Oxford Studies in Ancient Philosophy* 8: 19–65

(1992). (ed.) *Essays on the Philosophy of Socrates*, New York

Berkeley, George (1929). *Essay, Principles, Dialogues with Selections from Other Writings*, edited by Mary Whiton Calkins, New York

Beversluis, John (1987). "Does Socrates commit the Socratic fallacy?" *American Philosophical Quarterly* 24: 211–23, reprinted in Benson, 1992: 107–22

(1993). "Vlastos's quest for the historical Socrates," *Ancient Philosophy* 13: 293–312

Blass, Friedrich (1887–98). *Die attische Beredsamkeit*, 3 vols., Leipzig

Bloom, Allan (1968). *The Republic of Plato*, translated with notes and an interpretive essay, New York

(1987). "An interpretation of Plato's *Ion*," in Pangle, 1987: 371–95

Blundell, Mary Whitlock (1992). "Character and meaning in Plato's *Hippias Minor*," *Oxford Studies in Ancient Philosophy* Supplementary Volume: 131–72

Boutang, Pierre (1984). "Socrate," in Huisman, 1984, 2: 2654–64

Bowen, Alan C. (1988). "On interpreting Plato," in Griswold, 1988: 49–65

Braithwaite, R. B. (1932–33). "The nature of believing," *Proceedings of the Aristotelian Society* 33: 129–46

Brandwood, Leonard (1976). *A Word Index to Plato*, Leeds

Brès, Yvon (1973). *La Psychologie de Platon*, Paris

Brickhouse, Thomas C., and Smith, Nicholas D. (1989). *Socrates on Trial*, Princeton

(1994) *Plato's Socrates*, New York

Brisson, Luc (1997). *Platon: Apologie de Socrate, Criton*, traductions inédites, introductions et notes, Paris

Brun, Jean (1960). *Socrate*, Paris

Bruns, Ivo (1896). *Das literarische Porträt bei der Griechen*, Berlin

Burnet, John (1900–1907). *Platonis Opera*, 5 vols., Oxford

    (1920). *Greek Philosophy: Thales to Plato*, London

    (1924). *Plato: Euthyphro, Apology of Socrates, Crito*, edited with notes, Oxford

Burnyeat, M. F. (1971). "Virtues in action," in Vlastos, 1971: 209–34

    (1977a). "Examples in epistemology: Socrates, Theaetetus and G. E. Moore," *Philosophy* 52: 381–98

    (1977b). "Socratic midwifery, Platonic inspiration," *Bulletin of the Institute of Classical Studies* 24: 7–16, reprinted in Benson, 1992: 53–65

    (1987). "Plato," in Magee, 1987: 14–30

Bury, J. B. (1909). *The Ancient Greek Historians*, London

Calvin, John (1949). *Institutes of the Christian Religion*, translated from the Latin and collated with the author's last edition in French by John Allen, 2 vols., Grand Rapids

Canto, Monique (1987). Revised and updated 1993. *Platon: Gorgias*, traduction inédite, introduction et notes, Paris

    (1989). *Platon: Ion*, traduction inédite, introduction et notes, Paris

Canto-Sperber, Monique (1997a). (ed.) *Philosophie grecque*, Paris

    (1997b). "Platon." in Canto-Sperber, 1997a: 185–299

Cavell, Stanley (1987). *Disowning Knowledge in Six Plays of Shakespeare*, Cambridge

Cazeaux, Jacques (1989). *Platon: La République*, traduction et notes, Paris

    (1996). *Platon: Gorgias*, traduction nouvelle, introduction et commentaire, Paris

Chambry, Emile (1967). *Platon: Premiers Dialogues*, Paris

    (1989). *Platon: Oeuvres Complètes: La République*: Livres 1–3, texte établi et traduit par Emile Chambry avec introduction d'Auguste Diès, Paris

Châtelet, François (1980). *Platon: Protagoras ou Les Sophistes Gorgias ou Sur La Rhétorique*, traduit par Léon Robin avec notes par François Châtelet, Paris

Cherniss, Harold F. (1977). "Ancient forms of philosophic discourse," in *Selected Papers*, edited by Leonardo Taran (Leiden), 14–35

Chrétien, Claude (1987). *Charmide: Platon*, Paris

Chroust, A. H. (1957) *Socrates, Man and Myth: The Two Socratic Apologies of Xenophon*, London

Clay, Diskin (1994). "The origins of the Socratic dialogue," in Vander Waerdt, 1994: 23–47

Coby, Patrick (1987). *Socrates and the Sophistic Enlightenment*, Lewisburg

Cohen, L. Jonathan (1992). *An Essay on Belief and Acceptance*, Oxford

Cohen, S. Marc (1971). "Socrates on the definition of piety," in Vlastos, 1971: 158–76

Cook, Albert (1996). *The Stance of Plato*, Lanham

Coolidge, Jr., Francis P. (1993). "The relation of philosophy to *Sophrosune*: Zalmoxian medicine in Plato's *Charmides*," *Ancient Philosophy* 13: 23–38

Cooper, John M. (1997). *Plato: Complete Works*, edited, with introduction and notes, Indianapolis

Cornford, Francis Macdonald (1941). *The Republic of Plato*, translated with introduction and notes, Oxford

(1987). "Plato's *Euthyphro* or how to read a Socratic dialogue," in *Selected Papers of F. M. Cornford*, edited by Alan C. Bowen, New York, 221–38

Coventry, Lucinda (1990). "The role of the interlocutor in Plato's dialogues," in *Characterization and Individuality in Greek Literature*, edited by Christopher Pelling, Oxford, 174–96

Croiset, Maurice (1949). *Platon Oeuvres Complètes: Hippias Minor, Apologie de Socrate, Euthyphron, Criton*, texte établi et traduit par Maurice Croiset, Paris

Crombie, I. M. (1962). *An Examination of Plato's Doctrines*, 2 vols., London

(1964). *Plato: The Midwife's Apprentice*, London

Cross, R. C., and Woozley, A. D. (1964). *Plato's Republic: A Philosophical Commentary*, London

de Romilly, Jacqueline (1992). *The Great Sophists in Periclean Athens*, translated by Janet Lloyd, Oxford

Deschoux, Marcel (1980). *Plato ou le Jeu Philosophique*, Paris

Devereux, Daniel T. (1977). "Courage and wisdom in Plato's *Laches*," *Journal of the History of Philosophy* 15: 129–41

Diès, Auguste (1972). *Autour de Platon: Essai de critique et d'histoire*, deuxième tirage revu et corrigé, Paris

(1989). *Platon: Oeuvres Complètes: La République: Livres 1–3*, texte établi et traduit par Émile Chambry avec introduction d'Auguste Diès, Paris

Dilman, Ilham (1979). *Morality and the Inner Life: A Study in Plato's Gorgias*, London

Dixsaut, Monique (1994). *Le Naturel philosophie*, Paris

Dodds, E. R. (1959). *Plato Gorgias*, a revised text with introduction and commentary, Oxford

Dorion, Louis-André (1990). "Le subversion de l'elenchus juridique dans l'*Apologie de Socrate*," *Revue philosophique de Louvain* 88: 311–44

(1997). *Platon: Lachès, Euthyphron*, traduction inédite, introduction et notes, Paris

Dummett, Michael (1975). *Frege, Philosophy of Language*, London

Dümmler, F. (1889). *Akademika: Beiträge zur Litteraturgeschichte der sokratischen Schulen*, Giessen

Dupréel, Eugène (1922). *La Légende socratique et les sources de Platon*, Brussels

(1948). *Les Sophistes: Protagoras, Gorgias, Prodicus, Hippias*, Neuchâtel

Edwards, Paul (1967). (ed.) *The Encyclopedia of Philosophy*, 8 vols., New York

Elias, Julius A. (1984). *Plato's Defence of Poetry*, Albany

Ferguson, John (1964). "On the date of Socrates' conversion," *Eranos* 62: 70–3

(1979). (ed.) *Juvenal: The Sixteen Satires*, New York

Field, G. C. (1930). *Plato and his Contemporaries: A Study in Fourth-Century Life and Thought*, New York

Figal, Günter (1995). *Sokrates*, München

Flashar, Hellmut (1958). *Der Dialog Ion Als Zeugnis Platonischer Philosophie*, Berlin

Fontenrose, Joseph (1978). *The Delphic Oracle*, Berkeley

Frede, Michael (1992). "Plato's arguments and the dialogue form," *Oxford Studies in Ancient Philosophy* Supplementary Volume: 201–19

Friedlaender, Ludwig (1895). *Juvenalis: Saturarum Libro V mit Erklärenden Anmerkungen*, Leipzig

Friedländer, Paul (1964). *Plato: The Dialogues, First Period*, 3 vols., translated from the German by Hans Meyerhoff, Princeton

Garland, William J. (1976). "Notes on two Socratic arguments in *Republic* I," *Apeiron* 10: 11–13

Garrett, Jan Edward (1993). "The moral status of 'the Many' in Aristotle," *Journal of the History of Philosophy* 31: 171–89

Geach, P. T. (1966). "Plato's *Euthyphro*: an analysis and commentary," *The Monist* 50: 369–82, reprinted in P. T. Geach, *Logic Matters* (Oxford, 1972), 31–44

Gentzler, Jyl (1995). "The sophistic cross-examination of Callicles in the *Gorgias*," *Ancient Philosophy* 15: 17–43

Gigon, Otto (1947). *Sokrates, Sein Bild in Dichtung und Geschichte*, Bern

Goldberg, Larry (1983). *A Commentary on Plato's Protagoras*, New York

Gomperz, Theodor (1905). *Greek Thinkers*, 4 vols., translated by G. G. Berry, London

Gosling, J. W. C. (1973). *Plato*, London

Goulburn, Edward Meyrick (1858). "Socrates," A lecture delivered to the Young Mens' Christian Association in Exeter Hall, Tuesday November 30, 1858, London

Gould, John (1955). *The Development of Plato's Ethics*, Cambridge

Gower, Barry S., and Stokes, Michael C. (1992). (eds.) *Socratic Questions: The Philosophy of Socrates and its Significance*, London

Graham, Daniel W. (1992). "Socrates and Plato," *Phronesis*: 37/2: 141–63

Green, Peter (1967). *Juvenal: The Sixteen Satires*, New York

Griswold, Jr., Charles L. (1988). (ed.) *Platonic Writings, Platonic Readings*, London

Grote, George (1867). *Plato and the Other Companions of Sokrates*, 3 vols., 2nd edn., London

(1888). *A History of Greece from the Earliest Period to the Close of the Generation Contemporary with Alexander the Great*, 10 vols., London
Grube, G. M. A. (1980). *Plato's Thought*, Indianapolis
Gulley, Norman (1968). *The Philosophy of Socrates*, London
Guthrie, W. K. C. (1961). (tr.) Plato's *Protagoras*, in *The Collected Dialogues of Plato Including the Letters*, with introduction and prefatory notes, edited by Edith Hamilton and Huntington Cairns, Princeton, 308–52
(1971a). *The Sophists*, Cambridge
(1971b). *Socrates*, Cambridge
(1975). *A History of Greek Philosophy*, vol. IV: *Plato, the Man and his Dialogues: the Earlier Period*, Cambridge
Hackforth, R. M. (1933). *The Composition of Plato's Apology*, Cambridge
Hamilton, Edith, and Cairns, Huntington (1961). (eds.) *The Collected Dialogues of Plato*, Princeton
Hare, R. M. (1982). *Plato*, Oxford
Harrison, E. L. (1964). "Was Gorgias a sophist?" *Phoenix* 18: 184–92
Havelock, Eric A. (1957). *The Liberal Temper in Greek Politics*, New Haven
(1963). *Preface to Plato*, Harvard
Hazebroucq, Marie-France (1997). *La Folie Humaine et ses Remèdes: Platon Charmide ou de la Modération*, traduction nouvelle, notes et commentaire, Paris
Henderson, T. Y. (1970). "In defense of Thrasymachus," *American Philosophical Quarterly* 7: 218–28
Hermann, Karl Friedrich (1839). *Geschichte und System der Platonischen Philosophie*, Heidelberg
Hoerber, R. G. (1958). "Plato's *Euthyphro*," *Phronesis* 3: 95–107
(1962). "Plato's *Lesser Hippias*," *Phronesis* 7: 121–31
Holland, R. F. (1981–82). "Euthyphro," *Proceedings of the Aristotelian Society* 82: 1–15
Horneffer, Ernst (1904). *Platon Gegen Sokrates*, Leipzig
Hourani, George F. (1962). "Thrasymachus' definition of justice in Plato's *Republic*," *Phronesis* 7: 110–20
Hubbard, B. A. F., and Karnofsky, E. S. (1982). *Plato's Protagoras: A Socratic Commentary*, London
Huisman, Denis (1984). (ed.) *Dictionnaire des Philosophes*, Paris
Humbert, Jean (1967). *Socrates et les petits socratiques*, Paris
Hume, David (1980). *Dialogues Concerning Natural Religion and the Posthumous Essays "Of the Immortality of the Soul" and "Of Suicide,"* edited, with an introduction by Richard H. Popkin, Indianapolis
Hyland, Drew A. (1976). "Why Plato wrote dialogues," *Philosophy and Rhetoric* 9: 38–51
(1981). *The Virtue of Philosophy*, Athens
Irwin, Terence (1977). *Plato's Moral Theory: The Early and Middle Dialogues*, Oxford

(1979). *Plato Gorgias*, translated with notes, Oxford

(1986). "Coercion and objectivity in Plato's dialectic," *Revue internationale de philosophie* 40: 49–74

(1992a). "Socratic puzzles: a review of Gregory Vlastos, *Socrates, Ironist and Moral Philosopher*," *Oxford Studies in Ancient Philosophy* 10: 241–66

(1992b). "Plato: the intellectual background," in Kraut, 1992: 51–89

(1995). *Plato's Ethics*, Oxford

Jaeger, Werner (1943–45). *Paideia: The Ideals of Greek Culture*, translated from the Second German Edition by Gilbert Highet, 3 vols., New York

Joël, Karl (1893–1901). *Der echte und der Xenophontische Sokrates*, 3 vols., Berlin

(1921). *Geschichte der Antiken Philosophie*, Tübingen

Joseph, H. W. B. (1935a). "Plato's *Republic*: the argument with Polemarchus," in H. W. B Joseph, *Essays in Ancient and Modern Philosophy*, Oxford, 1–14

(1935b). "Plato's *Republic*: The argument with Thrasymachus," in H. W. B. Joseph, *Essays in Ancient and Modern Philosophy*, Oxford, 15–41

Jowett, Benjamin (1871). *The Dialogues of Plato*, translated into English with analyses and introductions, 4 vols., Oxford

Juvenal (1979). *Juvenal and Persius*, with an English translation by G. G. Ramsey, London

Kahn, Charles H. (1968). Review of Gilbert Ryle's *Plato's Progress*, *Journal of Philosophy* 65: 364–75

(1981). "Did Plato write Socratic dialogues?" *Classical Quarterly* 31: 305–20, reprinted in Benson, 1992: 35–52

(1983) "Drama and dialectic in Plato's *Gorgias*," *Oxford Studies in Ancient Philosophy* 1: 75–121

(1985). "The beautiful and the genuine: a discussion of Paul Woodruff's *Plato: Hippias Major*," *Oxford Studies in Ancient Philosophy* 6: 69–102

(1986). "Plato's methodology in the *Laches*," *Revue internationale de philosophie* 41: 7–21

(1988a). "Plato's *Charmides* and the proleptic reading of the early dialogues," *Journal of Philosophy* 85: 541–49

(1988b). "On the relative date of the *Gorgias* and the *Protagoras*," *Oxford Studies in Ancient Philosophy* 6: 69–102

(1988c). "Plato and Socrates in the *Protagoras*," *Methéxis: Revista argentina de filosophia antigua* 1: 33–52

(1991). "In response to Mark McPherran," *Oxford Studies in Ancient Philosophy* 9: 161–68

(1992). "Vlastos's Socrates," *Phronesis* 37: 233–58

(1996). *Plato and the Socratic Dialogue: The Philosophical Use of a Literary Form*, Cambridge

Kerferd, G. B. (1947). "The doctrine of Thrasymachus in Plato's *Republic*," *Durham University Journal* 9: 19–27

(1981). *The Sophistic Movement*, Cambridge

Kidd, Ian (1967). "Socrates," in Edwards, 1967, vol. VII: 480–86

(1992). "Socratic questions," in Gower and Stokes, 1992: 82–92

Kierkegaard, Soren (1989). *The Concept of Irony with Continual Reference to Socrates*, edited and translated with introductions and notes by Howard V. Hong and Edna H. Hong, Princeton

Kitto, H. D. F. (1966). *Poesis: Structure and Thought*, Berkeley

Klagge, James C. (1992). "Editor's prologue," *Oxford Studies in Ancient Philosophy* Supplementary Volume: 1–12

Klosko, George (1983). "Criteria of fallacy and sophistry for use in the analysis of Platonic dialogues," *Classical Quarterly* 33: 363–74

Kofman, Sarah (1983). *Comment s'en sortir?* Paris

Koyré, Alexander (1962). *Introduction à La Lecture de Platon suivi de Entretiens sur Descartes*, Paris

Kraut, Richard (1983). "Comments on Gregory Vlastos, 'The Socratic Elenchus'," *Oxford Studies in Ancient Philosophy* 1: 59–70

(1984). *Socrates and the State*, Princeton

(1992a). (ed.) *The Cambridge Companion to Plato*, Cambridge

(1992b). "Introduction to the study of Plato," in Kraut, 1992a: 1–50

Laborderie, Jean (1978). *Le Dialogue platonicien de la maturité*, Paris

Laertius, Diogenes (1950). *Lives of Eminent Philosophers*, with an English translation by R. D. Hicks, 2 vols., London

Lamb, W. R. M. (1925). *Plato*, with an English translation: *Charmides, Alcibiades, Hipparchus, The Lovers, Theages, Minos,* and *Epinomis*, London

Lee, E. N., Mourelatos, A. P. D., and Rorty, R. M. (1973). *Exegesis and Argument: Studies in Greek Philosophy Presented to Gregory Vlastos*, New York

Leggewie, Otto (1978). *Platon: Euthyphron*, Stuttgart

Lehrer, Keith (1990). *Theory of Knowledge*, Boulder

Levi, Albert William (1976). "Philosophy as literature: the dialogue," *Philosophy* 9: 1–20

Levi, Peter (1985). *The Pelican History of Greek Literature*, New York

Lewis, John Delaware (1882). *D. Iunii Iuvenalis Satirae*, 2nd edn., revised, 2 vols., London and New York

Lloyd, G. E. R. (1979). *Magic, Reason and Experience*, Cambridge

Louis, Pierre (1945). *Les Métaphores de Platon*, Paris

Lucian (1921). *The Dead Come to Life*, with an English translation by A. M. Harmon, London

(1936). *Lexiphanes*, with an English translation by A. M. Harmon, London

Lycos, Kimon (1987). *Plato on Justice and Power: Reading Book I of Plato's "Republic,"* Albany

Lysias (1892). "Against Eratosthenes," in *Ten Selected Orations by Lysias*, edited, with notes by George P. Bristol, Boston

Magalhães-Vilhena, Vasco de (1952a). *Le Problème de Socrate: le Socrate historique et le Socrate de Platon*, Paris

(1952b). *Socrate et la légende platonicienne*, Paris

Magee, Bryan (1987). (ed.) *The Great Philosophers: An Introduction to Western Philosophy*, Oxford

Maguire, Joseph, P. (1971). "Thrasymachus ... or Plato?" *Phronesis* 16: 142–63

Maier, Heinrich (1913). *Sokrates, sein Werk und seine geschichtliche Stellung*, Tübingen

Manon, Simone (1986). *Platon*, Bordas

Mazel, Jacques (1987). *Socrate*, Paris

McKim, Richard (1988). "Shame and truth in Plato's *Gorgias*," in Griswold, 1988: 34–48

McPherran, Mark L. (1985). "Socratic piety," *Journal of the History of Philosophy* 23: 283–309, reprinted in Benson, 1992: 220–41

(1990). "Kahn on the pre-middle Platonic dialogues," *Oxford Studies in Ancient Philosophy* 8: 211–36

(1996). *The Religion of Socrates*, University Park

McTighe, Kevin (1984). "Socrates on desire for the good and the involuntariness of wrongdoing: *Gorgias* 446a–468e," *Phronesis* 29: 193–236, reprinted in Benson, 1992: 263–97

Méron, Evelyne (1979). *Les idées Morales des Interlocutuers de Socrate dans les dialogues platoniciens de Jeunesse*, Paris

Momigliano, Arnaldo (1971). *The Development of Greek Biography*, Cambridge

Montuori, Mario (1981). *Socrates: Physiology of a Myth*, Amsterdam

(1988). *Socrates: An Approach*, Amsterdam

Moraux, Paul (1968). "La joute dialectique d'après le huitième livre des *Topiques*," in *Aristotle on Dialectic: The Topics*, edited by G. E. L. Owen (Oxford), 277–311

Morris, T. F. (1990). "Plato's *Euthyphro*," *The Heythrop Journal* 31: 309–23

Mulhern, J. J. (1968). "*Tropos* and *polytropia* in Plato's *Hippias Minor*," *Phoenix* 22: 283–88

Munk, Eduard (1857). *Die natürliche Ordnung der platonischen Schriften*, Berlin

Murdoch, Iris (1977). *The Fire and the Sun: Why Plato Banished the Artists*, Oxford

Murphy, N. R. (1951). *The Interpretation of Plato's Republic*, Oxford

Murray, Penelope (1996). *Plato on Poetry: Ion, Republic 376e–398b, Republic 595–608b*, Cambridge

Nagy, Gregory (1989). *The Cambridge History of Literary Criticism*, vol. 1, edited by George A. Kennedy, Cambridge

Nails, Debra (1993). "Problems with Vlastos's Platonic developmentalism," *Ancient Philosophy* 13: 272–91

(1995). *Agora, Academy, and the Conduct of Philosophy*, Dordrecht

Navia, Luis E. (1985). *Socrates: The Man and his Philosophy*, Lanham

Nehamas, Alexander (1986). "Socratic intellectualism," *Proceedings of the Boston Area Colloquium in Ancient Philosophy* 2: 275–316

Nettleship, Richard (1929). *Lectures on the Republic of Plato*, London
Newquist, Roy (1964). "Peter De Vries," in *Counterpoint*, Chicago: 146–52
Nicholson, P. P. (1974). "Unravelling Thrasymachus' arguments in the *Republic*," *Phronesis* 19: 210–32
Nielsen, Kai (1961). "Some remarks on the independence of morality and religion," *Mind* 70: 175–86
Nozick, Robert (1981). *Philosophical Explanations*, Cambridge
Nussbaum, Martha (1980). "Aristophanes and Socrates on learning practical wisdom," *Yale Classical Studies* 26: 43–97
O'Brien, Michael J. (1958). "Modern philosophy and Platonic ethics," *Journal of the History of Ideas* 19: 451–72
   (1963). "The unity of the *Laches*," *Yale Classical Studies* 18: 133–47, reprinted in Anton and Kustas, 1971: 303–15
   (1967). *The Socratic Paradoxes and the Greek Mind*, Chapel Hill
Ovink, B. J. H. (1931). *Philosophische Erklärung der platonischen Dialoge Meno und Hippias Minor*, Amsterdam
Pangle, Thomas, L. (1987). (ed.) *The Roots of Political Philosophy: Ten Forgotten Platonic Dialogues*, translated with interpretive studies, Ithaca
Pappas, Nickolas (1995). *Plato and the Republic*, London
Parry, Richard D. (1996). *Plato's Craft of Justice*, Albany
Partee, Morriss Henry (1981). *Plato's Poetics: The Authority of Beauty*, Salt Lake City
Patzer, Andreas (1987). (ed.) *Der historische Sokrates*, Darmstadt
Penner, Terry (1973a). "Socrates on virtue and motivation," in Lee, Mourelatos, and Rorty, 1973: 133–51
   (1973b). "The unity of the virtues," *The Philosophical Review* 82: 35–68
   (1992a). "What Laches and Nicias miss – and whether Socrates thinks courage merely a part of virtue," *Ancient Philosophy* 12: 1–27
   (1992b). "Socrates and the early dialogues," in Kraut, 1992a: 121–69
Plautus (1928). "Pseudolus," in *Plautus*, with an English translation by Paul Nixon, 5 vols., London
Pohlenz, Max (1913). *Aus Platons Werdezeit, philosophische Untersuchungen* Berlin
Poulakos, John (1995). *Sophistical Rhetoric in Classical Greece*, Columbia
Press, Gerald A. (1993). (ed.) *Plato's Dialogues: New Studies and Interpretations*, Lanham
Price, H. H. (1969). *Belief*, London
Randall, John Herman, Jr., *Plato: Dramatist of the Life of Reason*, New York
Rankin, H. D. (1983). *Sophists, Socratics and Cynics*, London
Reeve, C. D. C. (1988). *Philosopher-Kings: The Argument of Plato's Republic*, Princeton
   (1989). *Socrates in the Apology: An Essay on Plato's Apology of Socrates*, Indianapolis
Riginos, Alice Swift (1976). *Platonica: The Anecdotes Concerning the Life and Writings of Plato*, Leiden

Ritter, Constantin (1933). *The Essence of Platos's Philosophy*, London
Roberts, J. W. (1984). *City of Sokrates: An Introduction to Classical Athens*, London
Robin, Léon (1910). "Les 'Mémorables' de Xénophon et notre connaissance de la philosophie de Socrate," *L' Année Philosophique* 21: 1–47, reprinted in Léon Robin, *La Pensée Hellénique des origines à Épicure: Questions de méthode, de critique et d'histoire*, deuxième édition, Paris, 1967, 81–137
Robinson, Richard (1942). "Plato's consciousness of fallacy," *Mind* 51: 97–114
   (1953). *Plato's Earlier Dialectic*, 2nd edn., Oxford
Roochnik, David L. (1986). "Socrates' use of the techne-analogy," *Journal of the History of Philosophy* 24: 295–310, reprinted in Benson, 1992: 185–97
Rutherford, R. B. (1995). *The Art of Plato: Ten Essays in Platonic Interpretation*, London
Ryle, Gilbert (1966). *Plato's Progress*, Cambridge
Santas, Gerasimos (1971). "Socrates at work on virtue and knowledge in Plato's *Laches*," *Review of Metaphysics* 3: 433–60, reprinted in Vlastos, 1971: 177–208
   (1972). "The Socratic fallacy," *Journal of the History of Philosophy* 10: 127–41
   (1973). "Socrates at work on virtue and knowledge in Plato's *Charmides*," in Lee, Mourelatos, and Rorty, 1973: 105–32
   (1979). *Socrates: Philosophy in Plato's Early Dialogues*, Boston
Saunders, Trevor J. (1987). (ed.) *Early Socratic Dialogues*, New York
Savan David (1965). "Socrates' logic and the unity of wisdom and temperance," in R. J. Butler, (ed.). *Analytical Philosophy*, Second Series, Oxford: 20–26
Sayre, Kenneth M. (1988). "Plato's dialogues in light of the *Seventh Letter*," in Griswold, 1988: 93–109
Schaper, Eva (1968). *Prelude to Aesthetics*, London
Schleiermacher, Friedrich E. (1836). *Introductions to the Dialogues of Plato*, translated by William Dobson, London
   (1858). *The Apology of Socrates, the Crito, and part of the Phaedo*, with notes from Stallbaum, Schleiermacher's Introductions, and his essay "On the worth of Socrates as a philosopher," edited by William Smith, London
Schofield, Malcolm (1992). "Socrates versus Protagoras," in Gower and Stokes, 1992: 122–36
Shorey, Paul (1903). "Plato's ethics," in Paul Shorey, *The Unity of Plato's Thought*, Chicago, 1903: 7–34
   (1933) *What Plato Said*, Chicago
   (1937). *Plato: The Republic*, with an English translation by Paul Shorey, 2 vols., London

Sidgwick, Henry (1872, 1874). "The sophists," *Journal of Philology* 4: 288–307; 5: 66–80

Sinaiko, Herman L. (1965). *Love, Knowledge, and Discourse in Plato*, Chicago

Souilhé, Joseph (1981). *Platon: Oeuvres Complètes Tome 13: Dialogues Suspects, deuxième partie*, texte établi et traduit par Joseph Souilhé, Paris

Sparshott, F. E. (1966). "Socrates and Thrasymachus," *The Monist* 50, 421–59

Sprague, Rosamond Kent (1962). *Plato's Use of Fallacy: A Study of the "Euthydemus" and Some Other Dialogues*, London

(1972). *The Older Sophists*, Oxford

Stewart, M. A. (1977). "Plato's sophistry," *Proceedings of the Aristotelian Society*, 21–44

Stock, George (1909). *The Ion of Plato*, with introduction and notes, Oxford

Stokes, Michael C. (1986). *Plato's Socratic Conversations: Drama and Dialectic in Three Dialogues*, London

(1992). "Socrates' mission," in Gower and Stokes, 1992: 26–81

Stone, I. F. (1988). *The Trial of Socrates*, Boston

Tatham, M. T. (1891). *The Laches of Plato*, with introduction and notes, London

Taylor, A. E. (1911). *Varia Socratica*, First Series, Oxford

(1924). "Aeschines of Sphettus," in *Philosophical Studies*, London

(1929). *Plato: The Man and His Work*, 3rd edn., London

(1932). *Socrates*, Edinburgh

Taylor, C. C. W. (1976). *Plato: Protagoras*, translated with notes, Oxford

Tejara, V. (1984). *Plato's Dialogues One by One: A Structural Interpretation*, New York

Teloh, Henry (1986). *Socratic Education in Plato's Early Dialogues*, Notre Dame

(1987). "The importance of interlocutors' characters in Plato's early dialogues," in *Proceedings of the Boston Area Colloquium in Ancient Philosophy* 2: 25–38

Thayer, H. S. (1993). "Meaning and dramatic interpretation," in Press, 1993: 47–59

Thesleff, Holger (1976). "The date of the pseudo-Platonic *Hippias Major*," *Acta Philologica Fennica* 10: 105–17

Tigerstedt, E. N. (1969). "Plato's Idea of Poetical Inspiration," Commentationes Humanarum Litterarium Societas Scientiarum, Fennica

Trédé, Monique and Demont, Paul (1993). Platon: *Protagoras*, traduction nouvelle, introduction et commentaires, Paris

Tuckey, T. G. (1951). *Plato's Charmides*, Cambridge

Untersteiner, Mario (1954). *The Sophists*, translated by Kathleen Freeman, New York

Van Der Ben, N. (1985). *The Charmides of Plato: Problems and Interpretation*, Amsterdam

Vander Waerdt, Paul A. (1994). (ed.) *The Socratic Movement*, Ithaca

Verdenius, W. J. (1949). *Mimesis: Plato's Doctrine of Imitation and its Meaning to Us*, Leiden

Versényi, Laszlo (1982). *Holiness and Justice: An Interpretation of Plato's "Euthyphro,"* Lanham

Vickers, Brian (1988). *In Defense of Rhetoric*, Oxford

Vidal-Naquet, Pierre (1984). "Le Société platonicienne des Dialogues: Esquisse pour une étude prosopographie," in *Aux Origines de L'Origines L'Hellenisme la Crète et Grèce*, Hommage a Henri Effenterre, presente par le Centre G. Glotz, Paris

Vlastos, Gregory (1956). Editor's Introduction to *Plato's "Protagoras,"* translated by Benjamin Jowett, extensively revised by Martin Ostwald, New York

  (1958). "The paradox of Socrates," *Queen's Quarterly* 64: 496–516, reprinted with minor changes in Vlastos, 1971: 1–21

  (1967). "Was Polus refuted?" *American Journal of Philology* 88: 454–60

  (1971). (ed.) *The Philosophy of Socrates: A Collection of Critical Essays*, Garden City

  (1981a). *Platonic Studies*, 2nd edn., Princeton

  (1981b). "The unity of the virtues in the *Protagoras*," in Vlastos, 1981a: 221–69

  (1981c). "What did Socrates understand by his 'what is *F*?' question," in Vlastos, 1981a: 410–17

  (1981d). "Justice and happiness in Plato's *Republic*," in Vlastos, 1981a, 111–39

  (1983a). "The Socratic elenchus," *Oxford Studies in Ancient Philosophy* 1: 27–58, reprinted with extensive revisions as "The Socratic elenchus: method is all," in Vlastos, 1994: 1–33

  (1983b). "Afterthoughts on the Socratic elenchus," *Oxford Studies in Ancient Philosophy* 1: 71–74

  (1985). "Socrates' disavowal of knowledge," *The Philosophical Quarterly* 35: 1–31, reprinted with minor changes in Vlastos, 1994: 39–66

  (1988). "Socrates," *Proceedings of the British Academy* 74: 89–111

  (1990). "Is the 'Socratic fallacy' Socratic?" *Ancient Philosophy* 10: 1–16, reprinted with minor changes in Vlastos, 1994: 67–86

  (1991). *Socrates, Ironist and Moral Philosopher*, Ithaca and Cambridge

  (1994). *Socratic Studies*, edited by Myles Burnyeat, Cambridge

Wardy, Robert (1996). *The Birth of Rhetoric: Gorgias, Plato and their Successors*, London

Weingartner, Rudolph H. (1973). *The Unity of the Platonic Dialogue: The Cratylus, the Protagoras, the Parmenides*, Indianapolis

Weiss, Roslyn (1981). *"Ho Agathos* as *Ho Dunatos* in the *Hippias Minor,"* *Classical Quarterly* 31: 287–304, reprinted in Benson, 1992: 242–62

  (1986). "Euthyphro's failure," *Journal of the History of Philosophy* 24: 437–52

(1994). "Virtue without knowledge: Socrates' conception of holiness in Plato's *Euthyphro*," *Ancient Philosophy* 14: 263–82

West, Thomas G. (1979). *Plato's* Apology *of Socrates: An Interpretation, with a new translation*, Ithaca

White, Nicholas (1979). *A Companion to Plato's* Republic, Indianapolis

Wills, Garry (1993). "Hanging out with the Greeks," *The New York Review of Books*, May 13, 1993: 37

Wittgenstein, Ludwig (1989). *Culture and Value*, edited by G. H. Von Wright, translated by Peter Winch, Oxford

Woodbridge, F. J. E. (1929). *The Son of Apollo*, Boston

Woodruff, Paul (1982). *Plato: Hippias Major*, translated with commentary and essay, Indianapolis

(1983). (tr.) *Plato: Two Comic Dialogues: Ion and Hippias Major*, Indianapolis

(1986). "The skeptical side of Plato's method," *Revue internationale de philosophie*, 156–57: 26–34

(1988). "Expert knowledge in the *Apology* and *Laches*: what a general needs to know," *Proceedings of the Boston Area Colloquium in Ancient Philosophy* 3: 79–115

Woozley, A. D. (1971). "Socrates on disobeying the law," in Vlastos, 1971: 299–318

(1979). *Law and Obedience: The Arguments of Plato's* Crito, London

Xenophon (1972). *Symposium*, with an English translation by O. J. Todd, London

(1979). *Memorabilia*, with an English translation by E. C. Marchant, London

Zehl, Donald (1980). "Socrates and hedonism," *Phronesis* 25: 250–69

Index of passages cited

Index of names

407

Index of modern authors

General index